Utilizing Virtual Communities in Professional Practice

Dana L. Smerda-Mason
New Jersey City University, USA

Douglas John Koch
NEDLA, USA

A volume in the Advances
in Multimedia and
Interactive Technologies
(AMIT) Book Series

Published in the United States of America by
IGI Global
Information Science Reference (an imprint of IGI Global)
701 E. Chocolate Avenue
Hershey PA, USA 17033
Tel: 717-533-8845
Fax: 717-533-8661
E-mail: cust@igi-global.com
Web site: http://www.igi-global.com

Library of Congress Cataloging-in-Publication Data

Names: Smerda-Mason, Dana L., 1984- editor. | Koch, Douglas J., 1966-
  editor.
Title: Utilizing virtual communities in professional practice / edited by
  Dana Smerda-Mason, Douglas Koch.
Description: Hershey, PA : Information Science Reference, [2024] | Includes
  bibliographical references and index. | Summary: "This book supports
  those interested in the latest theoretical frameworks that provide a
  basis of understanding for successful virtual communities, so that
  others may be able to consider how aspects of professional circles can
  be affected by virtual communities"-- Provided by publisher.
Identifiers: LCCN 2023056043 (print) | LCCN 2023056044 (ebook) | ISBN
  9798369311110 (hardcover) | ISBN 9798369311127 (ebook)
Subjects: LCSH: Online social networks. | Organizational learning. |
  Identity (Psychology) | Information technology--Social aspects.
Classification: LCC HM742 .U855 2024 (print) | LCC HM742 (ebook) | DDC
  384.3/8--dc23/eg/20240126
LC record available at https://lccn.loc.gov/2023056043
LC ebook record available at https://lccn.loc.gov/2023056044

British Cataloguing in Publication Data
A Cataloguing in Publication record for this book is available from the British Library.

All work contributed to this book is new, previously-unpublished material.
The views expressed in this book are those of the authors, but not necessarily of the publisher.

For electronic access to this publication, please contact: eresources@igi-global.com.

Advances in
Multimedia and
Interactive Technologies
(AMIT) Book Series

Joel J.P.C. Rodrigues
Senac Faculty of Ceará, Fortaleza-CE, Brazil; Instituto de Telecomunicações, Portugal

MISSION

ISSN:2327-929X
EISSN:2327-9303

Traditional forms of media communications are continuously being challenged. The emergence of user-friendly web-based applications such as social media and Web 2.0 has expanded into everyday society, providing an interactive structure to media content such as images, audio, video, and text.

The **Advances in Multimedia and Interactive Technologies (AMIT) Book Series** investigates the relationship between multimedia technology and the usability of web applications. This series aims to highlight evolving research on interactive communication systems, tools, applications, and techniques to provide researchers, practitioners, and students of information technology, communication science, media

Coverage

- Digital Images
- Digital Watermarking
- Multimedia Services
- Social Networking

IGI Global is currently accepting manuscripts for publication within this series. To submit a proposal for a volume in this series, please contact our Acquisition Editors at Acquisitions@igi-global.com or visit: http://www.igi-global.com/publish/.

Titles in this Series

For a list of additional titles in this series, please visit:
http://www.igi-global.com/book-series

The Rise of Over-the-Top (OTT) Media and Implications for Media Consumption and Production
Nithin Kalorth (Mahindra University, India)
Information Science Reference • copyright 2024 • 297pp • H/C (ISBN: 9798369301166) • US $245.00 (our price)

Transformed Communication Codes in the Mediated World A Contemporary Perspective
Hasan Gürkan (Girona University, Spain) and Aybike Serttaş (Istinye University, Turkey)
Information Science Reference • copyright 2024 • 407pp • H/C (ISBN: 9798369308967) • US $240.00 (our price)

Examining Multimedia Forensics and Content Integrity
Sumit Kumar Mahana (National Institute of Technology, Kurukshetra, India) Rajesh Kumar Aggarwal (National Institute of Technology, Kurukshetra, India) and Surjit Singh (Thapar Institute of Engineering and Technology, India)
Information Science Reference • copyright 2023 • 301pp • H/C (ISBN: 9781668468647) • US $225.00 (our price)

Handbook of Research on Advanced Practical Approaches to Deepfake Detection and Applications
Ahmed J. Obaid (University of Kufa, Iraq) Ghassan H. Abdul-Majeed (University of Baghdad, Iraq) Adriana Burlea-Schiopoiu (University of Craiova, Romania) and Parul Aggarwal (Jamia Hamdard, India)
Information Science Reference • copyright 2023 • 379pp • H/C (ISBN: 9781668460603) • US $295.00 (our price)

For an entire list of titles in this series, please visit:
http://www.igi-global.com/book-series

701 East Chocolate Avenue, Hershey, PA 17033, USA
Tel: 717-533-8845 x100 • Fax: 717-533-8661
E-Mail: cust@igi-global.com • www.igi-global.com

Table of Contents

Preface... xv

Chapter 1
Teaching, Learning, and Engaging: The Online Music Community..................... 1
    Michael Manuel Rivera, Wallington Board of Education, USA

Chapter 2
Communities of Practice in the Workplace 29
    Remberto Jimenez, New Jersey City University, USA
    Veronica E. O'Neill, New Jersey City University, USA

Chapter 3
Virtual Professional Learning Communities for Educators 49
    Sarah Martin, Bridgewater Raritan Regional School District, USA

Chapter 4
The Union of the Physical and the Digital in the Phygital Transformation:
Intangible Design Evidenced by Knowledge With Artificial Intelligence........... 64
    Neli Maria Mengalli, Faculdade São Bernardo do Campo, Brazil
    Antonio Aparecido Carvalho, Faculdade São Bernardo do Campo,
      Brazil

Chapter 5
Online Learning and Communities for the Visual and Performing Arts 94
    Melissa Welz, New Jersey City University, USA

Chapter 6
Addressing Diverse Learners' Needs Through Inclusivity 117
    Zhivi Williams, Rowan-Cabarrus Community College, USA

Chapter 7
Virtual Communities to Support STEAM Educators 140
    Dana Smerda-Mason, New Jersey City University, USA

Chapter 8
Collaborative Research Data Management Using ResearchGate 159
    Nadim Akhtar Khan, University of Kashmir, India
    Nowsheeba Ashraf Asmi, Government College for Women, Srinagar,
        India
    Aimen Nazir Bhat, University of Kashmir, India

Chapter 9
Virtual Communities of Practice as Mentoring Tools in Health Professions
Education and Practice 182
    Vistolina Nuuyoma, University of Namibia, Namibia

Chapter 10
The Media Plays On: How an Archives Company Leveraged Community
During a Time of Shutdown 206
    Christopher J. Mason, Iron Mountain Media and Archive Services, USA
    Dana L. Smerda-Mason, New Jersey City University, USA

Compilation of References 226

About the Contributors 284

Index 287

Detailed Table of Contents

Preface.. xv

Chapter 1

Teaching, Learning, and Engaging: The Online Music Community.................... 1
    Michael Manuel Rivera, Wallington Board of Education, USA

During the 2019-2020 school year, the COVID-19 pandemic resulted in schools across the globe transitioning from traditional, in-person instruction to virtual instruction. Students received instruction from home as teachers scrambled to replicate content, pedagogy, and community in a new platform. With technology as the centerpiece of instruction, can authentic, real-world learning occur online? This chapter will discuss the process and execution of virtual instruction of a music class during the COVID-19 pandemic through three main concepts: connecting Etienne Wenger's communities of practice, analyzing student learning through the four main learning styles, and looking at the constructivist teaching model and its impact on the virtual music class. The results show a positive virtual class environment with high levels of student learning and engagement.

Chapter 2

Communities of Practice in the Workplace 29
    Remberto Jimenez, New Jersey City University, USA
    Veronica E. O'Neill, New Jersey City University, USA

This chapter will focus on reviewing the core elements of communities of practice in the workplace through four case studies that illustrate examples of what can be done to support organizational learning. Any organization, or workplace, has practices, domains of knowledge, and communities of employees. Yet, the role of communities of practice allows these three dimensions to come together and support employee success, learning, and embedding key practices. This chapter will begin with a review of the workplace and workplace learning. The chapter will then focus on what constitutes a community of practice, and additional permutations of the concept, such as landscapes of learning, that support learning. Four case studies in this chapter will focus on communities of practice examples from the medical field, corporate environments, and education. Suggestions for future research will also be discussed.

Chapter 3
Virtual Professional Learning Communities for Educators 49
Sarah Martin, Bridgewater Raritan Regional School District, USA

A virtual professional learning community (PLC) has the potential to impact positive change in a variety of work environments. The PLC model fosters collaboration and community among educators while achieving learning goals and shaping professional practice. As educators, we are often presented with professional learning opportunities that feel irrelevant to our daily classroom practice. Professional development opportunities often miss their mark because the stakeholders do not feel vested in the learning. Professional development delivered through a PLC model leverages the collective experiences of the participants with the powerful reflection that comes through collaboration. Well-designed PLCs engage stakeholders because the PLC model takes into account adult learning styles and hinges on the meaningful contribution of each participant. Thus, PLCs are a powerful tool for delivering professional development and shaping positive outcomes. This chapter will examine the definition of a PLC, describe the logistics of designing and implementing a meaningful community of virtual learners, and offer a first-hand account of how a virtual PLC was implemented in a middle school to impact professional practice. While the anecdotal accounts are specific to a middle school environment, the fundamental aspects of PLC design and implementation can be applied across a wide array of professional environments. Thus, much of the chapter content will be applicable beyond the scope of a school.

Chapter 4
The Union of the Physical and the Digital in the Phygital Transformation:
Intangible Design Evidenced by Knowledge With Artificial Intelligence........... 64
Neli Maria Mengalli, Faculdade São Bernardo do Campo, Brazil
Antonio Aparecido Carvalho, Faculdade São Bernardo do Campo,
Brazil

This chapter was written based on bibliographical research, qualitative and exploratory studies. The objective of writing the chapter was to highlight theories regarding community of practice for productivity, environmental and social governance, and results in organizations; however, the written elements require further studies to include in research regarding community of practice. In the final considerations, among the conclusions are the combination of the physical with the digital for the phygital transformation in business and the design made with human knowledge for the improvement of businesses that are in full modification with automation, mechanization, with robotization and the use of artificial intelligence for the (co) creation of ideas, insights, or execution of tasks.

Chapter 5
Online Learning and Communities for the Visual and Performing Arts 94
  Melissa Welz, New Jersey City University, USA

This chapter seeks to dissect the multifaceted dimensions of personal online learning spaces, situating them within the larger canvas of contemporary educational practices in the visual and performing arts field. An extension of the pedagogical movement towards student-centered and self-directed learning is the emergence of personal online learning spaces. Learners have access to a wide variety of tools in the arts, including interactive courses, virtual galleries, and personal showcases. Online learning environment gives students the freedom to personalize their educational experience, take into account different learning preferences, and develop a stronger bond with their aspirations in the arts.

Chapter 6
Addressing Diverse Learners' Needs Through Inclusivity 117
  Zhivi Williams, Rowan-Cabarrus Community College, USA

Inclusive teaching in higher education emphasizes interactions, equal opportunities, and care, but Black, Indigenous, and people of color (BIPOC) students face challenges in the classroom. While online education allows all students access to education, it amplifies disparities, particularly for marginalized groups. BIPOC students face discrimination and technology gaps, impacting their academic experiences. Bridging the divide between BIPOC and non-BIPOC students, addressing biases in the classroom, and promoting diversity and inclusion are essential to ensuring that all learners feel valued and supported. Rethinking course design and providing necessary resources can help foster an inclusive educational classroom where every student has the opportunity to thrive.

Chapter 7
Virtual Communities to Support STEAM Educators 140
Dana Smerda-Mason, New Jersey City University, USA

The 21st century represents a time of exceptional growth, providing unprecedented technological innovation that continues to rely on the creativity of mankind. More than ever, thought leaders in the areas of science, technology, engineering, and math are needed to help lead modern innovation to meet the insatiable needs of the modern consumer market. To prepare the future workforce with the skills needed to successfully compete in the global market, the world looks to educators focused on developing the up-and-coming generation. The pressure of this monumental task faces educators in the 21st century on a daily basis. Modern workforce skills and the meaning of cutting-edge knowledge seem to change at a rapid pace, often leaving educators in a constant cycle of upskilling. Educators can benefit from the support of comprehensive professional development and powerful virtual communities.

Chapter 8
Collaborative Research Data Management Using ResearchGate 159
Nadim Akhtar Khan, University of Kashmir, India
Nowsheeba Ashraf Asmi, Government College for Women, Srinagar, India
Aimen Nazir Bhat, University of Kashmir, India

Research data management benefits the scientific community through data sharing and collaborations, and its importance is much more owing to concerns from publishers, funding agencies, the public, and research organizations focussed on the quality and impact of research. Academic social networking sites facilitate the achievement of this goal through sharing and collaborating on research and ideas. ResearchGate has emerged as a platform for research data management, revolutionizing the ways to store, share, and access research data sets. The chapter highlights the significance of research data management and explores the importance of academic social networking sites in this area. It further explores ResearchGate features, which research scholars use to reflect successful collaborations, research growth, and better communication with peers. It attempts to assess the impact of RG research matrics for retaining the quality and visibility of research, which significantly impacts RG's success through openness, effectiveness, and interconnectivity in the scientific domain.

Chapter 9

Virtual Communities of Practice as Mentoring Tools in Health Professions
Education and Practice 182

Vistolina Nuuyoma, University of Namibia, Namibia

Virtual communities of practice refer to people who form a group that meets virtually through online platforms. The purpose of the meeting is to share expertise, passion, interests, and that translates into an independent society. The concept of virtual communities of practice is derived from communities of practice, which is a term coined by Jean Lave and Etienne Wenger in the early 1990s and is underpinned by the theory of situated learning. Other theoretical and philosophical underpinnings of virtual communities of practices and mentoring are Vygotsky's sociocultural theory of human learning, legitimate peripheral participation, zone of proximal development, and scaffolding. Although there are benefits offered by virtual communities of practice, literature seems to be limited to how they are used as tools for sharing information and improving practices. Owing to that, this chapter describes how virtual communities of practices may be used as mentoring tools in health professions education and practice.

Chapter 10
The Media Plays On: How an Archives Company Leveraged Community
During a Time of Shutdown 206
    Christopher J. Mason, Iron Mountain Media and Archive Services, USA
    Dana L. Smerda-Mason, New Jersey City University, USA

The COVID-19 pandemic challenged people across the globe and forced change across every industry. Many people were home due to quarantine requirements and to help pass this time turned to media of many forms for their entertainment and social interactions. At a time where new content could not be professionally created due to safety requirements, the entertainment industry was forced to visit their archives and collaborate with specialists to solve this emerging concern. This chapter focuses on the virtual communities developed by the archivists at Iron Mountain Media and Archive Services to implement strategies to service this need through the digitization of legacy media and other assets that they manage for their customers. Through creativity and innovation, these professionals created 21st century solutions through virtual communities to challenges related to training, transportation, digitization, and developed a plan to provide social and emotional support to the masses through the ability to connect with newly available media streaming demands.

Compilation of References 226

About the Contributors 284

Index 287

Foreword

The other day, I was reflecting on my experience in one of my educational technology virtual communities. In this space of thousands of educators, I have been mentored by experienced teachers and collaborated on projects with others. Late night technical questions posts have led to rich conversations, as well as the sharing of resources and materials. As I scrolled through the countless forums, I wondered how this community had managed to facilitate such meaningful discourse and support for educators around the world, all within a virtual space.

We are living in a new age of professional growth, where connections are not limited to physical interactions and proximity. While face-to-face networking still exists, virtual communities are on the rise, eliminating the barriers of time and distance. In these virtual spaces, people can asynchronously connect with others. They can ask questions, seek mentorship, share resources and ideas, work on a project, or learn from the experiences of those around them. From the aspiring writer joining a community to receive feedback and support others to the company leader creating a space for their global employees to share expertise, virtual communities offer the convenience of access, while also providing a diverse range of perspectives and experiences for participants.

Building a thriving online community is not an easy task. The success of one of these spaces is dependent upon active participation, a welcoming atmosphere, appropriate management, and the facilitation of connections. It is not as simple as having individuals with a shared interest join the same designated space. Through my experiences as both a creator and a participant, I have seen the power of well-structured and engaging online communities of practice. Navigating through the robust research base on online community development to determine how to effectively create these spaces can be overwhelming, but this book serves as a support system for that process.

This book captures the many nuances of designing a virtual community, especially in the discussion of how these spaces can lead to a person's professional growth. Dr. Smerda-Mason and Dr. Koch have curated examples of these digital communities from different fields, including K-12 education, health, businesses, and higher education, to show how the power of virtual communities transcends professional disciplines. The chapters seamlessly combine theoretical frameworks with real-world examples of virtual communities. In the spirit of global collaboration that is often celebrated and encouraged in these spaces, the authors of each chapter come from all over the world with a diverse range of perspectives and experiences, including

India, the United States, Brazil, and Namibia. Reading through each example offers insight into what a successful virtual community looks like, and highlights how these communities have been effective in improving professional performance and growth.

As you read this book, I encourage you to consider how each example shared can be adapted for your field. The combination of real-life applications, research, and theoretical frameworks allows for a more comprehensive understanding of virtual community best practices. Creating and, most importantly, sustaining a virtual community can be both challenging and rewarding. Each author has illustrated and outlined their online community journey, sharing their insight and experience to help you on your own path. They provide the tools and strategies to help you replicate their successes. Whether you are a company leader looking to facilitate asynchronous collaboration and learning between employees, or a STEAM teacher looking to build a space for fellow teachers to connect and share project resources, this book provides a guide for building these types of virtual communities.

Utilizing Virtual Communities in Professional Practice encourages innovation within professional practice and highlights the importance of digital connection. I am excited for you to take this journey and discover the power of participating in or designing a virtual community within your professional practice.

Kathryn Nieves Licwinko
Wayne Township Public Schools, USA

Preface

At the heart of human existence is the need to grow and learn. This is evidenced by the innovation we enjoy in the modern world, which is continuously fueled by need, curiosity, and the collaborative nature of individuals sharing experiences. It can be formal as in a professional society, or informal as community organization. Much of this intrinsic exchange of ideas can be viewed formally as types of market research that informs innovation. Other times, it occurs naturally and informally and individuals pass on their knowledge in different areas of existence.

Social learning has been occurring since the beginning of time and continues through today in a variety of circles. For example, organizations that share and promote professional values key to their identities, such as Scouting where adults prepare youth to confront the challenges of adult life. Another can focus on a different aspect related to industry such as the American Welding Society, where individuals can earn certifications in different areas of the industry. The International Association of Medical Science Educators is an organization of professionals dedicated to the advancement of the excellence of innovation of teaching and medical education.

On the more informal side of this theory can also be community groups of like-minded individuals interested in a variety of topics from planting and maintaining trees in their communities, to church groups dedicated to passing down of cultural traditions. Each of these examples are uniquely impacting learning, while providing a space for experts and novices to learn and grow together through the practice of their common interest.

Communities of practice are now complimented by technological innovation and no longer are confined by proximity and time. As we have learned through the COVID-19 pandemic, technology can provide the pathway for us to find new ways to communicate and exchange so that we can continue to grow. Technology enhances this traditional sharing practice by providing new and creative ways for individuals to continue to support one another through the virtual world.

Virtual communities provide a space for all individuals to learn in a community setting conveniently, while also providing autonomy to decide how to engage at a time they need it most. Online learning, and other professional learning communities make this possible, and are a tributary of evolution in this arena that provides a means of support for all members of the community regardless of their experience level. Our hope, as editors and authors, is that this book serves as a place to explore the impact of social learning as it is used in practice across a variety of fields in the form of virtual communities.

Research and healthcare are areas that continue to inspire progress in our well-being. In her chapter, "Virtual Communities of Practice as Mentoring Tools in Health Professions Education and Practice," Dr. Vistolina Nuuyoma explores how aspects of healthcare professions rely on virtual communities to instill contemporary practices in all members of the professional community. A complimentary aspect to consider is how we develop the understandings that inform modern practice through the collaborative efforts of those in the research field. In their chapter, "Collaborative Research Data Management Using ResearchGate," Dr. Nadim Akhtar Khan, Dr. Nowsheeba Ashraf Asmi, and Miss Aimen Nazir Bhat, provide a view of what is possible in modern collaborative research practices with the use of ResearchGate.

We are not only able to observe the benefits of sharing knowledge in virtual communities in entertainment spaces, or among informal groups, but also professionally. Dr. Remberto Jimenez and Dr. Veronica O'Neill focus on the benefits of upskilling employees within an organization as well as maximizing support in learning and development through virtual communities in their chapter "Using Educational Technologies to Support Workplace Virtual Learning Communities." Dr. Neli Mengalli and Dr. Antonio Aparccido Carvalho share their knowledge of the business world by blending Artificial Intelligence with the intangible aspects of where the digital world and the physical nature of these aspects merge, which they describe as 'phygital transformation,' in their chapter "The Union of the Physical and the Digital in the Phygital Transformation: Intangible Design Evidenced by Knowledge With Artificial Intelligence." These two chapters provide unique insight into the utilization of virtual communities, and how they are relied upon within corporate professional practice.

Performing arts and technology came together in an essential way during the COVID-19 Pandemic for those working in the arts field. Melissa Welz describes aspects of industry changes and how they reflect the needs of student musicians during this difficult time in the arts and education. Christopher J. Mason and Dr. Dana Mason offer a unique look into what happened behind the scenes in digitizing content during this time, when Hollywood and other media industry producers were unable to produce video content safely in person. Michael Rivera provides the perspective of the incredible shift educators experienced, which began without a moment's notice in March of 2020, and how it impacted music education. With an educational view of inside an elementary music classroom, he showcases methods, technological integration, as well as successful outcomes in his chapter "Teaching Learning, Engaging: The Online Music Community."

Meeting the needs of all learners and establishing equity through differentiated professional practice in education is important in supporting each individual towards a successful future. To ensure this, diversity, equity, and inclusion must be at the forefront of our minds, informing decisions in education. In her chapter, "Addressing Inclusive and Diverse Learners' Needs," Zhivi explores important ways that these practices can be enhanced as we continue to meet the needs of all 21st century learners.

Educational professional development is another area that is positively impacted by the implementation of virtual communities. Dr. Sarah Martin explores professional development training from the perspective of launching a new school program, with successful practices among middle school educators in her chapter focusing on "Virtual Professional Learning Communities for Educators." Another aspect of educator professional training is discussed in the chapter "Virtual Communities Supporting Educators in STEAM Education." Here, Dr. Dana Smerda-Mason discusses the essential need for STEAM education in K-12 education, as well as the benefits to educators and students that integrate convergence education, while addressing the need for virtual communities to promote 21st century professional learning opportunities for educators.

Virtual communities are specifically important to us as editors, because the nature of life-long learning and development should be available to all. Our personal and professional pursuits have always been in support of this as one of our core values, and virtual communities continue to encourage learning in this endless capacity. It is our hope that the contributions in this book help provide awareness of new and exciting ways to integrate virtual communities, as well as inspire the innovation and development for new solutions in various fields

Dana L. Smerda-Mason
New Jersey City University, USA

Douglas J. Koch
NEDLA, USA

Chapter 1
Teaching, Learning, and Engaging:
The Online Music Community

Michael Manuel Rivera
https://orcid.org/0009-0004-7318-5111
Wallington Board of Education, USA

ABSTRACT

During the 2019-2020 school year, the COVID-19 pandemic resulted in schools across the globe transitioning from traditional, in-person instruction to virtual instruction. Students received instruction from home as teachers scrambled to replicate content, pedagogy, and community in a new platform. With technology as the centerpiece of instruction, can authentic, real-world learning occur online? This chapter will discuss the process and execution of virtual instruction of a music class during the COVID-19 pandemic through three main concepts: connecting Etienne Wenger's communities of practice, analyzing student learning through the four main learning styles, and looking at the constructivist teaching model and its impact on the virtual music class. The results show a positive virtual class environment with high levels of student learning and engagement.

Mr. Martinez begins his first year of teaching with a range of emotions: He is nervous, anxious, but most importantly, excited to begin a career about which he has been dreaming since he was in elementary school. He is the newest teacher at George Washington Elementary School, located in the same town and district in which he grew up. He is the definition of a first-year teacher: an excited, plucky youngster who is optimistic about making a difference in the lives of his students. He stays late at school, sometimes until 5 p.m., working on creative lesson plans that will, hopefully, engage the class. He is up until 1 a.m. brainstorming ideas and searching different resources he may utilize. The first year of teaching is anything

DOI: 10.4018/979-8-3693-1111-0.ch001

but easy and can feel "like a sink-or-swim experience" (Moir, 2013, p.7). Over the course of his first year, Mr. Martinez experiences ups, downs, successes, failures, and unexpected surprises. When those unexpected surprises occur, he must be prepared to deal with the situation, no matter how unsatisfying it may be.

The first year of teaching is a time of trial and error—figuring out what works and what does not; Mr. Martinez will experience this as the year goes on. For now, he focuses on what is important to him: the classroom. He plans on developing a positive classroom community, an essential element for student learning, which will result in minimal student behavior issues. He plans to create a safe space for students to express themselves without fear of judgement. He plans to create opportunities for students to work and learn from one another, while they offer their own support through the learning process. The students will be in control of their learning, resulting in engagement throughout the class.

Throughout his first few days, Mr. Martinez absorbs his new school environment. He learns the different school policies, procedures, and protocols that are in place: how to sign in and out from the main office, fire drill exits and lock down plans, maintaining sub plans, and so on. He learns the names of the other teachers, teacher aides, secretaries, custodial workers, and lunch monitors with whom he will be working. He then scurries to new teacher orientation, where he and the other new teachers in the building meet with their new administrators and discuss expectations that they have for their newest hires. It is then off to another meeting, taking away time from classroom setup.

Mr. Martinez comes across tedious paperwork that takes away time from teaching.

The school requires lesson plans that include 21st-century skills, learning targets and outcomes, interdisciplinary elements, a step-by-step plan with start and end times, different measurements of assessment, and a list of differentiation practices for each lesson, all due by Thursdays at 3 p.m. He creates his Student Growth Objectives, or SGOs: an academic goal that provides data on a group of students and their understanding of the knowledge and concepts taught to them during the year. This usually comes in the way of a pre-test in the beginning of the year, separating his students into a low, medium, and high performing group based on their score, and administering the same test again towards the end of the year, with the hopes that the students receive a higher score the second time around.

The SGO forms 20% of the teacher's end of year summative performance review, and the other 80% comes from the score of three observations—one announced and two unannounced—during the year. Mr. Martinez spends time writing his Professional Development Plan, or PDP, detailing how his three goals—a district, school, and personal goal—will lead to his own professional development as an educator. He is mandated by law to read and sign all required Individualized Education Plans, or IEPs, for students who are in special education or receive school services such as speech or occupational therapy, taking note of each case and the modifications the student is required to have. This is all but a small piece of what Mr. Martinez is expected to perform, on top of his teaching duty.

On the first day of school, Mr. Martinez shifts his focus to the best part of teaching: interacting with students. He learns their names while taking note of their personalities; he discerns who are the nice students, the ones who may cause trouble, and those in between. He figures out how he will teach the material according to the strengths and weaknesses of their students. Most importantly, he figures out how to create a classroom community with all the different personalities and learning capabilities. Mr. Martinez is excited to teach, learn from, and engage with his new students. It is extra special for him, not only as the new teacher, but as the school's new music teacher.

There are so many challenges in the role of a new educator, especially those that specialize in music education. Much of the development at this stage occurs through mentoring, and entering as a new member of the learning community (Wenger, 2011). The elders of the community are the veteran educators who can help fill in the gaps on working culture of the school, operational functions and expectations. An assigned mentor helps with more detailed things related to classroom functions and many of the points detailed in this introduction. At this time, they traditionally occur conveniently in-person, and the community of practice thrives in a face-to-face environment, and will be available and open to support Mr. Martinez as he develops in his new position.

THE DAY IN THE LIFE OF A MUSIC TEACHER

The music classroom gives students the opportunity to engage with one another through various activities and lessons that include the standards of performing, creating, responding, and connecting (Hewitt, 2018). Students are constantly performing in music class, from the foundational steady beat to complex rhythms or from singing in head voice to matching pitch with solfeggio syllables. The students perform different dance tutorials that are found on YouTube as well as dances from different countries around the world. Mr. Martinez is lucky enough to have a collection of instruments for his students to use, from rhythm sticks to hand drums, from Orff Instruments such as xylophones, metallophones, and glockenspiels to guitars, ukuleles, and keyboards. Not every school is lucky enough to have instruments, or better yet, a music classroom, as some music teachers are given a cart for materials and rove from classroom to classroom.

Students create music in a variety of methods, for example, music rhythm compositions, song lyrics, basing music off a picture or poem, and music loops and beats on a digital audio workstation (DAW) on school-issued Chromebooks. Students respond to music in different social-emotional learning activities such as coloring to music in order to describe how the music makes them feel or writing about a favorite song or performer in a music journal. Students connect music with culture and society, looking at how the beginnings of jazz music influenced other genres such as rock, R&B, hip-hop, and pop (Garlock, 2020), for example. The activities that can be found within the standards of performing, creating, responding, and connecting result in meaningful musical connections.

Mr. Martinez is one of the few teachers (including the art and physical education teachers and librarian) who see the entire school population every week. Because he teaches every grade level in the school, he teaches the same group of students year after year, some for more than four years. Depending on the size and make-up of the school—for example, a K-2 school or 3-5 school—the music teacher can see an average of over 300 to 500 students a week. In this case, Mr. Martinez teaches at a K-8 school with music instruction for students in Grades K-6. He teaches five to six classes a day, with class sizes ranging from as little as 15 students to as many as 25 or more students. A special education class may push in with a general education class, a common practice for special subjects; this results in raising the class number to almost 30 students in one class.

The daily schedule changes day by day, resulting in a drastic change of a lesson or age group. Mr. Martinez begins his Monday morning with a second-grade class on practicing different rhythms then performing to a song using rhythm sticks, hand drums, and shakers. A fifth-grade class follows, writing rap lyrics based on a 'Fifth-Grade Struggle' after listening to Run-D.M.C's hit "Hard Times." A Kindergarten class immediately follows, singing fun songs and playing exciting games under the guise of the learning target. It is a busy day filled with different activities and personalities, with little to no down time for the teacher.

Since he has the privilege of teaching the same group of students every year, Mr. Martinez sees his students grow. By allowing Mr. Martinez to foster positive relationships with students, this contributes to a classroom environment that produces positive social and academic skills and outcomes (Wentzel, 2010), which also results in less student behavior issues and more student engagement. He learns how to respond to student learning through visuals, auditory, reading and writing, or kinesthetic activities. He navigates his teaching style, seeing what works for him in his classroom.

In addition to his teaching duty, Mr. Martinez runs two extracurricular music activities open for students in grades four through eight: band and choir. A number of schools have a separate teacher for band and choir; however, it is not uncommon to have one music teacher who teaches all three. At the start of the school year, a massive recruitment effort for band takes place. This includes band sign-ups, instrument rental coordination, and instrument distribution. A lesson schedule is created in which students are pulled out of a general subject class once a week for their lesson.

One option is to do this on a rotating basis. For example, one week the student will miss science class, the following week they will miss math class, and the cycle continues. This ensures that the student will not miss the same class every week and potentially fall behind in their classwork. In other schools, students are not to be pulled out of language arts and math due to state testing requirements, or even physical education due to state requirements of mandatory 90-minute P. E. classes a week. This leaves Mr. Martinez with little flexibility on taking his students out of class for their band lesson, but he is expected to make it work. If a student is taking a test during the class period of a lesson or is absent on their lesson day, the possibility of a make-up lesson is slim, Mr. Martinez ends up sacrificing his lunch or planning period to have a make-up lesson with the student.

An after-school band rehearsal takes place once or twice a week depending on the level of ensemble, which band students are required to attend. Because of this, Mr. Martinez is generally one of the last teachers to leave school. The same is done for choir, for which recruitment takes place at the start of the school year. This may involve an informal audition in which Mr. Martinez listens to every student sing to hear their singing voice, and the students match pitch. Choir rehearsals are held before school; therefore, Mr. Martinez is one of the first teachers to arrive at school, sometimes before the principal.

Two concerts are held annually, the winter and spring concerts. Mr. Martinez prepares the ensembles for the performances and chooses music that the students can perform at their level. He practices the music in his own personal time, so he is prepared to teach the music to his students. He organizes the layout of the concert, with little to no outside help. Other class performances, such as a Veteran's Day show, Flag Day show, holiday tree lightings, or other small grade performances can be requested by administration at any given time, and he is required to prepare and execute such performances.

The day in the life of a music teacher varies by district and school, but generally the position entails planning and executing lessons between different grade levels, tailoring lessons that correspond to the student's mode of learning; work with hundreds of students with different personalities every day, creating and maintaining student relationships, directing multiple ensembles, and keeping up to date with paperwork.

Mr. Martinez keeps a busy schedule but is excited to build up a music program of which the students and the school can be proud. Considering the variables that could happen day to day, there is nothing that this new teacher cannot handle, even if a variable eventually ends up as an unexpected constant. He is developing his experience through each of these challenges, while also having the support of his professional learning community helping him expect the unexpected, and navigate the exciting changes that normally occur within the cycle of a school year. Unbeknownst to this community of practice, the needs of the students and community would drastically shift, ushering in a need for virtual communities across the culture of education.

A Global Pandemic Changes the Norm

Who would have thought that a global pandemic in the beginning of 2020 would have led to schools remodeling the way teaching has been done for centuries in a matter of days? The Coronavirus, or COVID-19, shut down in March 2020 closed all public meeting areas such as businesses, restaurants, sports arenas, and places of worship. Schools quickly transitioned from traditional in-person learning to virtual learning, whereby students received virtual instruction from their teachers in front of a screen from the safety of their homes. The students missed out on opportunities to develop their social skills such as community building, problem solving, and conflict resolution; they no longer can interact with their classmate or teacher in-person. This was certainly not what Mr. Martinez—or any teacher—had signed up for.

One day of professional development is given in preparation for virtual learning. Mr. Martinez begins searching for online resources as he and his other colleagues set up for their maiden voyage. He transfers hardcopy materials to digital copies and begins scheduling assignments on Google Classroom, a learning management system that is a one-stop shop for teachers to create lessons, collect student work, grade and return papers, and communicate with students and parents remotely (Main, 2022). As he sits around the table with his colleagues, the colleagues share a concern for having to shift their detailed duties from an in-person to a virtual learning environment.

The determined music teacher works through the weekend to prepare for virtual instruction. He ensures that his students are to receive quality music instruction, albeit from home. Questions he ponders include:
1. What activities and lessons can be taught virtually which will engage the students?
2. How will students still learn using different learning modalities online?
3. What will be my teaching style, even if it is online?
4. How can I still foster a music classroom community online as opposed to in person?

The community of practice that occurs naturally in-person was no longer at hand for these educators, and so the learning community began to shift into a virtual format to start solving these new challenges at the inception of the pandemic-related academic shift. Colleagues commiserated over the unfortunate circumstances through text and email, and started to work together as a team to develop successful solutions to meet their students' educational needs, and offer as much normalcy and stability as possible in these uncertain times. This was the beginning of how virtual communities not only helped support the professional learning needs of fellow educators, but also developed community for students at a difficult time in global history.

The district began with asynchronous learning, whereby the assignment posts to the classes on Google Classroom on the scheduled days, where the expectation was for students to work through and complete the assignment by the end of the day. Mr. Martinez checks in a few times to see if any student needs help. Although not in person, he is overjoyed about seeing their assignments and realizing that they are grasping concepts which they have learned throughout the year. A few weeks later, synchronous learning takes place, whereby students meet live with their teacher on Google Meets via a link and follow the normal schedule as if they were in school. When it is time for their scheduled music class, the students log on through their music Google Meet link and Mr. Martinez is overwhelmed when seeing their faces.

As the days, weeks, and months go by in this new era of teaching, Mr. Martinez keeps a journal and documents all that has happened. Through research, trial and error, he sees progress in his students' musical abilities. They remain engaged through various virtual activities and lessons, often asking questions that connect back to the key concepts. Lessons are tailored to ensure that different learning modalities were targeted. Mr. Martinez later discovers the teaching style that works best for him. What was thought to be the only way of teaching can be replicated and accomplished in a virtual environment as well, as the community of practice in the classroom and also one among educators were reestablished through virtual platforms.

This chapter will discuss the process and execution of virtual instruction in a music class during the COVID-19 pandemic through three main concepts:

- Connecting Etienne Wenger's *Communities of Practice*;
- Analyzing student learning through the four main learning styles; and
- Looking at the constructivist teaching model and its impact on the virtual music class.

Technology through the TPACK (technological, pedagogical, and content knowledge) framework will also be explained, adding to the depth and knowledge of virtual instruction. After implementing these concepts, the results showed a positive virtual class environment with high levels of student learning and engagement. Examples of virtual instruction music lessons will connect with each of the concepts above.

Technology Integration

Mr. Martinez was at a crossroads when preparing for virtual instruction. He knew the content he would teach his students and had idea on how to present the content. What presented as a challenge to him and other teachers, was the usage of technology in the lessons. Mr. Martinez primarily relied upon the utilization of worksheets, presentations, and music performances during in-person teaching. The few technological materials used were YouTube clips and PowerPoint presentations. Given the task of switching to fully virtual instruction in a matter of days, he and his colleagues had to consider what the integration of technology in music class would look like.

TPACK Model

The TPACK model, proposed by Punya Mishra and Matthew Koehler (Adams, 2019), play an important role when integrating technology within the classroom. *Technological knowledge* (TK) refers to having a general understanding of current technology available. Technology rapidly changes, and a device or program a teacher uses can become obsolete in a short amount of time. Nevertheless, teachers must figure out a way to integrate technology productively within their curriculum (Mishra & Koehler, 2006). *Pedagogical knowledge* (PK) refers to how the teacher will present the content (Adams, 2019). This involves knowing what teaching style they are to use in order to benefit their students (Mishra & Koehler, 2006). *Content knowledge* (PK) refers to the content—or "what"—the teacher will present to their students. They are expected to be experts in the field in which they teach (Adams, 2019). Lee Shulman introduced the Pedagogical Content Knowledge (PCK) framework, however Mishra and Koehler (2006) argue that "having knowledge of subject matter and general pedagogical strategies, though necessary, was not sufficient for capturing the knowledge of good teachers" (p. 1021). Technology integration was built upon the existing PCK framework proposed by Shulman.

In the ideal classroom situation, all three knowledges overlap, as seen in Figure 1. Technology integration is incorporated in both pedagogical and content-based knowledge, paving the way for meaningful materials for both teachers and students (Adams, 2019). With 21st-century skills embedded in curriculums, technology usage highlights the importance of real-world skills. However, steps should be taken to ensure new technology items or online resources are not used at the same but rather spread out over time. Teachers should request and attend professional development sessions that involve technology as part as the curriculum. For example, when a new math textbook with a technology-based program or a new district technology initiative in the district.

Figure 1. The TPACK model

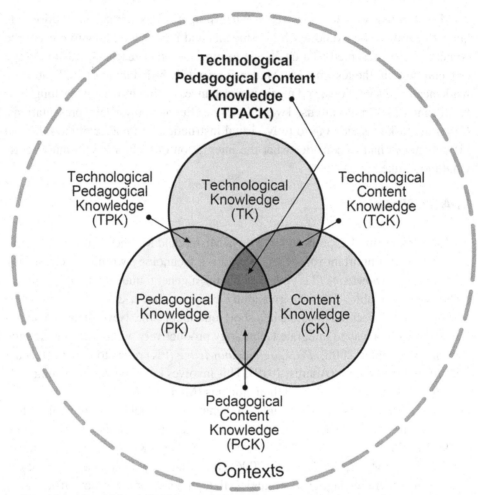

Note. Adapted from Mishra & Koehler. Reproduced by permission of the publisher, © 2012 by tpack.org.

In his research, Mr. Martinez found new online music resources, from music games, content-specific videos, lessons, and music creation websites. The resources located online helped with both content knowledge and pedagogical knowledge. Technology integration found its way into the music room, with the hope that it would enhance and support music instruction virtually by creating an online virtual learning community among the music students.

Establishing the Online Community

Establishing a classroom culture and environment should be the number one priority at the beginning of the school year, as it sets the tone for how the students are to interact with their teacher and classmates. Mr. Martinez's real-world approach to teaching connected with the students and helped establish a virtual community of practice. Music concepts and lessons were relatable to what they were experiencing in the moment at that particular time during the pandemic. Because of this, students were contributing to authentic learning, often leading to encouragement from others to participate.

This was accomplished in his first months of in-person instruction, but now that virtual instruction was underway, he wondered if this could be replicated online. He soon realized that students were contributing to their learning success not only as individuals but as a group and a natural sense of community began to develop. Learning online did not stop students from interacting with one other. Robert Plant (2004) describes this online community as "a collective group of entities, individuals, or organizations that come together either temporarily or permanently through an electronic medium to interact in a common problem or interest space" (p. 54). In this temporary virtual space, they all share a common goal, to learn and put into practice the musical skills taught as a community.

Communities of Practice

Etienne Wenger (2011) defines *communities of practice* as "groups of people who share a concern or a passion for something they do and learn how to do it better as they interact regularly" (p.1). Communities of practice include three characteristics that are important to the success of all involved: the commitment to the domain or topic of interest, interaction within the community, and practical resources that are shared among the members of the community.

Participating in a music ensemble, whether band or choir, is engaging in community practices. The musicians in each group—instrumentalists or vocalists—share their love of music and music making with one another. A symphonic orchestra, for example, prepares for a performance of Beethoven's Symphony No. 5 in C minor. The musicians, as individuals, rehearse their instrument partly at home, ensuring that the correct rhythm and pitch is played. As an ensemble, the group focuses on intonation, phrasing, and musicality to bring the piece alive.

On the other hand, a choir prepares for a performance of Carl Orff's "Carmina Burana." Similarly, the choristers as individuals rehearse their part at home, taking note of correct rhythm, pitches, and text. As an ensemble, the choir focuses on uniformity of the vowels and correct pronunciation of Latin and German. Each group partakes in discussions of interest within, for example, instrumentalists discuss their favorite Mahler symphony while vocalists discuss their favorite Eric Whitacre piece. They share resources amongst each other, for example, instrumentalists share their favorite recording of Stravinsky's *The Firebird* while vocalists share their favorite recording of Mozart's *Requiem*. Their commitment to discussion, interaction, and sharing resources establishes a successful community practice.

Knowledge is created amongst members based on shared goals. A formal group or committee may have goals that are set and limited by appointed members to complete a specific task (Angelle, 2008). Transferring this idea to the classroom, the teacher plays a passive role while students are at the forefront of their learning through collaborative work and social interaction. If the opposite were to take place, teachers would transfer knowledge from student to the student while not allowing for collaborative work to be done. Due to lack of peer interaction, students could not create their own knowledge that is meaningful to them. A classroom community cannot exist amongst students if meaningful interactions are not permitted.

Community Practices in the Online Music Classroom

Mr. Martinez laid ground rules for his students as virtual instruction began. The interactions, whether leaving a comment on Google Classroom or in the Google Meets chat, were to be respectful. If students had a question, they were permitted to type in the chat, which allowed Mr. Martinez one of their classmates to respond right away. Differences of opinion were welcomed in discussion boards, resulting in questions and debates on different music topics. Students answered each other while Mr. Martinez was a mere observer.

Fifth and sixth grade students worked on Soundtrap, a cloud-based digital audio workstation (DAW) that allows them to create their own music using pre-loaded loops and beats (About Soundtrap | Soundtrap, 2024). When assignments were completed, "listening days" were planned, much to the delight of the students and Mr. Martinez. Listening to their classmates' music using real-time sharing, they critiqued, then engaged in conversation either verbally or via comment in the chat. Many of the students took it upon themselves to learn advanced editing skills such as fade ins and outs and individual volume control and offered help to other students who wanted to incorporate these editing skills in their music. Everyone heard different beats and loops, which they were able to save and use in future projects.

Teaching band lessons during virtual instruction was not easy at first for Mr. Martinez. Although he had experience in band while a student in elementary school, his college training was in voice; nevertheless, he was determined to teach his students as much as he could on their instruments. One such instance was with fourth and fifth grade students, many of whom were learning snare drum for the first time. Going back and forth, he gave the students individual time to practice while meeting with them one by one. They listened as each one would perform and provided feedback in real time. Students were engaged in discussing their playing techniques and were supporting one another.

A decision was made to continue with choir during virtual instruction. In traditional in-person learning, 75 students were singing in the choir, but only five had signed up for this new virtual choir. What Mr. Martinez had planned for changed drastically and needed to be restructured. Creating a virtual choir transformed into a weekly mini voice lesson. Not only did students learn more about their singing voice, but this was also a chance for them to see each other and talk not only about music but their struggles of online instruction. Many of them had not interacted with other classmates for months; the students felt loved and supported, even from behind a screen.

The students' learning created meaning, shaping their shared music-making experience (Kenny, 2016). Rules were made by both teacher and students; membership was open to those in the class; roles were given out depending on the activity; identities were established by the students; and learning took place within the class environment (p. 1). While each class had students with a wide range of personalities and musical abilities, this layout was applied to all. Musical participation was formed online due to the shared investment between all parties involved (p. 87). A music community can exist both in-person and online; both are to be approached and executed in the same way.

Teaching Theories

In his first weeks of teaching, Mr. Martinez was struggling with pedagogical knowledge. He found no issues with content knowledge, because of his experience and expertise working the material that was to be taught. Execution and delivery as to the approach to the content were a different issue. He once gave a lecture on steady beat to a kindergarten class, much to the boredom and confusion of the little ones who desperately wanted to move around. Usually, there would be games in movement, and Orff instruments for students to interact with and physically experience these concepts, as opposed to listening to an explanation. Instead of capitalizing on the moment and having the students move to a steady beat, he had the students watch him perform one instead. After observing the reaction and lack of attention in class, he realized that there was room for innovation. The next day he taught the same lesson to a different Kindergarten class but with a different approach. This time, he had the students tap to the steady beat. Using what they had just learned, he then asked them to clap, stomp, march, and sing a steady beat by repeating "ta." The students executed this with ease, accompanied by with smiles and laughter.

The following week, after reviewing steady beat, they learned to perform four quarter-note beats by clapping, stomping, marching, and singing "ta" while keeping the steady beat. In short, the new concept of steady beat was taught in week one, and based off the prior knowledge of performing a steady beat, they added other layers such as tapping, clapping, stomping, marching, and singing, while performing a four-quarter-note beat pattern. The success and excitement of his students to participate was evidence that the right pedagogical approach had been taken.

Teachers adapt a style of teaching with which they not only resonate but that works for them in their classroom, by finding the right teaching style is a process of trial and error. Ozola and Purvins (2013) break down the different teaching and learning theories. Behaviorism, developed by the American psychologist B. F. Skinner, looks at how desired behavior contributes to learning. Cognitivism looks at how individuals make sense of and process information given to them (Yilmaz, 2011). In constructivism, students build upon prior knowledge and construct knowledge based on their experience. Student behavior is learned by imitation, resulting in learning, and it was evident that the constructivist approach could be successful in a virtual community setting for a music education experience.

Breaking Down Constructivism

Constructivism is broken down into two subsets: cognitive and social constructivism. Cognitive constructivism, associated with French Swiss developmental psychologist Jean Piaget, focuses on the individual and how they construct their knowledge through assimilation and accommodation (Powell & Kalina, 2009). Assimilation occurs when students take in new information in their own way of thinking; accommodation occurs when students change the way that they think in order to process new information (p. 243). Leo Vygotsky, the founder of social constructivism, believed that social interaction was an important part of the learning process, and social interaction from student to student promotes a higher level of learning (p. 243).

Constructivism in an In-Person Music Class

The constructivist teaching model in a music class is beneficial for several reasons. For one, students continuously build upon prior knowledge year after year. New information and skills are built upon, using previous information and skills already mastered. Using the example from earlier, Mr. Martinez built upon students' prior knowledge by performing a four-beat quarter-note rhythm while keeping a steady beat. As the year goes on, new rhythm patterns are added, building upon previous knowledge. Because he sees the same group of students every year in a different grade, another layer of difficulty is added, with more complex rhythm patterns, solfège notes, singing in pitch, and dividing beats into measures, among other musical skills. Even with new information processed year after year, the foundation of steady beat holds these new concepts in place. As students grow more proficient in music, they participate in ensembles such as band or choir. These skill sets go through the process of assimilation and accommodation over time; students add their own meaning to the taught concepts, applying then new information to their prior knowledge, enhancing their understanding.

Student interaction between other students leads to more meaningful instruction. While discussing a constructivist approach to teaching jazz music, Barron (2007) explains, "[a]lthough the developing jazz musician must inevitably devote the necessary time alone in the practice room, depth of understanding can be enhanced only through meaningful and repeated interactions with others" (p. 20). Learning does not have to be a one-person experience but rather a communal artform. Case in point, a second-grade class was learning solfège, a system that matches a syllable and hand signal with each pitch, creating a connection between three senses related to music: hearing, sight, and touch (Smith, 1934).

Mr. Martinez echoed back five different pitches: *low do-mi-sol-la-high do*. Students enthusiastically showed their hand signals while singing the correlating pitch. He then went on to show the students where the notes were on the music staff by way of flash cards created on a PowerPoint presentation. The prior knowledge was established, specifically that the signal and pitch of each note and their location on the music staff. Using this knowledge, the class went through a round-robin style of practicing, with different patterns of those five-note appearing before them. Students were given 30 seconds to practice the pitches, syllables, and hand positions of each note in student groups. The sense of learning communities occurred immediately as those who were struggling with hand signals were helped by their classmates around them.

Next, students were asked to perform individually, which resulted in variations on correct execution of the notes, hand symbols, and solfege syllables. After five random students performed, the entire class performed the solfège pattern before Mr. Martinez started the cycle again. Students were enthusiastic and engaged while performing this musical skill, one that develops over time. The social interaction between students, time given to practice and converse, and performing one-on-one while their classmates looked on, opened the opportunity for students to learn from each other in meaningful and impactful experiences.

Constructivism in a Virtual Music Class

How does the concept of student interaction work in a virtual music class? It is hard to imagine students interacting virtually for there is no way for them to learn from one other. The inclusion of technology is now a factor; how it is used can impact student learning (Johnson, 2017). Creative thinking is necessary when designing a constructivist virtual music class and shifting from the in-person experience.

As with the solfège lesson, Mr. Martinez went through the same process with rhythm with his second graders. As first graders, the students had learned a quarter note, quarter rest, and eighth note; it was a review of their prior knowledge. A new note was taught: the 16th note, adding onto their prior knowledge. Students had the opportunity to perform different rhythmic patterns one by one that included 16th notes while providing feedback to each other. This was done using virtual rhythm flashcards and sharing them on Google Meet. The students could be witnessed but not heard, as they were all on mute intently practicing the rhythms and moving their mouths.

When time was up, a myriad of emoji hands appeared on screen, eagerly waiting to be called upon to perform what they practiced. As students were called, they un-muted themselves and clapped out the rhythm, while their classmates watched from the screen. He then asked students to put a thumbs up if the rhythm was correct, a thumbs down if it was incorrect, or thumbs to the side if they were not sure. One by one, the students performed different rhythm patterns, while they gave instant feedback to each other. The teacher's role was first as a guide, using Socratic method to question students about their experience and evoke thoughtful answers. Students would answer with a thumbs up or down or in the chat, and after a while, they were providing the feedback to their classmates on their own while the teacher observed. Students engaged in constrictive critique and peer-review to perfect their skills. The students were not spectators but rather performers in their own learning.

Virtual learning communities were also impactful for instrumental learning. Students in band lessons tuned their instruments using a virtual tuner displayed by the teacher on a shared screen. They played their flute or clarinet on a concert B flat note; meanwhile, the tuner showed whether the note was flat, sharp, or in tune. If it was flat or sharp, the students knew how to adjust their instrument and would play again to doublecheck the pitch once more.

They then moved on to their lesson book, playing different exercises line by line. Whether in a woodwind lesson or a percussion lesson, the same order was followed each time: students were given 30 seconds to practice the musical line on their own. The teacher would watch the students practice as their sound was muted, which shed light on the different approaches that each student had to their individual practice. Some clapped the rhythm before playing the exercise while others went straight for it. After 30 seconds, the students stopped practicing, and one by one would unmute and play the exercise. Like the general music students, they provided feedback to each other in real time, with teacher support occasionally when necessary. Through this process, students learned ensemble, rehearsal, and performance skills all the while interacting virtually.

Soundtrap workdays were popular among the students, as students had the chance to work exclusively on project through this program and utilize different creative skills. On these days, the choice was given to conference with the teacher or work with peers online. From time to time, students asked for teacher support on projects, but for the majority of the time, students turned to each other for help, either unmuting themselves or typing their questions in the chat. Students gained knowledge and disseminated the information with others throughout their virtual learning community as a constructive practice.

Assignments and activities should be assigned in a way that connects with the students. Classwork must be based on real-world experiences instead of solely providing extra practice or to keep students busy. This results in meaningful learning experiences for all learners (Barron, 2007). When assigning a project on Soundtrap, the teacher designed the assignment in a way that would prompt student interest, connection, and engagement, as the language in the assignment mattered especially in engaging students while virtually learning.

For example, a common scenario provided could be considered as a routine chore, mandated as a requirement or formality of class participation:

Create a song that has an A section and B section, that is 16 counts long for each section, and be sure to include three to four sounds in each section with a fade in and out in the beginning and end.

The task lacks engaging in self-interest, which is always important but essential during virtual learning. Instead, the following scenario was given to the students to help promote interest and authenticity in learning:

You were hired by the music department of Kahoot to liven up the game music. Your new supervisor has given your first work assignment: Create new background music for Kahoot that is entertaining and will engage all players. You may share and discuss your creation with your co-workers.

Your music is to have the following:

- *An A section and B section, both with 16 counts each;*
- *Three to four sounds—not including a Bass and Drum—in each section; and*

- *Advanced editing skills, including fade in and out in the beginning and end.*

You are given one week to complete this task. A late submission means a deduction in your pay (in this case, grade point deducted for lateness).

The assignment written in this way accomplishes the following:
1. The assignment is now relatable to the students.
2. There is a connection between the students and video game music, many of whom play at home.
3. Students are placed in a real-life, problem-solving scenario. Students can approach this assignment however they see fit while following the requirements given.
4. Students can interact with other students. They can exchange ideas, listen to new sounds, and learn from each other.

In music class, meaningful connections and interactions formed through creating, performing, and responding allow students to take charge of their own learning. The teacher's role is to see the impact of the constructivist model in his music classes and continues with this concept online with high student engagement and performance.

Different Learning Styles

At this point of shifting to virtual learning communities during the pandemic, many music teachers have figured out how technology can be implemented in the classroom, established a virtual music community, and chose ideal pedagogical approaches to meet the needs of different grade levels. The next step brings focus on the art of teaching the material in this new environment. The challenges at hand at this stage include the number of students in different classes and environments, a productive plan for maximizing student learning in this virtual environment, while keeping in mind the different learning styles.

Why Is It Important?

Students process information in their own way. Gremli (1996) explains, "[a]n individual's learning style is the way that person begins to process, internalize, and concentrate on new material" (p. 24). Teachers tailor their lessons around the different learning styles of their students, adapting the lesson when necessary. Students are more than likely to retain information taught to them. Idrizi et al. (2018) state, "[l]earning is a complex process of achieving knowledge or skills involving a learner's biological characteristics/senses...[and] personality characteristics such as attention, emotion, motivation...[,] cognitive dimension, and psychological/individual differences" (p. 2). When a teacher can understand how their student learns, they then maximize their learning through different avenues. There are four widely accepted learning styles: visual, aural reading/writing, and kinesthetic, known as the VARK model (Fleming, 2011). These four distinct learning styles are to be taken into consideration when determining a student's learning style.

Visual Learners

Visual learners process information by demonstrations (Idrizi et al., 2018). Pictures, graphs, and demonstrations are utilized to enhance student learning. For example, in music class, the learners visualize the pulse of a steady beat by tapping; a YouTube video is used to reinforce the concept. They glance at a picture of the ocean, taking note of the up and down motion of the waves, making connections to how melody works including solfège notes going up and down on the music staff. Musical demonstrations such as watching a performance of Orff instruments, solfège hand-signals, and rhythm stick activities help visual learners process high performance skills.

Aural Learners

Aural learners process information by listening (Idrizi et al., 2018). They prefer to be provided with aural instructions and thrive in class discussions. In music class, auditory learners are most engaged through active listening activities. For example, students tasked with listening to music and analyzing different musical elements such as rhythm, melody, harmony, tempo, dynamics, timbre, and form. In solfège singing exercises, students perform different pitches by echoing back different solfège patterns they may hear. In a band class, they listen carefully to whether their instrument is flat or sharp.

Reading and Writing

Student learners under this category prefer to take and read notes (Idrizi et al., 2018), helping them remember information presented to them. They express and explain their understanding of the learned concept through writing. Music literacy is a large component of music class as they learn how to read notes on the music staff. Students feel that it is best to write notes for themselves so that they may use them when practicing outside of the classroom. These students may fear aural classroom discussions but thrive in writing activities.

Kinesthetic Learners

Kinesthetic learners process information by doing (Idrizi et al., 2018). Hands-on activities help more in processing information. Performing activities such as singing, playing an instrument, movement and dance, and composing music connect with them more. Other performance activities include tapping the steady beat on a body part in order to physically feel the beat or performing solfège hand signals to feel high and low pitches, connecting back to the ocean waves in melody.

Incorporating Different Learning Styles in the Virtual Music Classroom

Tasked with teaching students from kindergarten to eighth grade between general music, band, and choir, many music educators are challenged with delivering quality instruction across a vast area of expertise and domains within the music field. Experimenting with different ways of approaching student learning had to take place before they are able to execute a lesson with all four learning styles. To their advantage, they will be teaching the same group of students every year, and once the child's learning style is identified, the easier it became for to build lessons around it. There is no one size fits all solution. The described situation is unique to each music educator each year, and the approach must reflect that.

Examples of Visual Learning Activities

When learning virtually, visual examples are a primary means of supplementing lesson activities. For example, during a lesson for steady beat, students can follow along to the music while tapping their head to the beat. To reinforce the concept, students can use two pencils to tap along with the music as if they were rhythm sticks. The whiteboard tool becomes the substitute for the classroom board to write any information so that students could see the music staff or solfège notes, and have that live visual representation.

PowerPoint can primarily be used to provide a visual instruction of the lesson for the day. Songs can be matched with pictures with which students could connect. For example, a Thanksgiving song called "A Turkey Ran Away" could be matched with visuals of a turkey, an apple, a potato, and cranberries. Discussion and questioning techniques could be incorporated such as asking the class relatable questions like, "Why did the items run away?" Followed by a response from students, "Because they didn't want to be eaten!" The visuals help students to connect with the song with fun relatable discussion that incorporate their interests.

Soundtrap is a great visual learning platform, as students can see different beats layered on top of one another. This makes it easy for students to move beats around if needed. Students are able to see the beat travel as the song was played, connecting back to a moving beat. The same can be said for Chrome Music Lab, a website that had students creating music in fun, hands-on experiments (Chrome Music Lab, n.d.). The rhythm app on the website shows different rhythm patterns in beats of four, three, and two. Students can visually see the patterns that are played.

The virtual tuner can be an important part of band lessons. At the start of every lesson, the online tuner can be displayed on the shared screen so that students could see if they were in tune or not after playing their instrument, informing students if they were flat, sharp, or in tune. A virtual metronome is another great attribute for students to play their instrument in the correct tempo, not exceeding the intended speed and timing of the music. This is a huge support for individual practice, as well as during an ensemble rehearsal. This tool not only provides an auditory sound of the beat for students, but also employs a visual component to visualize the beat.

Examples of Aural Learning Activities

As a way for students to relax and enjoy and connect with the content before class begins, providing entrance music to fill the air such as jazz or unique recordings of other genres helps provide the human touch for a virtual music community. This give the opportunity for students to be exposed to different genres of music: from pop to hip-hop, classical to jazz, and Hispanic genres such as salsa, merengue, and bachata. Class discussions are then tailored to specific topics, such as Hispanic Heritage Month, Jazz History Month, or Women's History Month, and other cultural aspects related to curriculum. Students have the opportunity to engage with the content differently, and share how the music connected with them or how it made them feel.

There are times when events happen outside of the classroom that call for a teachable moment. Legendary Jazz pianist Chick Corea, whose compositions include "Spain," "La Fiesta," and "Windows," had passed away February 9, 2021, while Mr. Martinez's class was still being held virtually. Lesson plans were changed for the day, and instead there was a class discussion and spotlight honoring Mr. Corea's life and contributions to the music industry. After playing some of his performances on YouTube, including his 2004 live performance of 'Spain' from Montreux, Switzerland, students engaged in questions about his life, inquiring about topics related to his interest music, and the age he began learning piano. Some students commented on how his music was different, but enjoyed listening to it nonetheless. This is another example of how music listening exercises were a chance to know more about the students themselves and building community in virtual times. These types of activities allow the educator to learn about the student's interests in new ways, and work to incorporate their interests by customizing them into future activities.

Teaching music elements such as tempo or dynamics virtually is an exciting area to focus on with students. For example, a listening activity could be based on the piece "In the Hall of the Mountain King," by Edvard Grieg. Questioning exercises could include inquiries to the class focusing on the elements of tempo, such as describing the speed of the music in the beginning, and comparing to other parts. Dynamics questions would also relate to commenting on the volume of the music. Depending on the age level of the students involved in the discussion, answers will range from simply describing that the speed is slow, and the volume is soft, to the music is getting faster and louder. In time, students will confidently reply with specific music terminology, which are easily developed from this type of open discussion and critique within the virtual community.

Another virtual activity that is popular on student choice days, is a guess the rhythm game. Four different rhythms are displayed on their screen; a rhythm is played, and the students then guess which of the four rhythms was performed. Students are actively listening for and analyzing the correct rhythm being performed while choosing the correct rhythm displayed. Students can rely on their own manuscript paper at home to write what they think they are hearing, and compare their results to improve upon their aural comprehension skills. Having the shared screen option as an educator allows for an easy to display rhythmic options for students to analyze and choose from as this listen.

Examples of Reading and Writing Learning Activities

Not every student enjoys speaking aloud in class for personal reasons. They may have an introverted personality, afraid to say the wrong answer, or scared of judgement by other classmates. If those students do not like to speak in class, how is the opportunity given for them to participate and engage with the classroom environment? This is where the reading and writing activities in a virtual setting become a powerful tool for those students. Mr. Martinez thought carefully on how to accomplish this.

Policy should be considered, but making the decision to leave the chat feature of a virtual class on to allow students the opportunity to comment if necessary. It seemed dangerous at first because there is no control over what is typed in the chat, but it can accomplish several important points. First, it allows students who did not feel comfortable talking in class the opportunity to participate. In an in-person classroom environment, there are always some who are quiet and less participative, and it can be a challenge to ascertain their understanding of the material at hand.

This helps give voice to those in a modified way so that they can express themselves and show engagement in a way that is most comfortable for them.

Second, it is easy for students to type a question or a comment while instruction is going on. They did not have to wait to be called on and it ensures that the teacher would see important questions and comments at the time they were needed. This guides the teacher's approach to delivering content and is a helpful point to make adjustments in real-time to address the needs of the students as whole. This provides the opportunity for the teacher to modify instruction on-the-go, and help address the immediate needs of the students.

As with any type of virtual social interaction, guidelines need to be set to maintain appropriate use. This was a consideration that required checking with the policy of the school, and then developing classroom guidelines for the purposes of the class. Much like when classes meet in-person, the educator needs to clearly communicate this so that everyone in the class is aware of the expectations. It can be as simple as stating that the chat is to be used in a respectful manner with no inappropriate comments allowed, and followed up with consequences so all know what to expect if infractions occur. Based on the type of class, subject matter, and other factors, these should be developed by each educator to meet the needs of their students in the online environment.

Based on the environment that the student is logging on from, this may be the best mode of communication. During specific activities in the virtual music class-room, giving the students the option to type their thoughts in the chat or to verbally speak aloud, gives them the freedom of choice in how they want to communicate. The chat becomes especially useful during music listening activities, during which students can type their thoughts in real time as they listened to the music without having to verbally interrupt the listening example.

Writing assignments can include journal entries about the music listened to in class. Students can write paragraphs on their thoughts and feelings related to the music, which sometimes allows them to work through personal feelings. During the pandemic this not only included normal challenges for students, but also a death in the family or illness, keeping up with the workload of other classes, and the feeling of isolation caused by needing to say home. Music often opens these discussions of expression and helps students connect with their emotions, so journal assignments can be use sporadically as a way to check in with the students, giving them the opportunity to express themselves and address their social and emotional needs (Edgar, 2017).

Examples of Kinesthetic Learning Activities

During virtual learning, Mr. Martinez's day would begin at 8:40 a.m. and end at 1:10 p.m. with classes at 28 minutes long and a few minutes of break in between. It may be easy for an adult to sit behind a computer for that long, but it is nearly impossible to imagine a kindergartener sitting for four hours behind a computer, staying still, and focused on what was being taught. For students to learn, especially when they are young, movement is a must.

Movement activities can be integrated to begin every class meeting. These types of activities for a virtual music classroom can include freeze dancing to a video on YouTube, where when the guitar stops strumming everyone in the classes freezes. Another could include a spatial awareness activity to music, providing students the chance to stand, stretch, and express themselves through movement and music. When reinforcing steady beat, students can tap their heads, shoulders, legs, and heart, connecting that steady beat is the heart of music, which allows them to internalize the music and feel the beat in their body.

Soundtrap is a great program that provides students hands-on experience of how music is created, and allows them to make their own beats and digital compositions as they learn musical elements and incorporate AI. With this program, students can complete lessons that result in composing a cell phone ringtone or background music to a video game through project-based learning. When learning musical form, students can creat songs based off of a given structure, whether in binary or ternary form.

Chrome Music Lab is a great tool to reinforce musical element concepts such as these through hands-on music activities, by allowing students to start small and adapt a constructivist approach to developing their musical knowledge. Music educators can easily rely on these tools to help develop curricular-based alternate activities to support the new needs of online learning. With some research and planning, these suggestions help address various student learning styles, as well as modifications and differentiated needs that can be difficult to address through virtual learning. By helping students tap into their strengths through these tools and modifications, student engagement can be strengthened in a challenging virtual environment.

Engagement Unlocked

Establishing an online community, discovering the ideal virtual teaching approach, and discovering the individual learning styles and needs of all students, while integrating technology, can be challenging aspects that educators are tasked with throughout their virtual teaching experience. By constructing meaningful, real-world lessons, students are given the opportunity to take ownership of their learning in new ways as they learn in the setting of a virtual community. With the inclusion of different learning styles and activities—auditory, visual, reading/writing, and kinesthetic—student are given the arena to construct their own knowledge, while adding on to their existing and developing expertise. It is essential in a virtual learning community that educators find unique ways to create an environment in which students can interact with each other, and collaborate naturally. Most importantly, students must know that they are cared for, and this will positively impact student engagement and participation.

At the end of day, students receive a grade for the class and move on with their day. It should not be about grades, for they are just a number. It may say "85" or "95" or "100", but what does it all mean? How can educators ensure that their students leave their virtual learning community with the enduring understandings of the lesson at hand? An exit ticket can be a quick assessment that helps educators ascertain what students are taking away with them, and also provide essential and simple data so they can prepare to meet the needs of each student in the next class.

The real grade lies deeper is in the response to a simple "exit ticket" question: "What did you learn in music class today?" Essential questions can be easily utilized here, to help the educator grasp what needs review for next time, and what new material they can look forward to presenting. The role of a music teacher is not to simply pass along the knowledge of music, but rather to have students engage in a performance that is personal to them (Blair, 2009).

Three Takeaways

If there is anything to be learned from the COVID-19 shutdown, it is that there is no replacement for traditional in-person learning; students need in-person, peer-to-peer contact. The skills that are taught from a young age are built upon year after year. The virtual learning experience, through constant trial-and-error, was efficient because of the intentional thought process that was behind it. The goal—continue the education of the students by way of virtual learning when being in person was not possible—although simple, had many moving parts involved.

This experience has three takeaways as a result of virtual learning:
1. Activities incorporating the different learning modalities create meaningful instruction for students, resulting in high engagement and minimal behavior issues.
2. Students who have gone through virtual learning have experienced difficulty on many levels. There was, however, perseverance and strength that allowed the students to overcome this obstacle. If there was a need to transition back to virtual learning, students and educators will be better equipped to do so; they are resilient.

3. Authentic learning does not stop online. Students should continue to learn and grow from each other, and with a carefully curated virtual learning environment they can. Students are constantly surrounded with technology and it should be used to their educational benefit.

Follow-Up

As the Covid-19 pandemic started to come under control and schools reopened for in-person instruction once again, Mr. Martinez, now in his fifth year of teaching music, continues to implement lessons and concepts learned from virtual learning in his in-person music class, while keeping up to date on current educational trends. His knowledge of technology has grown drastically, with an online music curriculum that serves as the basis of instruction, supplemented by other online resources. Chrome Music Lab and Soundtrap have been successfully accepted and integrated into the district music curriculum, with new projects teaching students different compositional skills, connecting back to real-world experiences. Collaborative work is a major component of the class, with students working together to build on prior knowledge and create new information. Students tap into their strengths by way of their different learning styles. A community of learners is excited to make their way to music class each week where they create, perform, connect, and respond to music with high levels of participation and engagement. The techniques and resources that were developed and refined in virtual learning, are now blended with the established benefits of the return to in-person instruction. If virtual learning were to occur again, Mr. Martinez would be more than ready to tackle another unexpected surprise and be able to help his students continue to thrive in their music education.

REFERENCES

About Soundtrap. (2024). Soundtrap. https://www.soundtrap.com/about

Adams, C. (2019). TPACK model: The ideal modern classroom. In Power, R. (Ed.), *Technology and the curriculum: Summer 2019*. Power Learning Solutions.

Angelle, P. S. (2008). Communities of practice promote shared learning for organizational success. *Middle School Journal*, 39(5), 52–58. 10.1080/00940771.2008.11461654

Barron, J. (2007). Lessons from the bandstand: Using jazz as a model for a constructivist approach to music education. *Music Educators Journal*, 94(2), 18–21. 10.1177/002743210709400205

Blair, D. V. (2009). Stepping aside. *Music Educators Journal*, 95(3), 42–45. 10.1177/0027432108330760

Chrome Music Lab. (n.d.). https://musiclab.chromeexperiments.com/About

Edgar, S. N. (2017). *Music education and social emotional learning: The heart of teaching music*. G. I. A. Publishing.

Fleming, N. D. (2011). *Teaching and learning styles: VARK strategies*. Neil D. Fleming.

Garlock, L. (2020). Contributions of Jazz to Modern Music. *Copyright Alliance*. https://copyrightalliance.org/contributions-of-jazz-to-modern-music/#:~:text=Rock%2C%20R%26B%2C%20Hip%2Dhop,R%26B%20or%20Latin%20styled%20tunes

Gremli, J. (1996). Tuned in to learning styles. *Music Educators Journal*, 83(3), 24–27. 10.2307/3398974

Hewitt, D. (2018). Constructing informal experiences in the elementary general music classroom. *Music Educators Journal*, 104(3), 46–53. 10.1177/0027432117745361

Idrizi, E., Filiposka, S., & Trajkovik, V. (2018). VARK learning styles and online education: Case study. http://hdl.handle.net/20.500.12188/24558

Johnson, C. (2017). Teaching music online: Changing pedagogical approach when moving to the online environment. *London Review of Education*, 15(3), 439–456. 10.18546/LRE.15.3.08

Kenny, A. (2016). *Communities of musical practice*. Taylor & Francis. 10.4324/9781315572963

Main, P. (2022). Google Classroom: A teachers guide. *Structural Learning*. https://www.structural-learning.com/post/google-classroom

Mishra, P., & Koehler, M. J. (2006). Technological pedagogical content knowledge: A framework for teacher knowledge. *Teachers College Record*, 108(6), 1017–1054. 10.1111/j.1467-9620.2006.00684.x

Moir, E. (2013). Riding the first-year roller coaster. *Educational Horizons*, 92(1), 6–8. 10.1177/0013175X1309200103

Ozola, S., & Purvins, M. (2013) Teaching/learning theories: How They Are Perceived. *Bulgarian Comparative Education Society*, 133-138.

Plant, R. (2004). Online communities. *Technology in Society*, 26(1), 51–65. 10.1016/j. techsoc.2003.10.005

Powell, K. C., & Kalina, C. J. (2009). Cognitive and social constructivism: Developing tools for an effective classroom. *Education*, 130(2), 241–250.

Smith, M. (1934). Solfège: An essential in musicianship. *Music Supervisors' Journal*, 20(5), 16–61.

Wenger, E. (2011). Communities of Practice: A Brief Introduction. http://hdl.handle .net/1794/11736

Wentzel, K. R. (2010). Students' relationships with teachers. In Eccles, J. S., & Meece, J. L. (Eds.), *Handbook of research on schools, schooling and human development* (pp. 75–91). Routledge.

Yilmaz, K. (2011). The cognitive perspective on learning: Its theoretical underpinnings and implications for classroom practices. *The Clearing House: A Journal of Educational Strategies, Issues and Ideas*, 84(5), 204–212. 10.1080/00098655.2011.568989

KEY TERMS AND DEFINITIONS

Aural: Style of learning that favors to gather information by listening, such as audio recordings, podcasts, or lectures.

Communities of Practice: A group of people that come toegther because of shared interests and learn how to perform better as they interact with other people.

Constructivism: A theory in education that states learners must construct their own knowledge, building upon prior knowledge to understand and applying concepts and ideas. Student to student interaction plays an important role in creating knowledge.

Kinesthetic: Style of learning that favors hands-on activities to gather information.

Learning Styles: A wide range of theories that attempt to detail how a person learns and gathers information.

Reading and Writing: Style of learning that favors gathering information by reading (text, handouts, manuals) and writing.

TPack Model: 'Technological knowledge, pedagogical knowledge, and content knowledge.' Technological knowledge is the understanding of having knowledge of current available tecnhology. Pedagogical knowledge is the understanding of how to organize and present content for learners. Content knowledge is the knowledge of the subject matter.

Visual: Style of learning that favors information presented by pictures, charts, or various visual media options.

Chapter 2
Communities of Practice in the Workplace

Remberto Jimenez
New Jersey City University, USA

Veronica E. O'Neill
New Jersey City University, USA

ABSTRACT

This chapter will focus on reviewing the core elements of communities of practice in the workplace through four case studies that illustrate examples of what can be done to support organizational learning. Any organization, or workplace, has practices, domains of knowledge, and communities of employees. Yet, the role of communities of practice allows these three dimensions to come together and support employee success, learning, and embedding key practices. This chapter will begin with a review of the workplace and workplace learning. The chapter will then focus on what constitutes a community of practice, and additional permutations of the concept, such as landscapes of learning, that support learning. Four case studies in this chapter will focus on communities of practice examples from the medical field, corporate environments, and education. Suggestions for future research will also be discussed.

INTRODUCTION

Learning does not happen in solitude. Whether one is learning at home, in an office, in any sort of workplace, or even in online digital spaces, learning is an active process where meaning-making occurs. These interactions with others, regardless of whether they take place through synchronous or asynchronous channels, lead

DOI: 10.4018/979-8-3693-1111-0.ch002

to information and knowledge sharing. As people engage with the knowledge and information, learning occurs through active use of the information. This learning can be evidenced through the creation of artifacts, discussions, or some form of interactive engagement that leads to learning. This process takes us from just acquiring the knowledge of a practice and community, to participating in the creation and eventual evolution of this knowledge into the practices of a community. Learning comes from the participation and interactions with others as well as the knowledge that we bring based on our own past experiences.

Yet, learning from a community perspective is not just about learning for the sake of learning. Rather, it is about emerging ideas and thoughts that are immersed in beliefs and ideals, and even in the procedural understanding of a community. A community can be formal or informal. Communities can be temporary or long-lived. Communities can form as subgroups within a specific community. Regardless, communities blossom over time in the environments that they inhabit.

When we consider the role of learning, communities, and workplaces, we must consider the different ways that learning happens. The bodies of knowledge and practices of a community will vary greatly based on the industry, company, and roles defined within a given organization. Communities will emerge from the practices and norms derived from company policies, departmental mandates, standard operating procedures, and organizational norms and beliefs.

These communities ultimately lead to a landscape of experiences and knowledge making that support learners across their journey in the workplace cultures that emerge. As such, the role of these communities and the practices that both emerge and are reinforced by an organization can support the learning function, and support employee success. Therefore, the creation of communities that support such practices are seen as potentially desirable resources that can benefit employees across an organization. The practices, and how they are shared, updated and reinforced to support the needs of an organization, must also be considered when utilizing such avenues to support employee learning.

This chapter focuses on reviewing the core elements of communities of practice in the workplace through four case studies that illustrate examples of what can be done to support organizational learning. The concept of workplace is defined and examples are provided based on the recent literature. The chapter then focuses on what constitutes a community of practice, and additional permutations of the concept, such as landscapes of learning, that support learning. The four case studies this chapter focus on community of practices examples from the medical field, corporate environments, and education. Suggestions for future research are also discussed.

UNDERSTANDING THE WORKPLACE

In recent years, the word "workplace" has evolved and is no longer limited to a physical space or even a point in time (Cairns & Malloc, 2011). Today, work can happen at home, in an office, or any location where one can connect to their device and perform some form of work related to their role or function within an organization. All work requires the use of knowledge, procedures, and skills that that can run the gamut from interpersonal skills, including collaboration, active listening, and problem solving, to more technical skills, such as drawing blood from a patient, building a brick wall, rerouting cables to a new building, or using analysis database tools such as Python, R, or SQL.

When we think of the idea of work, there is learning that happens both to support the practices of an organization, as well as learning that emerges from the experiences formed through work. Cairns (2022) also looks at work as a learning process. Learning through work "involves meaning making and experiences that add to each worker" (Cairns, 2022, p.21). Both organizations and the role of an individual may dictate where work happens, and what knowledge and practices need to be learned to be successful in a given role or function. However, it is the individual and their engagement in the workplace that can have a profound effect on their short- and long-term success.

Engagement is not just about showing up and collecting a paycheck, although that can be seen as a result of working. Engagement at work means being a part of the community and engaging in their practices. O'Connor and Lynch (2011) note that "an empowered, engaged individual is a productive individual; an alienated or stagnant individual simply does not care" (p. 421). Engaged employees will be productive, but they must also become engaged in the community of practice to learn, contribute, and pivot as the workplace and practices evolve.

According to Wenger-Trayner and Wenger-Trayner (2015), the real body of knowledge of any profession is the "community of people who contribute to the continued vitality, application, and evolution of a practice" (p. 52-53). Engagement also means taking on the practices and contributing to the evolution of said practices. The practices of an organization may be both formal and documented. However, some practices may be informal and not necessarily obvious until interaction with other members of the community occurs. It is through these communities, both formal and informal, where the practices can be learned and honed over time.

Regardless of what constitutes the workplace for an individual, all workplaces have norms and requirements that every employee must learn. Therefore, success in the workplace requires the active engagement of its members. Active engagement means that employees use the tools, resources, and procedures available, to support employee immersion into the practices of the community. Procedures can change over time. The tools or applications used can evolve as new technology emerges. This means that the practices of a community can evolve, and we must evolve so that we can continue to contribute and inform what constitutes the practices of a community. We can only do this as engaged members of the community of practice. Through such active engagement, learning can be facilitated in the workplace.

LEARNING WITHIN THE WORKPLACE

Just like practice, learning in the workplace is also dynamic in that it can take on many forms as well. Learning can be part of a formal process, it can be informal, or it can be part of what happens on the job as employees go throughout their day. Learning can be just-in-time and as an employee engages in a particular situation or task. Hase and Blaschke (2022) describe learning as a "just in time phenomenon where opportunities to learn must be harnessed when the occasion presents itself, regardless of whether we are looking for them or not" (p.81). Cairns and Malloc (2011) define learning as "the outcome of an enabled active intentional interactional engagement in experiences and thinking" (p. 9). As such, opportunities for learning can happen at any time in the workplace.

Formal workplace learning usually falls into the purview of some form of a learning and development, or training function within an organization (Jimenez & O'Neill, 2023). These could be sub-teams within a division or department, such as the human resources department, or it can be a function within a specific part of the business, such as sales or marketing. Lui-Abel (2011) notes that "organizations have always relied on their training departments to ensure workers possessed appropriate skill sets to do their job" (p. 407). This can include teams that support the onboarding function for new hires, ongoing mandatory or compliance related training, as well as process and procedure related training sessions that are specific to a set of roles and or functions within the organization. Organizations are constantly looking for new ways to manage knowledge and new ways to support learning (Özdemir et al., 2022). However, being given the opportunity for learning is one thing. Actively engaging in that opportunity is another issue altogether.

Active learning strategies are used to help employees learn more through non-passive engagement with content and with others (Jimenez & O'Neill, 2023; Jimenez & O'Neill, 2022; Ueckert and Gess-Newsome, 2008), while also supporting opportunities for reflection, critical thinking and conceptual understanding (Jimenez & O'Neill, 2023; Jimenez & O'Neill, 2022; Colomer, et al. (2020); Mendez-Carbajo, 2020). In short, when learners can experience the knowledge, processes, and procedures related to their job firsthand, through these experiences, meaning-making and new ideas are formed. The modalities used can vary from engagement with digital content to interaction with other members of a community, whether synchronous or asynchronous. What matters is that through active engagement, learning occurs and can immerse that employee further into the practices of an organization.

For example, if a project manager reads the instructions on how their team keeps track of their projects but does not actively engage with this information and apply it, it is considered a passive form of learning. It is not active and will have a lower chance of being remembered. However, if the project manager logs into the project management tool and walks through the experience of what it is like to enter a task or milestone related to a project, then greater levels of learning, and retention, are occurring through these actions.

Therefore, employees must also take an active role in learning the practices needed to do their jobs. Active community members learn through engagement through their work and the work based on the practices of the community (Pyrko et al., 2017). These experiences help employees to develop the knowledge and skills needed to be successful, while also immersing them into the practices of the community. Over time, as the employee becomes more experienced and immersed in the practices of the community. They begin to add new ideas, new ways of thinking, and enhanced practices that can be shared by the rest of the community. Learning is not just a transfer or sharing of knowledge, but a continuous cycle to add and evolve the processes of the community (Wenger-Trayner, et al., 2022, p. 14).

Pyrko et al. (2017) describe learning as a "social formation of a person rather than as only the acquisition of knowledge" (p. 391). Through these social interactions, the identity of the individual is changed as part of a meaning making experience (Pyrko et al., 2017). This is in contrast to the original version of communities of practice focused on individuals building competence in practice and becoming members of a community (Lave and Wenger, 1991). From a practical perspective, as community members engage in the practices of a community, there will be a change for each individual's personal growth.

It is impossible to retain every bit of knowledge that could be possibly relevant to a community. However, it is possible to immerse oneself into the practices of a community to become immersed in a given role or function in a community. For example, a new nurse who starts in a new role at a hospital will need to immerse themself in the practices of their profession and in the practices of their new assignment. Over time as they repeatedly engage in these practices, they become further immersed in what it means to be a nurse and to be an employee of that particular hospital. They gain knowledge, but they also form relationships, and potentially influence or recommend changes to practice as they continue to grow in their role and in their understanding of the practices.

Employees must understand how to do their job, but also acquire the skills needed to support potential transitions into other roles or even promotions that may arise over time. Some organizations may offer formal organizational programs to support employee onboarding and reinforcement. Some communities create their own localized programs to support the knowledge sharing needed to support their ongoing learning. While still other communities may offer both formal and informal mentorship to guide and support employee learning as well. In addition, there is also a need for localized, community-specific learning that should also be included as part of ongoing learning as well. Therefore, communities, and the practices within a community, become critical components to any workplace.

COMMUNITIES OF PRACTICE

Grounded in the work of Lave and Wenger (1991) and social learning theory, Communities of Practice have existed for over 30 years in corporate and educational environments. Communities of practice are groups of people that share a common interest in a specific subject, and actively engage with each other to form new levels of ideas and understanding (Seddon, 2022; Wenger et al., 2002; Pyrko et al., 2017). Communities of practice serve as a way for employees to immerse themselves into the myriad aspects of a role or function. These communities can thrive in any organization, regardless of the number of employees or the industry/category that the organization serves.

To better understand the role of communities of practice, one must first understand what is meant by the words community and practice. Krogh (2012) defines 'community' from "a classical sociological premise where people form social bonds through shared norms, traditions, identity, and solidarity" (p. 412). A community can therefore be as small as a task force, a team, a division, a department, or as large as a hospital, school system, or even a corporate workplace. The underlying theme is that the community forms around individuals who share an interest in the ideas or norms of a group. For example, consider a person who just started a new role working at a concession for a local stadium. The employees of that concession stand form a community. The norms, traditions, and identity of the concession stand workers unite them in a set of experiences and practices that are unique to that role and to the members of that group.

In terms of practice, it refers to a collection of activities within the confines of a group or system, while learning continues as an active process within the confines of this group (Gherardi, 2000; Pyrko et al., 2019). Practice is also not just the established rules and activities of a group, but the negotiated new meaning and understanding that emerges over time from the active participation of these members in a given community. (Gherardi, 2000; Pyrko et al., 2019). For example, when a new cashier works for a supermarket, they learn the practices inherent in the role of a cashier. That community of cashiers learn through the legitimate peripheral participation in the activities of their community.

Legitimate peripheral participation serves as the means to acquire skills and put them into use (Lave and Wenger, 1991, p. 100). Over time that cashier can help reinforce the practices of that community in their daily tasks. They can also engage in activities that change the way that a task of function is performed. This new change in procedure could then be added to the practices, resulting in a dynamic community of practice that can change and evolve over time.

When combined together, the idea of community and practices form the operating guidelines that individual members follow and use in their day-to-day activities. Through these day-to-day activities, learning happens. These communities of practice are seen as effective modalities to support knowledge sharing and creation (Kim et al., 2012; Kasemsap, 2016). It has also achieved a level of legitimacy in the social science and organizational bodies of knowledge (Kasemsap 2016; Perron & Duffy, 2012).

Consider how adults learn by doing. Communities of practice provide the knowledge needed to support learning through the knowledge that is captured by the community. However, the knowledge in a community must be maintained and modified in order to support the processes and practice of any community. This knowledge is maintained both locally and across the organization; with some organizations opting to use knowledge creations and management strategies to store the institutional knowledge for the various communities (Gairin, et al., 2016). As members engage in a practice, the knowledge is reinforced through the repeated actions that the knowledge affords. Active engagement and learning occur through the maintaining, as well as the modification, of these practices.

DOMAIN, PRACTICES, AND COMMUNITIES

In addition, communities of practice focus on three core dimensions: Community, practice, and domain. The domain refers to the ideals and capabilities that members of a community identify with and care about, for example, their role and function in an organization(Wenger-Trayner & Wenger-Trayner, 2015). This is the tacit knowledge that members use to perform their day-to-day roles and functions. It can be technical, operational, or even aspirational depending on the organization. These domains can be therefore focused on a specific or very broad set of skills for the community to succeed both at an individual and organizational level (Wenger-Trayner & Wenger-Trayner, 2015).

Some roles may have practices that are unique to a specific discipline, while some roles may have broader responsibilities and may involve multiple domains of practice that must be learned. For example, the leader of a learning and development team needs to understand the domain knowledge of the learning and development function. In addition, that leader also must be familiar with the operational practices of the organization since that individual also possesses leadership practices to which they must adhere.

Some roles may also need to have additional domain knowledge when it comes to how the company makes money, and how the learning and development team operates to support corporate level objectives. As such, the role of an individual will play a significant role in the body of domain knowledge that will be relevant for both short- and long-term success. This in turn supports the communities in an organization to understand what is expected of them through the standard and agreed upon practices. The community becomes the keeper of knowledge who maintain and reinforce potentially dynamic practices that can change at the speed of business.

LANDSCAPES OF PRACTICE

Another layer to consider from the literature is that these more complex domains, and roles in a community of practice, lend themselves to the idea of a landscape of practice. Landscapes of Practice can be seen as the totality of local communities of practice and situated learning (Wenger-Trayner et al., 2014). In other words, think of a landscape of practice as a collection of multiple communities of practice that combined together form an all-encompassing body of knowledge (Keane et al., 2022). The members of a local community of practice form through the local, situated practices inherent in a community; these practices of a community may not necessarily be harmonious or devoid of conflict and tension (Wenger-Trayner, et al., 2014; Contu and Willmott, 2003; Wenger, 1999). As such, landscapes may have communities that may share common goals and interests but may not be aligned in terms of their practices or beliefs.

The individual and their beliefs play a role through any landscape of practice. It is the individual who finds their way through a landscape of practice and therefore develop relationships in practice within distinct communities across the landscape (Wenger-Trayner, et al., 2014). Consider a global corporation such as American Express. They have multiple communities of practice that exist across the various roles and departments that exist within the organization. They also have additional domains of knowledge that are unique by division, customer types, as well as by country. In such cases, the individuals share both local and non-local practices that support their learning and continued success. Each person must travel through these landscapes and travel from community to community to get work completed, to grow as an individual, and contribute to the bottom-line for their organizations.

In other cases, there may be overlapping communities that exist across various organizations. For example, human resource professionals exist across various organizations. They have their own inherent practices within their place of work. There are also standardized practices that they get from industry organizations such as the Society of Human Resource Management (SHRM). These industry specific organizations provide the standardization across key practices that are shared with other human resource professionals across the globe. Those localized professionals take these practices and embed them into the practice so their local communities as applicable.

Regardless of how many communities exist within a given landscape of practice, the individual plays a role in what practices from these external organizations can be embedded into their local practice. The individual becomes critical to the formation, modification, and use of bodies of knowledge in their own practice and in the practices formed across the landscapes (Jimenez & O'Neill, 2023; Wenger Trayner and Wenger-Trayner, 2015). The individual makes a conscious choice to either follow or disregard practice; they may do this in solitude or as part of their social interactions with others. Communities live and die through the actions of the members involved.

When looking at the concept of communities and landscapes of practices, it may seem overwhelming with all the myriad situations that could exist for an individual. It is not possible to become competent in all the inherent practices of an organization (Wenger-Trayner, et al., 2014). However, through the negotiating of what is important and what is not, one can engage in meaningful activities that still support employee success. Many organizations understand this and offer knowledge-sharing databases and resources to support the ongoing community. Competence is supported through the daily activities that help one problem solve and become more knowledgeable practitioners (Wenger-Trayner et al., 2014; Pyrko et al., 2019). Competence will grow as we repeat practices and reflect on what is and is not working.

Through these actions, landscapes and communities are social constructs that are critical to community development. Communities of practice develop in part through the relationships that we build at work, the collaborations that occur through our interaction with others, and even the problems that we solve together (Holland, 2018; Saldana, 2014; Wenger, 2009). These interactions help us to shape the ideals, best practices, and communities in which we work. Through these interactions, engage with each other and in the domains of knowledge that are most relevant to us, to our community, and to our landscapes.

These relationships are grounded in the concepts and ideals of situated learning and social learning theory, where learning happens through engagement with others and with the practices of a community (Anderson, et al., 2020, Brooks, et al., 2020; Lave & Wenger, 1991; Bandura, 1991). Based on these ideas, individuals learn in situated context through legitimate peripheral participation (Lave & Wenger, 1991). This idea undergirds the core concepts of how learning occurs through the use of communities of practice. Research on organizational environments indicates the important role of colleagues, mentors, managers, or professional contacts within a learner's personal and professional contexts (Anderson et al., 2020).

Therefore, the social aspects inherent to these communities and learning should not be minimized. This can be the case for employees collaborating in-person, on-line, and hybrid environments. By working together and through the use of relevant practices, we can upskill employees, instill the ideas and norms that are critical for success, and we also help further support their immersion into the community and or landscape. These ideas are not just relevant to corporate and medical enforcement. They can also be relevant to the academic sector as well.

COMMUNITIES OF PRACTICE IN EDUCATION

It is appropriate to note that there are variations on the communities of practice theme, called professional learning communities (PLCs) that are common in education. Typically, educational goals are led by the principal of the school, directing teachers in how to collaborate to achieve student learning goals, especially those prescribed by state regulations. However, this tends to stifle teachers, making them more concerned with covering material than fostering effective learning. By instituting a PLC, teachers can shift to a more collaborative role, coaching each other and sharing ideas to help students master their learning goals (Gaskins & Williams, 2022).

In higher education, students are sometimes arranged into PLCs. For example, the College of the Holy Cross in Massachusetts places all incoming freshmen into a program called Montserrat, an interdisciplinary cluster, with a corresponding residence hall and a first-year seminar. The students are immersed in a liberal arts approach to real-world issues. By living, working and studying with other cluster members, students experience deeper learning and make lifelong friends (College of the Holy Cross, 2023).

Similarly, all incoming freshmen at San Diego State University are required to participate in the Living Learning Communities (LLC) program. Students select an LLC seminar course each semester of freshman year. These courses combine a first-year seminar course with an advising component. The program continues the next semester, with the selection of a second LLC course. LLC students live in housing specific to the theme of the LLC course they are undertaking (University of San Diego, 2023).

REAL WORLD EXAMPLES

Communities of practice exist in a variety forms across multiple industries. The following sections detail some applications of the concepts described above, set-in real-world situations.

Ann: New Employee Experience

Ann was just hired as an entry level clerk at Megacorp, a large corporation located in her town. She is a recent college graduate, and this will be her first real job after years of part-time work in fast food. Ann was a good student, on the honor roll throughout high school, and cum laude in college. She majored in English literature and took a selection of liberal arts and business courses. Ann had two interviews before she was offered the job. Today is her first day of work, and she is understandably nervous. She does not know anything about what Megacorp does, or about how she will fit in, and is starting as an entry level employee. Ann's new manager, Eileen, is looking forward to onboarding her newest employee. She sees a lot of potential in Ann and is excited to get started on building Ann's future.

There are many ways to orient a new employee to a workplace. Some companies present new hires with hours of in-person training, to explain the history of the company, its position in the market, and its workplace rules. Other companies present the same information using programmed instruction on the Internet. As each module is completed, a brief quiz is presented so the company can document employee achievement.

Megacorp has opted to combine this type of training, for the basics and required compliance training, with team-specific training known as a Community of Practice (Wenger, 1999). In this model, new employees are embedded with more experienced teammates. As they encounter situations, and understand how to handle them, they can become mentors for that circumstance. No one is assumed to know everything, and leading is not limited to the most experienced team members.

One hallmark of this strategy is the concept of legitimate peripheral participation. This means that a newer teammate is still participating even if they are primarily learning. As they learn more and more, they will be able to take the lead in future situations.

In today's world, work is often accomplished by inputting information into computer systems, which translate that input into coding and subsequent action. The input is critical, because mistakes cause delays in processing and rejected work. When a new agent begins to work in such an area, they rely on their training and reference materials to guide them. If they are still unsure, they can reach out to another agent nearby to get a second opinion. However, the rookie agent soon learns that it is often more efficient to walk over to the most experienced agent in their area for a second opinion. The experienced agents have encountered such situations with greater frequency, and can greatly reduce the risk of delays and rejection. This extremely informal example is cost effective and useful (Lave & Wenger, 1991).

Patrick: Training New Nurses to Become Part of the Team

Patrick is the Director of the Center for Professional Development, Innovation, and Research for a major hospital. In this position, he oversees the training of recent graduates, training of experienced nurses who are transferring to specialty units in the hospital and addressing potential issues by creating and delivering training sessions in response to identified needs. In addition, he oversees the education of other healthcare professionals in the hospital. Patrick leads a team of seven full-time educators including the educators for the specialty units, such as operating room, emergency department and critical care.

As you might imagine, the needs of these three major groups vary greatly. For the most part, even though new nurses have graduated from nursing school and passed a licensing examination, their hands-on experience is limited to closely supervised clinical hours during nursing school. The orientation process for new graduates is typically three months, while specialty nurses such as operating room staff can be in orientation for up to a year.

In addition to being the nurse educator for the unit, each trainee is assigned to a nurse preceptor, who works with the orientee one-on-one to ensure the effectiveness of the training. All trainees meet weekly with their nurse manager, the nurse educator for the unit, and their own preceptor, to ensure clear communication about progress and upcoming goals. Each orientee has their own orientation plan, reviewed constantly to ensure progress is being made.

In the event that the orientee's preceptor is not available on a given day, the nurse manager and nurse educator will assign a substitute preceptor so the orientee is never left alone. The orientee has access to a broad community of practice within their specialty. Additionally, due to a high number of new graduates being hired, the hospital has developed a nurse residency program. This program continues the relationship with the preceptor, but there are also structured classes dealing with issues common to new graduates. Patrick feels that this orientation process is effective and is not looking to make any major changes at this time.

James: Building a Global Learning Organization

James is head of learning and development for a global organization. His primary focus is on their US business. He is responsible for all learning related initiatives, ranging from technical business processes, soft skills development, and regulatory/compliance initiatives. New employees join this team with widely different backgrounds and experience profiles. Depending on their new role, there are variations in the onboard training. However, all receive an invitation to sign up for the company's learning management system and are assigned a learning curriculum. For example, there are different learning paths for sales, marketing, finance. There is also a Standard learning path for roles that don't fit into these paths.

Once a new team member is onboard, they are assigned a buddy by their leader. This is a more experienced team member who guides them on day-to-day functions. Some areas hold group meetings including discussions about issues and concerns. These groups provide opportunities for new employees to meet peers and form their own support groups. Other team members also help and answer questions during the onboarding process.

If a buddy is not around or is not engaged, it can derail the training process. The new hire may take the initiative to find a substitute buddy, or may accept the situation, which harms the new hires' learning. If Patrick could improve anything about the onboarding process, he would ensure that the entire global landscape was reflected in training materials giving all team members access to specialized experience.

Joan: Operating in an Ever-Changing Global Landscape

Joan works for a major, global bank, in a highly regulated operations area. In brief, every publicly held corporation is required by local law to hold an annual shareholder meeting, where shareholders can vote on various issues critical to the corporation. In the largest markets, such as the United States, Canada and the European Union, the rules for these meetings are well known. In fact, corporations outsource these meetings to a vendor, as they are straightforward, and easy to track systematically.

However, many companies are organized in other jurisdictions. Each of these markets has its own regulations for notifying shareholders, disclosure of shareholder identity, and privacy. The companies also hire different agents to collect and tabulate votes, each of which has its own procedure.

As you might imagine, the bank would be happiest if the staff could input the country of incorporation, and a procedure would be presented. That is not realistic considering the complexity of the process. Joan is an expert in this process, with over 25 years of experience handling international meetings. If there is a meeting that is not handled by the vendor, there is a standard set of questions that she researches, using the answers to lead to the next question. The options are far too complex to be reduced to a decision tree or similar document. As Joan trains new staff members, she ensures that they understand why the choices were made, and that any new information is added to the database. She also makes herself available to all staff to guide them through the process and provide support as needed. This is just another example supporting the understanding that there are multiple ways to implement the concept of the community of practice, but all are marked by communication among fellow employees, not just with managers.

DISCUSSION AND AREAS OF FUTURE RESEARCH

The preceding cases showcase the importance and roles that community of practices can play towards workplace and organizational success. The practices inherent to any type of workplace must be spelled out and understood by the community members. The domains of knowledge must also be agreed upon and standardized across the workplace as well. However, the one element that is critical to the success of any community of practice is the people.

The community members are critical to both sustaining and evolving the practices and domains of knowledge across any organization. The individual becomes critical to the formation, modification, and use of bodies of knowledge in their own practice and in the practices formed across the communities and landscapes (Jimenez & O'Neill, 2023; Wenger-Trayner & Wenger-Trayner, 2015). As such, the workplace must also take into consideration the importance of having all its members aware of the practices within their domains and within the confines of the practices that are presented. This means that it is important that employees, the members of the communities, must understand that they are all in a community and all are responsible for helping each of the members thrive and succeed. This may pose a problem in some work environments where members are prone to withholding information due to the benefit of their longevity, and or trajectory that they want their careers to take to the detriment of others.

Everyone in a community must understand that they share responsibility to help maintain the norms, change practices and domain information, and evolve with the processes and procedures required of their roles. This also includes helping their fellow members, even if it is as simple as pointing them in the right direction to someone who can help and answer their questions. Some organizations may have codes of conduct or other behavioral expectations and standards that are communicated to others. It is one thing to have these codes of conduct, but it is another thing to make sure that employees are not just aware of them but take these codes of proper conduct as part of the practices of their communities. A community is only as strong as its weakest link. Therefore, all community members must not just be immersed in the practical knowledge of their role and community but must also share the willingness to impart such information as well for the success of their organization.

Future research is recommended when it comes to understanding the personal perspectives of individual employees in a community of practice. In some organizations, some individuals may not realize that they are in a community of practice and what that entails, especially in more informal communities that emerge. Informal organizational structures, there are learning and development, or training roles that are assigned to support and help the members of a community. But in more informal communities, these structures may not exist, or are seen as something other than does not pertain to their specific role of function. This will impact the role of learning in communities of practice and how learning is seen within these landscapes. Further research to support the individual perspective of community members will be needed both across formal and informal communities.

Further research will be needed to understand future knowledge management strategies to support domain knowledge and key practices of a community. Some organizations invest in knowledge management systems to formally store their bodies of knowledge. However, these depositories can quickly become outdated if not maintained by the members of a community. There are many tools that organizations of all sizes can consider to support their knowledge management strategies. This can include wikis, formal knowledge databases in platforms such as ServiceNow, as well as in their respective learning management and content management systems.

Depending on the organization, there may be some cost consideration when it comes to formal knowledge management applications. Some of these platforms may be outside of the budgetary constraints of an organization. However, relying on undocumented knowledge that resides in the mind of an employee is also not feasible, especially at the rate that employees are changing jobs thanks in part to the recent phenomenon of quiet quitting and the great resignation. Further research is recommended to understand how this knowledge can best be maintained and shared across varying industries and roles.

Finally, domain knowledge and practices are also being affected by the proliferation of artificial intelligence and machine learning. Organizations are looking at these tools to automate practices and use domain knowledge to completely restructure operational functions. This will in turn impact what roles and functions may exist in the coming years, including roles that may not even exist today. This change will have a great impact on communities of practice and their members. It is important to understand how communities of practice will evolve due to these changes and what these communities and landscapes will look like in the coming years. We also need to look at how learning in the workplace changes due to the further inclusion of these tools and resources.

CONCLUSION

Communities of practice serve a purpose in supporting organizational success through the support and learning of its membership. The role of individual members within a community of practice plays a significant role in the success or decline of a community. Communities of practice offer rich opportunities to be immersed in the practices and knowledge of specific domains. Regardless of whether one is working in a community of practice, a landscape of practice, or a professional learning community, the benefits are worth the effort needed to maintain and evolve such groups.

The example of the nurse educator and nurse preceptors shows the importance that individual members play within a community. The individual members of a community are instrumental in supporting the learning, both formal and informal, that transpires within such communities. The individual is also the beneficiary of a community of practice in that it helps to support their understanding of the norms and practices within their domain of knowledge. Their interactions, grounded in the theories of social learning theory and situated learning, showcase the importance of human interaction not just in the workplace, but in all facets of life. Regardless of whether the workplace is in person, or remote, the interactions between people is in how we learn and thrive in any community.

Regardless of what the future holds for the workplace, communities of practice, in all their forms, will continue to play toward individual and organizational success. As new generations begin to enter the workforce, and more seasoned professionals are looking to retire, the role of knowledge management strategies to capture the practices and domains of knowledge will become critical. The transfer of knowledge and practices from the retiring employees needs to be distilled and shared with the next generation to support organizational continuity. Finally, the immersion of the newer generation into current practice, and the new knowledge that they can bring to the evolving practice will also be critical for long term success.

REFERENCES

Anderson, V., Gifford, J., & Wildman, J. (2020). An evaluation of social learning and learner outcomes in a massive open online course (MOOC): A healthcare sector case study. *Human Resource Development International*, 23(3), 208–237. Advance online publication. 10.1080/13678868.2020.1721982

Bandura, A. (1991). Social Cognitive Theory of Self-regulation. *Organizational Behavior and Human Decision Processes*, 50(2), 248–287. 10.1016/0749-5978(91)90022-L

Brooks, J., Grugulis, I., & Cook, H. (2020). Rethinking Situated Learning: Participation and Communities of Practice in the UK Fire and Rescue Service. *Work, Employment and Society*, 34(6), 1045–1061. 10.1177/0950017020913225

Cairns, L., & Malloch, M. (2011). Theories of work, place and learning: New directions. In M. Malloch, L. Cairns, K. Evans, & B. N. O'Connor (Eds.), *The SAGE handbook of workplace learning* (First ed., pp. 3 - 16). SAGE Publications Ltd.

Cairns, L. G. (2022). Learning and work: theories and developments. In M. Malloch, L. Cairns, K. Evans, & B. O'Connor (Eds.), *The SAGE handbook of learning and work* (pp. 5-33). Sage Publishing. 10.4135/9781529757217.n2

College of the Holy Cross. (2023). Montserrat. https://www.holycross.edu/holy-cross-approach/montserrat

Colomer, J., Serra, T., Cañabate, D., & Bubnys, R. (2020). Reflective learning in higher education: Active methodologies for transformative practices. *Sustainability (Basel)*, 12(9), 3827. 10.3390/su12093827

Contu, A., & Willmott, H. (2003). Re-Embedding Situatedness: The Importance of Power Relations in Learning Theory. *Organization Science*, 14(3), 283–296. 10.1287/orsc.14.3.283.15167

Gairín, J., Rodríguez-Gómez, D., & Barrera-Corominas, A. (2020). Hints for rethinking communities of practice in public administration: An analysis from real practice. In I. Management Association (Ed.), *Open Government: Concepts, Methodologies, Tools, and Applications* (pp. 342-363). IGI Global. 10.4018/978-1-5225-9860-2.ch018

Gaskins, R., & Williams, A. (2022) *Set your team on fire: The three elements of a professional learning community.* Academic Press.

Gherardi, S. (2000). Practice-based theorizing on learning and knowing in organizations. *Organization*, 7(2), 211–223. 10.1177/135050840072001

Hase, S., & Blaschke, L. M. (2022). Heutagogy, work and lifelong learning. In M. Malloch, L. Cairns, K. Evans, & B. O'Connor (Eds.), *The SAGE handbook of learning and work* (pp. 80–98). Sage Publishing. 10.4135/9781529757217.n6

Holland, E. (2018) Mentoring communities of practice: what's in it for the mentor?. *International Journal of Mentoring and Coaching in Education.* 10.1108/IJMCE-04-2017-0034

Jimenez, R., & O'Neill, V. E. (2022). Strategies to Maximize Asynchronous Learning. In Durak, G., & Çankaya, S. (Eds.), *Handbook of Research on Managing and Designing Online Courses in Synchronous and Asynchronous Environments* (pp. 499–521). IGI Global. 10.4018/978-1-7998-8701-0.ch025

Jimenez, R., & O'Neill, V. E. (2023). Workplace Learning Trends: Third-Party Resources as Part of an Organizational Learning Content and Knowledge Strategy. In R. Jimenez & V. O'Neill (Eds.), *Handbook of Research on Current Trends in Cybersecurity and Educational Technology* (pp. 390-405). IGI Global. 10.4018/978-1-6684-6092-4.ch021

Kasemsap, K. (2016). Utilizing communities of practice to facilitate knowledge sharing in the digital age. In Buckley, S., Majewski, G., & Giannakopoulos, A. (Eds.), *Organizational Knowledge Facilitation through Communities of Practice in Emerging Markets* (pp. 198–224). IGI Global. 10.4018/978-1-5225-0013-1.ch011

Keane, J. T., Otter, M., & Violette, J. (2022). Impacting Practice: The Role of Digital Credentials in Social Learning Communities. In Huang, Y. (Ed.), *Handbook of Research on Credential Innovations for Inclusive Pathways to Professions* (pp. 194–213). IGI Global. 10.4018/978-1-7998-3820-3.ch010

Kim, S., Hong, J., & Suh, E. (2012). A diagnosis framework for identifying the current knowledge sharing activity status in a community of practice. *Expert Systems with Applications*, 39(18), 130893. 10.1016/j.eswa.2012.05.092

Krogh, G. V. (2012). Knowledge sharing in organizations: The role of communities. *Handbook of organizational learning and knowledge management*, 403-432.

Lave, J., & Wenger, E. (1991). *Situated learning: legitimate peripheral participation (Learning in Doing: Social, Cognitive and Computational Perspectives).* Cambridge University Press. 10.1017/CBO9780511815355

Lui-Abel, A. (2011). Identifying and classifying corporate universities in the United States. In M. Malloch, L. Cairns, & K. Evans (Eds.), *The SAGE handbook of workplace learning* (pp. 407-419). SAGE Publications Ltd. 10.4135/9781446200940.n30

Mendez-Carbajo, D. (2020). Active learning with FRED data. *The Journal of Economic Education*, 51(1), 87–94. 10.1080/00220485.2019.1687377

O'Connor, B. N., & Lynch, D. (2011). Partnerships between and among education and the public and private sectors. In *The SAGE Handbook of Workplace Learning* (pp. 420–430). SAGE Publications Inc. 10.4135/9781446200940.n31

Özdemir, İ. H., Sarsar, F., & Harmon, S. W. (2023). Blended Learning in Higher Education. In R. Jimenez & V. O'Neill (Eds.), *Handbook of Research on Current Trends in Cybersecurity and Educational Technology* (pp. 365-389). IGI Global. 10.4018/978-1-6684-6092-4.ch020

Perron, G. M., & Duffy, J. F. J. (2012). Environmental and business communities of practice: graduate students comparing community-relevant language: Assessing community of practice identity through language. *Business Strategy and the Environment*, 21(3), 170–182. 10.1002/bse.725

Pyrko, I., Dörfler, V., & Eden, C. (2017). Thinking together: What makes communities of practice work? *Human Relations*, 70(4), 389–409. 10.1177/0018726716 66104028232754

Pyrko, I., Dörfler, V., & Eden, C. (2019). Communities of practice in landscapes of practice. *Management Learning*, 50(4), 482–499. 10.1177/1350507619860854

Saldana, J. B. (2014). Comparison of community, practice, domain, and leadership expressions among professional communities of practice [PhD dissertation]. University of Phoenix, ProQuest LLC, Ann Arbor, Michigan.

Seddon, T. (2022). Liquid learning: re-conceiving the lived-in-world. In *The SAGE handbook of learning and work* (pp. 158–172). SAGE Publications Ltd. 10.4135/9781529757217.n11

Ueckert, C. W., & Gess-Newsome, J. (2008). Active learning strategies. *Science Teacher* (Normal, Ill.), 75(9), 47–52. https://search.proquest.com/docview/214624210 ?accountid=12793

University of San Diego. (2023). Living Learning Communities. https://www .sandiego.edu/learning-communities/

Wenger, E. (1999). *Communities of practice: Learning, meaning, and identity*. Cambridge University Press.

Wenger, E. (2009). Communities of Practice and Social Learning Systems: the Career of a Concept. In Blackmore, C. (Ed.), *Social Learning Systems and Communities of Practice*. Springer., 10.1007/978-1-84996-133-2_11

Wenger-Trayner, E., Fenton-O'Creevy, M., Hutchinson, S., Kubiak, C., & Wenger-Trayner, B. (Eds.). (2014). *Learning in Landscapes of Practice: Boundaries, Identity, and Knowledgeability in Practice-Based Learning* (1st ed.). Routledge., 10.4324/9781315777122

Wenger-Trayner, E., & Wenger-Trayner, B. (2015). Learning in a landscape of practice: a framework. In Wenger-Trayner, E., Fenton-O'Creevy, M., Hutchinson, S., Kubiak, C., & Wenger-Trayner, B. (Eds.), *Learning in landscapes of practice* (pp. 51–78). Routledge.

KEY TERMS AND DEFINITIONS

Communities of Practice: Groups of people who share a passion or interest in a given domain and engage in activities that lead to the expansion of their understanding of this topic area.

Community: Groups of people that share a common interest, belief, or share some form of commonality that unites them as members of a group, such as members of a town, school, or work location.

Domain: Domains are bodies of knowledge that can consist of knowledge and practices found in the context of a team, group, or organizational body.

Knowledge Management: The process of organizing, creating, using, and sharing collective knowledge within an organization.

Landscape of Practices: A collection of communities of practice and the spaces between them that could hold various domains of knowledge and practices.

Practice: The processes or actions of a group that are explicitly and implicitly linked to some form of group or role identity of both formal and informal environments.

Professional Learning Communities: The educators version of a community of practice; a group of educators who collaborate and towards the improvement of student learning and their profession.

Situated Learning: A learning theory that is focused on grounding learning within authentic activities within a given context and culture.

Social Learning Theory: A learning theory proposed by Albert Bandura that emphasizes the importance of observing, modeling, and imitating the behaviors, attitudes, and emotional reactions of others.

Workplace Learning: Any formal or informal learning that occurs in a workplace that supports the processes and knowledge needed to perform a role or function.

Workplace: Any place where work is performed.

Chapter 3
Virtual Professional Learning Communities for Educators

Sarah Martin

Bridgewater Raritan Regional School District, USA

ABSTRACT

A virtual professional learning community (PLC) has the potential to impact positive change in a variety of work environments. The PLC model fosters collaboration and community among educators while achieving learning goals and shaping professional practice. As educators, we are often presented with professional learning opportunities that feel irrelevant to our daily classroom practice. Professional development opportunities often miss their mark because the stakeholders do not feel vested in the learning. Professional development delivered through a PLC model leverages the collective experiences of the participants with the powerful reflection that comes through collaboration. Well-designed PLCs engage stakeholders because the PLC model takes into account adult learning styles and hinges on the meaningful contribution of each participant. Thus, PLCs are a powerful tool for delivering professional development and shaping positive outcomes. This chapter will examine the definition of a PLC, describe the logistics of designing and implementing a meaningful community of virtual learners, and offer a first-hand account of how a virtual PLC was implemented in a middle school to impact professional practice. While the anecdotal accounts are specific to a middle school environment, the fundamental aspects of PLC design and implementation can be applied across a wide array of professional environments. Thus, much of the chapter content will be applicable beyond the scope of a school.

DOI: 10.4018/979-8-3693-1111-0.ch003

A TEACHER'S TYPICAL DAY

The concept of professional learning is not unique to the vocation of education. In many fields, professionals are expected to grow their knowledge via professional development through attending conferences, completing continuing education courses, participating in in-house training, and taking part in out-sourced seminars and courses. What makes professional learning in the field of education unique, is that it needs to be tempered with the demands of a teacher's schedule, specifically the commitment to delivering in-person instruction to students.

Teachers spend the bulk of their professional day engaging with students. There is no substitute for the consistent classroom presence of an experienced educator. Student success is directly impacted by daily, in-person exchanges with teachers. As a nation, our experiences with on-line and virtual learning during the pandemic underscored just how vital in-person learning is for intellectual development, academic achievement, and social and emotional learning of students of all ages. Taking time away from classroom instruction is disruptive to the student experience and detrimental to student success.

Herein lies the challenge of professional development for educators. How do schools support teacher development and growth while maintaining continuity of instruction for students? While it may sound wonderful to attend a three-day professional conference with colleagues in your field; that will be three days out of your classroom. Engaging in the academic side of the teaching profession has value, to be sure, but it comes at a cost to the students who miss out on having access to their teacher.

The same can be said for in-house development. In many schools, teachers are pulled throughout the year for half-day or full-day professional development sessions within their districts. While many of these sessions provide value, they still remove the teacher from the classroom. The challenge to providing meaningful professional development opportunities for educators begins with how to schedule the activities within the scope of the teacher's day, without upending classroom instruction.

Here is an example of one teacher's typical day. Ms. Kopp, an eighth-grade social studies teacher in a large suburban school district, arrives at school by 7 o'clock each morning. This is a full hour before she is contractually obligated to be at school. In this first hour, Ms. Kopp grades papers, makes copies, and readies her room for the day's learning activities. She will not have time to attend to these tasks once her students arrive. At 8 o'clock, she begins homeroom. There is attendance to be taken, notes to be collected, fliers to be distributed. She has roughly fifteen minutes of student contact time during homeroom.

Ms. Kopp has three minutes from the end of homeroom until her first teaching period. Her twenty-five homeroom students exit, and her twenty-seven social studies students arrive. For the next forty minutes she is engaged in instruction. Classroom instruction looks different depending on the day. She may be delivering a whole class lesson, meeting one-on-one with students who need individual support, facilitating small groups, guiding a project, or hosting a seminar. No two days are ever the same, but every day is busy. With just three minutes between teaching periods, Ms. Kopp's day moves quickly. One class leaves, another arrives. She teaches five periods of social studies and one period of study hall. Ms. Kopp has twenty-five minutes to eat her lunch.

Built into her day is one period free from student-contact. This is considered a prep period. It is the same length as the teaching periods. During this period, Ms. Kopp might be contacting parents, prepping lessons, or meeting with colleagues. Every Monday, Ms. Kopp and her colleagues are required to stay one hour after the students leave for a meeting. The meeting may be a faculty meeting with the principal and the whole school, a department meeting with her social studies colleagues and their supervisor, or a district-led meeting with administrators from the central office. During department meetings, there is sometimes an opportunity for professional development.

Ms. Kopp's schedule is tightly packed from the time she arrives at school at 7 o'clock until she leaves at 3 o'clock. Often, she takes home papers to grade because there is simply not enough time during her day at school. This is not uncommon. Most teachers work several additional hours at home on lesson planning and grading. Many teachers' schedules are further constrained with coaching or club advisory duties. There is little time for much else.

In addition to time constraints, there is also the challenge of providing professional development to educators that is relevant to their content-area practice. Ms. Kopp's school serves only seventh and eighth graders, but there are roughly seven hundred students in each grade. At each grade level, there are twelve English teachers, six social studies teachers, six science teachers, six math teachers, and multiple special education teachers, some of whom teach small groups of students in resource room settings and some of whom co-teach with general education teachers.

The professional development needs of a math teacher are different from the needs of an English teacher. Each content-area has a different classroom protocol. The science teachers facilitate labs with students, there is a lot of group work and investigation. This classroom functions differently from an English classroom where students are not working on labs, but might be meeting in book clubs or doing a guided reading assignment. In an effort to deliver professional development to an entire school faculty, schools often fall short on delivering differentiated and meaningful opportunities for real professional growth. Often, educators are lumped together as one large group and fed presentations about topics that feel unrelated to their practice or redundant due to their experience and expertise.

Ms. Kopp's most recent professional development involved sitting through a presentation from her administrators about facilitating classroom discussions using a Socratic seminar model. In this model, the students take ownership of the discussion. It is a technique for engagement that works best when implemented by experienced educators. This model is not something that you would expect to see a first-year teacher attempting, and requires a high degree of classroom management and a comfort level that is honed over many years of working with students.

The entire school faculty was part of this session, led by the building's assistant principals. The faculty was first asked to complete a warm-up; a technique that many educators use to get their students ready for learning. While it may seem like a solid idea to create engagement, asking educators to behave like children can also feel condescending. This is certainly not going to create buy-in from the target audience. Much of the development offered to teachers involves this kind of misguided role play. Teachers know what goes on in the classroom; they do it each day.

The first problem with Ms. Kopp's last professional development involved the delivery. Most of her colleagues felt that the administrators were speaking down to them and insulting their professionalism. The second problem with this professional development was the content. Ms. Kopp is a veteran teacher. With over twenty years of teaching experience, she is well-versed in the Socratic seminar. It is a routine part of her classroom plans. She could have led the professional learning that day. Ms. Kopp was not alone in feeling this way. Most of her colleagues in the social studies department already know how to implement the seminar.

This professional training did not only alienate veteran social studies teachers who were already familiar with the content, it also alienated teachers whose classrooms don't rely on discussion of academic texts. Mrs. Laroach, who teaches physical education in Ms. Kopp's school could not see herself implementing a Socratic seminar. It simply doesn't fit with her classroom practice. Both Ms. Kopp and Mrs. Laroach would have benefited from spending this precious time on growing in a way that was meaningful to their lived experiences.

Implementing school-wide professional development is challenging. In most schools, you will find a diverse array of educators from myriad backgrounds with varying levels of experience. The professional development on the Socratic seminar would have been better rolled out to a small group of second- or first-year teachers who use discussion techniques in their classroom or offered as an optional session for educators who specifically wanted to learn about this strategy.

The session did not provide differentiation to meet the needs of the diverse body of learners. These educators were now in the seats of their students, but were not afforded the same basic requirements in instruction that they themselves are expected to provide when teaching classes. Designed differentiation opportunities added to professional development experiences for educators can help anticipate the need for choice or collaboration among fellow educators that help each contribute in meaningful training experiences (Johnson, 2009), and would have been a great alternative to the aforementioned professional training.

Choice in topics, are an easy way to ensure that the needs of many educators are being met, as well as providing hands-on or collaborative sessions to layer learning experiences. It also addresses the needs of veteran and novice educators serving on the same professional team. Developing a sense of collaboration through Professional Learning Communities (PLC) can also help develop support among educators that remains for the entire school year as they implement new techniques in the classroom.

What Is a Professional Learning Community?

Professional learning communities (PLCs) are sometimes referred to as professional development communities (PDCs) or professional learning networks (PLNs). These communities are essentially groups of professionals who meet over a set timeframe to grow knowledge about a particular topic related to their profession. Communities may look different and function differently across professional environments in order to meet the individual needs of the group, but all PLCs are centered around the idea of colleagues learning together with a common goal of growing as professionals in a given area.

Collaborative and cooperative in nature, these communities of professionals rely on the collective experiences of the participants (Riggins & Knowles, 2020). This model values the lived professional experiences of each participant and is well suited to meet the unique needs of the adult learner (Roumell, 2018). The most successful PLCs support participants in not only developing new understandings, but also in applying that new learning to professional practice (Roumell, 2018). Professional learning communities are informed by social learning theory (Johannesson, 2020). Inherent in the definition of community, social learning theory is grounded in the notion that new learning happens as a result of interactions between people.

The PLC Model in Educational Settings

The PLC model has great potential for transforming the way we implement professional learning for educators. Imagine how much more relevant Ms. Kopp's professional learning would have been had she been able to determine the focus of her study based on her individual professional strengths and weaknesses? Svendsen (2020) identifies the PLC as being one method of sustainable improvement in learning conditions and culture. Educators like Ms. Kopp and her colleagues are commonly fed professional development that feels irrelevant to classroom practice.

Often, the learning objectives have been designed without all stakeholders' input. The traditional conference-style or one-day workshop is perceived by teachers to be the least impactful method of professional learning that actually shapes classroom practice (Avidov-Unger & Zion, 2019). This creates a lack of engagement on the part of participants, as the learning is disconnected from their lived experiences.

Further, in the field of education, there is sometimes a tendency to be over-didactic in interactions between colleagues. This is what happened when Ms. Kopp's administrators tried to engage the faculty with an activity designed for students. Treating teachers like the students they teach is not a way to build buy-in or engagement. A PLC affords a unique opportunity for learners to become active participants in goal setting. This type of environment fosters true professional discourse that values the participants' expertise. When teacher-participants feel valued, they also feel vested (Avidov-Unger & Zion, 2019).

A review of the literature yields some common characteristics of successful PLCs within educational environments. While these studies are specific to the field of education, the big ideas that emerge from the findings are applicable to professions other than education. At its heart, a successful PLC is collaborative (Avidov-Unger & Zion, 2019; Burns, et al., 2018; Riggins & Knowles, 2020). There are peers and participants, but no one should be singularly guiding the discussion or direction. In some cases, one person may act as facilitator or secretary to guide organization and materials, but this is mostly a team effort. No one voice should dominate the group.

A successful PLC is also inquiry-based (Burns, et al., 2018; Svendsen, 2020). Asking questions is an important tool for digging deeper into any topic. Inquiry acts as an important motivating factor in the functioning of a PLC. When colleagues are engaged in active questioning about issues related to professional practice, there is space for reflection. Focusing on inquiry also provides a clear focus for the work of the PLC as well as a framework for evaluating the efficacy of the group's progress and growth in a given area (Svendsen, 2020).

Finally, successful PLCs are given the time and space they need in which to function efficiently (Avidov-Unger & Zion, 2019; Burns, et al., 2018; Riggins & Knowles, 2020). The PLC is not a one-time opportunity, but rather an on-going professional conversation within an established community that is carried out over the course of a set amount of time. In order for this to happen, the group needs to function with autonomy. Treating the PLC with professionalism affords the group credibility within the larger organization.

When implemented with care, PLCs afford teachers the opportunity to engage in action research as a method for improving practice (Johannesson, 2020). Action research is noted as a powerful tool for empowering teachers to shape and change their professional practice (Black, 2021). Action research, like the PLC model itself, is inquiry-based. With action research, the educator is involved with evaluating the problems within their own organization.

As such, the researcher and other stakeholders are active participants in a process that evaluates outcomes within their control (Arslan-Ari, et al., 2018). The action research model fits beautifully with the tenants of a PLC; educators investigating their professional practice within their own organization, asking questions about where they see room for improvement, making plans for how to implement change, and working together to evaluate the outcomes and hopefully impact positive change.

The idea of action research, where teachers are leading their own inquiry into a given topic and then creating strategies for recontextualizing their practice, is an enormously powerful motivator for participants within a PLC (Avidov-Ungar & Zion, 2019). Action research focuses on observation and investigation in order to make improvements at an organizational level rather than theoretical research which seeks to fill a gap in the literature (Vaughan, 2020). By fostering profession-alism through agency and inquiry, the PLC model of professional learning affords teacher-participants the freedom to explore topics that are relevant to their own professional practice (Black, 2021).

Not only do PLCs lend themselves to supporting the best practice of action research, PLCs are noted as having a positive impact on both system-wide change and student outcomes within a school (Svendsen, 2020). Organizational change is complicated. In order to bring about meaningful change, organizations must consider the embedded perceptions, beliefs, and practices of stakeholders (Cooper, et al., 2016). Teachers are consistently identified as the most influential factor on student achievement (Black, 2021). It would stand to reason that educators should be active participants in any efforts towards systematic change. Educators working as part of a PLC are uniquely situated to lead efforts to improve outcomes.

Cooper et al. (2016) present findings from a case study examining outcomes of teacher leaders implementing PLCs to bring about organizational change using Kotter's eight steps for leading organizational change. The eight steps encompass developing a sense of importance around the problem, building buy-in among stakeholders, removing barriers to empower action, maintaining participant moti-vation, and finally enacting change (VanWyk, 2020). Kotter's steps are applicable to any PLC, even if the goal of a PLC is not to bring about organizational change, but simply to impact professional practice.

The opportunities for growth and improvement in professional practice are maximized when teacher-participants feel vested in their learning (Avidov-Ungar & Zion, 2019). As noted earlier, the impact of buy-in from the participants cannot be overstated. In order to be successful, the PLC must have a focus that is relevant to the participants daily practice. Reading articles about topics unrelated to the daily instructional practices of the group will not create excitement about the learning.

Benefits of a Virtual PLC

Prior to COVID, the concepts of collaboration and virtual communities seemed incongruous. There was often the assumption that collaboration inherently involved in-person meeting. One positive outcome from collective experiences of teaching and learning during the pandemic is that many educators reshaped and challenged our thinking on this topic. While few will argue that in-person instruction between educators and students in a K-12 setting, is by far the most impactful kind of instruction, new understandings emerge related to the benefits of virtual collaboration when it comes to teacher professional development. There are a host of benefits to engaging in virtual communities in order to build understanding and shape professional practice.

The proliferation of opportunities for virtual or online professional development (PD) have been well-documented in the literature. Parsons et al., (2019) investigated US teachers' perceptions about virtual PD. Their findings offer significant insight into the efficacy for this type of PD. To begin with, the majority of educators they surveyed identified having participated in virtual PD. And the majority of those who engaged in virtual PD found it extremely effective. They also found that teachers who voluntarily participated in online PD reported better outcomes. This speaks not only to the benefits of virtual PD, but also supports the PLC model where participants have autonomy over their professional learning.

Parsons et al., (2019) also raise important points about social learning. Namely, they observe that the idea of participating in PD that involved being part of an interactive online community of practice, as opposed to virtual PD that was non-interactive, was especially appealing to the participants in their study. This speaks to the idea of learning as a social construct and informs the notion that collaboration with colleagues is an important motivating factor for educators.

Theory into Practice

In order to be effective, the topic of the PLC needs to be relevant to all participants. This is not a one-size-fits all model. The diverse needs of educators as professionals must be taken into consideration. A veteran math teacher may not need to sit through a presentation on classroom management, but they may benefit from a session on differentiation. Many veteran teachers feel comfortable in their content-area knowledge, but may look to develop their practice in other areas. Remember Ms. Kopp sitting in a professional development session about a topic she was already well-versed in. Her learning time would have been better spent learning about a topic she wanted or needed to explore.

Differentiating professional learning allows school districts to stand behind their beliefs in what makes strong pedagogical practices, and transfer some of these techniques to how they train their educators by blending them with andragogy. To support classroom-based instructional change, educators need to be exposed to training that supports their interests, as well as small group collaborative spaces to work with colleagues in developing a plan for applying new techniques (Grierson & Woloshyn, 2013). This type of collegial support can be an important factor that continues to support educators throughout the course of the school year, address-ing challenges, student abuses, and successful methods so they can be refined and modified for all grades and subject domains.

In the case of the independent reading PLC, members of the English department in a large suburban middle school completed a needs-assessment prior to the devel-opment of the PLC. This tool is invaluable in establishing a common need among a group of professionals. Determining the difference between individual needs and those of the wider community is important in planning (Wright, Williams, & Wilkin-son, 1998), and carrying out professional development training. Where learning and problem-solving may follow a template at times, there is no one approach that can account for individual challenges and personalization. It seems so simple, ask the people what they need. Yet, this is often where professional learning misses the mark.

The needs assessment yielded a common concern among the colleagues. They were all looking to improve their classroom practices around the topic of student-selected independent reading. Many participants felt that they were being expected to deliver instructional outcomes in this area without receiving clear guidance on best practices.

Once they established a common need, they set about to create a routine for meeting. In this case, the length of the learning community was predetermined. The group of about 22 English teachers decided to meet for a total of six sessions. This process of mapping out a PLC, was important for all stakeholders to establish a routine prior to beginning, because it set expectations and was helpful for reserving time for collegial support. The beginning of the independent reading PLC coincided with the return to in-person instruction after the pandemic. The shift from virtual to in-person instruction was challenging at best and created its own set of scheduling challenges, so the PLC met virtually to garner wide participation and considerably cut back on scheduling conflicts.

Having just experienced the challenges of virtual instruction in the K-12 setting, some participants worried that virtual meetings would be a stumbling block; that their collaboration would feel less authentic and that participants' voices would get lost in the whirl of a Google Meet. These fears were well founded in light of the lived experiences of students and teachers during the pandemic. The reality of this virtual PLC turned out to be quite the opposite of this initial assumption. Because the group was meeting virtually, people had greater flexibility with meeting times.

Issues like childcare, second jobs, and meeting space did not impact them. During the actual meetings, there was a palpable sense of freedom among participants. Participants were not being held in a room for a set amount of time, worried that once the meeting ended they still had to contend with the task of getting themselves to the next place they needed to be.

The group created their own Google Classroom as an online virtual community, and facilitated meetings via Google Meet. This afforded easy sharing of materials and the participants had a place to also share experiences in-between meetings. Once they identified their big topic to be independent reading, they needed to hone in on a focus related to independent reading.

Each participant was asked to generate a list of concerns related to the main topic of student selected independent reading. Those results were analyzed for common themes, which later informed the focus for one of their six PLC meetings. In turn, each meeting became its own thread on the Google Classroom, to streamline the organization of articles reviewed during that session and provide a space for participants to share the implications noted in their practice.

For each session, the group's facilitator selected current, academic literature related to the topic of that session. This usually included two articles with a strong focus on practice, as opposed to theory. It was powerful to see participants feeling excited about seeing their specific concerns addressed in a professional and meaningful way. This proved to be the most important factor in making participants feel like professionals.

The group's meetings were an opportunity for participants to share elements of their own professional practice as well. The true collaboration came when participants were able to offer practical solutions to each other. The group set the expectation that each participant would arrive at the meeting having already read and annotated the articles for that day. During the meeting, participants shared what they learned in the article and how they saw that as being relatable or useful to their own practice. As a community, they were able to decide what was feasible, and what detracted from their goals in the classroom.

The Google Classroom learning management system (LMS) proved extremely useful in the sense that even when the session was finished, if a participant developed materials related to that topic, they could easily share with the group. There are many LMS options to choose from, but they are advantageous to organizations in education and beyond. They are able to support learning and development programs that members of the community can access autonomously, and receive collegial support when they need it, not just during a training session (Braunston, 2018). Thus, the learning and collaboration continued long after the session ended, as did the professional support and collegiality. Participants were engaged in practice shaping discussions.

At the end of the PLC experience, the administration in their organization was supportive of the initiative; the value of which, could not be overstated. All participants were able to use the time in their PLC sessions as part of their professional development hours. Having administrative backing for their work not only lent credibility to their efforts, but also served as a motivating factor for participants to continue their professional practice.

Guide to Implementing a PLC

Whether you are an administrator looking to support goals related to organizational improvement or you are a teacher looking to collaborate with colleagues about how to improve instructional practice, the PLC model has the potential to be a catalyst for change. For educators, professional goals are often determined by organizational goals or initiatives. This administrative practice has the potential to strip educators of professionalism and integrity, by setting objectives without teacher-input. This is the antithesis of the core tenants of a successful PLC. Remember, this is not top-down learning, but rather bottom-up learning. The goals of the PLC need to be closely connected to the participants' lived experiences, professional learning interests, and needs, while preserving autonomy.

An administrator who has determined a need for organizational change should begin by asking their educators what they notice about this perceived need. Do they observe the same challenges? This creates buy-in and makes participants feel vested–vital components for building a successful PLC. In cases where participants were not asked for their input, the outcomes were dismal.

Organizations that do not focus on needs assessments tend to undertrain, overtrain, or train on the wrong things (Centor, 2004). The Wall Street Journal states that 90% of skills in professional development are easily lost after just one year (Silverman, 2012), so it is important to operate with accurate knowledge of specifically what educators need when targeting training topics for solutions. Without the inclusion of the employees receiving the training, types of efforts are really just traditional PD opportunities masquerading as a PLC in order to make participants feel heard; it is not genuine and will ultimately falter. In cases like the independent reading PLC mentioned above, where participants were involved at all stages of development, design, and implementation, the outcomes were impressive.

Educators looking to improve their practice should consider the PLC model, because it offers a powerful opportunity for collaborative action within the scope of your professional practice. Professional needs surface naturally in this process, because educators are given the space to communicate their ideas and engage in critique and seek out new learning opportunities to help address needs. This process will also make it easy to find groups of educators with the same needs, and address their issues together as opposed to a generic whole-school professional development session.

Once a topic for the PLC has been selected, ask participants what they are hoping to change or improve. Asking each person to list five to six specific goals related to the topic will help the community map out the initial meetings. This can be completed via Google Form or through a simple needs assessment. If your topic is differentiated instruction, participants should reflect on how they are looking to grow related to the topic. Perhaps participants need a clearer understanding of the purpose of differentiated instruction. Maybe it's a need related to practical implications in the classroom. After all participants have articulated their personal goals, analyze the responses for overlap. The goals of the PLC should reflect the needs of as many participants as possible. These goals will inform the focus of the sessions.

Determining a meeting schedule and number of meetings that work for all participants is key to meeting with success and having as many participants as possible engaged at each meeting. The Google Classroom is an ideal platform for facilitating a virtual learning community. Materials can be shared easily and participants can access the group for support even when they are not on a formal Google Meet. The classroom takes on a life of its own, where the learning has a place to live and breathe. Google Classroom can also be a place where participants share resources from their own collections and reflect on their classroom practice related to the topic of the PLC.

Planning for each session is key, and can take the shape of offering professional literature related to the goal of the session prior to the meeting, or listing challenges in need of discussion in advance of the meeting time. These articles then provide a foundation for the meeting discussion. One member of the PLC may be elected to gather this information or, as a group, educators may decide to rotate accountability for materials. Preparing for the session is integral to success because it shows participants that the community is engaged in important work and their time as professionals is valued. Haphazard sessions without a clear focus detract from the importance of the community.

After two or three sessions, it is helpful to provide an opportunity for participants to evaluate the process and content of the PLC. Reflecting on what is working and what is not working is an important step to sustaining the community and making stakeholders feel vested and heard. After this reflection, changes may need to be made to meet the needs of all participants.

At the end of the initial sessions, the community should allow themselves space to reflect on the efficacy of the PLC. Did participants find value in the experience? Were there changes that could have been made to help the community run more smoothly? Were all the learning goals achieved by all participants? How was each participants' practice impacted by the new learning? At this point, the community should determine whether they will continue to grow in the selected topic or whether they want to move to a new topic. Some members may opt to leave the group and new members may decide to join. This is a participant-driven process.

In developing a successful professional development experience for educators, it is essential to consider a variety of factors to ensure that the needs of the target group are being met. Needs assessment should be conducted, even on a basic level to help gauge the needs of the educators who make up the target audience. Virtual communities are also an important element that should be purposefully designed to address the needs of community collaboration among all educators involved.

Having this opportunity to continue to interact from a distance helps ensure that the learning continues when the professional learning community meeting ends. Educators are also supported by a variety of differentiated content and means of communication, which helps support a more effective professional learning environment. Educators are expected to modify and differentiate to meet the various learning needs of their students, and this practice should continue from pedagogy through andragogy to support adult education professionals. Through the implementation of virtual communities, elements of flexible learning are provided to maximize professional learning for educators.

REFERENCES

Arslan-Ari, I., Ari, F., Grant, M., & Morris, W. (2018). Action research experiences for scholarly practitioners in an online education doctorate program: Design, reality, and lessons learned. *TechTrends*, 62(5), 441–449. 10.1007/s11528-018-0308-3

Avidov-Ungar, O., & Zion, R. (2019). The characteristics and perceptions of teachers engaged in leading professional communities. *Teacher Development*, 23(3), 325–344. 10.1080/13664530.2019.1607772

Black, G. (2021). Implementing action research in a teacher preparation program: Opportunities and limitations. *Canadian Journal of Action Research, 21*(2), 47-71.

Braunston, T. (2018). 10 ways to enhance professional development with an LMS. *Knowledge anywhere.*https://www.knowledgeanywhere.com/resources/article-detail/10-ways-to-enhance-professional-development-with-lms

Burns, M., Naughton, M., Preast, J., Wang, Z., Gordon, R., Robb, V., & Smith, M. (2018). Factors of professional learning community implementation and effect on student achievement. *Journal of Educational & Psychological Consultation*, 28(4), 394–412. 10.1080/10474412.2017.1385396

Centor, E. (2024). Why training needs assessment is important to an organization. *Trainsmart Inc.*https://www.trainsmartinc.com/why-training-needs-assessment/

Cooper, K., Stanulis, R., Brondyk, S., Hamilton, E., Macaluso, M., & Meier, J. (2016). The teacher leadership process: Attempting change within embedded systems. *Journal of Educational Change*, 17(1), 85–113. 10.1007/s10833-015-9262-4

Grierson, A. L., & Woloshyn, V. E. (2012). Walking the talk: Supporting teachers' growth with differentiated professional learning. *Taylor and Francis online.* 10.1080/19415257.2012.763143

Johannesson, P. (2022). Development of professional learning communities through action research: Understanding and professional learning in practice. *Educational Action Research*, 30(3), 411–426. 10.1080/09650792.2020.1854100

Johnson, B. (2009). Differentiated instruction allows students to succeed. *Edutopia.* https://www.edutopia.org/blog/differentiated-instruction-student-success

Parsons, S., Hutchison, A., Hall, L., Parsons, A., Ives, S., & Leggett, A. (2019). US teachers' perceptions of online professional development. *Teaching and Teacher Education*, 82, 33–42. 10.1016/j.tate.2019.03.006

Riggins, C., & Knowles, D. (2020). Caught in the trap of PLC lite: Essential steps needed for implementation of a true professional learning community. *Education*, 141(1), 46–54.

Silverman, R. E. (2012, October 26). So much training, so little to show for it. *The Wall Street Journal*.https://www.wsj.com/articles/SB1000142405297020442590 4578072950518558328

Svendsen, B. (2020). Inquiries into teacher professional development: What matters? *Education*, 140(3), 111–141.

VanWyk, A. (2020). Leading curriculum changes in schools: The role of school principals as perceived by teachers. *Perspectives in Education*, 38(2), 155–167.

Wright, J., Williams, R., & Wilkinson, J. R. (1998). Development and importance of health needs assessment. *National Library of Medicine, 316*(7140). 10.1136/bmj.316.7140.1310

Chapter 4
The Union of the Physical and the Digital in the Phygital Transformation:
Intangible Design Evidenced by Knowledge With Artificial Intelligence

Neli Maria Mengalli
https://orcid.org/0000-0002-3782-3807
Faculdade São Bernardo do Campo, Brazil

Antonio Aparecido Carvalho
Faculdade São Bernardo do Campo, Brazil

ABSTRACT

This chapter was written based on bibliographical research, qualitative and exploratory studies. The objective of writing the chapter was to highlight theories regarding community of practice for productivity, environmental and social governance, and results in organizations; however, the written elements require further studies to include in research regarding community of practice. In the final considerations, among the conclusions are the combination of the physical with the digital for the phygital transformation in business and the design made with human knowledge for the improvement of businesses that are in full modification with automation, mechanization, with robotization and the use of artificial intelligence for the (co) creation of ideas, insights, or execution of tasks.

DOI: 10.4018/979-8-3693-1111-0.ch004

INTRODUCTION

Company leaders and people who were designing new businesses before the health crisis, and they knew some concepts of digital transformation and disruptive technologies, but with the acceleration that occurred with the pandemic, some principles needed to be reviewed. On March 11, 2020, the World Health Organization characterized COVID-19 as a global pandemic.

The term pandemic had reference to the geographical distribution of a disease, however the severity was not yet fully known and studied in the most diverse areas, so the world of work and professions did not have the dimension of the speed that would change new businesses or digital transformation which, every day, brings together the physical with the virtual and the immersive through extended realities that include smell on mobile devices and is called phygital transformation.

The healthcare sector recognized COVID-19 outbreaks and businesses that were not remodeled experienced the financial and consumer market effects. The leaders were not trained for a transformation with a health crisis, since, in the contents of the academic curricula, there were bytes, personal computers, connection, computational components, world wide web, data culture, digital transformation, among other curriculum contents pre-COVID-19. The thinking was focused on face-to-face and hierarchical work with hiring people who went to offices, stores or jobs every day.

In the leadership culture, the physical and the digital were separate, even though the data culture and digital transformation were undergoing significant changes. Amid the health crisis and the business crisis, the acceleration was an element that many attributed to the pandemic. While some may attribute much of the responsibility for the acceleration to COVID-19 outbreaks, the way people led and how people worked was dissonant or out of step with reality.

Companies invested in physical space and people had personal and well-being needs that did not fit into the business, employees wanted different work models from those practiced by organizations, mainly by conservative companies that wanted people at work every day without the concern for the employee's mental health. In fact, collaboration, in many cases, was not joint work with shared merits, it was work that someone did for someone else to take the credit in presenting ideas and results.

It is not possible to declare that there was an evolution of workplaces from traditional to those that practiced in virtual communities, however, it is possible to affirm that there was a redefinition after the health crisis and virtual communities of practice were potential for redirecting business. Working a domain or subject in a central and peripheral core and with a specialist promotes reflections in the midst of a dynamic market that focuses on the consumer and employee experience, which is different from the traditional customer and employee before the pandemic.

The shutdown mobilized businesses in a way that promoted reinvention for regular business after March 11, 2020.

Lave and Wenger (1991) defined communities of practice as informal organizations that were naturally formed among practitioners who were close to organizational boundaries. In communities of practice, there was collaboration, cooperation, and in-person and remote and the subject or domain. In 2020, communities of practice were key components for sharing knowledge in the most different organizational configurations so that best practices were known and so that tacit knowledge generated business or the development of products or services.

In the early part of the 21st century, the meaning of work, collaboration, cooperation, and joint work was re-signified in remote, hybrid, and face-to-face settings. Meetings and orientations occupied various times and spaces. The phygital transformation highlighted a new design to unite people at the intersection of the physical and the digital, as Mengalli, Carvalho and Galvão (2023, p. 34) wrote in the chapter on the metaverse ecosystem. People worked in the most unusual places and productivity was more monitored and controlled. The synchronous and the asynchronous enabled a new way of working and artificial intelligence was included to be close to emotional intelligence.

Effectiveness and productivity are concepts that need people to exist, and belong to a place. This was expanded upon in an interview on the KMOL Portal (2001) by Ana Neves with Étienne Charles Wenger, one of the authors who coined the term communities of practice. The question was raised asking if an individual should always be aware that they belong to a community of practice. Dr. Wenger responded that many people belong to communities of practice and do not realize they belong, which leads us to believe that there are more communities of practice that are designed in organizations.

The distinguished interviewee exemplified, in his response to Ana Neves, that a colleague of his, at work in a hospital, saw nurses who got together at lunch time and talked about work cases. After exemplifying how people do not realize that they belong to the practical community, he stated that lunch had become the main source of knowledge and nurses were not aware of their belonging.

The community of practice is informal knowledge work that has proven to be productive and produced results. The community of practice is knowledge work in an informal way that has proven to be productive and produced results and, in this chapter, readers will find theories about communities of practice and possible solutions for increasing productivity, innovation and results from the central core and peripheral core in the most different configurations of communities of practice.

In the background, there is the scenario with the implicit elements, and, in the focus of the chapter, there is the theory that involves the community of practice, productivity, environmental and social governance, results and the employee experience. The methodology used was bibliographical research with qualitative and exploratory studies. The chapter contains solutions and recommendations, as well as directions for future research. In final considerations, communities of practice and the combination of physical and digital that transform businesses.

The introduction, aims to prepare the reader to understand the disruptive transformation of business that occurs both consciously and unconsciously. The chapter was written for those interested in creating and developing communities of practice and people who seek creativity for the implementation of virtual, physical, and phygital communities, and believe that professionals in companies, the business area, and the educational area, which includes corporate education are also interested in the subject. Undergraduate and postgraduate students and professors, interested in virtual communities and communities of practice, instructors, and training and development professionals are also audiences for this chapter.

After the so-called new normal in the health crisis set in, productivity, results, and environmental and social governance made academics and professionals concerned about the speed of disruptive technologies. The immersive worlds of business, economic, and social development, and knowledge in communities of practice has potential for focusing on the well-being of people in business, for problem solving, for changes in business models and for strategic decisions. Therefore, the market and professions of the future and the amount of days worked could not be left out of the introduction to reflect on the impact of the evolution of disruptive technologies in the security of jobs and careers. These contribute to the image of communities of practice which includes co-creation with generative artificial intelligence and immersive worlds.

BACKGROUND: THE PAINTING OF THE SCENE PRESENT IN THE IMAGE OF COMMUNITY OF PRACTICE

Nowadays, people are increasingly interested in studying the latest theoretical frameworks to gain an understanding of digital transformation that enhances productivity and satisfying business outcomes. It is noteworthy that people look for communities of successful practices, however successful practices are in the particularities of each space of belonging. People learn in the peripheral core from experts in the central core and solve problems from one domain. The richness is in inhabiting several communities of practice in the company.

It is necessary to remember that each community of practice has a single domain, which is the subject necessary for the interaction and integration of the participants. There is the practice which is the contribution, exchange, and learning with others, which builds the community itself through interaction, construction, and management of knowledge. The existence of the community of practice is at the intersection of the subject with the practice and with the space for interaction, therefore, if practitioners are in more than one community of practice, they will have access to more than one subject, more than one practice and more than one space for interaction.

Such an understanding tends to help people with innovative ideas and with the resolution of institutional problems, as well as in the customization of approaches for the implementation of future communities of practice in organizations. It is known that communities of practice have stages of development. In the beginning, there are people with similar interests, computational resources, such as whether virtual, synchronous, or asynchronous, as well as methodologies, leveling and searching for the environment for the community of practice. The project of the community of practice and the engagement in social learning activities is in solving problems and searching for best practices that the community of practice can begin in organizations.

In face-to-face, virtual and hybrid work environments, people seek to talk to other people to uncover best practices and solve problems that alone could not achieve an effective result. Another potential moment for the community of practice in organizations is the moment when new team members arrive, as they can be guided and can, in a peripheral nucleus, learn from experts. Companies tend to do onboarding as an integration that is usually in person, however, in the community of practice, there is a memory of what was worked on, interactions so that there is no re-work and dissemination of existing conclusions. Change, speed and disruptive technologies are responsible for increasingly different work environments for contemporary business needs and employee experiences. In this way, technological solutions promote new ways of integrating people and managing knowledge.

In computational resources, the metaverse is also a possible space for communities of practice. With Masterson's (2022) question about what to do in the metaverse for at least an hour a day and Gartner Press Release's (2022) statement that a 25% of people will spend at least an hour a day in the metaverse until 2026 for work, action of purchasing, education, social activities that may or may not be entertainment, the metaverse or commercial name of immersive worlds can be a collective and shared phygital space for the community of practice.

The understanding that metaverse is a digital and immersive world and can combine virtual, augmented, mixed and extended reality, according to Mengalli, Carvalho and Galvão (2023, p. 36), and can raise ideas for creating communities of practice with participants and users who interact phygitally. Even though digital humans are represented by three-dimensional images, their thoughts and creativity move them away from the actions of machines that reproduce through parameterization.

The metaverse and communities of practice, whether in person at the workplace, virtually or phygitally while conducting work, are compatible, although some people may think of the metaverse and games, or entertainment. In this gaming mindset, gamification can occur in missions for employees, in fact, it is a possibility for knowledge management in business and for employees' experience. Disruptive technologies are strategies and methodologies, and approaches are studies of methods for social learning that benefits the company.

Gamification refers to the mechanisms and dynamics of games in physical and digital spaces, however, they are not only in the form of traditional games. Kapp (2012, p. 23) wrote that "gamification is using game-based mechanics, aesthetics, and game thinking to engage people, motivate action, promote learning, and solve problems, and for the context of the chapter, problem solving." This can involve ethics and aesthetics, game mechanics and thinking so that people can learn and fulfill missions that are so necessary for organizations.

Within communities of practice in business, disruptive technologies are the strategies used in knowledge management organization methods. Gamification can be analog in face-to-face contexts, digital in platforms and phygital in immersive worlds. People can be subjected to techniques that use games in serious situations that involve competition, collaboration, problem solving, passing phases or levels and recognition for the most appropriate practice. Gamification in communities of practice is possible.

Gamification, as the application of game mechanisms and dynamics in non-game contexts, is explored as a way of motivating and achieving missions in organizations. In onboarding, newcomers, for example, can complete missions to find the purpose of the institution and connect with their own purpose to show how motivated they are to work at the company or they can relate what they want to learn at the company. The dynamics can be in person with post-it notes, or virtual with a digital collaboration platform, such as Miro [RealTimeBoard], to facilitate remote and distributed communication within teams or even in immersive spaces.

Long-time participants in the community of practice may have challenges after meetings in finding best practices for writing a piece. It is possible to interview production supervisors to find out how the piece is produced. The data collected could be part of the material for the next meeting with the specialist so that participants could select the best production practices for the piece.

In communities of practice, practitioners experience social learning and can be valued and rewarded for shared ideas or knowledge. The points obtained with the ideas or best improvement proposals for the organization could receive social or financial rewards, in addition to receiving badges, gifts, coupons, prizes or a message from the organization's president. People tend to have expectations regarding efforts and, in gamified dynamics in non-games, they can receive recognition that transcends the company and involves the family.

These three examples of non-game gamification usually involve people to recognize and strengthen the community as part of social learning. Members of the community of practice join together to form the community with people with similar interests, and then there is the expansion of the community of practice that provides computational resources and methodologies for accountability with the practice. After the expansion, the maturation of the community of practice usually occurs based on responsibility for the practice and functioning through cycles of activities in the central nucleus and peripheral nucleus.

Work methods will definitely no longer be conservative, they tend to be less than five days a week and co-creation, will gradually evolve to include replacement for certain things with generative artificial intelligence. Employee experiences are different in relation to in-person and well-being. People realized that mental health was not a plus, but an integral part of the employee's life and working just four days would allow them to have time to take care of their body and mind, in addition to including their family as a priority in their life context. People's contact with the communication of movements that advocate a four-day week is growing.

The Day Week Global (2023) team encourages companies, employees, researchers, and governments to create a new way of working to improve business productivity, physical and mental health outcomes, quality in family relationships and the strengthening of communities and for the sustainability of work and the environment. It is noteworthy that the economic impacts were not considered.

If on the one hand people understood that mental health and family could be part of professional life, on the other hand, Day Week Global (2023) communication becomes more effective in virtual media, which was the medium most used by employees after the health crisis. The combination of well-being and personal needs was a driver of the employee's experience in the company and business models would once again have to change beyond remote, hybrid, synchronous and asynchronous, the quality of life of employees and productivity would have to be a topic on the agenda for leaders, as there were academic studies on reducing working time.

Hopkins, Bardoel, and Djurkovic (2023, p. 14) wrote about the reduction of working hours as a strategic move and showed that one of the biggest challenges for any company that adheres to the four-day work week (4DWW) is how to increase productivity, by at least 25%, with a 20% reduction in working time. The authors sought strategies with the study participants.

4DWW is a possibility for contemporary work and a sustainable career because employees can complete the week's tasks in four days instead of five days, although some companies had the idea of creating models with four days of ten hours of work. There are many changes to business and employee experiences after the health crisis. The four-day week is an element that cannot be ignored in the context of work and career, however, in business models there is room for virtual communities, the metaverse, artificial intelligence and productivity. In this way, the employee experience and the business would have to be together for economic development amid disruptive technologies, the market and human health and this phenomenon productivity, disruption, and reduction in working days were both in studies by consulting companies as well as academic research.

In addition to reports from consulting companies and academic research, foundation observatories have, within their scope, documents that highlight the reality of the world of work. The research by Hopkins, Bardoel, and Djurkovic (2023), for example, is in the Analysis & Policy Observatory and, in the conclusion, it is stated that the reduction of meetings, the elimination of non-essential work activities to concentrate on the most important and urgent tasks and the projection of work around people could be eliminated with the fifth day of work.

All this to reduce the workload and switch to 4DWW. Cuello (2023, p. 7) verified the reduction of working hours in companies that have results considered successful and found that most organizations share little information publicly, a fact that makes detailed analysis difficult. The author also found the reduction of hours, a four-day job, in public sector pilots in the Nordic countries. The study highlights the impact on companies and governments.

In this introduction, it was possible to reflect on the transformation of business and the elements that comprise it, such as the number of days worked, productivity, the metaverse, artificial intelligence and communities of practice, after all, the objective of this chapter is to highlight theories regarding communities of practice for productivity, for environmental and social governance and for results in organizations and, at the junction of the physical with the digital in phygital transformation, it was realized that there is an intangible design that is evidenced by knowledge and, in contemporary times, by artificial intelligence. In fact, it is not possible to forget metaverses as immersive experiences for interaction between people and machines.

For many years, fiction and academic theories have highlighted businesses that are much more disruptive than people can perceive and, although 4DWW is believed to be new, projects to reduce working hours have been taking place since the 1970s. People seek effectiveness and organizations seek effectiveness in activities, doing more with fewer resources, whether financial or time.

The Day Week Global team encourages government and non-governmental organizations, as well as researchers and company employees, with the aim of improving productivity and business. Physical and mental health and the quality of family relationships are topics that include the economic impacts that communities of practice have the potential to add to business. In Iceland, 4DWW was evaluated and was quickly adopted as the norm with 90% of the workforce by 2022.

Social and labor issues are important for business and Iceland and the United Kingdom have advanced research into social, economic and climate impacts. In the article Four-Day Work Week Trial in Spain Leads to Healthier Workers, Less Pollution (Broom, 2023) published in the World Economic Forum reported that there is a study carried out in the United Kingdom in 2022 that the results benefited both employers and employees and the tested protocol aimed to not just finding a balance between employees' personal and professional lives, but also helped to take care of their mental health and avoid burnout.

Still in the aforementioned matter, Valencia, in Spain, evaluated a four-day week during April and May 2023. The impact on the lives of workers resulted in the use of sports activities, relaxation, and meal preparation. According to Broom (2023), the results showed reduced stress levels and increased happiness. There was no mention of communities of practice in business, however knowledge management in business, in addition to promoting learning, also involves sharing data and strategic information for companies and governments and the development of people who integrate as a group for the creation and innovation. The maturation of the community of practice can be the beginning of focusing on practice even with a four-day week worked.

The maturation of the community of practice is compounded by the commitment and stipulation of standards and use of agendas. The renewal of interests [with novices and focus on practice] usually generates responsibility in the project of the community of practice, and the full activity promotes the functioning through cycles of activities in the central nucleus and peripheral nucleus. However, the renewal of interests can also lead to the decline of the community because people can delve deeper into activities with colleagues who did in the community of practice phases.

A community of practice in decline can cause dispersion, and with a loss of focus, the community of practice is left without the domain. When this occurs, the practice and the community is no longer useful for the business. If the dispersion is due to the creation of parallel relationships, there will be continuity of social contact in common learning (Dutra, Santos, & Silva 2013, p. 12; Mengalli, (2005) to evidence how each stage of the community of practice is different in terms of processes, forms of interaction, and relationships among people.

It is noteworthy that the community of practice is at the heart of many elements. The reification element refers to documentation, resources, technologies that can be disruptive or not, and the community presentation interfaces that can be in person with scheduled dates can be virtual, or can even be in immersive worlds developed for phygital meetings.

Another important element is participation because it has the history of interactions. The various contributions of different people in the peripheral nucleus should be in connection with the dialogues with specialists in the central nucleus. This way all the construction of solutions and knowledge management have the experiences and the maturity that emerge from prior knowledge to be developed with the readings of words and the professional and personal world.

The texture of re-negotiations and re-significations is increasingly different because employees' experiences are focused on well-being and activities. Mitigating anxiety about pressure for productivity can lead to more solitary work and disconnection from other people, which reduces knowledge management and social learning in the organization.

In contemporary times, work is increasingly distributed and asynchronous. People are working in geographically distant places and connections and interactions with other people are increasingly scarce. Business models must include disruptive technologies and participatory work methodologies with interfaces that mobilize people, such as, for example, meetings in immersive worlds with a set time for the presentation of work.

To support the social and emotional well-being of employees within an organization could include relying on disruptive technologies to curate a different engagement experience. For example, the various scenarios developed for the metaverse tend to reveal people who would not speak with the cameras open or in person. The use of immersive worlds proves to be a possibility that avoids compromising creativity, inventiveness, and innovation in solving problems, and developing digital solutions for companies because meetings need the physical and the digital together to mobilize elements in the meeting.

It is harmful that learning and development in many cases occur on platforms with self-instructional courses. The purposes of people and organizations need convergence, and it is not enough to send hyperlinks for employees to click and work only on operationalization. The purposes are tactical and strategic for people and for business, and communities of practice can leverage common interests, in addition to promoting social learning in the peripheral core from the central core with specialists. In business and communities of practice, there are no spaces and times for commensalism. The community is a living organism and needs interaction and obtaining results with successful and innovative practices.

Focus of the Chapter: Productivity, Governance, and Results

Proven successful and innovative practices can often come from people belonging to the community of practice, and the sense of belonging is in the identification of employees for participation. Participation presupposes the existence of organized institutionalization for the effectiveness of the results and involves culture and time and, in contemporary times, face-to-face in spaces that can be digital or phygital. When there is a combination of the physical and the digital in the phygital transformation, in the intangible design there is evidence of human knowledge and co-creation with artificial intelligence. Initially, it will be clarified that phygital enhances the creation of environments that combine tangible elements with physical spaces and products and intangible elements with spaces designed by developers that include augmented reality, artificial intelligence, and mobile devices for sensations.

The commercial and Marketing areas usually offer consumers a personalized experience to meet consumer expectations in a market increasingly thirsty for innovation. In this way, sensations are offered from disruptive technologies, however best practices can be evaluated by participants in the community of practice to improve offers to consumers.

The training and human development area can provide support for such improvements, in addition to creating courses, it can create communities of practice so that employees are not eternal learners because they belong to an organization that legitimizes employees' practices. The areas in the organization are interconnected and, if you think about developing people, it is necessary to research. From apprentices to practitioners, the employee experience is modified, and the training and human development sector can be supported by a research area that investigates immersive universes with the company's digital twin so that employees can experience what it will offer to customers: customized experiences. If phygital has an impact on consumption, it must be used and understood by workers in their professional experiences.

Phygital, in addition to having an impact on consumption, changes businesses by strengthening public engagement and redefines interactions with brands in an imperceptible way for the practitioner and the consumer. Data collection and behavioral analysis are more extensive when working to improve products or services because it is possible to know the preferences of customers or users in a controlled, synchronous environment that highlights the individual journey in the immersive world.

By implementing immersive virtual reality or augmented reality experiences in the most different areas of companies or equipping employees for remote and synchronous work to provide innovation in the presentation of ideas, in the simulation of projects in immersive worlds and in meetings involving smells and sensations with participants in different locations will be promoting incremental innovation in the area of training and development, as modifications and updates are made to an existing service that can be the community of practice.

There are many methods for developing activities with employees, but within the scope of this chapter, the focus is on virtual or phygital communities with the essence of community of practice by the elements. As part of their work, employees can have interactive QR Codes at strategic points to use their own mobile devices to scan and access digital content or receive interactive videos or even be transported to immersive worlds in metaverses.

It is necessary to understand the motivation of employees in their experience in communities of practice, in addition to understanding their profile and preferences to better adapt platform development. Internal research with data collection can indicate the specific expectations of social learning in communities of practice in phygital environments integrated with disruptive technologies, such as augmented reality, virtual reality, mixed reality, extended reality, and artificial intelligence for co-creation with computational programming. In differentiated experiences, employees learn socially.

However, it is necessary to train people to work with new methods, such as virtual or phygital communities. Even though it is known that entry into communities of practice is voluntary, the methodology and disruptive technologies must be taught to participants, especially when interactions are phygital because participants know the support and functioning of the immersive environment. People management must prioritize personalization and engagement, in addition to collecting data with the authorization of participants to offer more personalized experiences and to create engagement in both physical and phygital environments so that there is a greater connection between employees and the purposes of business. Assessments must be continuous with specific metrics for feedforwards, and adaptations of actions according to changes in expectations and market trends.

It is possible to train participants to inhabit metaverses, to assume distinct roles within the community of practice, to co-create with other human beings and to co-create with generative artificial intelligences. Participants must know how to act in the community of practice in accordance with the business purpose because communities of practice have potential for productivity, governance, and business results.

In this chapter, one of the objectives was to highlight theories regarding virtual or phygital communities and productivity that were included in the intangible design that includes the human being who co-creates with other humans and with generative artificial intelligence. Productivity at work has elements that reflect the employee's experience and the consumer's experience, such as know-how and investment in human beings. The point of attention to understand is: there are factors that can compromise labor productivity, such as skills and abilities, behavioral profiles, technological changes, and management practices, among other factors.

Productivity is linked to economic performance which, in industry 4.0, compared the amount of production with the amount of work spent on producing products or services. However, Soekiman (2023, p. 86), in the study that examined the effect of sharing knowledge and individual innovation capacity on employee performance, wrote that the community of practice, in the format of employee conversations, highlighted several issues worked on in joint and resulted in many types of follow-ups and ideas to apply existing science and technology to products or production processes, leading to a result of a learning culture and organizational process in the company.

Before moving on to advancing communities of practice and knowledge management, it is important to understand the concept of industry 4.0, as the fourth industrial revolution includes automation and the integration of disruptive technologies into business. There is a promotion of typing or computerization of processes, therefore, an increase in productivity is implied. If mechanization, robotization and automation were part of the revolution in industry 4.0, artificial intelligence, the Internet of Things (IoT) and cloud computing were included in business and were present in digital transformation.

The term industry 4.0 was used in 2011, in Germany, during the Hannover Fair, and, in 2013, studies included the fourth industrial revolution with the combination of disruptive technologies, the Internet of Things and data culture with mechanization, robotization and automation. The aim was to transform with cyber-physical systems, however the fifth revolution or industry 5.0 fulfills the function better because it includes design, human beings for the development of digital and phygital, for measuring the impact of strategic decisions on the business and for orientation towards the future. The human being is the center of phygital transformation with circular and sustainable practices for planetary society.

If the way of managing knowledge has changed, more than three decades later, the virtual or phygital community of practice highlights a new way of managing knowledge, in contemporary times, with the combination of the physical and the digital. The community of practice originates from the work of Lave and Wenger (1991) in which the authors show a possible and legitimate participation in the peripheral nucleus with learning from situated social practice, because participation in communities of practice enables a gradual increase in the engagement of people. Lave and Wenger (1991, p. 49-50) contrast learning as internalization with learning as participation in the community of practice.

Learning is related to participation that aims at evolution and renewal. The base is relational that includes people, actions, contexts, and theory with social practice. The community of practice can be used by researchers and academic investigators, by professionals from the same area or multidisciplinary professionals as long as the domain [subject] is unique, after all, a community is an intrinsic condition for the existence of knowledge. According to Lave and Wenger (1991, p. 98) participation in the practical culture in which any knowledge exists is an epistemological principle of learning.

Knowledge and learning are ways to improve working conditions and productivity. Cooke and Rogovsky (2023, p. 92) edited a book that has as its motto the human-centered agenda and approach productivity with evidence from Asia, and the theme of communities of practice was in India. The editors highlighted reflection on practices in companies to mitigate gaps with recommendations, to improve resilience, for business profitability and to ensure competitiveness and advantage for national and international growth. Both investors and consumers prioritized environmental and social issues and governance principles. The editors describe the community of practice with participants and directors and the impact on the supply chain company of inclusive workplace practices.

The social structure of practice, the relations among powers and the conditions of legitimacy for learning are real. Communities of practice have three dimensions: institutional, functional, and dialogic. Institutionally, practitioners [professionals or scientists] renegotiate their own practices to solve a problem or generate information. In the functional dimension, the social and the cultural are shared along with the practices. In dialogicity, the form and format are configured in the shared repertoire, in the routines, in the vocabulary or jargon, in the responsibilities and attributions, in the styles and in the technological spaces and times.

Mengalli and Valente (2010, p. 302) wrote that such dimensions are related to the works of Paulo Freire because the defender of critical pedagogy wrote about learning as a social phenomenon that relates to experience, with practice and with people's life stories. A creative act emerges that is destined for the critical understanding of the practice that is historical, social, and cultural and for the learning process, individual and collective, as long as it is used for the purposes of certain actions.

Productivity, in contemporary times, must be linked to better working conditions, labor rights, and legality so that there is no exploitation and, consequently, no productivity. The human-centered agenda mentioned is related to a joint of people management policies and practices, as Cooke and Rogovsky (2023) wrote: human-centered approach. Such an approach focused on ethics to promote dignity and equality for vulnerable workers and their families in India and concern for reputation in local and global markets. The community of practice involved many people at the most diverse levels to transform people management.

The concept of community of practice coined by Etienne Charles Wenger in the 20th century together with Jean Lave evidenced learning situated in the peripheral nucleus and in the central nucleus with specialists. However, in the phygital transformation with immersive environments in metaverses and multisensory platforms, other learning can be inserted, such as learning landscapes, for example. It is understood that it is possible to develop immersive and personalized learning spaces and times for working with practice.

The experience of the phygital employee refers to interaction in a hybrid way with virtual worlds and the real universe, for example, if the employee needs to simulate a situation in a community of practice to show how possible it can occur and involves risks, there is no need exposing people to adverse conditions and the technological and disruptive journey is known to everyone in a totally immersive experience.

Another example of a phygital collaborator comes from medicine and may have a community of practice working in a gamified way for learning surgeries. The most experienced surgeons gather at the junction of the physical space and use the digital space for simulations. A phygital community can be a community of practice. For example, certain types of surgery bring together people online and offline to help work together and understand the best means of treatment or procedures for a medical case open for discussion by a core group of experts. As people are analog, digital and phygital experiences complement the understanding of practice. The global market has included gamification in social learning methods and disruptive technologies enable mental configuration to transform the abstract into the concrete and enable sharing.

It is possible to include gamification or the transform(active) methodologies that Mengalli and Carvalho (2023, p. 19) have discussed in their research. These refer to strategies used for teaching to transform paradigms for the mental configuration and growth mindset, in addition to stimulating the participation, responsibility and autonomy. However, in co-creation, data culture, and the organization of time, there is human emotion and practice necessary to participate in events in immersive worlds and for people to be citizens in the phygital transformation.

Leveraging business in contemporary times needs environmental and social governance, and in the modern age can also require a phygital approach. Governance has assumptions of longevity for the planet, supporting the well-being of people with quality of life through environmental and social focus. Chien (2023, p. 1611) wrote that the performance measurement scale for scoring environmental and social governance contains standards or mechanisms to monitor, evaluate and regulate the performance of companies within the scope of environmental and social governance and the main focus is in scoring awareness about responsibility and accountability to highlight what was done for the region's environment and for society or social members. The companies' efforts to achieve the proposed goals and effectiveness are important to demonstrate the corporation's environmental and social governance.

Antonello and Cook (2023, p. 407) wrote about the existence of a community of practice for environmental resilience, mostly made up of engineers, hydrologists, scientists, and architects. There is also a historian participating and members said he brings new knowledge as well as historical depth to discussions and working practices in relation to flood responses. It is the various knowledge that is managed in the community of practice, and these specialists are connected through a virtual community to share their expertise and problem-solve over environmental issues relying on a phygital space. Although it can be understood as a digression, in the state of Rio Grande do Sul, in Brazil, in May 2024, there was an environmental catastrophe that took out businesses and mobilized the Brazilian government to open financing for companies and the harvest agriculture that were submerged in river waters.

Disasters do not need to occur, members can tell stories of events that occurred to mitigate new occurrences. The participation of members in sharing tacit knowledge and lived practices as a way of collaborative learning enables the understanding and modification of a real-life problem. Situated learning can have personal learning spaces that can be online or hybrid to highlight creation with practice that evidences the representation of knowledge. The important thing is to increase the engagement and involvement of participants for their own development and prevent the organization from having to experience environmental catastrophes. Learning in the community of practice develops businesses and changes organizational culture.

Situated learning (Lave & Wenger, 1991) presupposes "apprenticeship learning" and has the addition of "legitimate peripheral participation", which is learning in the peripheral core legitimized by the organization and accepted by members of the community of practice, but without the emphasis on social. Learning in a community of practice means that employees come together to achieve practical results. After all, situated learning with the addition of legitimate peripheral participation is inseparable from practical and social relationships. In theory, it can be understood as a possibility of studying transmission of knowledge in society, but it is necessary to have technology to support legitimate peripheral participation in communities; virtual or phygital.

Bhalla, Bahar and Kanapathy (2023, p. 198) wrote that computational resources, hardware, and software, are important for collaboration, as they are potential for communication and bringing people together to share knowledge and ideas. The authors complemented processes such as presence, visibility, rhythm, variety of interactions, efficiency in involving people and connection with the world that are enhanced with technologies. However, there are challenges that can affect the behavior of members of the community of practice, as the researchers wrote in relation to the difficulties faced in capturing tacit knowledge sharing unless explicit or communicable knowledge is present.

Disruptive technologies, such as the metaverse and artificial intelligence, are realities in businesses that care for productivity and learning with peers and in virtual communities. These tend to leverage organizations in learning and in practice that solves problems and enables disruptive innovation. It is possible to perceive that the movements, even if not recognized and legitimized by the companies, have the expansion, maturation, full activity, and dispersion with the systematization elements. It is noteworthy that the network can cause dispersion in communities of practice.

Environmental and social governance highlighted leaders who cared for practices and knowledge management and the collaborative attitude strengthened and legitimized communities of practice. Christofi, Chourides and Papageorgiou (2023,

p. 10) wrote that in addition to contributions from the community of practice, companies focused on environmental, social and governance scores and add that there is a relationship between scores and investor attraction, because high scores have numerous benefits, such as reviews from environmentally conscious consumers, enhanced corporate image by employees, increase in the price of company shares, and greater profitability. Lave and Wenger (1991, p. 52) wrote that social practice, whether subjective or objective, focuses on the person, but on the person contextualized in the world and as a member of the sociocultural community. It is the promotion of the view that knowledge in action with specific people and in delimited circumstances enhances transformations in business paradigms.

Louafi, et al. (2023, p. 286), in the context of public policies, wrote that knowledge and practice and the production and use of knowledge cannot be confused. The authors researched the socio-cognitive aspects, political challenges and responsible data connections, both in data culture and such studies made it possible to know how to address data agency issues, as well as data dissemination. Therefore, it is possible to understand that there are learning processes in communities of practice for both collective organization and strategic decision making; however, the authors wrote, within the scope of socio-cognitive and normative political challenges, it is necessary to establish differences between using data and collectively produced knowledge.

Business seeks collectively produced knowledge and greater productivity. If the tendency is to work in a four-day week, the virtual community can enable people to do more in less time because knowledge management is systematized and resources enable the central core and the peripheral core to be aligned so that employees are committed to work within four days a week. In the article Four-Day Work Week Trial in Spain Leads to Healthier Workers, Less Pollution (Broom, 2023), employees rated the improvement in productivity at 7.7, almost ten points as incredibly positive, without the use of communities of practice. If a community of practice had been implemented in this situation, there would be the possibility of planning, concentrating time, identifying priorities, and mitigating meetings by leveraging the support of the community. In relation to the levels of stress, exhaustion, fatigue and reduced conflict between work and family, the classification of the four-day work experience with an integrated virtual community for support could possibly be elevated to a possible rating of 9.1 on this particular scale.

The four-day week showed a different employee experience because people reported exercising more and getting more hours of sleep. In the United Kingdom, it was revealed that male workers took more care of their children. Even though the documents analyzed about 4DWW did not mention the community of practice, it is possible to assume that knowledge management in organizations transcends borders, hierarchical structures, geographic aspects, and time. In contemporary times, business enables the generation of knowledge and the well-being of employees.

Knowledge retention and sharing between the central core and the peripheral core enable time and resource savings, as well as improved process quality. The consumer experience includes the employee experience. If the focus is on the health crisis, it is possible, in the article The Pandemic Has Made a Four-day Working Week More Attractive to Workers and Businesses, Study Finds (Walker & Fontinha, 2022), to understand why 32% of people interviewed prefer to have additional work in the day off in another sector or developing your own business. The health crisis has given people more time to have diverse ways of increasing their income.

Business is no longer the same, as is the economy and the planet. Both one less day of work and organizations in communities of practice can show that businesses are more aware of environmental and social governance. Global carbon emissions and the exchange of experiences that transcend geographic limits focus on what is necessary for the company. Sharing information and data is in the interest of the community of practice because a domain is restricted to participants. The productivity factor and the sustainability element are together in the intangible design evidenced by knowledge with artificial intelligence. However, more research must be done to develop increasingly sustainable businesses with employee experiences that are better suited to quality of life.

Path to Conducting Research: The Methods Practiced

From the first studies on communities of practice in 2004 to 2023, it was possible to notice that the technologies used in virtual communities of practice for documentation were chat interfaces, forums, emails, libraries, notes, markers, portfolios and agendas (Mengalli, 2006, p. 33), and over the years, the metaverse proves to be a potential immersive world behind the intangible design that was evidenced by knowledge. However, it was not only the metaverse that could be added as a noun related to communities of practice.

A noun and an adjective could be related to communities of practice, generative artificial intelligence was presented in a user-friendly interface in 2021. Generative artificial intelligence enabled people to co-create from texts, images, and media in various formats with parameters that showed that generative models learned patterns and structures from humans to generate new data and information. Many people even believe that all knowledge management problems have been solved, after all, the well-designed prompts provided answers that human beings liked and even left them with the feeling that they had not thought of that answer, because it helped in solving simple problems.

A search in academic engines with the words "communities of practice" and "metaverse", and "communities of practice" and "artificial intelligence" was conducted in 2023, but no theory was found about productivity, environmental and social governance, and results, elements contained in the objective of this chapter. Please see the table below, as it was drawn to illustrate supplemental literature in the field addressing the metaverse and artificial intelligence in relation to virtual communities of practice, as follows:

Table 1. Indication of Emerging Data in the Areas and Association With Technologies

Type	Topic	Title	Area
Chapter	Metaverse	Knowledge Management in the Metaverse	Knowledge Management
Article	Metaverse	Envisioning Architecture of Metaverse Intensive Learning Experience (MiLEx): Career Readiness in the 21st Century and Collective Intelligence Development Scenario	Computer Science
Article	Artificial Intelligence	Communities of Practice for Contemporary Leadership Development and Knowledge Exchange Through Work-Based Learning	Business Administration
Article	Artificial Intelligence	Could Wound Care from the Artificial Intelligence Storm Taking Place Worldwide	Biotechnology

Source: Authors' Selection

In 2023, metaverse and artificial intelligence were found to be closely related to virtual communities of practice. The bibliographical review as research methodology was fundamental for understanding and situating the community of practice in history and contemporary times, in addition to enabling the identification of the methodology from published works.

During the investigation, it was possible to read, reflect and write based on the studies conducted. In the writing process, the theory was reconstructed, and the theoretical foundations were improved to converge with the objectives of the book and chapter. In this way, there was the possibility of bringing new ideas and theories for the personalization and implementation of virtual or phygital communities that may or may not be "of practice" for strategic decisions in the most different areas of knowledge.

Phygital transformation and artificial intelligence are both phenomena that involve the junction of the physical with the digital and disruptive technologies present in contemporary times. Individually they include productivity, environmental and social governance, and results in business and virtual communities that both serve as interfaces for knowledge management in corporations.

Academic materials related to the combination of metaverse and artificial intelligence in virtual communities were not yet readily available, the search in academic mechanisms provided literature with themes of productivity, environmental and social management, which all yielded results in communities of practice. The table below illustrates the topics being researched in various parts of the world related to the junction of these areas, which is an indication of emerging data in the field.

Table 2. Indication of Emerging Data in the Field

Country	Element	Purpose of the Book or Article	Area
Indonesia	Productivity	Examine the effect of sharing, and individual innovation capacity on employee performance.	Economy
India	Productivity	Improve productivity through better working conditions, and respect for workers' rights.	Human Resources
Australia	Environmental and Social Governance	Verify how environmental historians can interact to develop institutional policies.	Humanities and Social Sciences
Republic of Cyprus	Environmental and Social Governance	Strengthen the discourse on strategic agility with a comprehensive view of the best practices framework.	Business Administration
France	Results	Check work with knowledge and data.	Public Policies in Agriculture
Malaysia	Results	Highlight how fashion designers engage in social learning.	Knowledge Management

Source: Authors' Selection

Disruptive technologies and the scientific revolution emerge in traditional paradigms and there are challenges for science. Methodologies change and different perspectives show that something new revolutionizes traditional science. Kuhn (1998, p. 25) wrote about the disintegrating complements of tradition that are part of the scientific revolutions. Science is linked to the application of methods and paradigm shifts are scientific developments and should not be labeled researchers' revolutions.

The writing of this chapter had a certain break with the traditional because science consisted of solving puzzles (Kuhn, 1998, p. 77) that had the precision of scientific knowledge to highlight facts and elements in the investigation. The exploratory study coexisted with bibliographical research due to having little academic material about phygitality and artificial intelligence in communities of practice that may also include human-machine interaction.

In this investigation, there was a reading of the word and a reading of the world of the researchers that Freire (1979, p. 10) wrote about the act of reading the particular world that moved him and that he had to repeat, recreate and revive the text that he wrote. The author showed that there is more than one reading when writing. During the research, the genuine purpose came from a desire or an impulse to characterize the community of practice in contemporary times, and phygital transformation.

Dewey (1979, p. 66) wrote that every genuine purpose begins with an impulse and that when passing through a railroad crossing it is necessary to stop, look, and listen and, in this investigation, it was necessary to revisit initial research on communities of practice, understand the current reality of communities of practice and transcend traditional paradigms to infer the existence of the community of practice in the metaverse and with generative artificial intelligence in the co-creation of the human with the machine.

Existing Solutions and Recommendations in Relation to Disruptive Technologies

It was not intended to exhaust the presence of people in the world and the ethics of sharing, although the need for people to create and co-create digital solutions in participating in the phygital transformation is inseparable and indisputable. There is no ignorance of people's decision-making capacity regarding reflection and professional citizenship with computational resources on mobile devices. However, anxiety and fears can be caused by the demand for productivity. Carvalho, Cirera and Mengalli (2023, p.129) wrote a technical note about Fear of Logging off - FoLo - and found through the responses that there are cases related to global public health.

The questions referred to access to the world wide web and applications and 183 students answered the question, 20.2% remained connected to the World Wide Web for more than five hours and 12.6% stayed connected for up to five o'clock. This is data that worries the global public health authorities and companies still require employees to be connected for a long time, instead of mitigating the fear of people being disconnected from mobile devices and organizations.

In virtual or phygital communities, people or the central nucleus assume the way of working with knowledge and practice, after all, it is people who develop virtual or phygital communities. Mengalli and Valente (2010, p. 302) when writing about the relationship between the ideas of Étienne Charles Wenger and Paulo Freire showed that virtual or phygital communities, like communities of practice, self-regulating systems that promote learning and the professional qualification of the participants according to the interests of the institution and the will of the participants.

It cannot be ignored that upskilling and reskilling are fundamental for companies in the phygital transformation in industry 5.0 because the focus is on the consumer experience, on hyper personalization in experiences, products or services enabled by both the consumer experience and disruptive technologies. In Industry 4.0, the focus was on connecting machines, mass customization and products and services were intelligent without focusing on the consumer.

The idea of industry 5.0 is intricately linked with the concept of society 5.0 launched in 2016 in Japan. Human capabilities and society 5.0 were written in the 5th Basic Science and Technology Plan that promoted social well-being. It is important to highlight that the fifth industrial revolution does not replace the fourth industrial revolution. Technological and economic advances still do not guarantee social development and environmental and social governance. There was an improvement in responses to economic, social, and environmental challenges, in the creation of new values for the development of social transformation and in the establishment of virtuous cycles related to human beings, knowledge and intangibles for innovations, in addition to supporting scientific and technological innovation.

These paragraphs refer to a memory of the past. Freire (2003, p. 38) wrote that there is only knowledge in invention, reinvention, and in the restless, impatient, and permanent search for what people do in with the world. This is the phygital transformation, which is carried out by the human being and with the hope of well-being and quality of life, otherwise, the absolutization of ignorance, alienation, and dystopias reign.

This transformation is social in the upskilling and reskilling process and occurs from the will of the participants and leaders in the critical and historical moment. Engagement is to help the business to transform, to make strategic decisions, to solve problems and to change paradigms. They are historical, social, cultural, and economic opportunities for the meaning and resignification of the organization's purpose, after all, it is necessary to justify the time invested in the community of practice, in the intimacy with the events and in the contradictions of the contexts.

In academic investigations with the theme of virtual or phygital communities, it is necessary to follow the set of academic rules, but new theories for the elaboration of new theoretical frameworks, which as Kuhn (1978, p. 78) wrote, must show new ways of thinking the phenomena studied, because it will affect all related areas. When remembering the areas that were in the tables, it is possible to read that there are the economy, knowledge management, human resources, computer science, among others, therefore, the legal world and related areas have to give new meaning in the phygital transformation and in the interaction between humans and machines in the ethics of co-creation.

FUTURE RESEARCH DIRECTIONS: A SIMILAR COMPASS ROSE FOR SCIENTIFIC ADVANCEMENTS

In the text Introduction to Communities of Practice: A Brief Overview of the Concept and its Uses (Wenger-Trayner & Wenger-Trayner, 2015), the authors write the question: Where is the concept of community of practice applied? There is an answer to the question, however, it is important to have more research in business, organizational design, government, education, professional associations, and development, as well as human social interactions.

If knowledge is a critical asset, it is necessary to show in research how knowledge management in business is strategically done in virtual communities. It is believed that research can contribute to corporate education in the context of social structures for learning within a community of co-workers. It is known that there are central and peripheral cores, but research can situate learning in both cores and in the intersection between them.

In business, virtual communities usually allow professionals to assume collective responsibilities in knowledge management. There are links between learning and performance, therefore, investigations can approach the transfer aspects of tacit attribute of knowledge, dynamics of creation.

In Brazil, Mendes and Urbina (2015) researched and published an analysis of the Brazilian academic production in communities of practice, it is understood that it is important to have a global analysis by country for mapping knowledge management in communities of practice. In contemporary times, the inclusion of metaverses and generative artificial intelligence in the way people work with knowledge management is important so that more people have insights for creating or improving virtual communities.

In qualitative research there is the development of concepts, principles, or insights, according to Taylor, Bogdan and DeVault (2016, p. 8). New business researchers must develop theories for reflection on the adoption of artificial intelligence and the use of metaverses as possible spaces for knowledge management so that areas related to the creation of immersive worlds and the development of parameters for interaction with human beings can understand the legacy. The existing legacy leaves the inheritance to new and the need to include human emotions and emotional intelligence as important points for the well-being of people who are integral parts of professional virtual communities need more studies.

Therefore, studies, both investigative and advisory reports, need to provide sufficient information about how the research was conducted so that readers understand the context and intent of the academic documents or reports. New businesses and professions of the future seem to be based on disruptive technologies, but the human being's wellness and mental health should be a consideration along the ethical journey based on finding in the current research.

Specific productivity requirements, revenue metrics and customer acquisition are present in the new business models and with the lockdowns from 2020 to 2022 on remote work, people have modified their mental settings in relation to the significant impacts on organizational attitudes, according to the report The Pandemic has Made a Four-day Working Week More Attractive to Workers and Businesses, Study Finds (Walker & Fontinha, 2022) which includes the quality of work, the ability to attract and retain talent and whether employees feel more stressed at work.

Research directions that link virtual communities, quality of life, and the four-day week are needed to understand financial issues for both businesses and employees. The health crisis has brought conversations to the forefront about fewer working days with more productivity and flexible working and recruiting and retaining people for companies. The certainty is that the virtual community is an opportunity, but investigations are essential to find out what can happen in business models.

FINAL CONSIDERATIONS

It was concluded that virtual or phygital communities of practice are opportunities and possibilities to work on knowledge in phygital transformation. Co-creation does not only occur with human beings, but it can also be done with generative artificial intelligence as long as it is ethical, and the space can be immersive with synchronous time in the metaverse. Therefore, scientific theories must include human actions in the experiences of employees and consumers, in addition to emotions and feelings based on emotional intelligence and the growth mindset in a psychological view, since the physical meets the digital.

At the junction of the physical and the emotional with the digital in the context of the phygital transformation, the design is intangible and evidenced by the knowledge and artificial intelligence that bypass the intersections in business that must mitigate human mechanization, the automation of being and the robotization of people. Disruptive technologies are strategies and within virtual communities need to be demystified to understand the desires and needs of employees and consumers.

Economic power cannot oppress human beings because dystopias cannot be a reality, based on science fiction. Otherwise, colonization would be elaborated from phygital experiences and the use of techniques without reflection. The metaverse, in the context of knowledge management, is an immersive world that can have a central core and a peripheral core for social learning, problem solving, strategic decisions and business improvement.

The co-creation between humans and machines is real, and it is possible to include insight from a prompt in observation and interaction with another human and with the knowledge management space in social or collaborative learning, after all, machines, robotization and mechanization are present in human behavior for new behaviors or new attitudes, as well as in the observation and imitation of others. People must understand artificial intelligence in the context of work and business so that it is not obsolete in processes of human reification by corporations.

The elements domain, community and practice designed by Mengalli (2005) and written by Wenger-Trayner and Wenger-Trayner (2015) are essential for the intersection of community of practice, because they are the pillars of the community of practice. The domain is the subject that the group shares and which may be a common passion or interest. The community is the element responsible for relationships and interactions that are based on learning that involves humans with humans in sharing information and data for strategic decisions. Shared practice among members helps people develop their own repertoires.

The human being will never be reified in the virtual community because it involves communication and creativity that are in the human varnish. The structure of the community of practice brings together people from a variety of experience and varying domains. All member of the community benefit from interacting with experts and novices to aggregate best practices whether for solving problems or for strategic decisions. Even though the virtual community is informal, the legitimization of best practices by the organization transforms people with business recognition.

As part of the conclusion, research is essential to know how organizations understand the impact that the health crisis has had on business, both in culture and management and how the virtual community can respond to greater flexibility in days worked in person and how the economics and environmental and social governance can mitigate business hardships to create a more well-being-focused employee experience.

Understanding the desires and aspirations of employees reflects on the consumer experience and those responsible for people management can keep people happy and productive whether in the workplace or in a week with just four days worked. Disruptive technologies are present in the market and large companies are able to create new experiences for employees, both in knowledge management and as a community of practice, which can be potential for employee well-being.

In these statements and in the content of the chapter, the objective of highlighting theories regarding the community of practice was achieved, and productivity, environmental and social governance, and results in organizations were present. There was mention of industry 4.0 and 5.0, in addition to the phygital transformation that highlighted the joining of the physical with the digital and co-creation with generative artificial intelligence.

In the metaverse, people can build institutional and personal knowledge in the intangible designs that the virtual community forms for businesses that move towards using artificial intelligence more intensively. Brands promote the revolution with the introduction of digital humans to be the four-dimensional ambassadors of business.

New business models will emerge on the market, many will pivot, and the experience of employees and consumers will be assets for companies. The existing virtual communities in companies will be the riches with human capital hired to improve business and adaptation of companies to the concepts of industry 5.0 and phygital transformation.

REFERENCES

AbuKhousa, E., El-Tahawy, M. S., & Atif, Y. (2023). Envisioning architecture of metaverse intensive learning experience (MiLEx): Career readiness in the 21st century and collective intelligence development scenario. *Future Internet*, 15(2), 53. 10.3390/fi15020053

Antonello, A., & Cook, M. (2023). Environmental historians, policy, and governance. In *The Routledge handbook of environmental history* (p. 399–412). 10.4324/9781003189350-32

Bhalla, S., Bahar, N., & Kanapathy, K. (2023). Knowledge collaboration among fashion designers: An A Priori conceptual model. *The Electronic Journal of Knowledge Management, 21*(3). https://academic-publishing.org/index.php/ejkm/article/view/2928/2180

Broom, D. (2023). Four-day work week trial in Spain leads to healthier workers, less pollution. *World Economic Forum*. https://www.weforum.org/agenda/2023/10/surprising-benefits-four-day-week/

Chien, F. (2023). The role of corporate governance and environmental and social responsibilities on the achievement of sustainable development goals in Malaysian logistic companies. *Ekonomska Istrazivanja*, 36(1), 1610–1630. 10.1080/1331677X.2022.2090407

Christofi, K., Chourides, P., & Papageorgiou, G. (2023). Cultivating Strategic Agility - An Empirical Investigation in Best Practice. *Global Business and Organizational Excellence*, 00, 1–17. 10.1002/joe.22241

Cooke, F. L., & Rogovsky, N. (2023). Human-centred approach to increasing workplace productivity: Evidence from Asia. *International Labour Organization*. https://www.ilo.org/wcmsp5/groups/public/---dgreports/---inst/documents/publication/wcms_906606.pdf

Cuello, H. (2023). Assessing the validity of four-day week pilots. *Joint Research Centre*.https://joint-research-centre.ec.europa.eu/system/files/2023-04/JRC133008_jrc133008_dclass_wp_assessing_four-day_week_pilots_final.pdf

Day week global (2023). https://www.4dayweek.com/

de Carvalho, A. A., Cirera, R. dos R. & Mengalli, N. M. (2023). FoLo - fear of logging off: Medo de ficar sem conexão. *26ª carta de conjuntura*.https://www.uscs.edu.br/boletim/1603

Dewey, J. (1979). *Experiência e educação*. Companhia editora nacional.

Dutra, D. L., Santos, H. R. M., & Silva, R. S. (2013). Inovação em processos de aprendizagem. https://www.researchgate.net/publication/263426362_Inovacao_em _Processos_de_Aprendizagem

Freire, P. (1989). A importância do ato de ler: Em três artigos que se completam. *Coleção Polêmicas do Nosso Tempo*. Autores associados: Cortez.

Freire, P. (2003). *Pedagogia da esperança: Um encontro com a pedagogia do oprimido*. Paz e terra.

Hopkins, J., Bardoel, A., & Djurkovic, N. (2023). Emerging four day work week trends in Australia: Preview report. *Swinburne University of Technology*. https:// apo.org.au/node/323150

Kapp, K. (2012). *The gamification of learning and instruction: Game-based methods and strategies for training and education*. Pfeiffer.

Kuhn, T. S. (1998) *A estrutura das revoluções científicas*. Editora perspectiva.

Lave, J., & Wenger, E. (1991). *Situated learning: Legitimate peripheral participation*. Cambridge university press. 10.1017/CBO9780511815355

Louaf, S. Thomas, M., Jankowski, F., Leclerc, C., Barnaud, A., Baufume, S., Guichardaz, A., Joly, H., Labeyrie, V., Leclercq, M., Ndiaye, A., Pham, J., Raimond, C., Rey, A., Saudiy, A., Temple, L. (2022, October 27). Communities of Practice in Crop Diversity Management: From Data to Collaborative Governance. In *Towards Responsible Plant Data Linkage: Data Challenges for Agricultural Research and Development*. (pp. 273-288). Springer.

Masterson, V. (2022) We could be spending an hour a day in the metaverse by 2026. But what will we be doing there? *World Economic Forum*. https://www.weforum .org/agenda/2022/03/hour-a-day-in-metaverse-by-2026-says-gartner

Mendes, L., & Urbina, L. M. S. (2015). Análise sobre a produção acadêmica Brasileira em comunidades de prática. *RAC, 19*, 305-327. http://dx.doi.org/10.1590/ 1982-7849rac20151754

Mengalli, N. M. (2005). *Intersecção para a comunidade de prática.*https://www .flickr.com/photos/nelimariamengalli/354357844

Mengalli, N. M. (2006). Interação, redes e comunidades de prática (CoP): Subsídios para a gestão do conhecimento na educação. Dissertação (Mestrado em educação: currículo) - Programa de pós-graduação educação: Currículo, pontifícia Universidade Católica de São Paulo. São Paulo.

Mengalli, N. M., & Carvalho, A. A. (2023). *Creation of digital solutions in higher education: Strategies with hands-on and disruptive technologies in phygital transformation. Perspectives on enhancing learning experience through digital strategy in higher education.* IGI Global. 10.4018/978-1-6684-8282-7.ch001

Mengalli, N. M., de Carvalho, A. A., & Galvão, S. M. (2023). *Metaverse ecosystem and consumer society 5.0: Consumer experience and influencer marketing in phygital transformation. Influencer marketing applications within the Metaverse.* IGI Global. 10.4018/978-1-6684-8898-0.ch003

Mengalli, N. M., & Valente, J. A. (2010). *The critical and historical view in communities of practice for the development in education. Cases on collaboration in virtual learning environments: Processes and interactions.* IGI Global. 10.4018/978-1-60566-878-9.ch019

Neves, A. (2001, June 1). Etienne Wenger. *Podcast da knowman KMOL con Ana Neves.*https://kmol.pt/entrevistas/2001/06/01/etienne-wenger/

Queen, D. (2023). Could wound care benefit from the artificial intelligence storm taking place worldwide. *International Wound Journal, 20*(5), 1337–1338. 10.1111/iwj.1417137039743

Ribiere, V. (2023). *Knowledge management in the metaverse: The future of knowledge management. Knowledge management and organizational learning* (Vol. 12). Springer. 10.1007/978-3-031-38696-1_15

Rimol, M. (2022). *Gartner predicts 25% of people will spend at least one hour per day in the metaverse by 2026.* Press Release, Gartner.

Rowe, L., Knight, L., Irvine, P., & Greenwood, J. (2023). Communities of practice for contemporary leadership development and knowledge exchange through work-based learning. *Journal of Education and Work, 36*(6), 494–510. 10.1080/13639080.2023.2255149

Soekiman, S. (2023) The effect of knowledge sharing an individual innovation capability on employee performance with work motivation as an intervening variable. *Oeconomia copernicana, 14*(2). http://repository.unitomo.ac.id/3465/1/10.pdf

Sutton, A. (2023). Cultivating global health: Exploring mindfulness through an organisational psychology lens. *Mindfulness.* Advance online publication. 10.1007/s12671-023-02228-y

Taylor, S. J., Bogdan, R., & DeVault, M. L. (2016). *Introduction to qualitative research methods: A guidebook and resource.* Wiley.

Walker, J., & Fontinha, R. (2022). The pandemic has made a four-day working week more attractive to workers and businesses study finds. *Henley Business School.* https://www.henley.ac.uk/news/2022/the-pandemic-has-made-a-four-day-working -week-more-attractive-to-workers-and-businesses-study-finds

Wenger-Trayner, E., & Wenger-Trayner, B. (2015). *Introduction to communities of practice: A brief overview of concept and its uses.* https://www.wenger-trayner.com/introduction-to-communities-of-practice/#:~:text=Communities%20of%20practice%20are%20groups,better%20as%20they%20interact%20regularly

ADDITIONAL READING

Abuhantash, A. (2023). The future of HR management: Exploring the potential of e-HRM for improving employee experience and organizational outcomes. *World Journal of Advanced Research and Reviews, 18*(2). 647-651. 10.30574/wjarr.2023.18.2.0883

Asante, . (2023). Optimization of consumer engagement with artificial intelligence elements on electronic commerce platforms. *Journal of Electronic Commerce Research,* 24(1). http://www.jecr.org/sites/default/files/2023vol24no1_Paper2.pdf

Bode, I. (2023). Emergent normativity: Communities of practice, technology, and lethal autonomous weapon systems. *Global Studies Quarterly.* https://findresearcher.sdu.dk/ws/portalfiles/portal/224959580/Bode_Emergent_Normativitity_GSQ_2023.pdf

Cohen, S., & Queen, D. (2023). Generative artificial intelligence community of practice for research. *International Wound Journal,* 20(6), 1817–1818. 10.1111/iwj.1427437344961

Frehywot, S., & Vovides, Y. (2023). An equitable and sustainable community of practice framework to address the use of artificial intelligence for global health workforce training. *Human Resources for Health,* 21(45), 45. Advance online publication. 10.1186/s12960-023-00833-537312214

Kuhn, T. S. (1970). *The structure of scientific revolutions* (2nd ed.). The University of Chicago Press.

Mengalli, N. (2005). *Estágios da comunidade de prática.* https://www.researchgate.net/figure/Figura-1-Estagios-da-Comunidade-de-Pratica-MENGALLI-2005_fig1_263426362/download

KEY TERM AND DEFINITIONS

Experience of Collaborators in Communities of Practice: The structure of communities of practice is legitimized by the institutions and, in the business model, is made effective by the participation of each member. Employees cannot be eternal learners in the sense of taking numerous courses to be recognized as responsible for managing knowledge in the company. It is possible for a collaborator to be a specialist in detailing a product, a process, or a service, to be a specialist in the central core to teach in the peripheral core and contribute to the learning of other collaborators. Knowledge management is the responsibility of all employees in the company and the courses can echo as opportunities for collective innovations in communities of practice. In this way, learning is alive and is part of a process that involves teaching and helping other people in reflections that generate co-creation and co-authorship in business in dynamic networks for the quality of collaboration and for the well-being of people with strategic productivity for the organization. The professional structure with dialogical support makes it possible for employees to experience a meaningful data culture and shows that the experience of each employee has strategic value for the company and has an impact on the consumer experience on business results. It is understood that employees are all those who work together for the purpose of the company to be conducted, therefore, productivity and assertiveness are inherent to the success of the business. People live immersive experiences and have contact with artificial intelligences and the experience of employees shows feelings and emotions in relation to work that tends to promote people into meta-influencers in the organization and outside it as business ambassadors.

Human Varnish: It is a term created in the business area and has been linked to the professions of the future, especially when it involves disruptive technologies. The human varnish shows that only human beings have characteristics that involve creativity, communication, and emotion. Work that requires repetition tends to be conducted by mechanization and robotization, however, when there is a need for creativity, communication and emotion, the human being will not be surpassed by computational parameters.

Phygital Transformation: It is the change that groups strategies that unite the real world and the digital universe with a fluidity that produces intangible results. The use of disruptive technologies must be transparent, that is, there must be no flaws that are visible to users or consumers. The focus is on instantaneity, immersion and interaction that make sense for the consumer or user. It is important to evaluate adherence and acceptance and analyze behavioral data to promote the best immersive experience.

Chapter 5
Online Learning and Communities for the Visual and Performing Arts

Melissa Welz
New Jersey City University, USA

ABSTRACT

This chapter seeks to dissect the multifaceted dimensions of personal online learning spaces, situating them within the larger canvas of contemporary educational practices in the visual and performing arts field. An extension of the pedagogical movement towards student-centered and self-directed learning is the emergence of personal online learning spaces. Learners have access to a wide variety of tools in the arts, including interactive courses, virtual galleries, and personal showcases. Online learning environment gives students the freedom to personalize their educational experience, take into account different learning preferences, and develop a stronger bond with their aspirations in the arts.

INTRODUCTION

Prior to the emergence of the novel coronavirus, the music industry was already experiencing an ascendancy sparked by the growth of online streaming services. However, the introduction of the pandemic necessitated the cancellation of live performances, tours, and new releases, resulting in a dramatic spike in streaming consumption. COVID-19 prompted a migration from in-person music instruction to remote learning modalities.

DOI: 10.4018/979-8-3693-1111-0.ch005

This resulted in a sharp increase in streaming demand as consumption behaviors shifted in response to the pandemic. In addition, COVID-19 unforeseen circumstances prompted a broad migration from in-person music pedagogy to remote instructional modalities. The rapid proliferation of streaming alongside public health measures accelerating the adoption of distance learning technologies have combined to fundamentally transform the music industry in a remarkably brief period.

During COVID-19, precipitated an unprecedented crisis for the live music industry, with global revenue losses exceeding $30 billion in 2020 alone. This financial devastation continued into 2021, as ongoing public health restrictions curtailed large gatherings and live events worldwide. For recording artists who rely heavily on income from live performances, these cancellations dealt a severe economic blow.

However, the growth of music streaming during this pandemic provided a partial salve for these wounds. While streaming royalties remain small in comparison to earnings from live concerts, this digital revenue stream helped offset losses and sustain artists through extended touring hiatus. Looking ahead, innovations in virtual performances and increased consumer adoption of streaming unlocked new monetization pathways. Major streaming platforms like Spotify, Tidal, Pandora, and Apple Music observed meteoric growth across key metrics, including subscriptions, artist participation, and user activity throughout the crisis. These digital services unveiled novel functionality to facilitate virtual concerts and interactive streaming.

Virtual performances and livestreams became an economic lifeline in 2020 and 2021. This rapid adoption hints that such practices are not a fleeting fad, but rather a permanent shift redefining the musical world experience. Many experts predict that even post-pandemic, virtual events will continue flourishing in tandem with in-person gatherings. Though irreplicable, live shows now face competition from more accessible streaming alternatives reaching global audiences. The music industry must integrate these emerging formats into sustainable business models moving forward. With the genie out of the bottle, virtual concerts and online communities are poised to permanently transform artist-fan connections.

Virtual online concerts are live music performances that are streamed over the internet, allowing audiences to experience the event remotely from the comfort of their own homes or any location with an internet connection. These virtual concerts have become increasingly popular in recent years, providing a unique and innovative way for artists to connect with their fans in the digital era.

One prominent example of a virtual online concert is Travis Scott's Astronomical event within the popular video game Fortnite in 2020. This groundbreaking performance featured a fully-rendered, digital version of the rapper performing a series of songs in the game's virtual environment. Millions of Fortnite players were able to log in and attend the concert, exploring the interactive stage and even purchasing virtual merchandise related to the event (Forbes, 2020).

The versatility of virtual online concerts has also allowed for the exploration of unique collaborative experiences. In 2021, the electronic music duo The Chainsmokers partnered with the metaverse platform Supersphere to host a virtual concert that blended live-action and computer-generated elements. The event featured the artists performing on a physical stage, with their digital avatars appearing alongside them in a fully-rendered virtual environment. This innovative approach allowed for a heightened level of visual and auditory immersion, as well as the incorporation of interactive features like virtual meet-and-greets and the ability for fans to control various aspects of the concert experience.

The advent of virtual concerts, livestreams, and social media has unlocked novel avenues for artists to engage audiences. Numerous digital platforms have debuted customized features and formats to facilitate more intimate artist-fan connections. Performers can now establish direct outreach channels via platforms like Instagram and Twitch. Though nascent before 2020, COVID-19 proved catalytic for this trend's exponential growth in followership. Concurrently, record labels have provided technological support and infrastructure to enhance production values on livestreams.

Certain streaming services pioneered new monetization tools surrounding virtual events, including paid virtual meet-and-greets or exclusive content access. Others introduced tiered membership models where fans pay premium subscription fees to unlock special artist content and interactions. While still evolving, these innovations reveal how virtual concerts can transcend financial losses from touring cancellations. By creatively merging technology, social media, and fan incentives, the music industry can nurture closer than ever artist audience relationships due to online learning and communities. Moving forward, virtual concerts, platforms, classes, communities and direct outreach will likely become cornerstones of sustaining visual and performing artist careers.

The internet and digital technologies have dramatically expanded the possibilities for self-directed and personalized learning in all fields and subjects. In the visual and performing arts field, students now have an unprecedented ability to create their own online learning spaces that will fit to their interests, needs, and creative goals. These personalized online environments allow students to take control of their own education and pursue artmaking in a way that is meaningful and relevant to them.

In this chapter, we will examine the rise of personal online learning spaces within the larger context of student-centered pedagogy and educational technology. We will briefly review the theoretical foundations and key tenets of student-centered learning. We will then discuss how the internet and participatory culture have enabled new forms of informal, self-directed learning online. We will then outline some of the unique affordances of online spaces for arts learning, such as access to open educational resources, connectivity and community building, exhibition and audience engagement, and interest-driven learning pathways.

We must consider how personal online learning spaces align with and extend theories of student-centered learning in the visual and performing arts careers. We will pay particular attention to how these spaces allow for artistic development that is driven by students' own passions, identities, and aspirations. While acknowledging their limitations, we will explore the potential of online spaces to fundamentally reimagine arts education in a digital age.

The Music Industry Prior to COVID-19

The increasing motion at which the world transitioned from the agricultural, industrial, and information ages is arguably one of the most significant shifts in world history (Toffler, 1981). In the years preceding COVID-19, the visual and performing arts field experienced significant changes as a result of disruptive technical breakthroughs and evolving consumer behavior. First of all, the paradigm for music consumption underwent a radical change with the introduction of digital streaming services, led by companies like Spotify, Apple Music, and Amazon Music. The ease of on-demand streaming services has gradually replaced the conventional practice of buying physical albums or single music. Because per-stream royalty rates were far lower than those of traditional sales, this move presented serious issues to the industry's revenue streams. As a result, both record companies and artists had to adjust to this new reality, looking for new ways to make money and reinventing their business strategies.

One of the main principles of the industry continued to be the search for new talent, with record companies and talent agencies constantly searching for the next big thing. A resilient concert industry is driven by audiences' insatiable hunger for live experiences, reinforcing the importance of live performances and traveling as a source of income for artists.

However, there was also a major transformation in the dynamics of marketing and promotion. The conventional dependence on radio play and physical record sales was replaced by a greater focus on social media visibility, viral advertising campaigns, and tactical alliances with streaming services.

Tracking listener preferences, consumption trends, and demographic information allowed for better focused marketing campaigns and well-informed creative decisions. Although this data-centric strategy presented new prospects, worries about standardization and the preference for financial success over artistic originality were also voiced. Nevertheless, the visual and performing arts field was already shifting away from live musical/ art performances and toward internet choices alongside online/distance education.

While virtual online concerts have captivated music fans and redefined the live performance experience, the transformative potential of virtual technologies extends far beyond the realm of entertainment. These innovative platforms have also made significant inroads into the field of education, offering new avenues for learning, collaboration, and immersive experiences. Much like the ways in which virtual concerts have brought the magic of live music to audiences worldwide, the integration of virtual tools and environments into the educational landscape has the power to revolutionize how students engage with course material, interact with their peers, and access learning resources. As we explore the evolving landscape of virtual online concerts, it is essential to also consider the parallels and opportunities presented by the application of these technologies within the educational sphere, where the potential to redefine and enhance the learning experience is equally profound.

The way students use new technology to learn can have a positive impact on the subject of music education (Purves, 2012). Online resources provide access to a wealth of recordings, performances, and materials from diverse musical traditions worldwide, broadening students' musical knowledge and appreciation. Also, with online learning/distance education, educators bring their prior teaching theories and experiences with them when they transition to an online learning environment.

This usually indicates that a person's idea of teaching music is found in the conventional cultural and collaborative conceptions of the music experience and traditional music education (Reimer, 2003). According to Picciano (2002), in order for online learners to feel like they belong, it is important to establish a community early on in their platform. By proactively nurturing an inclusive and interactive online classroom/community culture from the beginning, educators/leaders can mitigate feelings of isolation and alienation that online students may experience, thereby promoting a greater sense of belonging and commitment to their educational pursuits.

Visual and Performing Arts Online/Distance Education

Online Education Distance Education is a teaching and learning modality used in several areas of knowledge since the 19th century. Many researchers sought to categorize in phases the development of Distance Education based on the technological changes and theories of learning adopted in this modality. Moore and Kearsley (2012) divide it into five historical generations. The first generation used the letters as a medium of instruction, the second generation was mediated by radio and television.

The third generation, in turn, was not characterized by the adoption of another form of technology used in teaching and learning, but rather, it was marked by the institutionalization of Distance Education courses, such as those offered by "open universities." The fourth generation, started in 1980 with the first real-time distance interaction made possible by audio, video and computer teleconferencing, widely used in corporate training. Finally, for Moore and Kearsley (2012), the last generation is marked by online teaching and learning. This latest generation is defined by the dissemination of new Digital Information and Communication Technologies (DICT), which make countless technological resources available to us. In this sense, the popularization of the internet has potentiated the use of DICT, and not only revolutionized several aspects of our lives, but also played an important role in the changes that occurred in DE, causing the growth of this modality, allowing the circulation of information and interaction between geographically dispersed individuals.

According to Gohn (2009), there are various terms to define this educational format: distance education, e-learning, virtual education, remote teaching and learning, online distance education, online teaching, open learning, mobile education, among other terms. Based on the Moore and Kearsley (2012) classification, as all these researches sought to understand the teaching and learning processes mediated by Digital Information and Communication Technologies (DICT) via Web.

Throughout history, the field of visual and performing arts education has been characterized by a somewhat monolithic pedagogical approach. The traditional model, often described as a "sage on the stage" or "follow the master", dominated teaching and learning practices in this realm. In the theater arts, practitioners honed their craft through intense monologue rehearsal, meticulously adjusting facial expressions to align with the director's vision. This immersive process often resulted in participants breathlessly working to ensure precise emotional delivery.

Dance and music education mirrored this paradigm, relying heavily on observational learning. Students closely observed instructors' movements and playing demonstrations, diligently replicating and practicing these actions. Immediate feedback from teachers further refined their physical expressions. Notably, these classes exhibited minimal integration of technology, which may explain why dance, in particular, lagged in adopting technological applications (Calvert et al., 2005).

Distance Education has, for many years, been used as a teaching and learning modality for theoretical areas of knowledge. In the twenty-first century, due to the development of digital media and the popularization of the internet, there has been an increase in projects that use these resources in the teaching and learning of musical instruments. Research has been used in many types of forms by using different data collection methods, in which students involved in online teaching and learning modality demonstrated a very similar technical and musical development to those involved in face-to-face lessons.

The main challenges found refer to the lack of a superfast broadband, which demonstrates that teaching and learning strategies must also be adapted to the technical limitations imposed by the connection possibilities and equipment used in the action research. This occurred, for example, in research that used platforms where teacher and student could not play at the same time without latency, in this case, those involved had to adapt. It is important to point out that this teaching format goes beyond the choice of devices, software and platforms, it comes up against specific ways of building knowledge and approaches to content. Some characteristics related to pedagogical approaches, communication and behavior of teachers during online synchronous lessons are described in some of the works. The problem related to the online teaching and learning of musical instruments intensifies in front of the current moment in which the world is facing a pandemic generated by COVID-19.

This feeling of estrangement is understandable and demonstrates the importance of promoting research and the consequent training of professionals qualified to work in this specific modality of teaching and learning. In this perspective, this will have a great impact in the field of online teaching and learning, in relation to the development of new software and equipment as well as teaching strategies in the area.

In performing arts classes, teachers engage in hands-on activities, designing costumes, constructing props, manipulating curtains, and experimenting with special lighting effects—all conducted in the presence of attentive students documenting key concepts. In ancient art forms like Chinese Opera, the preservation of tradition involved not only teachers but also legendary artists imparting knowledge through studio sessions—a method aimed at safeguarding heritage and authenticity.

In the realm of film and television, educators have long dedicated their time to theoretical lectures, exploring concepts like Montage, GoogleMeet, and Zoom. However, the emergence of COVID-19 disrupted this conventional approach, leading to the cancellation of in-person classes, rehearsals, and live performances. This pivotal moment compelled the performing arts community to navigate the uncharted waters of remote pedagogy, replacing traditional face-to-face instruction with synchronous online learning.

Faced with this unprecedented challenge, educators had to rethink their teaching methods and find creative ways to engage students in a virtual setting. The familiar terrain of in-person demonstrations and critiques gave way to a new landscape where educators, despite the initial disorientation, embraced innovation. Technologies like video conferencing, digital whiteboards, and cloud-based collaboration tools became the pillars supporting interactive learning through screens.

Amidst the difficulties, the performing arts disciplines showcased remarkable resilience, using technology not merely to survive but to reshape instruction in an increasingly digital world. This adaptive spirit reflects the transformative power of embracing change and leveraging technology to enhance the educational experience.

The Rise of Student-Centered Pedagogy

Over the past few decades, a shift towards student-centered pedagogy has transformed arts education. This theoretical paradigm stems largely from constructivist learning theories that emphasize the active role students play in building their own knowledge (Vygotsky, 1978). Rather than passively receiving instructor-driven content, constructivism frames learning as an active process where students construct meaning through experience, reflection, and dialogue.

When we think of core tenets of student-centered pedagogy, we should keep in mind focusing on the interests, backgrounds, and developmental levels of individual students rather than adhering to a standardized curriculum. We must also provide open-ended experiences and creative problems for students to explore and interpret based on their perspectives. The educator should be a facilitator who guides and scaffolds self-directed learning rather than solely lecturing or transmitting knowledge. This allows students to share control over the pace, activities, and parameters of learning. This method helps in assessing students' depth of understanding through authentic tasks and demonstrations rather than traditional tests.

This learner-driven paradigm has thoroughly impacted arts education approaches (Baker, 2021). For instance, arts programs emphasize nurturing students' individual creativity over teaching codified techniques. Curricula prioritize immersive studio projects over lectures on formal elements. Assessments focus on portfolio reviews and critiques rather than objective tests.

While student-centered pedagogy has brought invaluable changes to arts education, it also presents challenges. Teachers must develop skills for mentoring self-directed learning and providing differentiated instruction within group settings. Open-ended learning requires strong intrinsic motivation from students. Striking a balance between structure and independence remains an ever-evolving endeavor. However, at its heart, student-centered arts education empowers students to shape their own artistic journeys.

In the realm of education, we witnessed the rise of webinars and inventive performance projects, born from the creative fusion of flipped classroom and 'outcome-based education' concepts. This convergence of blended learning, flipped classroom methodology, and outcome-based education is encapsulated in the term, hybrid learning. It's not just a buzzword; it represents a dynamic synthesis of diverse educational strategies geared towards elevating the overall learning experience and fostering adaptability in the face of evolving challenges.

For certain performing arts disciplines deeply rooted in personalized, real-time interactions, the feasibility and necessity of blended learning pose distinct challenges. Scholars such as Colombi and Knosp (2017), Power and Kannara (2016), and Li (2020) have observed that the additional time required for preparation can hinder the effectiveness of blended learning in these contexts. However, an alternative perspective comes from Ruokonen and Ruismäki (2016), who argue that blended learning opens up enhanced opportunities for independence and active learning among performing arts students.

Colombi and Knosp (2017) proposed a practical solution by suggesting that certain theoretical materials and references be made available to students before or after class. This approach frees up precious face-to-face class time for interactive activities, like the thoughtful selection and appreciation of specific music. However, they also underscore the significance of visual elements, such as displaying profile photographs, in fostering a sense of belonging during real-time teaching.

Searching through the intricacies of blended learning, Power and Kannara (2016) put forth a comprehensive framework encompassing external environment, technology, curriculum, and student considerations. This framework serves as the foundational basis for crafting a practical model for virtual learning environments (VLEs) within the creative arts. It is a thoughtful exploration into the factors influencing blended learning, paving the way for a more effective and tailored approach to virtual education in the creative realm.

Unpacking Personal Online Learning Spaces/Communities

Picture your online learning space/community as a versatile room designed to offer diverse virtual experiences, a departure from the traditional classroom or studio setup. This being said, we will delve into the intricacies through three key elements: content, communities, and technologies. Content serves as the foundation of personal learning, encompassing both tangible and intangible resources vital for cultivating knowledge.

In the realm of virtual art, content takes various forms such as multimedia tutorials, guides, project examples, commentaries, and interactive curricula. These open-licensed materials not only allow for self-paced learning but also spark innovative aesthetic expressions. User-generated productions, a significant aspect of content, are shared across online networks, fostering a collaborative environment. Platforms like DeviantArt and MindCafe, with their digitizations and behind-the-scenes glimpses, serve as sources of inspiration.

Interactive communities closely align with both informational and creative content. Members of virtual online communities, comprising like-minded creators, commentators, and audiences, contribute to personal learning through participatory engagements. Online forums become spaces for technical queries, peer evaluations, collaborative brainstorming, and celebratory milestones, cultivating a sense of belonging and stimulating artistic evolution. Social media further strengthens these networks, reducing virtual distances through interest-based followings and geotagged meetups.

The delivery of content and community facilitation undergo rapid advancements with advanced technologies. Emerging interfaces simplify access to diverse assets, enhancing the quality of virtual experiences. Smartphones and tablets, equipped with sophisticated software, bring learning to the palm of your hand, ensuring accessibility everywhere you go. Responsive websites streamline browsing, and platform-specific features like timestamped comments on YouTube and options on TikTok elevate the pedagogical relevance of multimedia. Augmented and virtual reality tools blur the boundaries between the physical and digital, immersing users in artistic scenarios. Undoubtedly, technological scaffolds contribute significantly to the fluidity and personalization of online independent study.

The visual and performing arts education unfolds as a rich tapestry interweaving theoretical and practical dimensions, illuminating their symbiotic relationship and the collective enrichment they bring to the discipline. While the practical facet, focused on honing performance skills, often takes center stage in music education programs, the fusion of theory and practice stands as paramount for a holistic comprehension of music, ultimately culminating in elevated artistic performance. Hence, both the theoretical and practical components prove indispensable, mutually fortifying each other within the realm of music education.

Across the globe, visual and performing arts departments in educational institutions struggle with challenges, notably concerning their size. The personalized attention demanded by vocal and instrumental instruction, tailored to accommodate diverse learning speeds, contributes to the intricacies faced. Additionally, the perception that musical talent or giftedness serves as a prerequisite for studying music can inadvertently foster exclusivity, hindering access for potential learners. Financial constraints further compound the predicament, placing limitations on the equipping of music rooms and expecting students to procure their own instruments, thereby constricting the pool of prospective students.

In the sphere of higher education, a notable trend towards online learning communities, marked by the establishment of Virtual Learning Environments (VLEs) and Managed Learning Environments. These online platforms offer a cohesive user interface for course management and content delivery, enabling remote instruction and collaborative endeavors. Virtual education, denoting courses delivered with physical separation between teachers and students, relies on diverse technologies such as course management applications, the internet, multimedia resources, and videoconferencing. Virtual classrooms, facilitated by personal computers, not only broaden access to advanced educational experiences but also foster collaborative learning processes, thereby enhancing the quality and effectiveness of education. Although e-learning cannot entirely supplant the impact of exceptional teachers, it stands as a significant evolution in the educational landscape. The amalgamation of e-Learning with traditional face-to-face instruction has given rise to blended learning, a widely embraced approach within music education.

Beyond traditional boundaries, online learning emerges as a service transcending geographical constraints through technological means. E-Learning opens avenues to blend computer-based strategies with physical classroom settings, allowing teaching and learning to extend beyond the confines of a campus. In the context of music education, various delivery modes, including blended learning, distance/open learning, virtual learning, and collaborative music activities, present extensive possibilities. Students gain access to course materials and engage with facilitators online, affording them the flexibility to pursue their studies from the comfort of their homes. Similarly, lecturers can maintain meaningful interactions with students while attending conferences or fulfilling professional commitments away from the campus environment.

Moreover, e-Learning acts as a catalyst for global collaborations among music departments, understanding knowledge sharing and research endeavors. Discussion forums, blogs, wikis, and online collaborative activities serve as platforms where students from diverse institutions converge, forming discussion groups. Collaborations among lecturers facilitate intercultural research endeavors, with faculty from various countries and continents conducting studies within their respective local contexts. The insights garnered from such collaborations represent a valuable synthesis of diverse cultural and economic settings, contributing to the multifaceted landscape of music education.

Ostashewski et al. (2016) and Li et al. (2018) state that the utilization of portable devices, such as iPads and mobile phones, for live demonstrations in small groups works well in online education. This innovative use of technology allows for student-controlled playback and practice activities, creating avenues for review and interactive engagement. Beyond its impact on individual learning, this approach proves beneficial in large-group settings outside the confines of the traditional classroom. In essence, the integration of online course management systems and portable devices not only caters to the diverse learning styles in dance education but also enhances interaction, engagement, and the overall effectiveness of teaching methodologies in both small and large group settings.

Challenges of Social Isolation in Online Learning

In the realm of online learning within the education sector, students often find themselves navigating a landscape characterized by self-reflection, isolation, and a notable absence of physical interaction. Prolonged engagement in virtual spaces tends to give rise to social isolation, as the lack of face-to-face communication becomes a breeding ground for stress, anxiety, and negative thoughts. Rovai, Wighting, & Liu (2005) underscore the significance of robust communication and active social interactions, emphasizing their correlation with both sustained engagement and learning satisfaction.

In a departure from this, visual arts embraces a practice-based approach as a pedagogical strategy. Here, small groups of students engage in learning under the close guidance of experienced mentors. This collaborative practice-based learning environment allows for the iterative exploration of ambiguous problems through multimodal analysis, proposition, and critique.

The emphasis lies on cultivating self-regulation in learning, nurturing personal teacher-student relationships, and spotlighting ethics and ideals over rigid rules and sanctions. The studio approach, rooted in practice-based learning, necessitates seamless interaction among students and lecturers for effective knowledge exchange and artistic expression. The efficacy of this method is inherently tied to face-to-face studio approach learning, as it proves fundamental to fostering creativity, critical thinking, and expressive skills. This distinctive approach stands in contrast to the challenges posed by prolonged online learning, providing a space that not only imparts knowledge but also nurtures the core elements of artistic development.

The asynchronous nature of online learning poses an ongoing challenge for providing students with timely and meaningful feedback. Without the immediacy of in-person interactions, students often struggle when periodic assessments offer little chance for prompt responses. Face-to-face instruction still reigns supreme for instant feedback that motivates and engages. Nowhere does this prove more crucial than in visual and performing arts critiques.

These lively sessions become a dynamic forum for the exchange of insights between teachers and students. Feedback fuels an iterative loop where artworks continuously evolve through reexamination and rethinking. In-progress critiques prompt critical decision making during studio experiments, catalyzing breakthroughs. The multidimensional suggestions, revisions, and reflections encompass both technical fundamentals and conceptual directions. Ultimately, this interplay of subjective perspectives and objective advice brings nascent creative visions to tangible fruition.

Another prevalent weakness in online learning is the disproportionate emphasis on theoretical knowledge over practical skills. While innovative online platforms attempt to address this issue, it remains unresolved. Visual arts, as a diverse field, places importance on learning by doing, where the construction and interpretation of visual texts are fundamental skills developed through practice. Sjöholm (2014) underscores the reliance on productive tension based on knowledge practices, contemplation, bodily engagement, and improvisation in the studio. Practical experimentation in the studio involves manipulating, transforming, improvising, and reconstructing ideas through the use of materials and techniques. The development of practical skills in visual arts necessitates hands-on learning under the close supervision of lecturers, emphasizing the impracticality of achieving effectiveness through online means.

While online learning excels at conveying theoretical knowledge and certain discrete skills, it struggles to cultivate more complex competencies. The very heart of active learning - experimenting, questioning, explaining - falters without in-person interactions. This poses particular challenges for practical disciplines where skills are honed through hands-on practice.

As Arkorful (2014) argues, e-learning has intrinsic limitations for fields demanding close collaboration and real-time engagement between students and instructors. Not every subject can transition seamlessly to a virtual format, especially those relying on tangible experiences to build mastery. Certain key skills simply resist replication through technology, constrained by the absence of face-to-face guidance and feedback. For these practical competencies, e-learning can complement but not entirely replace the value of learning by doing alongside mentors. While advantageous for conveying facts, online education alone falls short for fields requiring tactile proficiency.

Developing a highly effective online learning course necessitates extensive investments in time, financial resources, and specialized expertise. Successful online learning courses encompass a variety of elements, including multimedia integration, advanced web development, robust technical support, and the careful design of user interactions. However, if executed poorly, online courses can disrupt and have a detrimental impact on the learning process due to challenges such as limited time concentration and spatial constraints. Consequently, establishing the optimal practices for online learning courses remains an ongoing process, particularly when it comes to identifying learning methods that are both suitable and effective across various domains. In contrast, traditional training methods, which rely on direct instruction, standardized approaches, and hands-on experiential learning, have a well-established foundation and are generally acknowledged as more effective for teaching and learning in the visual and performing arts field.

Effective design in the e-learning context requires careful attention to various factors, such as the provision of rich learning activities, the incorporation of interesting storylines, opportunities for student reflection and feedback, appropriate technology selection, contextual suitability, and consideration of the personal, social, and environmental impact of the designed activities.

Careful lesson planning, instructional design, creative writing, and software specification is crucial for online learning and communities. The aim is to create engaging and appropriate learning experiences that are likely to be utilized and achieve the intended learning outcomes.

Online learning emphasizes the significance of incorporating multiple media types, such as text, images, and sound, to cater to different learning styles and enhance interactivity. One must pay attention to the core elements of e-learning design that can bridge the gap between educational intention and student experience.

Online learning communities should possess six key elements of effective e-learning design:

1. Activity
2. Scenario
3. Feedback
4. Delivery
5. Context
6. Impact

They are becoming a more common and significant way for people to further their education and career development. In order to guarantee the effectiveness and involvement of these online learning platforms, some fundamental design guidelines must be followed. Effective e-learning for online communities should include six key components, which have been determined by thorough research and real-world experience.

Activities are the first essential component. Delivering knowledge in a passive, lecture-style is insufficient for meaningful online learning to take place. High levels of interactivity are necessary for effective e-learning, as students must actively participate in accomplishing important tasks, resolving issues, and creating knowledge via their own experiences. Interactive simulations, group projects, discussion boards, and other active interactive activities might be examples of this.

The importance of scenario-based learning is closely related. Online courses should place learning objectives within realistic, contextualized scenarios that reflect the real-world problems and decision-making processes that students will encounter in their personal or professional life, as opposed to offering knowledge in an abstract manner. This makes the material more immediately relevant and meaningful by connecting the theoretical and practice gaps.

Furthermore, prompt and excellent feedback is crucial. Whether from peers, automated systems, or instructors, learners require regular, positive feedback on their performance and growth. Through this feedback loop, they may pinpoint their areas of strength and improvement and keep getting better at what they do. Multiple feedback modalities, such as personalized coaching and support or graded tests, should be offered by well-designed e-learning platforms.

Effective delivery is the fourth essential component. It is important that online courses be located on easily navigable and intuitive platforms that offer a smooth and uninterrupted learning environment. High-quality multimedia material, mobile device optimization, and ease of navigation are all essential for maintaining student interest and focus.

The fifth component emphasizes the significance of creating e-learning that is customized to the unique requirements, experiences, and learning styles of the intended audience. To guarantee relevance and accessibility, factors including industry, work functions, cultural contexts, and technical fluency should all be properly considered.

Ultimately, the ultimate objective of any e-learning activity is to have significant effects - for both the individual students and the larger community or business. Therefore, systems for monitoring and assessing behavioral modifications, learning outcomes, and concrete marketing or educational rewards should all be included in an effective design. This data-driven strategy guarantees an adequate return on investment for e-learning initiatives and permits ongoing development. Virtual learning environments can become effective catalysts for individual development, organizational transformation, and community improvement by strategically implementing these ideas.

THE USE OF BLENDED LEARNING IN VISUAL AND PERFORMING ARTS CLASSROOMS

The concept of blended learning made its inaugural appearance in the Finnish pedagogical discourse in 2005, when it was discussed in the online publication, "Piirtoheitin" In this work, the authors translated the English term "blended learning" into the Finnish "sulautuva opetus" (Joutsenvirta, 2010). A turning point in the development of teaching and learning approaches in the Finnish tertiary sector was the introduction of the "sulautuva opetus" concept. The rapid adoption of blended learning models by colleges and universities provides proof of the academic establishment's adaptability in implementing this revolutionary pedagogical strategy.

Though not without critics who examined the intricacies of meaning, "sulautuva opetus" gained popularity quickly, demonstrating Finland's adaptability to new trends and dedication to technologically enhanced education innovation.

In Finland, visual and performing arts education is an integral part of general education, with primary school teachers assuming responsibility for visual and performing arts education during the first six years of schooling. However, many student teachers face challenges in these areas due to their limited background in the subjects. Often, their knowledge is based solely on compulsory courses, which may hinder their understanding of complex concepts like music theory. For instance, comprehending the triad, a fundamental musical element, is crucial for teachers to effectively instruct students in various musical tasks. Therefore, it becomes imperative to explore effective methods to enhance student teachers' understanding of music theory.

Blended Learning as a Solution:

Blended learning combines various learning modalities, including face-to-face interactions, autonomous learning, peer learning, and e-learning opportunities. By incorporating these elements, a blended learning environment offers flexibility and personalized learning experiences that cater to the diverse needs of student teachers.

In Finland schools, most student teachers in the program actively engaged with the blended learning environment, leveraging the offered opportunities. They recognized the advantages of blended learning, such as flexibility and individualized support, compared to traditional teaching methods (Joutsenvirta, 2010). However, it is noteworthy that not all students found every blended learning element equally useful. This variation in perception highlights the importance of tailoring instructional approaches to meet the specific needs and preferences of learners.

The findings of this research hold significant implications for music teacher education. Blended learning environments can provide valuable tools and resources for student teachers to enhance their understanding of music theory, particularly complex concepts like the triad. By integrating practical music activities into the learning process, student teachers develop a more profound operational relationship with music, fostering motivation and competence in teaching music to future students.

The significance of blended learning supports primary school student teachers' study of music theory. Blended learning offers a promising approach to overcome challenges related to music education by providing flexibility, personalized learning experiences, and opportunities for practical application. Also, by incorporating blended learning principles into visual and performing arts education with the usage of technology, we can empower student teachers to develop a strong foundation in music theory and successfully impart their knowledge for the future world and the future generations of students. The fast implementation of blended learning models in Finnish universities predicted a broader transformation in instructional strategies facilitated by emerging digital technology. With the development of pedagogical approaches that leveraged the power of hybrid face-to-face and online modalities, educators from a variety of disciplines started investigating new ways to use social media platforms to improve student learning.

THE POTENTIAL OF SOCIAL MEDIA FOR TEACHING AND LEARNING IN THE PERFORMING ARTS

Social media has emerged as a powerful tool for learning, enabling learners to develop higher order thinking skills, engage in problem-solving, and foster communication and collaboration. It also facilitates connections between classroom learning and real-world experiences, making education more engaging and relevant. YouTube, with its audio-visual elements and social interaction features, has the potential to serve as an instructional medium, aligning with the current trends of collaboration and social networking in education.

Nowadays, YouTube, Instagram, and TikTok are valuable tools for teaching, learning and building online communities in the visual and performing arts. While numerous studies have explored the use of social media platforms in education, the focus has primarily been on academic subjects, leaving a dearth of research in the realm of performing arts education.

Videos as Social Media

The fundamental principle underlying our exploration is that learners have a higher level of understanding and retention when they engage in multisensory experiences: seeing, hearing, and doing. Studies have shown that learning with multimedia elements, such as videos, is highly effective. Educators can communicate concepts and information in a variety of ways while using multimedia learning environments. By carefully combining text, graphics, audio, video, and interactive simulations, teachers may create dynamic, multi-sensory learning environments that provide students autonomy over the pace and delivery of the material (Cairncross, 2001).

The success of instruction can be greatly increased by using video materials effectively. Research indicates that the strategic integration of videos throughout critical phases of the educational process enhances student involvement, expands comprehension, and streamlines the transfer of knowledge (Hsu, 2013). When video features are carefully incorporated, they engage learners' senses, grab their attention, and provide dynamic representations that enhance learning. Additionally, using videos wisely can improve lesson pacing by summarizing important takeaways, presenting themes with eye-catching graphics, and using animation to make complicated ideas easier to understand. Video becomes a revolutionary tool for improving student outcomes and teaching when it is strategically connected with learning objectives. YouTube, along with platforms like Teacher Tube, Instagram, TikTok and Vimeo, offers an extensive collection of videos encompassing various content genres, ranging from films and television shows to music and instructional materials. Moreover, YouTube transforms into a social media platform when users share videos and engage in interactive discussions through comments and other forms of interaction.

Videos have been successfully employed in various fields, such as Java computing, to facilitate learning while minimizing lecture time. They contribute to cognitive and social development, particularly in problem-solving tasks. However, the use of YouTube in education, particularly in the performing arts, remains relatively unexplored. While some studies have examined YouTube's instructional potential in academic subjects like medicine and architecture, further research is warranted.

In conclusion, social media holds immense promise as a tool for teaching and learning in the visual and performing arts. By harnessing its audio-visual capabilities and leveraging the power of social media, educators can create engaging and interactive learning experiences for students. However, further research is needed to fully understand and optimize the use of YouTube in performing arts education. As we strive to adapt education to the ever-evolving technological landscape, social media platforms' potential as an instructional medium becomes increasingly evident, paving the way for innovative and effective pedagogical practices in the performing arts realm.

ONLINE COMMUNITIES FOR VISUAL AND PERFORMING ARTS EDUCATION

The proliferation of online learning has opened new possibilities for accessing education in the visual and performing arts. Students can now engage with arts instruction and build creative communities without geographic restrictions. A leading force in online arts communities is the Rhode Island School of Design's (RISD) Digital + Media program. This graduate program offers specialized concentrations in areas like animation, user experience design, and virtual reality. Students collaborate on digital projects, network with industry partners, and exhibit work in a digital gallery. The online format expands access to RISD's prestigious arts education globally.

For performing arts, Broadway Dance Online stands out for its comprehensive video library of dance class instruction. Top Broadway choreographers teach classes in styles from ballet to hip-hop. Dancers can participate in forums, compete in "dance-offs," or even submit videos for feedback. The communal nature of the platform helps dancers feel connected, supported, and inspired.

Focusing on music education, the Online Conservatory at the Juilliard School provides pre-college students with private lessons, ensemble groups, and theory classes. This prepares young musicians for acceptance into elite music programs. The synchronous virtual classes enable students to have quality interactions with Juilliard faculty.

In the cinematic arts, the New York Film Academy offers online degrees that still capture the collaborative filmmaking process. Students pitch ideas, write scripts, share footage, and provide peer feedback using cloud-based platforms. The curriculum balances individual work with teams to simulate real production environments.

For visual arts students, SVASU is an online university dedicated to digital painting, sculpting, and game art. The project-based courses guide students from concept art to finished products using leading creative software. The emphasis is on developing professional-level digital portfolios to launch art careers. Some online arts communities cater to hobbyists and self-learners rather than offering accredited programs. The GiftEd online marketplace aggregates thousands of arts and crafts video workshops, allowing enthusiasts to pick individual classes à la carte. Skillshare also offers unlimited access to creative online classes in everything from watercolor to podcasting.

These innovative online platforms expand access to arts education in a flexible, engaging format. As technology evolves, so do the digital tools for collaborating, exhibiting, and learning alongside fellow creatives from around the world. The wealth of online communities is dismantling traditional barriers and transforming what it means to study the visual and performing arts. Skillshare and Udemy offer extensive catalogs of video workshops and tutorials taught by working artists and designers. Classes cover everything from oil painting techniques to graphic design software tips. Students can access these on-demand classes at their own pace and share their progress with classmates.

TikTok and Instagram provide vibrant platforms for visual artists to share their work and connect with followers. By using relevant hashtags and mentioning influencers in their field, artists can build engaged audiences and get discovered by art fans, galleries, and potential clients worldwide.

Online museums such as the Musée d'Orsay and Uffizi Gallery enable virtual visits and access to digitized collections. Dedicated museum social media accounts provide art history content, spotlight specific works, and host livestream events like curator talks. For photographers, Flickr and 500px are essential online communities offering opportunities to share photos, get feedback, and interact with professional photographers in niche genres. Photo contests, portfolio critiques, and awards are additional perks. Turning to performing arts, TikTok is a hub for dancers to take class together by following dance challenge hashtags. YouTube is loaded with free dance, singing, and acting tutorial videos by teachers at top studios like Millennium Dance Complex. MasterClass delivers celebrity-led video lessons.

The Music Conservatory offers private music lessons with elite faculty through an online conservatory. Broadway Dance Online streams dance classes filmed in NYC studios so students around the world can join live. Discord servers dedicated to the arts provide spaces for creatives to collaborate on projects, share works in progress, swap tips, and socialize informally through messaging and voice chat. Servers exist for game design, electronic music production, podcasting, and more. Reddit is home to in-depth discussions among artists spanning r/Art, r/Photography, r/Filmmakers, r/acting, and countless other communities tailored to creators' interests and crafts. The platform enables insightful Q&As.

By tapping into these online networks - from massive open courses to niche hobbyist forums - aspiring artists can find their people, unlock new skills, showcase their talents, and immerse themselves in creative communities no matter where they are in the world. The virtual landscape fosters connections vital to any artistic practice.

In conclusion, online learning classrooms and communities are growing widespread. Digital tools provide flexibility. However, at times, they struggle to fully replicate certain hands-on learning experiences. Ultimately, a blended approach combining online delivery of theory with in-person practical learning may provide the ideal arts education model for the digital age. COVID-19 has accelerated the need for creativity, experimentation, and reinvention of teaching practices to nurture artistic skills in a virtual world.

REFERENCES

Arkorful, V., & Abaidoo, N. (2014). The Role of e-Learning, the Advantages and Disadvantages of Its Adoption in Higher Education. *International Journal of Education and Research*, 2, 397–410.

Baker, L. R., Phelan, S., Woods, N. N., Boyd, V. A., Rowland, P., & Ng, S. L. (2021). Re-envisioning paradigms of education: Towards awareness, alignment, and pluralism. *Advances in Health Sciences Education : Theory and Practice*, 26(3), 1045–1058. 10.1007/s10459-021-10036-z33742339

Cairncross, S., & Mannion, M. (2001). Interactive multimedia and learning: Realizing the benefits. *Innovations in Education and Teaching International*, 38(2), 156–164. 10.1080/14703290110035428

Calvert, S. L., Strong, B. L., & Gallagher, L. (2005). Control as an engagement feature for young children's attention to and learning of computer content. *The American Behavioral Scientist*, 48(5), 578–589. 10.1177/0002764204271507

Colombi, E., & Knosp, S. (2017). Teaching Dance with Online Course ManagementSystems. *Journal of Distance Education*, 17, 73–76.

Crawford, R. (2017). Rethinking teaching and learning pedagogy for education in the twenty-first century: Blended learning in music education. *Music Education Research*, 19(2), 195–213. 10.1080/14613808.2016.1202223

Gohn, D. M. (2009). *Educação musical a distância: propostas para o ensino e aprendizagem de percussão* (Doctoral Dissertation). Universidade de São Paulo, São Paulo.

Hsu, C.-K., Hwang, G.-J., Chang, Y.-T., & Chang, C.-K. (2013). Effects of video caption modes on English listening comprehension and vocabulary acquisition using handheld devices. *Journal of Educational Technology & Society*, 16(1), 403–414.

Huang, E. Y., Lin, S. W., & Huang, T. K. (2012). What type of learning style leads to online participation in the mixed-mode e-learning environment? A study of software usage instruction. *Computers & Education*, 58(1), 338–349. 10.1016/j.compedu.2011.08.003

Joutsenvirta, T., & Myyry, L. (2010). *Blended learning in Finland*. Faculty of Social Sciences at the University of Helsinki.

Li, Z. (2020). Teaching Introduction to Dance Studies Online Under COVID-19 Restrictions. *Dance Education in Practice*, 6(4), 9–15. 10.1080/23734833.2020.1831853

Moore, M., & Kearsley, G. (2012). *Distance Education: A Systems View of Online Learning* (3rd ed.). Wadsworth.

Ostashewski, N., Reid, D., & Ostashewski, M. (2016). Utilizing Multimedia Database Access: Teaching Strategies Using the iPad in the Dance Classroom. *Journal of Distance Education*, 16, 122–128.

Picciano, A. G. (2002). 'Beyond student perceptions: Issues of interaction, presence, and performance in an online course'. *Journal of Asynchronous Learning Networks*, 6(1), 21–40.

Power, J., & Kannara, V. (2016). Best-Practice Model for Technology Enhanced Learning in the Creative Arts. *Research in Learning Technology*, 24(1), 30231–30316. 10.3402/rlt.v24.30231

Purves, R. (2012). Technology and the educator. In McPherson, G. E., & Welch, G. F. (Eds.), *The Oxford Handbook of Music Education* (Vol. 2, pp. 457–475). Oxford University Press. 10.1093/oxfordhb/9780199928019.013.0030

Reimer, B. (2003). *A Philosophy of Music Education: Advancing the vision* (3rd ed.). Prentice Hall.

Rovai, A. P., Wighting, M. J., & Liu, J. (2005). School climate: Sense of classroom and school communities in online and on-campus higher education courses. *Quarterly Review of Distance Education*, 6(4), 361–374.

Rucsanda, M. D., Belibou, A., & Cazan, A. M. (2021). Students' attitudes toward online music education during the COVID 19 lockdown. *Frontiers in Psychology*, 12, 753785. 10.3389/fpsyg.2021.75378534975646

Ruokonen, I., & Ruismäki, H. (2016). E-Learning in Music: A Case Study of Learning Group Composing in a Blended Learning Environment. *Procedia: Social and Behavioral Sciences*, 217, 109–115. 10.1016/j.sbspro.2016.02.039

Sjöholm, J. (2014). The art studio as archive: Tracing the geography of artistic potentiality, progress and production. *Cultural Geographies*, 21(3), 505–514. 10.1177/1474474012473060

Tassi, P. (2020, April 23). Fortnite's Travis Scott Concert Was A Stunning Spectacle And A Glimpse At The Metaverse. https://www.forbes.com/sites/paultassi/2020/04/23/fortnites-travis-scott-concert-was-a-stunning-spectacle-and-a-glimpse-at-the-metaverse/

Toffler, A. (1980). *The third wave*. Morrow.

Vygotsky, L. S. (1978). *Mind in society: The development of higher psychological processes*. Harvard University Press.

Chapter 6
Addressing Diverse Learners' Needs Through Inclusivity

Zhivi Williams

Rowan-Cabarrus Community College, USA

ABSTRACT

Inclusive teaching in higher education emphasizes interactions, equal opportunities, and care, but Black, Indigenous, and people of color (BIPOC) students face challenges in the classroom. While online education allows all students access to education, it amplifies disparities, particularly for marginalized groups. BIPOC students face discrimination and technology gaps, impacting their academic experiences. Bridging the divide between BIPOC and non-BIPOC students, addressing biases in the classroom, and promoting diversity and inclusion are essential to ensuring that all learners feel valued and supported. Rethinking course design and providing necessary resources can help foster an inclusive educational classroom where every student has the opportunity to thrive.

Today's college classrooms are diverse, with students from different cultural, ethnic, language, learning, and economic backgrounds. This diversity presents opportunities and challenges for faculty striving to create inclusive learning environments where students feel they belong and can thrive. With online education, learning has become more accessible to Black, Indigenous, and people of color (BIPOC) students, low-income individuals, and first-generation college students.

However, with the benefits of increased accessibility, online learning increases disparities and biases that can hinder a BIPOC student's experiences in the classroom. The design of any course, online or in-person, often fails to account for students' different backgrounds, learning styles, and needs; the feeling of not belonging; discrimination; and low academic achievement among BIPOC students.

DOI: 10.4018/979-8-3693-1111-0.ch006

In this chapter, we will look at developing an inclusive learning classroom in higher education, focusing on the experiences of BIPOC students in online classrooms. We will also explore the different natures of diversity, inclusion, and equity in the classroom and examine the challenges and opportunities of the growing diversity of student populations.

Based on research findings, this chapter will suggest strategies for faculty to support inclusive classrooms that put equity first, promote belongingness, and honor all students' diverse experiences and perspectives. From establishing clear communication and building relationships with students to addressing conflicts and biases, this chapter provides steps for faculty seeking to create a learning environment where all students feel valued, respected, and empowered to succeed.

Ultimately, this chapter serves as a call to action for faculty to support diversity and inclusion in the classroom and eliminate barriers to learning. By creating an inclusive learning classroom, faculty can enhance academic outcomes and cultivate a culture of belongingness and equity that prepares students to thrive in a diverse world.

According to De Wit (2011) and Kaur et al. (2017), in today's higher education environment, the classroom (online and in-person) includes students from different locations, religions, cultures, ethnicities, languages, educational backgrounds, socio-economic status, and work experiences, which creates a more complex classroom landscape. Galle and Mills (2013) noted that due to the diversity of today's classrooms, faculty should review their teaching styles. Kift et al. (2013) wrote that classroom practices, design, and ecosystem must ensure participation and equal opportunities for all students regardless of physical, cognitive, affective, and conative differences.

According to Allen and Seaman (2016) and Woodward and Larson (2017), with the growth of online learning, higher education has become more accessible to all students, including traditionally marginalized students, and the rates of Black (9% to 44%) and Latinx (43% to 54%) learners enrolled in online education have steadily increased. Garriott et al. (2023) stated that higher education has experienced an increase in the number of low-income and first-generation students. The increasing diversity in online classrooms provides an opportunity to consider online course design and create a classroom where every student is set up for optimal success.

According to Cochran et al. (2014), Figlio et al. (2013), and Jaggars and Bailey (2010), although online education offers accessibility, low achievement has been driven by student demographics indicated by poverty, academic obstacles, and lack of support. Students may not experience the full benefits that online learning has to offer. Chase et al. (2002), Salvo et al. (2019), Kutner et al. (2006), Kim and Bonk (2002), and Mavor and Traynor (2003) agreed that inadequate academic learning environments, technology gaps, and a lack of equity in learning environments have been identified as significant contributors to the experiences of traditionally marginalized students, including people from racialized backgrounds in online learning environments. Scheurich and Young (1997) stated that entrenched policies and practices in higher education also contribute to the marginalization of students based on class, race, ability, and gender. According to Lincoln and Stanely (2021), there is no definitive agreement regarding the extent of institutional discrimination, but there is notable agreement and research that supports the existence of institutional racism.

DEFINITIONS

When considering the online experiences of BIPOC students, it is vital to define words such as multiculturalism, diversity, inclusion, and equity. The Association of American Colleges and Universities (AAC&U) defined diversity as:

the variety created in any society (and within any individual) by the presence of different points of view and ways of making meaning, which generally flow from the influence of different cultural and religious heritages, from the differences in how we socialize women and men, and from the differences that emerge from class, age, and developed ability. (qtd. in Phillips, 2019, p. 3)

There are several ways to teach a diverse class. One way is to ensure that the instructor educates themselves on other racial, ethnic, and cultural groups other than their own. Instructors should incorporate examples, materials, and visual aids from other cultures as much as possible throughout the class. When assigning topics, they can encourage students to explore different authors that are not of their race or that are from the BIPOC community. In addition, an instructor can review the course syllabus or ask a BIPOC colleague to review it and share feedback on their experience. They can check to see if different approaches to learning are included in the classroom and think about how sensitive topics will be handled. Instructors can also create an opportunity for students to connect what they are learning to real-life experiences. Further, students can be asked to create a diverse study group that is open to anyone but has set rules to follow. For example, all students must participate in the group, no one person should solely be doing the work, and the groups should have time to work in class when the instructor can monitor student interaction. If there is a disconnection within the group, the instructor should speak with the students after class and express their concern. If a collaboration be formed with another class at a minority-serving college, the instructors from both classes can connect and determine how they can work together.

As revealed by Talbot (2003), multiculturalism is the development of a state of being in which an individual feels comfortable and communicates effectively with people from any culture, in any situation, because they have developed the necessary knowledge to do so. It also embodies proficiency in communicating effectively with individuals from diverse cultural backgrounds. While diversity is an underlying element within multiculturalism, its range extends further. Multiculturalism aims to support an environment that values diversity by recognizing and honoring the diverse contributions and perspectives of individuals from varied backgrounds. According to Avery and Thomas (2004), Rankin (2005), and Williams (2013), while diversity encompasses various attributes like race, ethnicity, gender, and sexual orientation, its presence does not guarantee that an institution has achieved equity and inclusion.

Promoting inclusion in the classroom means creating a culture in which all learners feel welcome, valued, and safe. Hammond (2015) asserted that inclusion allows examining how diverse thoughts and perspectives are included within an institution. There are different ways to incorporate inclusion into the classroom. One example is modeling inclusive language. Instructors should learn students' pronouns and avoid using masculine pronouns for both males and females. If they have students for whom English is not a first language, they can explain idioms such as *break a leg, hang in there, a dime a dozen,* and so on. Another example is to provide multiple ways to participate in the class. Participation may include journal writing, reading logs, a reflection on different works of authors, group work, online discussions, and many more. Instructors should avoid using the same type of participation during the course.

All students' opinions about a topic or subject should be respected. If a student has an emotional connection to a topic being discussed, the instructor should not let other students dismiss the student's feelings about the topic. Not addressing offensive, discriminatory, or insensitive comments in the classroom can make a student feel excluded and bring tension to the class.

Instructors can have the class perform a self-assessment, which can be beneficial in revealing gaps in approaches, habits of the instructor and students, and classroom practices. This can be done by recording the class. Prior to doing so, the instructor should inform students, explain the purposes of recording, and obtain their permission. The camera should record from the back of the classroom so that student's faces are not shown. The purpose of the recording is to improve the instructor's interaction with the class and the student's interaction with each other. When reviewing the recording, the instructor can look for ways to ensure students feel included in the classroom.

Equity entails ensuring all students have equal access, fairness, and impartiality to foster opportunities for success and flourishing. According to Bensiomon and Polkinghorne (2003), equity includes assessing the bias within systems and institutions that can potentially impact the distribution of opportunities and resources. Examples of ways equity can be incorporated are using anonymous grading. Unconscious biases and prejudices that we all have can impact a student's grade in class. Instructors can incorporate a system that will allow students' names to be hidden during the grading process. This will allow for fair and impartial grading of assignments. The round-robin technique can be incorporated into an online or in-person class; this technique allows for all students to participate in the classroom environment since each student is given time to share their thoughts or ideas before moving on to the next student. Some students dominate the classroom discussion, making it difficult for quieter students to participate in the class discussion. The round-robin technique prevents the dominant students from taking over the discussion and allows quieter students to share their thoughts. This also allows a student who may be the only person of their race in the class to participate.

Another way to create equity in the class is to invite diverse speakers to speak to the students. On a college campus, most instructors are white, and inviting diverse speakers to the class will expose all students to a world they know little about. Speakers can be invited to speak in person or virtually. More speakers may opt to speak virtually to a class due to not having to travel and only taking an hour out of their day to speak with them.

Equity can also be promoted by including readings from BIPOC authors. Instructors can shape the minds of their students and how they see the world, which is a unique position to be in, and they should make an effort to include readings from authors with different backgrounds. Instructors should complete an inventory of the assigned readings in the class and ask, Who are the authors? Are they all the same race? If so, then they can find readings written by authors of a different race on the same topic or subject. This will help students view the world differently and to gain a better understanding of society in general.

Finally, equity can be improved in the classroom by soliticiting anonymous feedback from students. Students can be afraid to speak with the instructor or share their concerns about their teaching style or classroom format. These feelings can be intensified for BIPOC students. Instructors can assess how the class is going by allowing students, throughout the course, to share their feedback anonymously. This can be done by creating an anonymous survey through Google or other available quiz platforms (in the class LMS) to assess what needs to be modified in the course. If possible, instructors should incorporate the suggestions before the end of the semester. This will allow the students to see that their feedback matters.

Curriculum Infused With Diversity

It is assumed that classes that teach about diversity are the only ones that have to supply diverse content. This is not true. Regardless of the discipline, all instructors can incorporate diverse content and backgrounds that represent the diverse makeup of a class. This helps to create a more inclusive learning experience for all students.

A curriculum with a high degree of diversity includes different perspectives, cultures, and experiences in work and practice. It involves acknowledging and embracing the strength of diversity within the curriculum to promote inclusivity, foster understanding, and prepare students to thrive in a multicultural world. This means that diversity is not just a topic to be addressed independently but an integral part of the classroom experience that increases learning outcomes and strives to promote diversity, equity, and inclusion.

This objective is achieved in the classroom by including diversity in the curriculum; in training sessions for students, faculty, and staff; and in orientation programs for first-year students. Viewing diversity as an integral part of the curriculum goes beyond mere representation among faculty, staff, and students. According to Brown (2004), the curriculum should be:

Underlying assumptions and perceptions that rigidify the institution against ideas perceived to be contentious to the status quo. It has to be actively pursued, put in place, and constantly analyzed, nurtured, and supported during and after implementation (pp. 26).

Including diversity is not a one-time thing; instead, it is a continuous process that begins with the initial inclusion of individuals from diverse backgrounds. However, the college structure should promote and facilitate the retention of diverse individuals by fostering a sense of belonging. Additionally, it is necessary to encourage a culture that embraces and celebrates diversity. Viewing diversity as part of the curriculum not only gives the means to offer diverse perspectives and challenge dominant norms but also offers an opportunity to reshape culture and promote a particular vision for an inclusive culture. Since colleges play a critical role in shaping future leaders, their output guides every discipline and filters through every layer of society.

Krishnamurthi (2003) delineated three manifestations of diversity within the curriculum: additive, which incorporates select multicultural elements into the existing curriculum; integrative, which establishes multiculturalism as a fixed component of curricular requisites; and transformative, which positions multiculturalism as the central tenet of the curriculum. Regardless of its form, diversity as a curriculum offers a comprehensive, truthful portrayal of reality, equips students to navigate a multicultural society, and addresses a wide range of learning needs. Ross (2014) presented empirical evidence suggesting that structured interactions among diverse students, facilitated through curricular interventions, yield favorable cognitive and democratic outcomes. Furthermore, research indicates that enrolling in a diverse course can lessen intolerance and bias. Students on campus tend to associate with students who are like them. Efforts to foster diverse student interactions and promote skills associated with democratic citizenship are framed as components of a diverse education. This educational approach involves guiding students through critical reflection on desensitizing sociopolitical circumstances and empowering them to enact change. Ross (2014) stated that a diverse curriculum represents a pedagogical strategy forging connections between diversity and an ongoing process of democratization, which evolves as diverse perspectives are continually integrated.

When using images or examples, it is important to include diverse representations of all students, even if they are not in your class. Remember, not all students know American culture and may not understand an image or example used in the classroom. When creating tests or class material, instructors should ensure they represent a variety of different backgrounds (i.e., race, ethnicity, gender, learning styles, and country of origin). When creating tests, case studies, or course material, use names from other cultures, not popular or standard American names. Also, consider incorporating examples of different cultures, religions, disabilities, ages, and so on into the course material. Since BIPOC individuals are underrepresented in society, instructors might have difficulty finding images to incorporate into course materials. To find images of BIPOC individuals or groups, instructors can search online for free images or contact someone at the school who works with images— for example, the library or marketing department. If it is difficult to find diverse content, it may be useful to discuss the history of your field. Discuss or highlight the contributions of a BIPOC person to the field. Other ways to incorporate diversity into the classroom is to include diversity as a course learning goal and link it to current or historical events that can be added to classroom activities. Instructors can also include a diversity and disability statement in the class syllabus. If the syllabus cannot be changed and the class uses an LMS, that information can be included on the LMS or as an addendum to the syllabus. Universal design can be incorporated into the course material to increase accessibility for all students at different levels. Later in this chapter, universal design will be discussed in greater detail.

Other ways to incorporate diversity into the classroom include letting the students talk and introducing new material that addresses diversity each semester or year. This can be accomplished by bringing in one new article and introducing a new topic to the class. Including a short video is a great way to bring up issues dealing with diversity and will open up the classroom for a great class discussion. To ensure diversity is being met in the classroom, answer the following questions:

- How can I find time to discuss diversity in my class when there is so much content to cover?
- Does the course material assume that all students have the same level of background knowledge?
- To what extent are the learning objectives related to diversity?
- What is the benefit of including diverse course material in the class?
- What gender or race is being represented in the class material?
- Are classroom expectations and requirements clearly stated?
- How will conflict be discussed and addressed in the class?
- Do the class discussions allow for all students to participate?
- Do the classroom readings and assignments include diverse authors and backgrounds?
- How can I be a better ally for all my students through the class curriculum?

Experience of BIPOC Students in Online Classrooms

According to Rovai and Gallien (2005), the number of BIPOC students attending online classes is increasing yearly. Few studies discuss the experiences of students, but in those that do discuss student experiences, the findings are contradictory. According to Smith and Ayers (2006), and Hussain and Jones (2021), several research studies have examined the disconnect between the design of online courses and the diverse backgrounds, learning requirements, and encounters with discrimination among students. Many online courses have been designed without sufficient consideration of the cultural backgrounds and learning preferences of BIPOC students. They often reflect a faculty-centric approach or align predominantly with the dominant culture's values.

According to Walton and Cohen (2011), scholarly literature addressing BIPOC students in online classes underscores the importance of fostering a sense of belonging. Cohen et al. (2009) wrote that engaging in active learning experiences, including collaborative work with peers and interaction with instructors, is pivotal in promoting sustained academic achievement and overall well-being. Research has indicated that Black, Latinx, and Asian online students tended to participate more frequently in course discussion boards compared to White students. Correa and Jeong (2011) stated that interactive tools facilitated connections for students to engage with communities where they felt acknowledged and valued.

According to Tucker (2014), a research study revealed that Black students found online learning appealing because of its flexibility, the color-blind context, and the prompt interactions with instructors. Hart (2012) stated that online students who successfully thrive and persist in their coursework are those who perceive a strong social presence and a feeling of connectedness. Studies by Ke and Kwak (2013) and Moore (2014) suggested that individuals from racialized communities may discontinue participation in online programs because of inadequate interaction with instructors and peers, coupled with a preference for verbal communication and occasional face-to-face interaction. According to Ashong and Commander (2012), some researchers argue that online learning environments have not been structured with the learning needs of racialized people in mind, therefore creating barriers to their success. According to Rovai and Wighting (2005) and Okwumabua et al. (2011), other research suggested that racialized people have more negative experiences compared to their White counterparts in online learning environments.

Rovai and Gallien (2005) said it is important to realize the presence of discrimination or bias in an online class for BIPOC students. Rovai and Wighting (2005) stated that in predominantly White online classrooms, Black students often express feelings of isolation from both the social and academic community. Hussain and Jones (2021) identified discrimination and bias as significant contributors to a diminished sense of belonging among BIPOC students. Barber et al. (2020) stated that for students attending predominantly White institutions (PWIs), fostering more diverse peer interactions and demonstrating institutional commitment to inclusivity and diversity can help alleviate the negative impacts.

Sieck et al. (2021) suggested that when designing online and in-person courses, it is important to recognize the digital divide among BIPOC students, especially since many courses integrate different technologies like VoiceThread and Flipgrid (Sieck, et al., 2021). According to the National Digital Inclusion Alliance (2024), some students face limitations in accessing internet services, which can hinder their participation in the classroom. To bridge this gap, according to Summey and Guitierrez (2012), many colleges have implemented laptop lending programs to assist the digital divide.

In the classroom, BIPOC students encounter different stressors that affect their classroom experience. These stressors include stereotype threat, microaggressions, racism, and other factors that not only create a difficult climate for BIPOC students but also affect the classroom for White students.

What is a stereotype threat? According to the University of Colorado Boulder Center for Teaching and Learning (n.d.), stereotype threat refers to the risk of confirming negative stereotypes about an individual's racial, ethnic, gender, or cultural group, which can create a high cognitive load and reduce academic focus and performance.

What are microaggressions? Microaggressions are statements or actions that someone thinks are innocent but, in reality, are a form of discrimination against BIPOC individuals. Microaggressions could include, but are not limited to, the following.

- White students think BIPOC, specifically Black, students are not as smart as them.
- Black students are not invited to join study groups.
- White instructors have low expectations of BIPOC students.
- Black students are the last to be called on in class.
- Black students present ideas, and their ideas are taken by White students.
- Black student comments are ignored or dismissed, or white students and instructors are surprised that Black students are smart and well-spoken.

Griffith et al. (2019) discovered that Black students at PWIs often carry significant emotional and cognitive worries due to stereotype threats and related microaggressions, which can hinder their learning process. For support, Black students may find mentors or others like them outside the PWI setting to discuss what they are experiencing. However, some responses by Black students are misunderstood by their instructor as being unprepared for class or not being present. For example, students may think they need to work harder to counter the negative stereotypes, especially when the number of Black students in the class is low. These stressors often lead Black students towards navigating a challenging class environment, compared with the ease some White students experience in the same class.

Stereotype threats manifest differently for Spanish-speaking students, as observed in Ruvalcaba's (2020) qualitative study of Hispanic undergraduates at a PWI. Stereotype threats for Hispanic students include different types of behaviors, such as being labeled as speaking "broken English," which stereotypically suggests a lack of intellect or education. Additionally, Spanish-speaking students are sometimes seen as outsiders, regardless of their citizenship, making the students feel like they do not belong. Hispanic students are sometimes asked to be the person who speaks on behalf of their community in class discussions because the instructor assumes that all Hispanic students are the same and ignores the diversity within their community.

Just like Black students, Hispanic students carry an emotional and mental load as they navigate a climate of stereotypes and microaggressions, impacting their academic performance. In response to these stressors, Ruvalcaba (2020) stated that if they participate in class discussions, Hispanic students may meticulously calculate their responses (countering the "broken English" stereotype), or they may self-censor and not participate at all.

Proposed Strategies for Fostering an Inclusive Classroom

Maintaining an inclusive classroom throughout your teaching is important as an instructor. One way to incorporate inclusion in the classroom is to include cultural content that increases student achievement. Including cultural content in the classroom is called culturally responsive teaching (CRT).

CRT builds a bridge between a student's real-life experiences and their experiences in school by integrating content from diverse backgrounds and recognizing how course content shapes the student's mind, attitude, and learning style. Implementing diversity specific to different learning styles encourages students to appreciate and celebrate their differences and those of other students. Including diverse classroom content, resources, and materials ensures a balanced and inclusive classroom.

There are a number of ways an instructor can build inclusion within the classroom. Instructors can take the following steps to apply culturally responsive teaching. First, introduce yourself as the instructor. Students should get to know you as someone who is there to support them and should feel comfortable coming to you for questions they may have or other assistance. When introducing yourself to your students, give them some background information about yourself. For example, tell them where you attended college, a little about your childhood, and maybe a few things you struggled with when you attended college. If you were the first person to go to college in your family, explain to your students what your experience was like. Also share what you wish you would have known that you did not know to help them navigate their college journey.

Next, get to know your students by using a confidential survey, which can be a great way to learn more about them. The survey should not pry into their personal lives but allow students to share how they would like to be addressed (sharing their pronouns), their goals, their learning style, and their access to technology. For example, do they have a computer/laptop or internet service? It could be beneficial to know if a student is working, as this could affect their class attendance and when they are able to do assignments. The survey should clearly stated that it is confidential and for the instructor's use only. When an instructor learns more about their students, they are able to make suggestions to help the students. For example, students could be encouraged to go to the writing center for assistance. If the college has a laptop loaner program, this could be suggested to student who do not have laptops.

Tell students how they will work with each other and the instructor. Will students be working in groups? Will the class come up with ground rules when working with each other? Some examples of ground rules that are inclusive are: do not interrupt the person speaking; do not claim anyone else's ideas as your own; be respectful of other's opinions, especially if they are different from your own; and try to keep an open mind. It is a good idea to come up with the ground rules as a class; this will allow all students to participate and feel included. This information can be collected verbally in class or through a discussion board for those students that do not like to speak in a classroom setting.

How will conflict be addressed? Is the conflict interpersonal? Was a microaggression or stereotype directed at someone? Are there various levels of readiness to discuss the topic? Did someone have an intense emotional response? Will the conflict be addressed in the classroom, or does it need to be addressed with a student outside of the classroom? Students should never be made an example of in the classroom. Depending on the conflict, this could also be a learning opportunity for the students. It is a great opportunity to explain what a microaggression is and why what was said should not have been said or explain a different way of saying what was said.

If you are not sure how to address the conflict in the class, you can let the students know the conflict will be addressed after getting feedback from colleagues. You may state that as the instructor you are not sure how to proceed but that you invite continued feedback from students; then share what steps they can expect next. Not all conflict needs to go beyond acknowledgment and listening, but instructors must explore whether more needs to be done.

Sometimes, students are able to devise different ways to resolve the conflict on their own. Listen to the voices and feelings of students affected by the conflict. The instructor may decide to allow the affected students the opportunity to share what is troubling without rebuttals or interruptions. Or, the instructor and students may address what was written in an anonymous, writing prompt.

If the conflict continues, consider meeting with the students privately. Or, create an in-class or online activity that will explore the issue. For example, the instructor could provide an example of the conflict and ask students to come up with as many solutions as possible rather than seeking a common agreement. Sometimes, the in-class or online activity causes more harm rather than being helpful. Check in with the students affected by the conflict. Ensure the students are not being triggered by the solutions that are given by others.

Students are diverse in many different ways that cannot be seen. Their differences may be related to race, national origin, socioeconomic status, ethnicity, physical disabilities, neurodisabilities, sexual orientation, religion or spiritual beliefs, or many other factors. If students are working in groups, the groups should be assigned so that students are working with students they would not work with on their own. This allows students to get to know one another and for students not to be isolated or feel like they do not belong. If students create their own groups, encourage or help them to set up diverse study groups.

The tone for inclusiveness can be set in the course syllabus or other areas in the LMS. Richardson and Yang (2015) provided examples of approaches that can set the tone for respectful conversations in the course. One example is to address the importance and value of classroom discussion. Let the students know that everyone can share their opinion but, when opinions are shared, they should be respectful to one another. Tell students to listen to others' opinions and perspectives that are different than theirs and that it is okay to disagree with someone else's opinions.

Another example is to explain that students in the class come from different backgrounds and no one is expected to know all the history of one group's background, regardless of whether the student is from the United States or not. Let students know that different topics deal with the background of others through readings and discussions, and everyone should be prepared to share their thoughts and opinons. Also, let students know that current events will be discussed in class, that respecting someone's opinions on the subject is important, and that being disrespectful to someone will not be tolerated.

Inform students that the class prioritizes mutually respectful relationships and is inclusive for all students. There is to be no discrimination, and everyone should feel comfortable and be able to share in the classroom learning experience. If students want to share their concerns or improvements with the class, let them know to bring it to your attention.

A final example is to explain that the work that is accomplished in class is achieved through the respect of oneself and others. Discussions in class will be difficult and complicated at times. Encourage students to show their passion for the questions that arise in the class and that possible debates may occur. Let the students know that everyone is going to be held accountable for what is being said and to be mindful of how they are expressing their opinions. Difficult conversations can be held in class with respect and sometimes with humor but, during these conversations, everyone should be open to listening to one another's different opinions and perspectives on the topic. Students should also be aware that if a difficult discusson begins to become disrespectful, a break will be taken for all to regain composure and discuss why the conversation became highly intense.

Motivational Framework for CRT

According to Ginsberg and Wlodkowski (2009), CRT aims to create compelling learning experiences through which learners can maintain their integrity as they attain relevant educational success. This can be done by incorporating inclusion into the classroom. For example, instructors can assign students to work in small groups that allow for them to interact in a meaningful way with one another. This also allows students the opportunity to see different perspectives and learn from someone who is not like them. In addition, students can choose a research paper or topic that is relevant to them that will align with the class work. This helps to bring diversity to the course assignments, and if students have to present their work to the class, this always helps the students to learn about diversity in the classroom. CRT also creates challenging and engaging learning experiences that allow students to actively engage in questioning, posing problems, conducting research, and completing projects. Along with having challenging and engaging learning experiences, students learn how they are learning something valuable to them and their community through writing, reflect on what they learned through their own experiences, and are given multiple ways to present the knowledge or skills they have learned.

Universal Design for Learning?

Incorporating universal design for learning (UDL) elements can further improve understanding and inclusive practices. UDL aims to reduce barriers and enhance learning opportunities for all students, promoting engagement in diverse ways of thinking. Baldwin and Ching (2021) asserted it strives for accessibility and equity, encouraging the creation of goals, methods, tools, and assessments to benefit everyone.

UDL is used to help improve and enhance teaching and learning for all students based on how students learn and highlights the different ways in which students access and interact with classroom content across different subjects. UDL consists of three major pillars: engagement, representation, and action and expression. Each pillar gives students opportunities to meet their learning styles.

Engagement is the "why" of learning. It makes sure there are different ways provided for students to access the material. It allows for active learning in the classroom while preventing different opportunities based on the students' differences and interests. UDL makes sure that students can access class materials differently, encouraging active participation while supporting diverse learning. Instructors can increase student motivation by setting class and assignment objectives that prioritize accessibility, which helps create equality in the classroom and provides motivation to students. CAST (2018) stated that student self-regulation is enhanced when extrinsic motivation is fostered throughout a course through varied support. Peterson-Ahmad and Luther (2022) maintainted that investing time in promoting the purpose of learning within the course environment is key to fostering increased student engagement.

Representation is the "what" of learning and considers that students have various ways of perceiving and understanding the course material. When students are given different ways of interacting and accessing the course material, they will have more ways to construct meaning and learn for increased clarity and understanding of the course material. Peterson-Ahmad and Luther (2022) stated that faculty who provide varied means for students through multiple representations of learning gives students heightened opportunities to access and learn course content.

Expression is the "how" of learning and is seen through action and expression. It ensures that students have the opportunity to navigate the course material and react to their learning in varied ways. Providing students with materials to better interact with course content provides inclusive access to the different ways students learn knowledge. Peterson-Ahmad and Luther (2022) claimed that by addressing the "how" of learning, college faculty can better allow various students opportunities for successful navigation and completion of course objectives based on the specific needs of the students.

How Can UDL Be Incorporated Into the Classroom?

The following details provide an overview of the UDL pillars and suggestions for incorporating them into the college classroom.

- Provide multiple means of engagement.
- Make sure that class work, regardless of the delivery method, aligns with the Americans with Disabilities Act (ADA) standards. For example, videos should have captions, color schemes consisting of light text on dark back backgrounds or dark text on light backgrounds, and clear visual layouts.
- Offer clear and detailed feedback to students and explain how the feedback can assist them on future assignments.
- When reviewing the class material, make sure diverse methods are included. Are readings from authors of different races or nationalities included?

What Should Be Avoided?

It is important to avoid thinking that BIPOC students should educate White students and faculty about their lived experiences. While asking BIPOC students to share their experiences or thoughts during class may seem respectful, this dismisses the students' environment, culture, history, and classroom experiences. BIPOC students can feel stressed when they feel that they have to speak on behalf of everyone in their community, which can promote the misconception that BIPOC communities are homogenous. Instructors should not think that the lack of participation relates to a student's intellect. Understanding the stress experiences by BIPOC students sheds light on how the stress may hinder their participation and cause additional problems in the classroom and with their learning.

The Center for Educational Innovation (2022) advised not to assume that treating all of your students "the same" is equitable. Once we view the university through the PWI lens and consider the dynamics of identity and positionality, we can see that treating all students identically reproduces the inequities of the PWI. In fact, the PWI context has never treated all students "the same." We should avoid using majority rules when teaching and during class activities. The majority rule approach suggests that White students are superior to BIPOC students. This can be seen when working in teams in the classroom, in person, or online. Working within a team, BIPOC students can easily be overlooked or their viewpoints ignored or even stolen.

It is very important not to make assumptions about the backgrounds of students. Thinking that all students have the same or similar experiences can lead to issues in the class because each student's experiences are unique. No two students have the exact or similar experiences, not even within the same culture. This is why getting to know students is very important. Colleges with diverse populations have students from different racial and economic backgrounds and gender identities. Always approach students with an open mind about their background.

Explicit and implicit bias should be avoided. Eberhardt (2019) explained implicit bias as a distorting lens that is a product of our brain's architecture and our society's disparities. Individuals form ideas or biases about race, weight, ethnic origin, accent, religion, gender, and disability by their past experiences, where they live, and dominant norms in their society. These biases can shape one's perception, attention, memory, and actions, often unconsciously or contrary to one's intentions. According to Banaji and Greenwald (2019), hidden biases can plant "mindbugs" or ingrained habits of thought that lead to errors in how one perceives, remembers, reasons, and makes decisions. Those habits come from unknown feelings and beliefs about different groups.

Microaggressions should also be avoided. They can occur unintentionally but can also come from one's own biases. Microaggressions were mentioned in this chapter, but here are other microaggressions to avoid: continuing to mispronounce a student's name even after being told the correct pronunciation several times; asking a BIPOC person to teach you words in their native language; stating, "When I look at you, I do not see color"; saying to someone, "I am not racist. I have several Black (Asian, Indian, Native American, Hispanic, etc.) friends"; asking a Black person, "Can I touch your hair?"; consistently calling on one gender in class; saying, "you people"; or complimenting non-White students on their use of "good English."

Microaggressions can make a person or group of people feel less significant than they are; they feel threatened, intimidated, like they do not belong, or as thought their culture is invalidated.

CONCLUSION

In conclusion, as we navigate the landscape of education in online and classroom environments, it becomes apparent that promoting diversity, inclusion, and equity is necessary. The journey toward creating an inclusive classroom for BIPOC students requires multiple approaches that require different dimensions of diversity and consistently address biases and barriers.

Defining terms such as diversity, inclusion, and equity sets the tone for understanding the difficulties in creating an inclusive classroom. Diversity contains many facets, including race, ethnicity, gender, and sexual orientation, while inclusion promotes a culture where all learners feel welcomed and valued. Equity ensures fairness and impartiality in the classroom and strives to provide all students with the same access to opportunities and resources. Sharing these definitions with your students will help them to understand the importance of an inclusive classroom.

A diverse curriculum promotes inclusion and prepares students to thrive in a diverse world. The curriculum should incorporate all students' perspectives, cultures, and experiences. Multiculturalism offers a pathway to challenging dominant norms and promoting social justice.

The experiences of BIPOC students in online or in-person classrooms highlight the importance of encouraging a sense of belonging and addressing barriers students may face. Including cultural content through CRT, implementing UDL principles, and acknowledging and addressing the stress of BIPOC students are important steps in creating an inclusive classroom.

However, it is crucial to approach these strategies with mindfulness and sensitivity, avoiding expecting BIPOC students to serve as teachers for their peers and instructors or continuing microaggressions through conscious or unconscious biases. By continuing to break down these barriers, instructors can foster an inclusive classroom where all students feel valued, empowered, and equipped to succeed.

Ultimately, the journey toward inclusivity in education requires reflection, continuing to learn, and action. It demands a commitment to breaking down barriers, making diverse voices known, and encouraging a culture of respect, empathy, and understanding. Through collective efforts and unwavering dedication, we can create educational spaces that reflect diversity, equity, and inclusion and empower all students to thrive and be successful on their educational journey.

REFERENCES

Allen, I. E., & Seaman, J. (2016). *Online report card: Tracking online education in the United States.* Babson Survey Research Group and Quahog Research Group, LLC. https://files.eric.ed.gov/fulltext/ED572777.pdf

Ashong, C. Y., & Commander, N. E. (2012). Ethnicity, gender, and perceptions of online learning in higher education. *Journal of Online Learning and Teaching*, 8(2), 98–110. https://jolt.merlot.org/vol8no2/ashong_0612.pdf

Avery, D. R., & Thomas, K. M. (2004). Blending content and contact: The roles of diversity curriculum and campus heterogeneity in fostering diversity management competency. *Academy of Management Learning & Education*, 3(4), 380–396. 10.5465/amle.2004.15112544

Baldwin, S. J., & Ching, Y.-H. (2021). Accessibility in online courses: A review of national and statewide evaluation instruments. *TechTrends*, 65(5), 731–742. 10.1007/s11528-021-00624-6

Banaji, M. R., & Greenwald, A. G. (2019). *Blindspot: Hidden biases of good people.* Random House Publishing Group.

Barber, P. H., Hayes, T. B., Johnson, T. L., & Marquez-Magana, L. (2020). Systemic racism in higher education. *Science*, 369(6510), 1440–1441. 10.1126/science.abd714032943517

Brown, L. (2004). Diversity: The challenge for higher education. *Race, Ethnicity and Education*, 7(1), 21–34. 10.1080/1361332042000187289

CAST. (2018). Universal design for learning guidelines version 2.2. https://udlguidelines.cast.org/

Chase, M., Macfadyen, L., Reeder, K., & Roche, J. (2002). Intercultural challenges in networked learning: Hard technologies meet soft skills. *First Monday*, 7(8). Advance online publication. 10.5210/fm.v7i8.975

Cochran, J. D., Campbell, S. M., Baker, H. M., & Leeds, E. M. (2014). The role of student characteristics in predicting retention in online courses. *Research in Higher Education*, 55(1), 27–48. 10.1007/s11162-013-9305-8

Cohen, G. L., Garcia, J., Purdie-Vaughns, V., Apfel, N., & Brzustoski, P. (2009). Recursive processes in self-affirmation: Intervening to close the minority achievement gap. *Science*, 324(5925), 400–403. 10.1126/science.117076919372432

Correa, T., & Jeong, S. H. (2011). Race and online content creation. *Information Communication and Society*, 14(5), 638–659. 10.1080/1369118X.2010.514355

De Wit, H. (2011). *Trends, issues and challenges in internationalisation of higher education*. Centre for Applied Research on Economics and Management, Hogeschool van Amsterdam. https://www.eurashe.eu/wp-content/uploads/2022/02/wg4 -r-internationalization-trends-issues-and-challenges-hans-de-wit.pdf

Eberhardt, J. L. (2019). *Biased: Uncovering the hidden prejudice that shapes what we see, think, and do*. Penguin Books.

Figlio, D., Rush, M., & Yin, L. (2013). Is it live or is it internet? Experimental estimates of the effects of online instruction on student learning. *Journal of Labor Economics*, 31(4), 763–784. 10.1086/669930

Gale, T., & Mills, C. (2013). Creating spaces in higher education for marginalised Australians: Principles for socially inclusive pedagogies. *Enhancing Learning in the Social Sciences*, 5(2), 7–19. 10.11120/elss.2013.00008

Garriott, P. O., Ko, S.-J., Grant, S. B., Jessen, M., & Allan, B. A. (2023). When race and class collide: Classism and social-emotional experiences of first-generation college students. *Journal of College Student Retention*, 25(3), 509–532. 10.1177/1521025121995483

Ginsberg, M., & Wlodkowski, R. (2009). *Diversity and motivation: Culturally responsive teaching in college* (2nd ed.). Joseey-Bass.

Griffith, A. N., Hurd, N. M., & Hussain, S. B. (2019). "I didn't come to school for this": A qualitative examination of experiences with race-related stressors and coping responses among Black students attending a predominantly White institution. *Journal of Adolescent Research*, 34(2), 115–139. 10.1177/0743558417742983

Hammond, Z. (2015). *Culturally responsive teaching and the brain: Promoting authentic engagement and rigor among culturally and linguistically diverse students*. Corwin Press.

Hart, C. (2012). Factors associated with student persistence in an online program of study: A review of the literature. *Journal of Interactive Online Learning*, 11(1), 19–42.

Hogan, K. A., & Sathy, V. (2022). *Inclusive teaching: Strategies for promoting equity in the college classroom*. West Virginia University Press.

Hussain, M., & Jones, J. M. (2021). Discrimination, diversity, and sense of belonging: Experiences of students of color. *Journal of Diversity in Higher Education*, 14(1), 63–71. 10.1037/dhe0000117

Inclusive teaching at a predominantly White institution.(2022). Center for Educational Innovation. https://cei.umn.edu/teaching-resources/inclusive-teaching -predominantly-white-institution

Jaggars, S. S., & Bailey, T. (2010, July). *Effectiveness of fully online courses for college students: Response to a Department of Education meta-analysis.* Community College Research Center. https://ccrc.tc.columbia.edu/media/k2/attachments/ effectiveness-online-response-meta-analysis.pdf

Kaur, A., Awang-Hashim, R., & Noman, M. (2017). Defining intercultural education in Malaysian context for social cohesion. *International Journal of Multicultural Education*, 19(2), 44–60. 10.18251/ijme.v19i2.1337

Ke, F., & Kwak, D. (2013). Constructs of student-centered online learning on learning satisfaction of a diverse online student body: A structural equation modeling approach. *Journal of Educational Computing Research*, 48(1), 97–122. 10.2190/EC.48.1.e

Kift, S., Nelson, K., & Clarke, J. (2010). Transition pedagogy: A third generation approach to FYE – A case study of policy and practice for the higher education sector. *The International Journal of the First Year in Higher Education*, 1(1), 1–20. 10.5204/intjfyhe.v1i1.13

Kim, K.-J., & Bonk, C. J. (2002). Cross-cultural comparisons of online collaboration. *Journal of Computer-Mediated Communication*, 8(1), JCMC814. Advance online publication. 10.1111/j.1083-6101.2002.tb00163.x

Krishnamurthi, M. (2003). Assessing multicultural initiatives in higher education institutions. *Assessment & Evaluation in Higher Education*, 28(3), 263–277. 10.1080/0260293032000059621

Kutner, M., Jin, Y., Greenberg, E., & Paulsen, C. (2006). *The health literacy of America's adults: Results from the 2003 National Assessment of Adult Literacy* (Report No. NCES 2006483). National Center for Education Statistics. https://nces .ed.gov/pubs2006/2006483.pdf

Lincoln, Y., & Stanley, C. A. (2021). The faces of institutionalized discrimination and systemic oppression in higher education: Uncovering the lived experience of bias and procedural inequity. *Qualitative Inquiry*, 27(10), 1233–1245. 10.1177/10778004211026892

Mavor, S., & Traynor, B. (2003). Exclusion in international online learning communities. In Reisman, S. (Ed.), *Electronic learning communities: Current issues and best practices* (pp. 457–488). Information Age Publishing.

Moore, J. (2014). Effects of online interaction and instructor presence on students' satisfaction and success with online undergraduate public relations courses. *Journalism and Mass Communication Educator*, 69(3), 271–288. 10.1177/1077695814536398

National Digital Inclusion Alliance. (n.d.). *Definitions*. National Digital Inclusion Alliance. https://www.digitalinclusion.org/definitions/

Okwumabua, T. M., Walker, K. M., Hu, X., & Watson, A. (2011). An exploration of African American students attitudes toward online learning. *Urban Education*, 46(2), 241–250. 10.1177/0042085910377516

Peterson-Ahmad, M. B., & Luther, V. L. (2022, July 18). *Fostering inclusivity in the college classroom: Looking through a universal design for learning lens*. Faculty Focus. https://www.facultyfocus.com/articles/equality-inclusion-and-diversity/fostering-inclusivity-in-the-college-classroom-looking-through-a-universal-design-for-learning-lens/

Phillips, A. (2019). The Quest for Diversity in Higher Education. *Pepperdine Policy Review, 11*(4), 1-28. https://digitalcommons.pepperdine.edu/ppr/vol11/iss1/4

Rankin, S. R. (2005). Campus climates for sexual minorities. *New Directions for Student Services*, 2005(111), 17–23. 10.1002/ss.170

Richardson, C. R. (2023). *Diversity and inclusive teaching*. University of Delaware Center for Teaching and Assessment of Learing. https://bpb-us-w2.wpmucdn.com/sites.udel.edu/dist/c/6655/files/2014/03/Culturally-Responsive-Teaching-1jy7hnk.pdf

Richardson, C. R., & le Blanc, S. (2023). *Diversity and equity in learning*. University of Delaware Center for Teaching and Assessment of Learning. https://bpb-us-w2.wpmucdn.com/sites.udel.edu/dist/c/6655/files/2014/03/Diversity-and-Equity-in-Learning_Jan2016-zm93qx.pdf

Richardson, C. R., & Yang, F. (2015). *Course syllabi: Suggestions for statements to include on your syllabus*. University of Delaware Center for Teaching and Assessment of Learning. https://bpb-us-w2.wpmucdn.com/sites.udel.edu/dist/c/6655/files/2014/03/Course-Syllabi_statements_January2016-2gs8wet.pdf

Ross, S. (2014). Diversity and intergroup contact in higher education: Exploring possibilities for democratization. *Teaching in Higher Education*, 19(8), 870–881. 10.1080/13562517.2014.934354

Rovai, A. P., & Gallien, L. B. (2005). Learning and sense of community: A comparative analysis of African American and Caucasian online graduate students. *The Journal of Negro Education*, 74(1), 53–62. https://www.jstor.org/stable/40027230

Rovai, A. P., & Wighting, M. J. (2005). Feelings of alienation and community among higher education students in a virtual classroom. *The Internet and Higher Education*, 8(2), 97–110. 10.1016/j.iheduc.2005.03.001

Ruvalcaba, A. (2020). *I can be myself, [almost] always: A Latinx microclimate in a predominantly White institution of higher education* (Publication No. 27994297) [Master's thesis, Michigan State University]. ProQuest Dissertations Publishing. 10.24059/olj.v23i1.1390

Salvo, S. G., Shelton, K., & Welch, B. (2019). African American males learning online: Promoting academic achievement in higher education. *Online Learning : the Official Journal of the Online Learning Consortium*, 23(1), 22–36. 10.24059/olj.v23i1.1390

Scheurich, J. J., & Young, M. D. (1997). Coloring epistemologies: Are our research epistemologies racially biased? *Educational Researcher*, 26(4), 4–16. 10.2307/1176879

Sieck, C. J., Sheon, A., Ancker, J. S., Castek, K., Callahan, B., & Siefer, A. (2021). Digital inclusion as a social determinant of health. *Digital Medicine*, 4(1), 52. Advance online publication. 10.1038/s41746-021-00413-833731887

Smith, D. R., & Ayers, D. F. (2006). Culturally responsive pedagogy and online learning: Implications for the globalized community college. *Community College Journal of Research and Practice*, 30(5–6), 401–415. 10.1080/10668920500442125

Stereotype threat. (n.d.). University of Colorado Boulder Center for Teaching & Learning. https://www.colorado.edu/center/teaching-learning/inclusivity/stereotype -threat

Sue, D. W. (2010). *Microaggressions in everyday life: Race, gender and sexual orientation*. Wiley & Sons.

Summey, T., & Gutierrez, A. (2012). Laptops to go: A student assessment of a library laptop lending service. *Journal of Access Services*, 9(1), 28–43. 10.1080/15367967.2012.629929

Swain, S. (2013). *Diversity education goals in higher education: A policy discourse analysis* (Publication No. 1957) [Doctoral dissertation, University of Maine]. University of Maine: Electronic Theses and Dissertations. https://digitalcommons .library.umaine.edu/etd/1957

Talbot, D. (2003). Multiculturalism. In Komives, S. R., & Woodard, D. B.Jr., (Eds.), *Student services: A handbook for the profession* (pp. 423–446). Jossey-Bass.

Walton, G. M., & Cohen, G. L. (2011). A brief social-belonging intervention improves academic and health outcomes of minority students. *Science*, 331(6023), 1447–1451. 10.1126/science.119836421415354

Williams, D. A. (2013). *Strategic diversity leadership: Activating change and transformation in higher education*. Routledge., 10.4324/9781003447122

Woodyard, L., & Larson, E. (2017). *2017 distance education report*. California Community Colleges Chancellor's Office. https://www.cccco.edu/-/media/CCCCO -Website/docs/report/2017-DE-Report-Final-ADA.pdf

Chapter 7
Virtual Communities to Support STEAM Educators

Dana Smerda-Mason
New Jersey City University, USA

ABSTRACT

The 21st century represents a time of exceptional growth, providing unprecedented technological innovation that continues to rely on the creativity of mankind. More than ever, thought leaders in the areas of science, technology, engineering, and math are needed to help lead modern innovation to meet the insatiable needs of the modern consumer market. To prepare the future workforce with the skills needed to successfully compete in the global market, the world looks to educators focused on developing the up-and-coming generation. The pressure of this monumental task faces educators in the 21st century on a daily basis. Modern workforce skills and the meaning of cutting-edge knowledge seem to change at a rapid pace, often leaving educators in a constant cycle of upskilling. Educators can benefit from the support of comprehensive professional development and powerful virtual communities.

INTRODUCTION

The 21st century represents a time of exceptional growth, providing unprecedented technological innovation that continues to rely on the creativity of mankind. More than ever, thought-leaders in the areas of science, technology, engineering, math, and science are needed to help lead modern innovation to meet the insatiable needs of the modern consumer market. To prepare the future workforce with the skills needed to successfully compete in the global market, the world looks to educators focused on developing the up-and-coming generation.

DOI: 10.4018/979-8-3693-1111-0.ch007

The pressure of this monumental task faces educators in the 21st century on a daily basis. Modern workforce skills and the meaning of cutting-edge knowledge seem to change at a rapid pace, often leaving educators in a constant cycle of upskilling. Education is an aspect of professional practice that can specifically benefit from the reliance of online social learning communities to help meet the timely need for new information, as well as impactful means of engagement with their students.

Online social learning communities could provide an important solution to serving educators in the field in regards to their professional development needs. Learning is not an action that occurs independently, and historically has functioned as a social experience, because humans are intrinsically social beings (Wenger-Trayner, 2024). Humans have been passing down knowledge to one another both in practice and observationally for centuries, and as new technology emerged in civilization, humans adapted how they passed on this information to the next member of the community. The masters and apprentice relationship is overtly present in a variety of professions, as well as the mentoring process in other types of professional communities. People continue to rely on the expertise of those around them to learn, grow, and share knowledge.

This practice continues as the advent of social media influences how society communicates and consumes information, and the opportunity for new pathways to learning and growth takes shape with technology. Many of these aforementioned existing relationships are integrating technology to improve the transfer of skills and information and utilizing the tool of social media to improve STEAM education skills among educators is no different. To design effective online social learning spaces for educators, it is important to understand the growing needs of the profession, and explore the educational initiatives of the past to bring together more complete view of the challenge at hand.

FROM STEM TO STEAM

Education has taken a variety of shapes over the course of many centuries. Historically families passed on skills and traditions, while the wealthier people had access to more of a formalized education for the children that met their position in life. Academic studies were based on curricula developed around guidance from developing educational theorists of the time. The advent of public education has provided the opportunity for more students to achieve an academic education, and it continues to adapt to modern day needs to best support the future benefit of students. As the academic community looked forward to the second half of the 20th century, it became apparent that adjustments in pedagogy and educational theory would need to occur.

In the 1960's and 1970's technological innovation was on the rise, and required the development of more qualified employees to help navigate the needs of the time. It was at this time that the workforce began to develop collaborative experiences in industry with professionals that had different and complimentary professional expertise (Herr et.al, 2019). The earliest form of this collaboration incorporated professionals that could represent their skills in the fields of science, technology, engineering, and math, which lead to the familiar title known today as the STEM fields (Dalton, 2019). The collaborative nature of these domains emerged as a workforce theme, and helped individuals with this particular background contribute to a more innovative and efficient workforce, ultimately rewarded with higher earning potential (Reitenback, 2015).

To better prepare students for the future, educators adopted a convergence approach to learning that integrated knowledge, techniques, and experience from different domains to provide real-world experience in solving modern-day challenges (Herr et al., 2019). Schools started focusing on STEM education, by grouping these subjects together in ways that would help students develop experience reflective of professional expectation, and they would be competitive in the job market. This convergence education model thrived and served as the basis of educational innovation at this time in history.

Around the late 1980's into the 1990's, advancements in innovation started to accelerate, and the STEM fields required a different approach to be able to keep up with the needs of the market. Although professionals trained in the STEM subjects had different domains of expertise, they were all trained with a similar way of thinking. This similarity in training and approach started to impede their ability to communicate brilliant innovations to become solutions of popularity in the mainstream world (Reitenbach, 2015). They all shared strong competency in convergent thinking, where they would solve for one specific correct answer when presented with a challenge (Markov, 2017). This ultimately limited the ability to engage in deeper problem solving, and have a more effective communication even among their professional collaborative teams.

To help integrate a solution to this challenge, Massachusetts Institute of Technology (MIT) produced their own publication as a student reading requirement entitled *Learning to Communicate in Science and Engineering*, to help prepare their students for a more successful collaborative experience (Reitnebach, 2015). What was missing from the process was divergent thinking in the collaborative experiences of these brilliant professionals. Divergent thinking is a process where individuals brainstorm many different solutions until they find the most efficient one, which is determined by the needs of the market or the research-based needs assessment for the challenges they are working to solve (Reiter-Palmon & Hunter, 2023). This is an attribute that is naturally taught in the area of the arts subjects, and was the missing piece for STEM education.

It is important to remember that neither convergent thinking nor divergent thinking models are solely superior to one another. Like convergence education, the benefits occur when both of these methods are combined in a collaborative process. Collaboration among a diverse group of subject matter experts helps lean on a variety of expertise, which serves to produce a stronger solution having had the inclusion of people with different processes to identify and address all the shortcomings of a solution to prepare the most effective one possible.

With the necessity for a divergent thinking approach that incorporated the arts and design into learning (Land, 2013), the STEM learning method was expanded to the 21st century model known as STEAM education by integrating the divergent thinking process of the arts and design fields into the technical fields of education. STEAM can effectively be taught as a transdisciplinary, arts-integrated method (Hunter-Doniger, 2018), and is touted as a cutting-edge approach to learning in the 21st century. Regardless of this understanding, transdisciplinary learning remains a challenge to implement for many committed and experienced educators. Back in 2013, A Partnership for a New American Economy uncovered in their research that only 4.4% of American undergraduates were enrolling in higher education technical programs (Land, 2013). In comparison, China and Singapore had a higher enrollment with upwards of 31% of students pursuing these areas of studies. Without proper intervention, American students' low interest in the technical fields will have a negative impact on the nation's ability to innovate and maintain its place in the global market.

There is evident need for modern professional development solutions in the area of STEAM education, to help prepare educators with techniques and knowledge of what they will need to provide a strong STEAM foundation for students in the 21st century. Based on a 2022 educator study, 73% of participants stated that they had experience teaching STEAM education, but later in the study only 50% were able to define STEAM education with accuracy (Smerda-Mason, 2022). Educators often reverted to the old STEM approach, which differs in that it focuses on a convergent thinking process, where students work to develop a singular correct solution. By teaching the underutilized STEAM model, the element of arts and design help integrate divergent thinking skills, which strengthen collaboration and critical thinking in a way that develops students as stronger problem solvers (Land, 2013). This helps illuminate an initial area of confusion and misunderstanding that is making the implementation of this methodology a problematic one for educators in the 21st century.

THE EDUCATOR'S CHALLENGE

The issue of low enrollment in the STEM fields is mirrored among the professionals in education, who are required to have a bachelor of arts degree to obtain certification, and can seek optional certifications or a different degree for advanced courses (Education-Colleges.com, 2021). Many professionals in the technical fields possess a bachelor of science or master of science degree to work in their field, and are paid at a higher rate than educators. Educators are required to obtain a bachelor of arts, or master of arts degree. In a 21st century world, educators are expected to prepare to inspire students to pursue higher education in an area that they themselves may not have had interest or expertise, leaving room for inviting technical professionals to join the field of education.

Although this does happen from time to time, it is less common that a technical professional would be enticed to switch careers to pursue education. In many states, they would be required to obtain teaching skills and certification, which would result in the investment of time and money as they enrolled in additional college courses, and practical application field study as a student teacher. When they finally achieved their certification and were hired in the field full-time, these efforts would be coupled with a decrease in salary compared to the field that they had recently left behind.

To address this need, incentive programs such as loan forgiveness (U.S. Department of Education, n.d.), or Alternate Route Teacher Certification Program had been put in place to attract professionals to apply their specialized skills in education (Field, 2018). Loan forgiveness programs promise to absolve small parts of college loan debt after five years teaching in the field at an approved school district to help ease the burden on education professionals or those obtaining additional education to join the field. The Alternate Route Teacher Certification Program was developed at a time where the education world wanted to attract experts from various professional fields to become teachers. As long as the professional had a bachelor's degree in their field and graduated with a GPA above a 2.7, some states would require them to take a course during their first year as an educator. During this time, they were also provided with a mentor and could work through a full school year with experienced guidance, and at the end of the year they would obtain their teaching certification.

Time during the school day is dedicated to an action-oriented, active instruction schedule, with short and limited time for preparation that is often utilized to prepare for upcoming classes and communicate with parents. Lesson planning and curricular development are other responsibilities that generally occur on an educator's personal time before or after school due to the lack of available time during the day. Grading and assessment feedback are also included in the after-hours responsibility, which can leave little opportunity for seeking formalized professional growth opportunities.

It is especially difficult when it is in a technical field, and educators are tasked with upskilling themselves in an unknown area.

Some educators have expressed that they do not use the STEAM model primarily because it was not required by their school administration, and they were already overloaded with other curricular responsibilities and the pressures of standardized testing, not to mention the lack of funding for specialized supplies (Smerda-Mason, 2022). If educators were required to implement STEAM, and provided the necessary materials and training time, they may be more willing to incorporate that approach with their students. This is an all-too-common theme in 21st century education, where educators operate on tight schedules managing overflowing plates of responsibilities. It is a valid concern that leaves educators with little to no time to develop new activities and to be infused into their existing curriculum schedule.

The educators of the 21st century require solutions as unique as their challenges, to support them with creativity and effective training practices. Educators are expected to prepare their students for future positions of employment that have yet to be created (Robinson, 2010), and do so in a lasting way. Educators are facing many difficult dynamics from classroom conditions, lower salary guides, and overall lack of respect from students, families, and sometimes administration and policy makers. In Pennsylvania, 16,000 teaching certificates were issued in 2012-13, and only 6,000 later in 2021-2022 (Greene, 2022). Upskilling in the 21st century adds to the burden and contributes to recruitment and retention issues in the field, which only adds additional pressure on those who remain in the field.

EFFECTIVE PROFESSIONAL DEVELOPMENT

These challenges point to a growing need to find innovative approaches to support educators as they upskill and blend technical understanding to develop a convergence education approach for their students. Educator preparation for a convergence education setting will only be successful if the challenge of educator professional development is efficiently addressed. With limited time, and other daily concerns, educators need effective and efficient means of upskilling to prepare for a convergence education approach.

Social online learning communities could meet this need by providing a unique support that addresses specific needs expressed by educators in the field related to the implementation of STEAM education. It is important to first itemize an effective approach to 21st century professional development for educators, to provide guidance in driving the discussion to an efficient solution. Before developing a virtual community such as this, it is important to examine the aspects of successful strategies to address specific professional development needs from this area of the field of education. Many unique barriers are emerging for educators tasked with implementing this cutting-edge model of learning within their classroom environments.

Desimone (2009) has provides a background of successful strategies to support this particular issue. This researcher developed a five-element system that could be incorporated into all educator professional development opportunities to ensure that they would be impactful. These points include clear content focus, active learning, coherence, sustained duration, and collective participation. The framework aims to address critical issues in traditional professional development training models that affect teacher knowledge and beliefs, classroom practice, and student outcomes (Conradty & Bogner, 2020).

Traditional professional development training focuses on important concepts, but it seems that this content is often delivered independent of other curricular connections (Chai, 2018). *Content focus* should be considered in the planning of educator training. It must incorporate learning activities that are based on the curriculum and classroom expectations so content addressed can be practical and easily tested and experimented with by those in attendance at the training. Having activities and training modules that focus specifically on different lessons and projects from the classroom experience will help educators make a direct correlation to successful implementation and will also help raise their self-efficacy while they attempt to practice this after the training session has ended (Conradty & Bogner, 2020).

Active Learning should be incorporated into professional development environments. Having opportunity to engage in experiences where educators are able to interact with the material in a variety of ways helps layer experiences for lasting results, as opposed to passive participation (Conradty & Bogner, 2020). For educator professional development, this could include peer review, present materials within the peer group, analyze information in a collaborative setting, or hands-on approaches to training sessions. This is something that educators are encouraged to do in the daily classroom environment because of its efficacy on retention of material, and educators should have the same benefits afforded to them as well in their training experiences.

Each school has different goals for the academic year. Many are mandated by the district or state level, and gleaned from specific student-driven data. It is not uncommon for professional development experiences to lack the customization for their particular audience. If training is not properly targeted and customized for the individuals attending, it will be hard to implement and ultimately a less impactful session. As a result, Desimone (2009) suggests *Coherence* in educator training to ensure that the content for the session is in alignment with goals established by the school, district, state, as well as in support of the current curricular content being used.

A relatively unique consideration refers to *Sustained Duration* in professional development training. It is common to see content delivered as a one-time workshop. This guideline of the framework suggests that training should occur in a series, and often throughout the year to support the needs of educators as the school year continues. This also encourages timely implementation of newly learned content or strategies from training. Twenty consecutive sessions are ideally encouraged to properly give educators the support they need throughout the school year for new curriculum implementation.

The element of community is one that has been found to be impactful for successful implementation, and so Desimone (2009) recommends *Collective Participation* as the final element of this framework. Having the opportunity to develop one's professional understanding through collaborative activities with professional peers provides collegial support that continues long after the training has ended. This could include common preparation time among grade level partners or content partners to help develop strategies for success. When districts provide room for this sort of interactivity to be prioritized, professional learning communities build among educators that will create lasing collaborative support.

The field of education is aware that students do not all learn in the same way. As individuals, we have a variety of experiences, predispositions, and other factors that influence our ability to learn. The teaching profession assumes the expectation to modify and differentiate instruction to meet the needs of their students, yet many aspects of traditional professional development remain static. Educators are expected to learn in silos of one-size-fits-all instructional delivery of information, and then pressure is applied when educators are unsure how to implement this into the field. What makes a positive impact on students, can also empower educators, and so it is essential to consider an andragogical approach that supports the diverse needs of educators in the field (Schaffauser, 2019). Incorporating this type of framework, as well as social online learning communities can aid in addressing the needs of all types of professionals within the field of education, which ultimately will help service students effectively.

SOCIAL LEARNING COMMUNITIES AS A SOLUTIONS

Educators work towards employing cutting-edge solutions to meet the diverse needs of their students. If it is expected of them utilize a variety of tools at hand to be effective educators, then it is essential to employ all helpful techniques, technology, research, and tools to meet the professional development training needs of 21st century educators. By combining resources, varying domains of content knowledge, pedagogical design, and collegial support with technology, it is possible to develop an online social learning community that meets the needs of educators in an impactful 21st century professional development training solution.

A social learning community can be developed to support educators in their need for a modern training solution. Designing this space should take into considerations elements of Desimone's five-element 21st century professional development guidelines, as well as employ technology, collaboration, and differentiation techniques for learning. It can take the form of whatever platform best suits the needs of the educator community, but for the purposes of this chapter, the idea of utilizing a website will be the example focused on.

If it is based on a website, it can be a space where content, materials, and ideas can be shared across the group. Media such as videos and pictures, all shared by members of this virtual community, would serve as a diversified content offering, and over time this content will gradually grow to contain a diverse representation of content knowledge within the online social learning community. Professionals would have the opportunity to post webinars and upcoming conferences, or training sessions that they come across to help share information about learning opportunities that will help them connect with new skills and individuals to broaden their personal practice.

It is important that the online virtual community have a discussion board, forum, or a place to make posts and comments. Opportunities to collaborate with professional peers are often difficult to establish within the traditional K-12 schedule. Educator mentoring and regular feedback loops play an important part in the continuous role of improving and developing new skills and techniques (Desimone, 2015). The egalitarian nature of this type of group will thrive on collaboration that is instantly accessible, making guidance available when members of the group need it most.

It can be difficult to build training that has a consistent focus on continued collaboration, and collective participation when working only in-person environments (Desimone-Garet, 2015). Online virtual communities with the ability to participate in interactive forms or message boards address this challenge with a solution. Within this virtual space exists a community of practice. Each member brings an important contribution towards growth by sharing their expertise. It also serves as a non-recursive model benefitting that serves all members of the community. Members who lack any experience are welcomed to the group to look through and suggest resources, as well as benefit from questions being posed and answered by others.

In time, as these new members build their confidence and their experience develops, they themselves will be asking questions of the group, and gradually sharing their experience as they help others. The experts within the community with the most experience benefit by refining their tried-and-true practices, and creatively problem-solving through the collaboration and support of the newer community members. They also have the opportunity to emerge as thought leaders in their area of expertise and are broadened by the collaboration and collegial support. Regardless of what level of professional experience an individual possesses, they have a place to grow and develop as they share their knowledge among this community of education professionals.

A group of educators can respond differently to the same session of professional development training, much like how different students retain and comprehend uniquely in the very same classroom experience. Understanding the diversity of educators' abilities, skillsets, personal experiences, and experience in the education field can be important to helping contour a differentiated approach to learning within an andragogical environment. Professional development training needs to be designed to meet the personal and changing needs of the individuals in the audience (Desimone-Garet, 2015).

Online social learning communities address this by inviting a community of experts into one place, and allowing individuals to self-direct their experience through collaborative interaction with one another. Not all districts are the same, with some districts existing in a highly populated urban area, and others in a desolate rural location. As a result, their operational needs and expectations will be very different, and the diversity of the field must represent the diversity within the community for it to thrive and provide a comprehensive learning experience for all (Desimone-Garet, 2015).

Within this type of online learning community, it requires the use of 21st century learning skills, similar to elements that educators are using to reinforce with their students in the classroom. The Four C's is a concept in STEAM education that encourages the use of four important design thinking and problem-solving elements: critical thinking, collaboration, creativity, and communication (Zimmerman, 2018). Each of these elements can be evidenced within online social communities by the active problem-solving in the forum or chat areas of a group like this. Community members can also submit training videos, demonstrations, or other helpful media for others to search for on specific topics of interest for continued self-directed engagement.

Incorporating elements from how educators seek to teach their students is a great consideration for teachers to approach professional development for 21st century learning and STEAM education. Although this type of a group is focusing on the needs of adult learners and therefore would require an andragogical approach to learning, we can modify this to incorporate successful aspects of pedagogical practices that can be differentiated to meet the varying needs of adult learners. By providing modern learning techniques for educators in their professional training experiences, educators will have more support in understanding the benefits of STEAM education first hand, and help provide a new perspective on how to integrate elements such as these into their daily classroom practice.

Educators in this situation need unique solutions, and it is important to review a variety of examples of how ideas can be shared through these types of online professional learning communities. Educators that are currently implementing the STEAM approach share media with examples of activities that they use successfully with their students, and how they were able to gradually implement them in to their teaching practice to improve their confidence teaching STEAM activities in the classroom. The STEAM model is aimed to be integrated into an existing curriculum regardless of the subject, so other educators can benefit from these examples. With this support, individuals can slowly develop pathways towards integration by connecting a hand-full of their favorite lessons that they feel confident delivering with new STEAM activities that meet their learning objectives. They would then update these lessons with project-based or inquiry-based learning activities, arts and design components that complimented their content, as well as collaboration and real-world problem-solving opportunities. When getting started it is important to begin with what is working and take small steps towards STEAM integration.

A variety of factors contribute to the inhibition or encouragement of STEAM implementation, and have been discussed throughout this chapter. Many of these individual concerns can be grouped into the areas of discipline and content knowledge, pedagogical design, administrative support, collegial support, and professional development (Dong, et. al, 2018). Online social learning communities can help raise teaching self-efficacy by allowing educators the ability to self-direct through a platform of resources, while also providing live expertise of the community to support them with any of these challenges at their convenience. This helps gradually demystify and dissolve the intimidation factor that troubles many educators as they struggle with where to begin their professional upskilling (Geng, et. Al, 2018).

Another option among online social learning communities is the sharing of events that have professional development training sessions from reliable and effective providers. Community members benefit from the experience of others who have attended and are able to recommend impactful training of which other members in the group may have never heard about because they are new to the STEAM fields. These can come in a variety of forms that may not be advertised in a national capacity and it helps to spread the word to potentially interested educators.

For example, sessions that occur as a series throughout the school year to offer continuous support as new things are implemented within the classroom happen to be highly impactful and quite common among STEAM training opportunities. Some school districts offer summer camps for students, and Carnegie Melon used the summer camp model as an opportunity to train teachers in their robotics program. In an informal camp setting, educators received professional development, then taught what they learned to participating students, ultimately making them stronger with the material and setting when the school year arrived (Schaffauser, 2019).

Educators benefit from already having an expertise in their specialized content area, so when a transdisciplinary approach is implemented their level of self-efficacy is threatened (Dong et al., 2018). STEAM education is not as much about being the expert in every field, as it is about providing a space for students to learn 21st century skills in each of their classes through convergence education (Conradty & Bogner, 2020). Engineering is the domain that educators express the need for the most help in implementing in the classroom (Smerda-Mason, 2022), and also an area where educators can seek immediate support. Organizations of retired engineers exist in virtual communities as well, such as The American Academy for Environmental Engineers and Scientists, are willing to actively partner with schools to bring practical and technical knowledge to the classroom (The American Academy for Environmental Engineers and Scientists, 2022). There are many other types of virtual communities beyond engineering throughout the United States that educators can partner with, for example The Retirees School Volunteer Association, based on their declared commitment to partnering with administrators, educators, and students to help with academic success (The Retirees School Volunteer Association, 2022).

The Next Generation Science Standards were initially designed to help bridge the gap in pedagogical design between various subjects for a convergence education approach to learning, but instead it started to illuminate these very differences (Chai, 2018) since they had been designed according to individual domains initially. Coupled with the need for integrating non-science domains, and the number of gaps grew. Educators working through this pedagogical challenge can benefit from partnering with their colleagues by creating a professional learning community (PLC) representative of all domains, including at least one colleague with special education expertise. Together colleagues will model the collaborative design process in the planning stages, which not only can produce a comprehensive pedagogical approach, but grow their comfort level in teaching with collaboration for their students. Gradually, this can help shift the culture of the school by having commitment from a variety of colleagues involved in the process.

Administrative support can be a powerful element in the success of STEAM implementation, and an added area to online social communities. Educator beliefs and attitudes about curricular changes are directly impacted by their leaders, which can affect the success of newly implemented initiatives (Dong et al., 2018). Administrators are often tasked with mandates and additional responsibilities less obvious on the teaching level. Some educators found data to share with staff and administrators to understand how beneficial STEAM can be for students' test scores, achievement, attendance, or another area administration may want to improve. By offering support and solutions for the success of the school, it may be possible to shift towards meeting individual educator needs as well. This is something that can be developed and shared through a dynamic online professional learning community to enhance the partnership between educators and administrators, and inform collective policy based on modern trends being implemented in the classroom.

Educators have also found value in communicating their needs in advance, and discussing initiatives with their administrators. The fruit of these types of discussions helps everyone understand what is happening in other areas of the school, and work towards supportive solutions. Where some schools are able to provide flexible scheduling solutions, adjustments for new space requirements, other educators might be successful in receiving support for individual professional training needs, available technologies, and flexible planning time with colleagues (Smerda-Mason, 2022).

In addition to this, collegial support and collaboration in various forms can emerge as an important element, yielding positive effects on teaching self-efficacy (Dong et al., 2018) when addressed through the implementation of an online social learning community or in-person experiences. This may look different to each educator, but can come in the form of faculty meetings, coaching, departmental professional learning groups, or mentoring. Not every school culture has these elements structured in with regularity, and for educators in this situation, these types of collaborative experience can broaden one's scope of peers through online professional learning communities.

There are online groups to join through Facebook, LinkedIn, and other websites and social media platforms that are great places to start when seeking other STEAM educators to share ideas with and develop new ideas. For example, online message boards, Google groups, and websites such as the STEAM Learning Lounge can serve as spaces to autonomously browse STEAM technologies, as well as recorded webinars, as well as strike up fruitful conversation on the forum to reach out for community collaboration (www.steamlearninglounge.com).

Others such as the North East Digital Learning Association, more commonly known as NEDLA, provide professional development in the form of educational programming through webinars and virtual learning series. In these sessions, experts and novices from a variety of domains including education, corporate industry, and healthcare can convene for 21st century discussions on contemporary issues affecting them in the field. Although they are all designed in different ways, these communities have many commonalities as they act as support for educators and learning professionals through the creation of a community of practice where individuals can meet other growing professionals with similar interests to share information together (Wenger, 2000).

CONCLUSION

Professional development can be difficult to find the time for, and educators express two favorite formats for learning: hands-on training, as well as professional development training in virtual settings (Smerda-Mason, 2022). Many of the afore-mentioned forums and online PLCs are a great way to compliment and differentiate within professional learning. Where it can be great to learn in a live setting as a student, it also helps to have less formal sessions, which can be joined from home or recorded and reviewed later. This provides greater freedom to adult learners who can benefit from conveniently browsing content or joining the community discussion anywhere they find a few minutes or hours of free time in their personal lives.

The nature of a social learning community is one that supports lifelong growth and learning for individuals of any age or experience level. It addresses the need for urgent solutions, while being able to explore and grow at the convenience of the educator. The collaborative nature helps the community thrive as individuals rely on one another's strengths to learn and grow in their unique ways. Wenger-Trayner (2024) encourages this means of collaborative learning across a variety of iterations with certain key elements present that set the stage for authentic development and growth interactions:

"A community of practice is not defined by the medium through which members connect. Mutually relevant challenges of practice are much more important than modes of interaction. They key to a community of practice is the ability of partici-pants to recognize the practitioner in each other and that basis, to act as learning partners. If online interactions alone allow people to do this in meaningful ways (and by now there is enough evidence that it is possible), then the result is an 'online' community of practice" (Wenger-Trayner, 2024).

There are many ways to grow into STEAM education and these suggestions serve as a starting point towards exploring transdisciplinary learning through STEAM integration. With the proper support educators can successfully and confidently bring new experience to their classrooms for their students. Developing a uniform understanding of what educators are working with in terms of method and approach prior to attempting STEAM integration will help strengthen the efforts being made. This may be difficult initially, but the first step for educators in fortifying this un-derstanding for educators would be to immerse themselves in a supportive online learning community to begin the journey. In time, students and educators will grow into this form of learning and prepare for exciting trends of future growth in 21st century education.

REFERENCES

Babette, A. (2018). The development of STEAM educational policy to promote student creativity and social empowerment. *Arts Education Policy Review*, 119(2).

Barni, D., Daioni, F., & Benefene, P. (2019, July). Teacher's self-efficacy: The role of personal values and motivations for teaching. Frontiers in psychology. Retrieved from https://www.frontiersin.org/articles/10.3389/fpsyg.2019.01645/full#:~:text =Teachers'%20self%2Defficacy%2C%20namely,being%20in%20the%20working %20environment

Bhandari, N. A. (n.d.). Using a professional development model to enhance instructional models. Virginia Tech. Retrieved from https://higherlogicdownload.s3.amazonaws .com/SPED/04bdc7a0-1ec9-4eaa-b61c-677439532d1a/UploadedImages/Journal _2012/CEC%20Art%202%20Bhandari%20Using_a_PD_Model_to_Enhance _Instructional_Practices%5B.pdf

Chai, C. S. (2018). Teacher professional development for science technology engineering and math (STEM) education: A review from the perspectives of technical pedagogical content. *The Asia-Pacific Education Researcher*, 28(1). 10.1007/ s40299-018-0400-7

Conradty, C., & Bogner, F. X. (2020) STEAM teaching professional development works: Effects on students' creativity and motivation. *Smart Learning Environments, 7*(26).

Dalton, W. (2019). What is STEM? Pearson accelerated pathways. Retrieved from https://pearsonaccelerated.com/blog/stem

Davis, M. D., Witchcraft, S. M., Baird, S. O., & Smits, J. A. (2017). *The science of cognitive behavioral therapy*. Academic press., 10.1016/B978-0-12-803457-6.00003-9

Desimone, L., Garet, M. (2015). Best practices in teachers' professional development in the United States. *Psychology, Society, and Education, 7*(5). DOI:10.25115. PSYE.V7I3.515

Desimone, L. M. (2009). Improving impact studies of teachers' professional development: Towards better conceptualizations and measures. *Educational Researcher*, 38(3), 181–200. 10.3102/0013189X08331140

Dong, Y., Xu, C., Song, X., Fu, Q., Chai, C. S., & Huang, Y. (2018). Exploring the effects of contextual factors on in-service teachers' engagement in STEM teaching. *The Asia-Pacific Education Researcher*, 28(1), 25–34. 10.1007/s40299-018-0407-0

Education-Colleges.com. (2021). Retrieved from https://www.education -colleges.com/bachelors-degree-ba- bs/#:~:text=All%20states%20in%20the%20 U.S.,and%2C%20eventually%2C%20 for%20teaching.

Field, A. (2018). Solutions to the STEM teacher shortage. *The network: CISCO's technology news site.* Retrieved from https://newsroom.cisco.com/feature-content ?type=webcontent&articleId=1916176

Geng, J., Jong, M. S., & Chai, C. S. (2018). Hong Kong teachers' self-efficacy and concerns about STEM education. *The Asia-Pacific Education Researcher*, 28(1), 35–45. 10.1007/s40299-018-0414-1

Girl Scout Research Institute. (2019). Decoding the digital girl: Defining and supporting girls' leadership. Retrieved from https://www.girlscouts.org/content/ dam/girlscouts-gsusa/forms-and- documents/about-girl-scouts/research/GSU-SA_GSRI_Decoding-the-Digital- Girl_Full-Report.pdf

Greene, P. (2022). There is no teacher shortage. So why is everyone talking about it. *Forbes*.

Guyotte, K., Sochacka, N., Costantino, T., Walther, J., & Kellam, N. (2014). STEAM as social practice cultivating creativity in transdisciplinary spaces. *Art Education*, 67(6), 12–19. 10.1080/00043125.2014.11519293

Herr, D. J. C., Akbar, B., Brummet, J., Flores, S., Gordon, A., Gray, B., & Murday, J. (2019, August). Convergence education- an international perspective. J Nanopart Research. *Vol. 21*(229). *Journal of Nanoparticle Research*, 2019(21), 229. 10.1007/ s11051-019-4638-7

Hunter-Doniger, T. (2018). Art infusion: Ideal conditions for STEAM. *Art Education*, 2(71), 22–27. 10.1080/00043125.2018.1414534

Land, M. H. (2013). Full STEAM ahead: The benefits of integrating the arts into STEM. *Procedia Computer Science*, 20, 547–552. Advance online publication. 10.1016/j.procs.2013.09.317

Learning Lounge, S. T. E. A. M. (2024, January 10). Links and resources. www .steamlearninglounge.com

Liao, C. (2016). From interdisciplinary to transdisciplinary: An arts-integrated approach to STEAM education. *Art Education*. 10.1080/00043125.2016.1224873

Markov, S. (2017). *Joy Paul Guilford: One of the founders of the psychology of creativity*. Geniusrevive.com

McComb. (2015, January 3). *Improving teaching through collegial support*. Huffpost. Retrieved from https://www.huffpost.com/entry/improving-teaching-through-collegial-support_b_6089654

North East Digital Learning Association. (2024, January 10). *Events*.https://nedla.org/page-969292

Office of the U.S. department of education. (n.d.). Wondering if you can get your loans forgiven for your service as a teacher? *Federal student aid*. Retrieved from https://studentaid.gov/manage-loans/forgiveness-cancellation/teacher

Reichenbach, G. (2015). From STEM to STEAM education. *Power*, 159(6), 6–6.

Reiter-Palmon, R., & Hunter, S. (2023). Handbook of organizational creativity: Individual and group level influences. Science Direct. https://doi.org/10.1016/C2020-0-04164-0

Robelen, E. (2011, December 7). STEAM Experts make case for adding the arts to STEM. *Education Week*, 1(6).

Robinson, K. (2009). *The element. How finding your passion changes everything*. New York, NY: The Penguin Group.

Robinson, K. (2010, November 4-5). *Keynote address* [Conference presentation]. NJEA 2010 Convention, Atlantic City, NJ, United States.

Schaffauser, D. (2019). Getting trained to TEACH ROBOTICS: This professional development opportunity helps you with the basics and even includes freely available curriculum. *T H E Journal (Technological Horizons in Education), 20*(6).

Silva, E. (2009). Measuring skills for 21st century learning. *Phi Delta Kappan, 90*(9), 630-634. .10.1177/003172170909000905

Smerda-Mason, D. (2022). Professional development concerns and solutions in STEAM education [Doctoral dissertation, New Jersey City University].

The American academy of environmental engineers and scientists. (2022). AAEES website. Retrieved from https://www.aaees.org/studentchapters/

The retirees school volunteer association. (2022). RSVA website. Retrieved from https://rsva.org/

Wenger, E. (2000). Communities of practice and social learning systems. *Organization, 7*(2), 225-246. 10.1177/135050840072002

Wenger, E., White, N., & Smith, J. D. (2009). Digital habitats: Stewarding technology for communities. CPsquare.

Wenger-Trayner, E., & Wenger-Trayner, B. (2015). Introduction to communities of practice. Retrieved from https://wenger-trayner.com/introduction-to-communities -of-practice/

Wenger-Trayner, E., & Wenger-Trayner, B. (2024, January 9). *Can a community of practice exist only online?* Wenger-Trayner: Global theorists and consultants. https:// www.wenger-trayner.com/online-communities-of-practice/

Wenger-Trayner, E., & Wenger-Trayner, B. (2024, January 11). *What is social learning?* Wenger-Trayner: Global theorists and consultants. https://www.wenger -trayner.com/what-is-social-learning/#:~:text=Etienne's%20work%20on%20social %20learning,others%20or%20use%20certain%20tools

Zimmerman, E. (2018, July 27). The 4 c's of learning in a connected classroom. Edtech focus on K-12. Retrieved from https://edtechmagazine.com/k12/article/2018/ 07/4-cs-learning-connected-classroom

Zollman, A. (2012). Learning for STEM Literacy: STEM Literacy for Learning. *School Science and Mathematics*, 112(1), 12–19. 10.1111/j.1949-8594.2012.00101.x

KEY TERMS AND DEFINITIONS

21st Century Skills: In a time when the world continues to change at a rapid speed, it is difficult to predict what skills students will need to be successful after graduation. As a result, instead of focusing on what pieces of knowledge they have, 21st century learning is helping students develop specific skills to help to creatively problem-solve, and figure out things for themselves. The skills associated with 21st century education include intrapersonal, life, workforce, non-cognitive, and applied skills (Silva, 2009).

Communities of Practice: Groups of individuals that share an interest and collaboratively learn to develop their skills in this interest through their interaction (Wenger-Trayner, 2015).

Convergence Education: Integration of knowledge, techniques, and expertise from various domains to more efficiently solve social and scientific challenges that arise in the modern world (Herr et al., 2019).

Convergent Thinking: The path to develop one single correct answer to solve a challenge (Markov, 2017).

Divergent Thinking: The process of problem-solving where individuals brainstorm many different solutions until they find the most efficient one (Reiter-Palmon & Hunter, 2023).

Social Constructivism: Teaching and learning successfully occurs when the focus is on interpersonal interaction and the student's ability to understand and participate in the discussion (Davis et al., 2017).

STEAM Education: This stands for Science, Technology, Engineering, Arts and Design, and Math. The missing element in preparing students for the 21st century was the element of creativity. This model of education marks a shift in learning priorities which incorporates teaching creativity and problem-solving to help students become competitive with the innovative needs in the 21st century workforce (Liao, 2016).

STEAM Literacies: The ability to identify, apply, and integrate concepts from science, technology, engineering, arts and design, and math as a means of developing collaborative problem-solving skills to engage a wider variety of learners and meet the needs of issues in the 21st century (Zollman, 2012).

STEM Education: This stands for Science, Technology, Engineering, and Math and is a 20th century model of education. It is a form of pedagogy that incorporates the learning from these areas in which all subjects are taught at the same time. (Reitenbach, 2015).

Teaching Self-Efficacy: The teacher's belief in their ability to handle tasks, responsibilities, and challenges related to their professional responsibilities (Barni et al., 2019).

Chapter 8
Collaborative Research Data Management Using ResearchGate

Nadim Akhtar Khan
University of Kashmir, India

Nowsheeba Ashraf Asmi
Government College for Women, Srinagar, India

Aimen Nazir Bhat
University of Kashmir, India

ABSTRACT

Research data management benefits the scientific community through data sharing and collaborations, and its importance is much more owing to concerns from publishers, funding agencies, the public, and research organizations focussed on the quality and impact of research. Academic social networking sites facilitate the achievement of this goal through sharing and collaborating on research and ideas. ResearchGate has emerged as a platform for research data management, revolutionizing the ways to store, share, and access research data sets. The chapter highlights the significance of research data management and explores the importance of academic social networking sites in this area. It further explores ResearchGate features, which research scholars use to reflect successful collaborations, research growth, and better communication with peers. It attempts to assess the impact of RG research matrics for retaining the quality and visibility of research, which significantly impacts RG's success through openness, effectiveness, and interconnectivity in the scientific domain.

DOI: 10.4018/979-8-3693-1111-0.ch008

INTRODUCTION

Research involves interlinked and systematic scientific steps for minutely, objectively, and scientifically identifying and solving a research problem (Singh, 2021). It includes discovering, interpreting, and developing practical, sequential actions and steps to solve a research problem (Kothari, 2004). The foundation of scientific research in the form of theories and perceptions depends on how data are selected, collected, transformed and understood using appropriate processes for data selection, Annotation, generation, and data refinement (Wang et al., 2023). Therefore, data collection and analysis are central to developing a better understanding and knowledge of scientific discoveries (De Regt, 2020).

The availability of vast amounts of machine-readable scientific data facilitates the utilisation of efficient methods to collect, organise, visualise, and model these data to increase the reliability, speed, and transparency of knowledge creation (Leonelli, 2020). Therefore, managing this data becomes more crucial for researchers, research institutions, and universities to enrich their scientific profiles. Research Data Management, as such, brings fascinating change and benefits the scientific community for actively engaging in activities concerning data sharing and collaborations (Chawinga & Zinn, 2021). The importance of RDM is much more due to pressure from publishers, funders, the public and research organisations to improve the quality and impact of research (Kinde et al., 2021).

Besides, this change is primarily associated with technological infrastructure developments, evolving information needs and seeking behaviour, and the inception of services like RDM through libraries for diverse communities in higher education (Ashiq et al., 2022). Libraries actively support research throughout its process, from brainstorming ideas and conception, data collection, processing and interpretation, storage and data preservation, result publication, and impact evaluation (Hamad et al., 2021). Thus, the libraries, with funding organisations and other academic units, play a vital role in supporting research needs through RDM (Xu, 2022). Effective management of data is such a vital precursor in making data Findable, Accessible, Interoperable and Reusable (FAIR); for this reason, researchers should develop Data Management Plans (DMPs) in the initial stages of the research (Jones et al., 2020). The RDM focussed on FAIR principles can be significantly enhanced by utilising the competencies and capabilities of Social Media features supporting the research culture based on openness, thus resulting in the evolution of open science, open research, open education, open data and governments, etc.

METHODOLOGY

The literature survey focusing on research data management and the importance of social media, especially Academic Social Networking Sites with a particular focus on utilising the existing competencies of ResearchGate in data management is carried out using reputed databases and search engines like EBSCOhost, Web of Science, Google Scholar, DOAJ: Directory of Open Access Journals, publishing houses like Wiley, Emerald, Taylor and Francis, and ResearchGate etc.

The survey attempts to identify the modern trends in Research Data Management through the identification of significant research works about RDM, the role of social media, especially ASNSs, in RDM and exploring prominent features and tools of ResearchGate for enriching the user experiences through openness, one-to-one connectivity, sharing and exploring research interests and works. The literature survey, coupled with exploring the ResearchGate website, helped identify and explore many essential facts and features of the RG platform to support a more vibrant online research ecosystem discussed in subsequent parts of this work.

Research Data Management and Its Significance

Whyte and Tedds (2011) define Research Data Management (RDM) as "the organisation of data, from its entry into the research cycle through to the dissemination and archiving of valuable results." According to Tang & Hu (2019), RDM includes provisions for information consultation, diligence in data management planning, training in data management during research documentation and metadata enrichment, research data sharing and curation. Thus, RDM is developing as the core area of research activities on which the entire research process depends (Patel, 2016).

The interest in research data management at the global level is rising, and researchers ensure quality output, including publications and datasets (Perrier et al., 2017). Wittman and Aukema (2020) state that data management promotes the reusability of the data, saving time and resources. More scientific areas, including mathematics, natural sciences, medical sciences, engineering, etc., are evolving as data-driven sciences produce lots of data for supporting research. Besides, document-driven sciences like digital and artefact-based sciences rely on digital infrastructures for digital documents, including historical texts and associated metadata, which generate much data with potential value for future research. Thus, research data management becomes more crucial for stakeholders, including professors, researchers and their collaborators, students, the economy, governmental bodies, and society (Andrikopolou et al., 2020; Heuer,2020).

RDM offers different benefits, including data sharing to avoid research duplication and safeguarding valuable data sets through preservation and curation activities. It fosters research insights based on co-assessment and correlation of data deduced from different sources. Besides, it imparts research integrity through the verification and validation of results. It further fosters interdisciplinary research by cross-examining the data (Andrikopoulou et al., 2022).

Driven by funding and publishing requirements to open and reuse data, RDM has become a crucial part of a researcher's role (Birkbeck et al.,2022). Researchers need to understand RDM, especially its importance in supporting their research projects and fostering satisfying funders' requirements for sharing (Netscher et al.,2020). The stakeholders, especially faculty members and researchers, are not fully aware of RDM and must be aware of data management templates, RDM policies and guidelines (Kinde et al., 2021).

The requirements for quality in RDM systems depend on designing scalable and reliable solutions for research-identity data focused on readers, Personal Record Managers, and community members developing, hosting and using such data through institutional repositories and RDM systems (Wu et al.,2017). They provide and curate their research by maintaining their profiles in these systems and acting as primary data providers, resulting in online curation and sharing of such data (Wu et al., 2016).

RDM Using Social Networking Sites (SNSs)

Social media has emerged as a fast-adapted networking technology and has found its application in research activities. It has gained importance among researchers to strengthen their networks and enhance research visibility and has significantly impacted the world of research communication (Edosomwan,2011). Social networking sites have reached the peak of popularity and are used by all generations and genres (Pfeil et al.,2009). SNSs provide provisions for research scholars to network and publish their research. Academicians can communicate and collaborate with groups, departments, and locations, connecting with researchers and finding resources, thus creating and joining research groups (Williams & Woodacre, 2016). They can discover best practices, papers, people, and public groups and explore research usage worldwide. Thus, they utilise these to search efficiently for expertise, methods, and materials for their research. Their use focuses on contacting other researchers, disseminating research results, and following other scholars by employing social media features, including citation indexes, document creation, edition, and sharing and communication tools (Nández & Borrego, 2013).

Thus, these Social Networking Sites facilitate research scholars to build social communities in which they connect with scholars who share their research interests. They can create their profiles, update their professional achievements, share their research papers, and later export them as CVs for finding jobs and recognition. Research scholars can add files to their profiles and fully control their access. They can add video files, images, audio, PDFs, research papers, findings, and questions related to their research. Several ASNSs are available on social media sites, each with features and tools for various research activities.

Institutional Research performance has become essential to competitive rankings, funding, and student recruitment, resulting in many research performance indicators (Yu et al., 2016). Thus, most researchers are adopting research data management practices for data sharing. They are preserving and sharing their research data in their networks by publishing in research journals, sharing through ASNS like RG and providing data through an open data repository or upon request to peers. The reasons for sharing the research data include enhanced scientific progress, increased citations and visibility of research. Researchers engage in data sharing, but training and institutional support are needed to encourage strong data management practices and open data sharing (Kaari, 2020).

Role of Academic Social Networking Sites (ASNSs) in RDM

Academic Social Networking Sites (ASNSs), specifically, are designed to cater to the needs of users associated with academics. For research scholars, ASNSs are a medium where they can create and share their ideas. They provide a platform for interaction, communication, collation, and collaboration. ASNSs allow research scholars to create communities and engage in interesting professional conversations (Yan et al., 2023). They facilitate future collaborations, stimulating creativity and easing the complexity of research problems. In addition to other benefits, ASNSs are where research scholars can make their work accessible and control what to share with whom and to what extent. They also help research scholars track demand for published articles, find the impact of published papers, follow colleagues, and find related research papers and career opportunities (Okeji, 2019).

The popularity of ASNSs and their usage among researchers owing to features like experts' contact details, citations, links to resources, articles, images and so on stimulate scholarly interactions by eliminating confusion, improving the clarity of questions, and promoting scholarly content management (Jenget al., 2017). ASNSs encourage rapid, informal communication without the delays imposed by formal journal publishing or peer-review process" (Tartari, 2015).

ASNSs like ResearchGate, Academia.edu, Google Scholar, LinkedIn, etc., are predominantly created for scholars to set up their profiles, upload their scholarly publications, and convey them to peers (Naushad et al.,2022). RG users mainly follow others from institutions of higher research activity, forming virtual networks around revered institutions. ASNS, like RG, can facilitate the evaluation of research activities among research institutions, and such sites can be helpful and credible for acquiring resources, keeping informed about research, and promoting academic influence (Yan & Zhang, 2018). Majumdar (2022) reveals professional visibility as one of the motivating factors for academicians and researchers to join ASN sites. Other important motivators include seeking scholarly answers, accruing citations and experts, sharing research using self-archiving facilities of ASN sites, enhancing research collaboration and job seeking, and thus providing alternative metrics for measuring research impact.

ASNSs assist scholars in conducting research, including identifying research problems, methodology, data collection, data analysis and interpretation, expert advice, and sharing of research (Hailu & Wu, 2021). They help generate in-text citations and bibliographies, create footnotes and endnotes, capture sticky notes and highlights, import and organise PDF files, and manage publication lists, notes, and annotations (Majhi et al., 2023). ASNSs are places where research scholars can discover papers, people, and public groups, bookmark articles, and manage publication lists (Anyim, 2021; Asmi & Margam, 2018).

Researchers' behaviour of sharing research data on ASNSs remains inadequately explored and can be viewed from underdeveloped social activity around self-archived research data in ResearchGate showcasing reads and citations. Besides, it requires literacy and innovation to engage with data practices across digital systems, providing adequate support for the researchers to use them significantly (Raffaghelli & Manca, 2023).

Privacy Concerns in RDM

Recent work in the literature has exhibited the alacrity of academic professionals in data sharing with the research community which is increasing the need for data privacy. Since data is constantly being shared, it is possible for professionals to lose control over it and calls for privacy concerns. The major privacy concerns in RDM are:
1. Sensitive and Restricted Data
Professionals are obliged to assure they are not disclosing any sensitive and restricted data specifically when proceeding with human subjects. There is a possibility of risk of data disclosure or consent for data sharing was not bestowed.
2. Secondary and Proprietary Data

Professionals need to be attentive while working with secondary and proprietary data to ensure they are entitled to disseminate it and they should only disseminate it when there are no legal deterrents.

3. Copyright and Ownership

Copyrighting data has also become an arduous task. A researcher needs to comprehend who holds the data, who claims the ownership and what are their expectations concerning the sharing of data. All these call for clarification before ethically sharing the data (Ivey et al., 2023).

4. Data storage and volume

Large amount of data produced from fluorescence imaging or MRI and are frequently archived in diverse locales in different formats demanding a substantial amount of time and endeavor to administer the data proficiently. Professionals need constant support for storage of such data to prevent data integrity and accessibility issues (Mittal et al., 2022).

Security Issues in RDM

Since data is a vital asset and is administered appropriately to avoid any data breaches or loss. Security issue includes numerous phases encompassing data collection, processing storing, sharing, communicating, securing, archiving and reusing. Some of the common security issues are:

1. Authentication access

It ensures that only authorized users can access the data by implementing user validation methods such as passwords, biometric authentication to prevent data breaches (Zahid et al., 2023).

2. Data Loss

It refers to the loss of data due to technological obsolescence or improper data curation. Inadequacy in proper backup procedures can result in permanent data loss. Professionals are not well-equipped to avoid cyber attack or phishing attempts which can also result in loss of data (Evering & Brodeur., 2022).

3. Data Integrity

It is important for professionals to ensure the accuracy and reliability of data. They need to be vigilant while collecting, managing and curating data concerning its precision and credibility.

Possible Means Towards Addressing These Issues

Professional training programs concerning RDM activities such as metadata creation, data curation, Information technology tools and equipment, legal and ethical considerations, security and privacy and storage of research data needs to be imparted at different levels.

Robust and extensive RDM laws and policies need to be devised to address privacy concerns of users concerning ethical considerations. (Masinde et al., 2021).

Workshops and seminars engaging professionals towards developing a better understanding about security and privacy concerns in RDM can also help to overcome these issues.

Besides training modules and courses focusing on instructing professionals about RDM and best practices in adressing the challenges associated with RDM. Few such examples include Digital Humanities Data Curation (DHDC),New England Collaborative Data Management Curriculum (NECDMC) and MIT Libraries RDM workshops.

The professionals need to step out of traditional spaces into virtual world to deliver services more efficiently. Since social media increases the visibility of research data and helps to collaborate with others. It makes easy data easily available for professionals to collect and curate because of its increased visibility. Various social media platforms used to find research work and researchers for collaboration are: ResearchGate, ORCID, and Google Scholar. Other social media platforms used for networking, share ideas, information are: Facebook, Twitter, Blogs, LinkedIn.

ResearchGate (RG) for Collaborative Research

Collaboration means sharing responsibilities, risks, rewards, and resources to accomplish shared objectives and improve mutual abilities (Camarinha-Matos & Afsarmanesh, 2008), an opportunity to build new relationships under defined values and vision (Pun & Kubo, P2022). The most important aspect of collaboration is collective agreement on practising choices in practical projects (Griffiths et al. 2021). Research Collaboration is a "social process whereby human beings pool their experience, knowledge, and social skills to produce new knowledge" (Bozeman & Boardman, 2014). Collaborators may include individual researchers, laboratories, groups, departments, institutions, sectors, or countries. In research, multiauthor or multi-address papers are often used to gauge collaboration (Katz & Martin 1997), and the three broad research collaboration patterns in research are project-based, learning-based, and institution-based (Chen 2020). Through research collaboration, academics benefit considerably from sharing skills, experiences and specific expertise (Gorska et al.,2020). Research collaborations thus include sharing ideas, new learning techniques, data collection across a broad spectrum, wide coverage area, sharing of experience, and research funding. These partnerships maximise human resources by combining expertise and abilities(Roberts, Van Wyk, & Dhanpat 2016).

ResearchGate: An Overview

ResearchGate was started as an ASNSs in 2008 to address scientific knowledge creation and sharing concerns. It connects more than 20 million research scholars, scientists, and academicians across 190 countries to collaborate, share their works, and search for answers (ResearchGate, 2023).

RG has 83 Nobel laureates as its members, including all three winners of the 2021 Nobel Prize in Physics, and each day, approximately 6400 new members post their publications, questions, ideas, and collaborations. RG has maintained publisher partnerships with reputed publishers like Springer Nature, Wiley, Rockefeller University Press, and Hindawi since 2019. Through these partnerships, RG has brought millions of Versions of Record directly to the ResearchGate platform with the full knowledge and approval of the original publishers.

RG content partnership ensures adding new articles, making an article base of about 1.3 million with new additions daily. Through its publisher partnership, RG provides access to 2400 Journals, making their content discoverable to the researchers. RG allows its members to add many types of research from different stages of the research cycle, including negative results, datasets, posters, presentations, preprints, accepted manuscripts, and some published articles. Thus, sharing research content, not only in the form of positive outcomes but also negative results, failed experiments, failed applications, or other shortcomings, helps avoid repeating the same mistakes and have expert supervision throughout various stages of the research. The benefits of such networking help them explore the benefits of this platform, leading towards an open, connected, and researcher-centric community.

In 2021, RG started building Publisher Solutions, thus playing a pivotal role in connecting publishers with the research community. Through these collaborations, research data has been shared on a common platform, and publishers have been kept informed, sparing the research scholars from facing legal problems (ResearchGate, 2021).

RG Features and Tools for Research Data Management

Research scholars can create a profile or personal website on Researchgate. Upon registering on the website, each researcher creates a unique profile containing the researcher's contact information, research interests, institutional affinities, accomplishments, and allied information. Data collection and analysis are fundamental to scientific understanding and discovery, two of the central aims in science as RG serve the noble goals of open science in addition to providing a free and open platform for researchers to showcase their work (Ward, Bejarano,& Dudás, 2014). Research-Gate uses a recommendation system to filter information and recommendations for scholars looking to connect with others in similar fields. These connections create meaningful conversations that, in turn, may lead to collaborations. (Rodrigues, Brandão, & Zárate 2018).

Many metric parameters available in RG increase the impact of the research work. RG assists researchers by providing information from harvested databases and other sources, thus helping them develop connections and promote online discussions between authors. RG member benefits include connectivity achieved using the "Following" feature of Researchgate. It allows research scholars to follow other research scholars, groups or activities they are interested in. The research scholars can keep track of all the research initiatives and questions they've been following on ResearchGate.

Another way to connect is by asking questions. A separate 'Questions section' exists where research scholars can pose technical questions or start a discussion. They can answer the questions based on their expertise suggested by the site and keep track of the questions they follow or the ones they ask. In this way, the research scholars can clear doubts regarding their research by posting queries online and finding solutions from experts or people working on the same projects. The discussions help broaden the knowledge on a subject and avoid failures.

Researchers must use the appropriate subheading for presenting their research under the "Research" tab. They can also locate and save the research projects of other researchers in their field or relevant ones. The "Saved List" feature facilitates the creation of a private list of research publications, projects, and debates saved by the scholar. ResearchGate features a semantic search engine to identify research papers that search internal resources and critical external free research databases such as PubMed, CiteSeer, arXiv, and others. Researchers can also request full articles directly from the author. ResearchGate searches the text of the papers a research scholar has uploaded to see who they have cited and those who've cited them across their institution's network, as well as other networks they're following, followers, 'cited by', cites, or top co-authors (ResearchGate, 2023).

The newsfeed presents recommendations based on academic researchers' areas of interest, including recommendations for who to follow, related research papers, and job suggestions. It notifies researchers about activities on the projects they share. They manage messages and respond online and offline by accepting or rejecting requests from other research scholars. The members get in-depth stats about who is reading their research and also track citations. RG contributes to a statistics overview of publications updated by the research scholar under "Stats" and "Scores". Under this feature, the research scholar displays the research interest score, a combination of reads, citations, and recommendations.

RG developed the Research Interest (RI) Score to offer a more intuitive, transparent, robust, and relevant metric. It measures the performance, popularity and scientific impact of a research scholar. This new statistic offers research scholars a clearer idea of other scientists' interest in their research topics. This enables a research scholar to keep track of interest in all their research things in one place and compare their research items to others in their field or year of publication.

The reads are identified based on geographical demography, discipline, institution and seniority. The progress of publications' reach can also be traced graphically by the weekly research report generated by RG. To offer a more comprehensive performance measure for researchers and institutions, RG blends bibliometrics with altimetrics. An autonomous crawling method is used by RG indexing to gather bibliographic information, citations, and other details about academic publications from various sources (Singh, Srichandan, & Lathabai, 2022).

Thus, researcher profiles created on these platforms allow authors to share the bibliographic data of their publications in peer-reviewed journals and their nontraditional scholarly output, such as grey literature, datasets, presentations, and educational materials, including syllabi. The preferred scholarly social media platform among scientists, ResearchGate, is one application that serves the scientific community.

ResearchGate (RG) for Performance Measurement

The proper organisation and communication of research are essential for research scholars' professional and moral growth. ASNSs are helpful tools that guide research scholars in finding the impact of their published work. They can get stats about views, downloads, and citations of research, track times cited counts and h-index, review publication lists, and find impact points (Amees & Singson, 2015). These are the places for scientific presentation, discourse, and academic knowledge transfer where research scholars can add detailed tags for establishing a new collaboration, aggregate content via RSS, collect all the research in a single, searchable interface, get free access to selected journal articles, book chapters, etc., and encourage them to identify quality resources (Haris et al., 2023).

Researchers are thus quickly embracing social media channels like RG to provide broader coverage of research papers from their universities and enhance the impact of their research and the resultant rankings of their institutions (Onyancha, 2015). RG includes provisions for providing information catering to users' areas of interest, including connecting to other researchers and uploading research data and articles. It is becoming a hub for marketing research materials and job advertising (Professor Facebook, 2012).

The study by Lee et al. (2019) explores the motivations behind self-archiving research items on RG and reveals that accessibility was the most highly rated factor, followed by altruism. The other motivating factors include reciprocity, trust, self-efficacy, reputation, and publicity. In their study, Gorska et al. (2020) reveal that the international collaboration of the research teams is positively associated with the presence of the first author on ASNSs like ResearchGate and Academia.edu. Thus significantly raising the personal, professional and social factors, demonstrating that RG motivations for self-archiving could increase or decrease based on several factors.

Research shows that the publication-sharing metric had the highest correlation with the RG score, significantly impacting it. Furthermore, RG metrics also significantly relate to Scopus indicators, with shared publications having the highest correlation compared to other RG metrics. Thus, researchers' participation in the RG effectively increases citations and significantly improves university rankings (Valizadeh-Haghi et al., 2022). RG aims to connect researchers to publicise their work, and studies reveal that RG is dominated by recent articles with about three times as many views as older articles. It also varies in scholarship coverage, with poor representation from the arts and humanities, health, and decision sciences. Thus, view count is evolving as a new audience indicator on RG (Thelwall & Kousha, 2017)

The use of RG for academic exchanges thus is gaining wider acceptance among academics, with features like RG score and RG impact points as potential indicators for universal research performance metrics. Results show a strong correlation between the research grants and RG scores (Kuo et al.,2017). RG employs a comprehensive performance measure, the ResearchGate score, the flagship indicator for measuring scientific reputation through individual researcher performance (Yu et al., 2016). Thus, Scholars use RG to share publications, seek collaboration, communicate work in progress, and build a scholarly reputation.

It realistically showcases the research activity level of institutions resulting from increased research activity of their affiliate RG users, who tend to have higher RG scores, more publications and citations, and more profile views and followers (Yan & Zhang, 2018). The study by Ali et al. (2017) reveals no direct correlation between an institution's ranking and its respective RG score, but lower-ranked institutions can have a lower RG score. Therefore, institutions must strive to lift their rankings through improvised research profiles.

DISCUSSION AND CONCLUSION

Using RG for Research Data Management provides significant advantages, including enhanced collaborations, research visibility and accessibility at the global level. Its members benefit from its features, enabling sharing, discovering, and citing datasets, fostering a more open and interconnected scientific landscape. These features further facilitate collaborations at different levels for efficient RDM and improved research workflow. However, many issues persist as researchers attempt to get involved in RDM practices, including training and institutional support to encourage strong data management practices and open data sharing, data privacy, standardisation of data formats, data security and licensing information. Addressing these issues can ensure the credibility and integrity of shared research. Besides, creating widespread awareness about adopting best practices in RDM using RG will further enhance its effectiveness and usage.

RG, thus, expressly meets research scientists' present and future academic needs through which they communicate their research with colleagues and other experts to advertise and advance their research and keep up with their field's most recent findings. RG's content partnership with publishers ensures content availability from reputed journals. Furthermore, RG ensures access to harvested databases and other sources mapped to researcher profiles. Through features like Stats and Scores, RG also provides an overview of the statistics for publications and enhances research impact.

Despite its emergence as a prominent ASNSs for RDM for collaborating, sharing, and accessing research data sets, there are prominent issues concerning openness, such as data privacy, licensing, security, and standardisation. Besides, focusing on addressing these issues coupled with enhancing the existing capabilities like research workflows, interoperability with existing systems, and harvesting potentialities will result in a more vibrant research ecosystem with user-friendly features. The user experiences can be enriched through extensive training manuals and programs exploring the existing features to their best capabilities. Furthermore, the technological enhancements and evolving new comprehensive metrics for establishing the impact of shared research will further contribute to the success of RG and foster more openness, effectiveness and interconnectivity in the scientific domain, resulting ultimately in quickening scientific discovery and innovation,

Future Research Areas

The present work explores RDM in the context of using ASNSs to create a compelling and robust research ecosystem. However, further research can focus on developing robust frameworks for effective research exchange addressing concerns about research content, ownership and confidentiality. Although there is a lot of research on social networking sites, the potential of academic social networking sites is yet, in part, untapped. Researching the use and effects of academic social networking sites is necessary, as academic social networking sites' ethical, intellectual, and legal ramifications need to be analysed.

Besides, research can be conducted to reveal the researcher's experiences using RG for RDM and identify areas for further improvements. Research focusing on emerging areas such as Artificial Intelligence, Big Data, Linked Data and blockchain and their role in enhancing the efficiency and security of RDM on platforms like RG can add more value to the existing knowledge base. Besides, new frameworks for measuring research impact using these platforms can be designed to develop comprehensive metrics for accessing the impact of shared research data.

REFERENCES

Aguillo Caño, I. F., Uribe Tirado, A., & López López, W. (2017). Visibilidad de los investigadores colombianos según sus indicadores en Google Scholar y ResearchGate. Diferencias y similitudes con la clasificación oficial del sistema nacional de ciencia - COLCIENCIAS. *Revista Interamericana de Bibliotecologia, 40*(3), 221–230. https://doi-org.nassdoceresources.remotexs.in/10.17533/udea.rib.v40n3a03

Ali, M. Y., Wolski, M., & Richardson, J. (2017). Strategies for using ResearchGate to improve institutional research outcomes. *Library Review*, 66(8/9), 726–739. 10.1108/LR-07-2017-0060

Amees, M., & Singson, M. (2015). Faculty contributions and activities on Academic Social Networking Sites: a study onResearchGate. In *Proceedings of National Conference on Future Libraries*. Issues and Challenges. Retrieved from https://www.researchgate.net/profile/Mangkhollen-Singson/publication/284726628_Faculty _contributions_and_activities_on_Academic_Social_Networking_Sites_a_study _on_ResearchGate/links/565830cb08aefe619b208da6/Faculty-contributions-and -activities-on-Academic-Social-Networking-Sites-a-study-on-ResearchGate.pdf

Andrikopoulou, A., Rowley, J., & Walton, G. (2022). Research Data Management (RDM) and the Evolving Identity of Academic Libraries and Librarians: A Literature Review. *New Review of Academic Librarianship*, 28(4), 349–365. 10.1080/13614533.2021.1964549

Anon. (n.d.-a). Data Management & Open Science. *Vrije Universiteit Brussel*. Retrieved December 15, 2023 (https://www.vub.be/en/our-research/our-vision-and -mission/optimal-research-environment/data-management-open-science)

Anon. (n.d.-b). What Is Research Data Management. Retrieved December 15, 2023 (https://datamanagement.hms.harvard.edu/about/what-research-data-management)

Anyim, W. O. (2021). Use of academic social networking sites among lecturers in state universities. *Journal of Media, Culture and Communication, 1*(1), 1-13.

Ashiq, M., Usmani, M. H., & Naeem, M. (2022). A systematic literature review on research data management practices and services. *Global Knowledge. Memory and Communication*, 71(8/9), 649–671. 10.1108/GKMC-07-2020-0103

Asmi, N. A., & Margam, M. (2018). Academic social networking sites for researchers in Central Universities of Delhi: A study of ResearchGate and Academia. Global Knowledge. *Memory and Communication*, 67(1/2), 91–108. 10.1108/ GKMC-01-2017-0004

Barker, P., & Campbell, L. M. (2016). Technology Strategies for Open Educational Resource Dissemination. In *Open Education: International Perspectives in Higher Education* (pp. 51-71). Cambridge, UK: Open Book Publishers. 10.11647/OBP.0103.03

Birkbeck, G., Nagle, T., & Sammon, D. (2022). Challenges in research data management practices: A literature analysis. *Journal of Decision Systems, 31*(sup1), 153-167. 10.1080/12460125.2022.2074653

Bozeman & Boardman. (2014). *Research Collaboration and Team Science: A State-of-the-Art Review and Agenda.* SpringerLink.

Camarinha-Matos & Afsarmanesh. (2008). Concept of Collaboration. Academic Press.

Chawinga, W. D., & Zinn, S. (2021). Research Data Management in Universities: A Comparative Study from the Perspectives of Librarians and Management. *The International Information & Library Review*, 53(2), 97–111. 10.1080/10572317.2020.1793448

Chen, P.-Y. (2020). Academic Social Networks and Collaboration Patterns. *Library Hi Tech*, 38(2), 293–307. 10.1108/LHT-01-2019-0026

Danish National Forum for Research Data Management. (n.d.). The FAIR principles. Retrieved from https://www.howtofair.dk/what-is-fair/

De Regt, H. W. (2020). Understanding, values, and the aims of science. *Philosophy of Science*, 87(5), 921–932. 10.1086/710520

Echeburúa, E. (2013). Overuse of social networking. In Miller, P. M. (Ed.), *Principles of Addiction* (pp. 911–920). Academic Press. 10.1016/B978-0-12-398336-7.00092-9

Evering, D., Pratt, I., & Brodeur, J. J. (2022). The current state of research data management (RDM) at McMaster. Academic Press.

Facebook, P. (2012). *Economist*, 402(8771), 80.

Gorska, A., Korzynski, P., Mazurek, G., & Pucciarelli, F. (2020). The role of social media in scholarly collaboration: An enabler of international research team's activation? *Journal of Global Information Technology Management*, 23(4), 273–291. 10.1080/1097198X.2020.1817684

Griffiths, A.-J., Alsip, J., Hart, S. R., Round, R. L., & Brady, J. (2021). Together We Can Do So Much: A Systematic Review and Conceptual Framework of Collaboration in Schools. *Canadian Journal of School Psychology*, 36(1), 59–85. 10.1177/0829573520915368

Hailu, M., & Wu, J. (2021). The use of academic social networking sites in scholarly communication: Scoping review. *Data and Information Management*, 5(2), 277–298. 10.2478/dim-2020-0050

Hamad, F., Al-Fadel, M., & Al-Soub, A. (2021). Awareness of Research Data Management Services at Academic Libraries in Jordan: Roles, Responsibilities and Challenges. *New Review of Academic Librarianship*, 27(1), 76–96. 10.1080/13614533.2019.1691027

Haris, M., Ali, N., & Vaidya, P. (2023). Assessment of ResearchGate to Unfurl the Academic Pursuits of Physics Scholars. *Journal of Scientometric Research*, 12(2), 490–500. 10.5530/jscires.12.2.045

Heuer, A. (2020). Research data management. *Information Technology, 62*(1), 1-5. 10.1515/itit-2020-0002

Ivey, S., Lafferty-Hess, S., Ossom-Williamson, P., & Barrick, K. (2023, January 1). Managing, sharing, and publishing data. http://hdl.handle.net/2451/69653

Jeng, W., DesAutels, S., He, D., & Li, L. (2017). Information exchange on an academic social networking site: A multidiscipline comparison on researchgate Q&A. *Journal of the Association for Information Science and Technology*, 68(3), 638–652. 10.1002/asi.23692

Jones, S., Pergl, R., Hooft, R., Miksa, T., Samors, R., Ungvari, J., Davis, R. I., & Lee, T. (2020). Data Management Planning: How Requirements and Solutions are Beginning to Converge. *Data Intelligence*, 2(1–2), 208–219. 10.1162/dint_a_00043

Kaari, J. (2020). Researchers at Arab Universities Hold Positive Views on Research Data Management and Data Sharing. *Evidence Based Library and Information Practice*, 15(2), 168–170. 10.18438/eblip29746

Katz, J. S., & Martin, B. R. (1997). What Is Research Collaboration? *Research Policy*, 26(1), 1–18. 10.1016/S0048-7333(96)00917-1

Kinde, A. A., Addis, A. C., & Abebe, G. G. (2021). Research data management practice in higher education institutions in Ethiopia. *Public Services Quarterly*, 17(4), 213–230. 10.1080/15228959.2021.1879707

Kothari, C. R. (2004). *Research Methodology: Methods and Techniques*. New Age International.

Kuo, T., Tsai, G. Y., Jim Wu, Y.-C., & Alhalabi, W. (2017). From sociability to creditability for academics. *Computers in Human Behavior*, 75, 975–984. 10.1016/j.chb.2016.07.044

Lee, J., Oh, S., Dong, H., Wang, F., & Burnett, G. (2019). Motivations for self-archiving on an academic social networking site: A study on researchgate. *Journal of the Association for Information Science and Technology*, 70(6), 563–574. 10.1002/asi.24138

Leonelli, S. (2020). Scientific research and big data. Retrieved from https://plato .stanford.edu/entries/science-big-data/?ref=hackernoon.com

Liu, X., & Ding, N. (2016). Research data management in universities of central China. *The Electronic Library*, 34(5), 808–822. 10.1108/EL-04-2015-0063

Majhi, S., Sahu, L., & Behera, K. (2023). Practices for enhancing research visibility, citations and impact: Review of literature. *Aslib Journal of Information Management*, 75(6), 1280–1305. 10.1108/AJIM-11-2023-532

Majumdar, S. (2022). Studies on the use of academic social networking sites by academics and researchers: A review. *Annals of Library and Information Studies*, 69(2), 158–168. 10.56042/alis.v69i2.61141

Masinde, J., Chen, J., Wambiri, D., & Mumo, A. (2021). Research librarians' experiences of research data management activities at an academic library in a developing country. *Data and Information Management*, 5(4), 412–424. 10.2478/dim-2021-0002

Merriam-Webster. (2024, May 21). Social media. In Merriam-Webster.com dictionary. Retrieved from https://www.merriam-webster.com/dictionary/social%20media

Mittal, D., Mease, R., Kuner, T., Flor, H., Kuner, R., & Andoh, J. (2022). Data management strategy for a collaborative research center. *GigaScience*, 12, giad049. Advance online publication. 10.1093/gigascience/giad04937401720

Nández, G., & Borrego, Á. (2013). Use of social networks for academic purposes: A case study. *The Electronic Library*, 31(6), 781–791. 10.1108/EL-03-2012-0031

National Library of Medicine. (n.d.). Research Data Management. Retrieved from https://www.nnlm.gov/guides/data-glossary/research-data-management

Naushad Ali, P. M., Zehra, S., Vaidya, P., & Mohsin, S. M. (2022). Role of Academic Social Networking Sites in Knowledge Sharing and Research Collaboration among Research Scholars. *DESIDOC Journal of Library and Information Technology*, 42(5), 309–317. Advance online publication. 10.14429/djlit.42.5.18239

Netscher, S., & Katsanidou, A. (2020). Understanding and Implementing Research Data Management. In Wagemann, C., Goerres, A., & Siewert, M. B. (Eds.), *Handbuch Methoden der Politikwissenschaft* (pp. 79–96). Springer VS. 10.1007/978-3-658-16936-7_4

Onyancha, O. B. (2015). Social media and research: An assessment of the coverage of South African universities in ResearchGate, Web of Science and the Webometrics Ranking of World Universities. *South African Journal of Library and Information Science*, 81(1), 8–20. 10.7553/81-1-1540

Patel, D. (2016). Research data management: A conceptual framework. *Library Review*, 65(4/5), 226–241. 10.1108/LR-01-2016-0001

Perrier, L., Blondal, E., Ayala, A. P., Dearborn, D., Kenny, T., Lightfoot, D., Reka, R., Thuna, M., Trimble, L., & MacDonald, H. (2017). Research data management in academic institutions: A scoping review. *PLoS One*, 12(5), e0178261. 10.1371/journal.pone.017826128542450

Pun, R., & Kubo, H. (2022). What Collaboration Means to Us: Advancing Equity, Diversity, and Inclusion Initiatives in the Library Profession. *Collaborative Librarianship, 13*(1), 2. Retrieved from https://digitalcommons.du.edu/collaborativelibrarianship/vol13/iss1/2/

Raffaghelli, J. E., & Manca, S. (2023). Exploring the social activity of open research data on ResearchGate: Implications for the data literacy of researchers. *Online Information Review*, 47(1), 197–217. 10.1108/OIR-05-2021-0255

ResearchGate. (2021). Progress Report 2021. Retrieved from https://www.researchgate.net/progress-report-2021/publisher-solutions

ResearchGate. (2023). About ResearchGate. Retrieved from https://www.researchgate.net/about

Roberts, Van Wyk, & Dhanpat. (2016). *Exploring practices for effective collaboration*. Academic Press.

Rodrigues, Brandão, & Zárate. (2018). Recommending Scientific Collaboration from ResearchGate. Academic Press.

Sanjeeva. (2018). *Research data management: A new role for academic/research librarians*. Academic Press.

Singh, A. (2021). Basic Steps of Doing Research. SSRN *Electronic Journal*. 10.2139/ssrn.3925363

Singh, V. K., Srichandan, S. S., & Lathabai, H. H. (2022). ResearchGate and Google Scholar: How Much Do They Differ in Publications, Citations and Different Metrics and Why? *Scientometrics*, 127(3), 1515–1542. 10.1007/s11192-022-04264-2

Tang, R., & Hu, Z. (2019). Providing Research Data Management (RDM) Services in Libraries: Preparedness, Roles, Challenges, and Training for RDM Practice. *Data and Information Management*, 3(2), 84–101. 10.2478/dim-2019-0009

Tartari, E. (2015). *The Use of Social Media for Academic Purposes in Student' Learning Process*. Academic Journal of Interdisciplinary Studies. 10.5901/ajis.2015.v4n2p393

Thelwall, M., & Kousha, K. (2017). ResearchGate articles: Age, discipline, audience size, and impact. *Journal of the Association for Information Science and Technology*, 68(2), 468–479. 10.1002/asi.23675

University of Reading. (n.d.). Open and FAIR data. Retrieved from https://www.reading.ac.uk/research-services/research-data-management/preserving-and-sharing-data/open-and-fair-data

University of Toronto Libraries. (2024). Academic Social Networks. Retrieved from https://guides.library.utoronto.ca/researchimpact/networks#:~:text=Academic%20Social%20Networks%20(ASNs)%20are,are%20typically%20free%20to%20use

Valizadeh-Haghi, S., Nasibi-Sis, H., Shekofteh, M., & Rahmatizadeh, S. (2022). ResearchGate Metrics' Behavior and Its Correlation with RG Score and Scopus Indicators: A Combination of Bibliometric and Altmetric Analysis of Scholars in Medical Sciences. *Information Technology and Libraries*, 41(1), 1–12. 10.6017/ital.v41i1.14033

Wang, H., Fu, T., Du, Y., Gao, W., Huang, K., Liu, Z., Chandak, P., Liu, S., Van Katwyk, P., Deac, A., Anandkumar, A., Bergen, K., Gomes, C. P., Ho, S., Kohli, P., Lasenby, J., Leskovec, J., Liu, T.-Y., Manrai, A., & Zitnik, M. (2023). Scientific discovery in the age of artificial intelligence. *Nature*, 620(7972), 47–60. 10.1038/s41586-023-06221-237532811

Ward, J. H., Bejarano, W., & Haggis, W. (2015). "Open during renovation": Open science and libraries. Substance Abuse Library and Information Studies, 2, 82-89. DOI: https://doi.org/10.7282/T3TM7DGN

Whyte, A., & Tedds, J. (2011). Making the case for research data management. DCC Briefing Papers. Digital Curation Centre. Retrieved from https://www.dcc.ac.uk/resources/briefing-papers

Williams, A. E., & Woodacre, M. A. (2016). The possibilities and perils of academic social networking sites. *Online Information Review*, 40(2), 282–294. 10.1108/OIR-10-2015-0327

Wittman, J. T., & Aukema, B. H. (2020). A Guide and Toolbox to Replicability and Open Science in Entomology. *Journal of Insect Science*, 20(3), 6. 10.1093/jisesa/ieaa03632441307

Wu, S., Stvilia, B., & Lee, D. J. (2016). Exploring researchers' participation in online research identity management systems. *Proceedings of the Association for Information Science and Technology*, 53(1), 1–6. 10.1002/pra2.2016.14505301105

Wu, S., Stvilia, B., & Lee, D. J. (2017). Readers, Personal Record Managers, and Community Members: An Exploratory Study of Researchers' Participation in Online Research Information Management Systems. *Journal of Library Metadata*, 17(2), 57–90. 10.1080/19386389.2017.1348783

Xu, Z. (2022). Research Data Management Training in Academic Libraries: A Scoping Review. *Journal of Librarianship and Scholarly Communication*, 10(1). Advance online publication. 10.31274/jlsc.13700

Yan, W., & Zhang, Y. (2018). Research universities on the ResearchGate social networking site: An examination of institutional differences, research activity level, and social networks formed. *Journal of Informetrics*, 12(1), 385–400. 10.1016/j.joi.2017.08.002

Yu, M.-C., Wu, Y.-C. J., Alhalabi, W., Kao, H.-Y., & Wu, W.-H. (2016). Research-Gate: An effective altmetric indicator for active researchers? *Computers in Human Behavior*, 55, 1001–1006. 10.1016/j.chb.2015.11.007

Yu, M.-C., Wu, Y.-C. J., Alhalabi, W., Kao, H.-Y., & Wu, W.-H. (2016). Research-Gate: An Effective Altmetric Indicator for Active Researchers? *Computers in Human Behavior*, 55, 1001–1006. 10.1016/j.chb.2015.11.007

Zahid, R., Altaf, A., Ahmad, T., Iqbal, F., Vera, Y. A. M., Flores, M. A. L., & Ashraf, I. (2023). Secure data management life cycle for government big-data ecosystem: Design and development perspective. *Systems*, 11(8), 380. 10.3390/systems11080380

ADDITIONAL READING

Afolabi, I. T., Ayo, A., & Odetunmibi, O. A. (2021). Academic collaboration recommendation for computer science researchers using social network analysis. *Wireless Personal Communications*, 121(1), 487–501. 10.1007/s11277-021-08646-2

Bullinger, A. C., Hallerstede, S. H., Renken, U., Soeldner, J. H., & Moeslein, K. M. (2010). Towards research collaboration–a taxonomy of social research network sites.Retrieved from https://aisel.aisnet.org/amcis2010/92

Hemphill, L., Hedstrom, M. L., & Leonard, S. H. (2021). Saving social media data: Understanding data management practices among social media researchers and their implications for archives. *Journal of the Association for Information Science and Technology*, 72(1), 97–109. 10.1002/asi.24368

Hoang, D. T., Nguyen, N. T., Tran, V. C., & Hwang, D. (2019). Research collaboration model in academic social networks. *Enterprise Information Systems*, 13(7-8), 1023–1045. 10.1080/17517575.2018.1556812

Palsdottir, A. (2021). Data literacy and management of research data–a prerequisite for the sharing of research data. *Aslib Journal of Information Management*, 73(2), 322–341. 10.1108/AJIM-04-2020-0110

Rafiq, M., & Ameen, K. (2022). Research data management and sharing awareness, attitude, and behavior of academic researchers. *Information Development*, 38(3), 391–405. 10.1177/02666669211048491

KEY TERMS AND DEFINITIONS

Academic Social Networks (ASNs): are similar to social networking sites, but designed for the academic community. These online platforms allow you to develop a profile and connect with other researchers, while also allowing you to share academic related content (University of Toronto Libraries,2024).

Data Repository: "A data repository is a service that exists to preserve and provide access to research data. It is a future-proof vehicle that ensures data remains accessible and usable over the long term" (University of Reading,n.d).

FAIR principles: "The FAIR principles, first published in 2016, contain guidelines for good data management practice that aims at making data FAIR: findable, accessible, interoperable, and reusable" (Danish National Forum for Research Data Management,n.d.).

Repository: "Any service hosting a collection of resources, especially one organised thematically and facilitates resource discovery through structured resource descriptions. For making resources available, repositories may disseminate resource descriptions in machine-readable formats" (Barker & Campbell, 2016).

Research Data Management: "Research data management is the organisation, documentation, storage, and preservation of the data resulting from the research process, where data can be broadly defined as the outcome of experiments or observations that validate research findings and can take a variety of forms including numerical output (quantitative data), qualitative data, documentation, images, audio, and video" (National Library of Medicine,n.d.).

Social Media: "forms of electronic communication (such as websites for social networking and microblogging) through which users create online communities to share information, ideas, personal messages, and other content (such as videos)" (Merriam-Webster,2024).

Social Networking Sites: A social networking site is an online place where a user can create a profile and build a personal network that connects him/her to other users. (Echeburúa, 2013).

Chapter 9
Virtual Communities of Practice as Mentoring Tools in Health Professions Education and Practice

Vistolina Nuuyoma
https://orcid.org/0000-0002-5744-1355
University of Namibia, Namibia

ABSTRACT

Virtual communities of practice refer to people who form a group that meets virtually through online platforms. The purpose of the meeting is to share expertise, passion, interests, and that translates into an independent society. The concept of virtual communities of practice is derived from communities of practice, which is a term coined by Jean Lave and Etienne Wenger in the early 1990s and is underpinned by the theory of situated learning. Other theoretical and philosophical underpinnings of virtual communities of practices and mentoring are Vygotsky's sociocultural theory of human learning, legitimate peripheral participation, zone of proximal development, and scaffolding. Although there are benefits offered by virtual communities of practice, literature seems to be limited to how they are used as tools for sharing information and improving practices. Owing to that, this chapter describes how virtual communities of practices may be used as mentoring tools in health professions education and practice.

DOI: 10.4018/979-8-3693-1111-0.ch009

INTRODUCTION

The ability to communicate effectively is one of the social competencies that are becoming increasingly significant in contemporary professional environments, including healthcare settings (Skarbalienė et al., 2019). Moreover, communication is one of the generic competencies required for collaboration, problem-solving, and social interaction among health professionals (Pramila-Savukoski et al., 2024). This implies that communication is at the heart of all healthcare interventions, and alongside teamwork, it is required for high-quality healthcare (Dietl et al., 2023). Ineffective communication in healthcare settings has consequences such as inappropriate use of valuable resources, discontinuity of care, compromise of patient safety, dissatisfaction in patients and overworked professionals (Vermeir et al., 2015). This calls for health professionals to continue learning through regular interactions with others, attend formal and informal training, and learn by being part of multidisciplinary communities found in healthcare settings. On the other hand, the transformation of health systems that occurred as an adaptive response to disruption in health professions education during the COVID-19 pandemic emphasized more professionals to undertake an "education for life" approach (Frenk et al., 2022). This requires professionals to be learning throughout life, learning new ways to live their own lives, promote and restore healthy life. These may be better achieved through forming communities of learning with other professionals.

This chapter aims to explore the concept of virtual communities of practice (VCoP), and its philosophical and theoretical underpinnings. The concept of VCoP is derived from communities of practice (CoP), which is a term coined by Jean Lave and Etienne Wenger in the early 1990s, through the theory of situated learning. Therefore, situated learning theory, which is under the umbrella of constructivism will be discussed as one of the theoretical and philosophical underpinnings in this chapter. The main section of this chapter will help readers understand fundamental aspects and different forms of VCoP that are broadly used in healthcare settings and/ or in health professions education and practices, and their relationship to aspects of mentoring/mentorship. In addition, it will analyze the benefits, facilitators, and barriers of VCoP. Due to technological advancement in the health professions' education and practices, there will be tips and strategies on how virtual communities of practice may be utilized as mentoring tools in healthcare settings. This will equip mentors and mentees with knowledge and skills as well as come up with workable plans with possible solutions to common barriers or hindrances to virtual mentoring in a VCoP. As implications to the field of health professions education and practice, this chapter may be used as a framework or an agenda that may be adopted in mentoring novice professionals who are placed in remote, under-served and far to reach area, where suitable mentors are not available locally for in-person mentoring endeavours.

Lastly, this chapter included recommendations and suggestions for future research to advance knowledge and skills on how mentoring can be done virtually using VCoP.

Chapter Objectives

After you have worked with this chapter, you should be able to;

- Define virtual communities of practice.
- Understand the theoretical and philosophical underpinning of virtual communities of practice.
- Analyze the benefits, facilitators, and barriers of virtual communities of practice.
- Discover how virtual communities of practice may be utilized as mentoring tools in health professions education and practice.

BACKGROUND

Health professions education and practice have recognised the need for interprofessional learning environments and collaborative practices. However, this requires formal and informal structures to be put in place for continuous interaction and engagement among health professionals. One such engagement is the use of communities of practices, which may be done through face-to-face interactions, and or via virtual and online platforms. The latter is known as virtual communities of practice. Due to the benefits and affordances of many platforms used in VCoP, it is suitable to use as a mentoring tool in health professions education and practice.

Development and gaining independence of individuals, in both aspects of life, including academic, emotional, social, and organizational, requires the cooperation of several actors (Ziegler et al., 2021). This implies that self-development is not autocatalytic because it does not occur by itself. Therefore, requires mentoring. Moreover, adult learners have an increased demand to understand the expectations of an educational process. This should be fulfilled in a safe and stress-free environment which provides positive feedback, reward, encouragement, and the creation of a sense of belonging in a team (Koutsoukos et al., 2020). Health professionals are adult learners who should be assisted to achieve this through the act of mentoring. With this background, the overarching aim of this chapter is to conceptualize and analyse how virtual communities of practice may be used as mentoring tools in health professions education and practice.

THE MAIN FOCUS OF THE CHAPTER

As a main focus of this chapter, this section is divided into four sections, namely; understanding virtual communities of practice, its theoretical and philosophical underpinnings; benefits, facilitators, and barriers of virtual communities of practice in health professions education and practice; understanding mentoring, its theoretical and philosophical underpinnings; and use of communities of practice as mentoring tools in health professions education and practice. The literature used in this chapter was searched with various search engines and was discussed with consideration of the author's personal experiences and opinions.

Understanding Virtual Communities of Practice, Its Theoretical and Philosophical Underpinnings

Virtual communities of practice (VCoP) refer to people who form a group that meets virtually through online platforms. People meet to share expertise, passion, interests, and that translates into an independent society (Ghamrawi, 2022). The concept of VCoP is derived from communities of practice (CoP), which is a term coined by Jean Lave and Etienne Wenger in the early 1990s, through the theory of situated learning. Lave and Wenger defined CoP as groups of people who share passion or concerns over something they do and learn how to do it better through regular interactions (Wenger, 1998). This implies that there should be an interest in a common practice to qualify as a community (Ranmuthugala et al., 2011).

The concept of CoP can be applied in organizations, education, government, associations, the web, and social sectors. Although CoP has been widely used in business and education sectors, its use in healthcare settings is generally described to be associated with inconsistent structures and has been limited. Despite that, the healthcare setting is one sector that may get advantages from the CoP approach. Forming CoP may occur naturally in a healthcare setting owing to the fact that professions such as nursing and medicine function as a network and are connected by referral pathways (Mcalpine et al., 2023). Moreover, the use of CoP in health professions practice and education is greatly supported because these individuals provide a suitable, safe, and supported learning environment. Peer-to-peer relationships in both professional and social aspects are promoted due to the sense of support among peers (Terry et al., 2020). Generally, CoPs are established in healthcare settings for learning, exchange of knowledge and information, and also for sharing and promoting evidence-based practice (Ranmuthugala et al., 2011).

While CoP is a multifaceted program operated using different models, which are complex (Ranmuthugala et al., 2011), Wenger, (1998) indicated that CoP consists of four components. The four components are practice, community, meaning and identity. Practice implies that members of the group learn by doing, for example in healthcare settings, they learn through performance of skills and role-modelling. Community denotes learning through belongingness and interactions with other members of the group. For example, health professionals become part of an inter-professional or multidisciplinary team where members interact with one another. Meaning refers to learning by experience which takes place in the social environment as well as interaction with the group. In healthcare settings, interaction with other members of the team enriches both work and social experiences which have a positive impact on professional growth. Identity denotes learning by becoming, in the process of learning, members share and adopt social identity. Health professionals learn by becoming part of the team, embracing shared identity, and forming a sub-culture within wider society.

Moreover, in their first publication, Wenger and Lave explained that CoP is identified by three aspects, which are; the domain, the community and the practice (Lave & Wenger, 1991). The domain signifies a shared area of interest among members. In a CoP, the domain acts as an area of members' overlapping expertise, which acts as an initial and a pulling unifying factor for individuals who might want to join the group. This can be individuals who interact daily or otherwise can be those who work in separate organizational units, disciplines, or locations (Bentley et al., 2010). For example, in healthcare settings, members can have daily inter-actions through patient care, or professionals from separate healthcare facilities, disciplines or from different countries, and cities. The community is represented by interactions among the CoP members. The practice is a shared profession that members pursue to develop further through participation in the CoP. To strengthen practice, membership in CoP is multilayered and this is due to inevitable variances in individual abilities, needs, and willingness to devote their time to the negotiation of practice with other members in the community (Pyrko, 2019). As one of the primary endeavours of CoP, the learning process takes place through regularly thinking together with members about real-life problems or hot topics, and unitedly finding solutions to them (Pyrko, 2019).

In their critique of the evolution of the CoP concept, Li et al., (2009) revealed that CoP groups are associated with four characteristics, which are also known as essential characteristics of CoP. These are;

* members interaction with each other in formal and informal settings
* sharing of knowledge among members
* collaboration among members for new knowledge creation
* development of a shared identity is fostered among members of the CoP group.

CoP, which is a precursor of VCoP is underpinned by situated learning theory as its theoretical and philosophical basis (Fig 1). Situated learning theory embraces delivering knowledge in an authentic context. This implies that learners should be involved in authentic settings of daily practice for knowledge application (Hajah et al., 2018). For example, for health professionals, authentic settings are hospitals, clinics, health centres, and community-based organizations where the actual practice of health care service provision occurs. Situated Learning is a particular form of learning in which the learning environment is "situated" in a specific context (Gonen et al., 2016). It is principally a social-cultural process, which usually requires collaboration and social interaction within the "community of practice". Situated learning postulates learning as a process which entails collaborative participation within context. Collaboration and interaction emphasized in situated learning theory is in line with Vygotsky's sociocultural learning theory which postulates that social interaction is central to cognitive development, which is required for learning (Moore, 2011). Vygotsky's theory argues that cognitive abilities are socially constructed and guided. Therefore, interaction with others in social-cultural contexts facilitates the growth and development of specific capabilities, problem-solving, memory, attention and learning in general. Vygotsky's sociocultural learning theory promotes the notion of "zone of proximal development" (ZPD) as one of its constructs. ZPD is defined as the learner's actual level of development and the next level attainable through the use of capable adults, mediation, environmental tools, mediation, and peer facilitation (Vygotsky, 1978). ZPD can be promoted via collaboration and interaction with others within a learning community. This is because individuals learn better when working together with others, and that is through such collaborative efforts where internalization of new concepts occurs and skills are developed (Shabani et al., 2010).

Learning is not seen as an individual endeavour which can be solely situated in an individual's mind, environmental issues also have influence (Zakrajsek & Schuster, 2018). Therefore, the situated learning theory has three fundamental elements, which are the context, participation of a learner, and community of practice (Lave & Wanger, 1991). Due to interactions that occur in situated learning through communities of practice, Lave and Wenger (1991) described this process as legitimate peripheral participation. Legitimate peripheral participation is conceptualized as a process through which an individual becomes a member of a CoP and eventually transitions from being a marginal practitioner to a central practitioner (Woo, 2015). This explains the process of how newcomers to the CoP become a full part of the community. Legitimate peripheral participation is a vital process in CoP as it facilitates growth and sustains the community. However, for smooth legitimate peripheral participation to occur in a CoP, unequal power relations should be identified between individuals, and how such obstacles impact on individuals' opportunities to learn and become central practitioners or members. For learning to be successful in CoP, new members should progressively adopt the identity of a full member (Grosik & Kanno, 2021), by becoming central members.

Situated learning theory has been adopted in various fields of study and professional disciplines. In health professions education, the emphasis is on clinical practice or placements which is done to bridge the gap between theory and practice. This is because situated learning supports apprenticeship and practical learning. Learning is contextually bound, meaning it does not simply entail gaining decontextualized knowledge and skills but is linked to context and participation in a community (Grosik & Kanno, 2021). Moreover, understanding the origin of knowledge requires people to immerse themselves in a context where knowledge is originally generated (Chang, 2021). In the case of health professions education, knowledge originates in clinical practice and, therefore provides an environment where learning should take place, which defines situated learning. Other contexts where situated learning is displayed in health professions education are online and e-learning environments, interprofessional education, peer and professional groups and societies, live or virtual simulation and environments (O'Brien & Battista, 2020).

Situated learning has the potential to integrate current and future developments as well as wider applications of innovative clinical skills and education initiatives in health professions education and practice. This is because it provides genuine context that promotes reflections, authentic experiences, and encounters with experts in clinical settings. Moreover, it allows for learning from multiple settings and has great support for collaborative learning and coaching of learners (Gonen et al., 2016). Those are some characteristics of VCoP because situated learning provides its theoretical basis and its philosophical underpinning. Learning from notions of Vygotsky's sociocultural theory, situated learning theory, communities of practice, and legitimate peripheral participation, there is great potential for communities of people who already have contact with each other, either face-to-face or virtually to form a VCoP. This is because people in the community already have common interests, they learn in the same social, cultural, and sometimes physical context. What they need is regular contacts to share knowledge, and skills and create virtual platforms to be used for regular meetings. The theoretical and philosophical assumptions that underpin VCoP are displayed in Figure 1.

Figure 1. Theoretical and Philosophical Underpinnings of VCoP

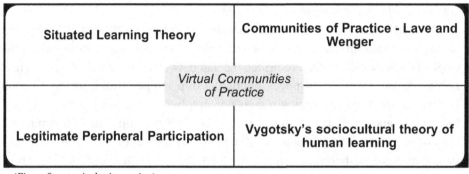

(Figure Source: Author's creation)

There is great growth in the use of VCoP among professionals in various disciplines who use online platforms to share knowledge and impact on their members' practice in the physical world (Qutab et al., 2022), including health professionals. This could be due to advancements in digital technologies and artificial intelligence that facilitate virtual communication. Due to the manner of interactions in VCoP, they are also known as networks of practice. The benefits, facilitators, and barriers of VCoP are described in the following section.

Benefits, Facilitators, and Barriers of Virtual Communities of Practice in Health Professions Education and Practice

Healthcare sectors experience challenges such as shortage of personnel, dissatisfied personnel, unmet patients' needs, and lack of coordination between different units. At times, new technologies and innovations are introduced but they take longer time to be fully implemented (Vaisshalli et al., 2022). In some healthcare settings, tasks and duties at hand do not match the number and skills of personnel available, and working conditions are unfavourable, worsened by poor recognition and support from supervisors. Communities served by health professionals have unrealistic expectations, and professionals feel this has a negative impact on their work, socioeconomic status and private life (Jaeger et al., 2018). For health professionals to find solutions to challenges experienced in healthcare settings, there is a need for harmony through learning communities.

VCoP may help to change the nature of individualized and isolated learning to incline to a more connected and collaborative culture (Ranmuthugala et al., 2011). Therefore, facilitating collaborative clinical practice is ideal for an interprofessional team. It should be noted that most VCoPs are formed to facilitate professional knowledge sharing, smoothen communication, and advance the implementation of evidence-based practices among professionals and in geographically dispersed communities (Shaw et al., 2022). Due to the use of technology and web-based applications, VCoP facilitates communication and rapid sharing of documents (Valenti & Sutton, 2020). It is known that professional groups are prone to contextual gaps commonly due to age, gender, and occupation differences. VCoP is likely to narrow these contextual gaps (Gammelgaard, 2010). Moreover, joining of, and engagement in VCoP may reduce structural and professional isolation (Barnett et al., 2012).

On the other hand, the use of VCoP surrogates interdisciplinary dialogue, and this could be because members join online platforms from their comfort zones, not in-person attendance and therefore may feel less intimidated (Yang, 2020). VCoP is one of the effective knowledge management initiatives that can be used by health professionals and researchers to improve the quality of healthcare services. This is due to perceived usefulness, satisfaction with the systems used and quality of knowledge shared via VCoP (Alali & Salim, 2013). It should be noted that informal and loosely structured VCoP are deemed more suitable for many practitioners due to full-time work (Valenti & Sutton, 2020). Owing to the collaborative nature of VCoP, such platforms promote collaborative learning. This has advantages as it creates synergy in a way that the impact and output of activities are greatly influential in comparison to individualized initiatives. VCoP also has benefits in supporting the retrieval of information and processes due to better coordination of knowledge (Gammelgaard, 2010). Additionally, VCoP has advantages in a way that it allows health professionals to motivate for resources needed by their patients, interact, share tips and demonstrations, exchange experiences, and reflect on their clinical practice (Bermejo-Caja et al., 2019).

A variety of VCoP forms are used in healthcare settings, which allow members to engage in either synchronous or asynchronous platforms. A scoping review by Shaw et al., (2022) revealed virtual platforms used for VCoP are live online discussions for hot topics and case-based discussion platforms for different forum posts, case studies, and clinical questions. There is the provision of web-based resources, online meetings, emails with news, updates and notifications, provision of recorded meetings, live presentations on YouTube videos and Webinars, blog posts, implementation registry. Tele-mentoring, guest speakers and clinical expert speech on podcasts are also considered as VCoP in healthcare settings. Struminger et al., (2017) reported there is a non-profit project in the name of Extension for Community Healthcare Outcomes (ECHO), which is an example of a VCoP used on six continents, covering more than 23 countries. This health professions education and care management collaborative initiative brings together international, regional, and local specialists, and interprofessional teams from rural and underserved communities to virtual learn and form a case-based community of practice (Struminger et al., 2017). Owing to that VCoP provide a platform for health professionals to update their knowledge and skills on updated guidelines, and care practices, and share best practices, and innovative ways in post-and undergraduate training, this brings improvement in health professions education and practices. Improvement in care practices may result in a reduced number of deaths and admissions due to a specific disease and reduced maternal and child mortality rates. At the same time, improved education practices result in competent graduates who are innovative and critical thinkers.

While there are benefits and facilitators of VCoP as outlined in the previous paragraph, numerous VCoP do not succeed due to the lack of engagement of collaborators or members of the community (Haas et al., 2021). In their paper on strengthening VCoP as an evidence-based approach, Valenti and Sutton, (2020) have identified three major challenges associated with VCoP, these are lack of access to systems, lack of structure and contracts, and lack of full-time faculty participation. Issues related to concerns for privacy, lack of trust, lack of motivation and, encouragement, and technology-related issues are reported to be barriers and challenges associated with VCoP in interprofessional collaboration and education (McLoughlin et al., 2018). Moreover, even though the use of unfamiliar language can be challenging to new members joining the groups, the use of 'community slang' suggests that a concession of meaning processes has taken place within the VCoP (Gammelgaard, 2010). This is a good indicator of synergy and collaborative learning among group members.

In their study on the acceptability and feasibility of a VCoP to primary care professionals, Bermejo-Caja et al., (2019), revealed barriers to the use of VCoP. This encompasses technological difficulties associated with the use of inappropriate or/ outdated hardware and software which may restrict and hinder participation as well as accessibility to the VCoP platforms. Due to the use of resources and documents in non-native languages, it poses difficulty for some members to understand information. The time restrictions in work environments can limit access to a VCoP. Practitioners usually have no time to access VCoP platforms while in the work environment, at the same time, it is not easy to access from the home environment (Bermejo-Caja et al., 2019). As a supportive intervention, technologies may support these difficulties by giving people options of asynchronous platforms to participate in group discussion forums at their convenience or avail recordings from live sessions.

Another gap identified in the VCoP arena is on evaluation of its activities and processes. This is because many VCoPs are complex, and have multifaceted structures, which may be wrongly interpreted when observed from different points of view (da Silva et al., 2020). On the other hand, when evaluation of VCoP's activities and processes is conducted, feedback is not directed to an individual or specific people, making it difficult to implement what is suggested. To bridge the gap, members of the VCoP should be allowed to evaluate one activity at a time, instead of waiting to evaluate after a longer period or after several activities. For example, professional organizations that offer continuous professional development activities evaluate at the end of sessions for feedback to be directed to the facilitators and organizers. Most professional organizations should use evaluation tools that are simple and with easy-to-follow instructions. For example, using online tools with functionalities to summarize responses.

Understanding Mentoring, Its Theoretical and Philosophical Underpinnings

Mentoring is a personal development learning tool which denotes the relationship between two people who are in any way not linked within a line management structure (Dowling et al., 2018). In mentorship, there is a mentor and a mentee. The mentor is usually an experienced person, who guides a mentee to develop skills and knowledge for professional advancement. Therefore, the focus is on mutually agreed goals which are related to a career plan. To emphasize its importance, mentoring is one of the approaches required to strengthen health systems (Manzi et al., 2017). This is because it has the potential to be beneficial as a clinical training, and a development strategy for health personnel (Schwerdtle et al., 2017). A more formal mentorship, which is usually a work-related requirement, goes through stages of initiation, cultivation, transition, and redefinition. It also involves the signing of a contract with mutual goals, and expectations, handling confidentiality issues, boundaries, formal regular meeting schedules and reporting (Hill et al., 2022). Informal mentorship starts with a mentee recognizing their readiness to learn, identifying the need to seek a mentor and thus type of mentoring they need to seek (Klinge, 2015). For example, in higher education institution settings, there are two broad categories of mentoring, which are career and psychosocial mentoring (Anafarta & Apaydin, 2016). Career mentoring involves offering opportunities for professional visibility, exposure, protection, coaching, and giving challenging assignments. Psychosocial mentoring encompasses role modelling, counselling, friendship, acceptance, and confirmation.

Although mentorship is required for professional growth, not all professionals may act as good mentors. Effective mentors are characterized by being available, approachable, supportive, experienced, trustworthy, active listeners, enthusiastic, encouraging, collaborative, facilitator of networking, a provider of wisdom, shapes skills and a role model for mentees. At the same time, a good mentee is characterized by being proactive, committed, willing to learn, open-minded, self-aware, reflective, excited and communicative (Hill et al., 2022).

According to Ziegler et al., (2021), mentoring entails activities of persons in their role as mentors. The role usually involves different educational actions and plans to improve the mentor and mentee who are in the mentorship relationship. The act of mentorship provides a platform to improve staff performance and engagement, promote learning culture and encourage collaborative practice. This could be due to its bidirectional nature as it benefits both mentors and mentees and is therefore considered as a fundamental step in professional and personal development (Burgess et al., 2018). A good mentorship programme should have mutual benefits, which are career-focused and empowering (Schwerdtle et al., 2017). On the mentors' side, mentorship provides an opportunity to have a learning partner, promotes creativity, a sense of purpose and fulfilment, skills enhancement and feedback (Klinge, 2015). Moreover, mentoring offers a rewarding experience, promotes recognition by others, improves job performance, and rejuvenation (Grima et al., 2014). Mentees benefit from mentorship through the enhancement of knowledge and skills, receiving feedback, sense of cohesion and responsibility, assimilation culture, creativity, leadership skills development, professional values clarification, increased job satisfaction, and boosting of sense of power and confidence (Klinge, 2015). In addition, the essential knowledge and skills of mentees are improved through mentoring, in terms of decision-making in health care services, actions made will be mentee-driven, which prepares them for future actions (Manzi et al., 2017). Overall, mentoring benefits the healthcare industry by improving the quality of care delivery, improving service utilization and satisfaction, and improving health systems and public health (Manzi et al., 2017).

Mentoring or the practice of mentorship may be conducted virtually and with in-person endeavours. Virtual mentoring supports the development of skills, knowledge acquisition, confidence building and cultural competence while equally nurturing relationships between mentors and mentees (McReynolds et al., 2020). That means the mentor and mentee do not have to be at the same geographical location. Like other educational and workplace initiatives, mentoring is also underpinned by theoretical and philosophical assumptions.

The ZPD is identified as a theoretical and philosophical basis for mentoring in health professions education and practice. As one of the constructs for Vygotsky's sociocultural learning theory, ZPD is defined as the learner's actual level of development and the next level attainable through the use of capable adult, mediation, environmental tools, mediation, and peer facilitation (Vygotsky, 1978). This simply pronounces the difference between what the learners can learn on their own without assistance, and what they can learn with the direction of a facilitator or other learners (Clapper, 2015). Although Vygotsky's concept of ZPD was originally developed to describe how cognitive growth occurs in children (Fani & Ghaemi, 2011), it is widely used and applied to the learning process in adults. In the case of mentorship, the capable mentor can be an effective mentor, while ZPD activities denote what is conducted for mentoring purposes. Similarly to ZPD, mentorship allows a mentee to assimilate and accommodate new skills and information, into their practice (Clapper, 2015). The good aspect of ZPD is that it does not merely refer to the amount of support needed for new skill acquisition but to the steps required to transition to the next developmental stage of ability (Groot et al., 2020). In terms of how ZPD actions are conducted in the learning environment, scaffolding can be steered as part of the activities in the ZPD. This means a facilitator can assist a learner with an understanding of content or mastering skills by availing additional resources needed to support the learning process (Clapper, 2015). With that in mind, scaffolding can also be steered as part of mentoring, whereby a mentor may provide extra resources needed to master a specific part of the work component. Due to the reason that this chapter describes VCoP as a mentoring tool, ZPD and scaffolding are conducted with the assistance of web-based applications and online platforms.

Use of Virtual Communities of Practice as Mentoring Tools in Health Professions Education and Practice

VCoP in healthcare settings are characterized to be self-directed, professional outcome-based, experience-centred, and problem-centred with opportunity for life-long learning. In addition, some are goal-oriented and self-motivated (Abedini et al., 2021). Moreover, evidence is available to support that VCoP healthcare professionals provide a flexible learning mode with up-to-date resources that are applicable to use in daily practice and afford participants the opportunity to exchange experiences (Bermejo-Caja et al., 2019). Owing to those characteristics, VCoP could be suitable to use as a mentoring tools in healthcare settings. Moreover, virtual communities are one of the suggestions made to improve interprofessional education to enhance inclusivity for students where internet access and electronic devices are available (Samarasekera et al., 2022). Similarly, virtual mentoring communities may improve interprofessional practice which is required for successful outcomes of healthcare interventions.

Virtual mentoring entails a teaching-learning process and mentorship which is technology-assisted and takes place through a reciprocal, career-developing relationship between a mentor and mentee, who are diverse in professional status and credentials (Clement, 2018). Considering that mentoring is for professional development, role modelling and nurturing of the mentee, it can be conducted despite the fact that the mentor and mentee are in geographically dispersed settings. This can be facilitated through the use of tools such as the internet, emails, electronic media, and telephones, to provide positive learning outcomes for virtual mentoring. Similarly, these are tools utilized for engagement, interaction, and sharing of information in VCoP. However, similar to other technologically facilitated activities, in virtual mentoring, mentees and mentors find it difficult to establish rapport when meeting virtually. There is decreased engagement from the mentees, which can be attributed to virtual meeting fatigue and difficulties with virtual technologies. Despite those challenges, virtual mentoring offers convenience in terms of scheduling and reduced travel burden (Patel et al., 2023).

In health professions education and practice, there are formal and informal VCoP. The formal VCoP has renewable permanent memberships, structures, and regular meetings. Just to mention a few, international and regional associations that provide for VCoP in nursing and health professions education are such as Sigma Theta Tau International (STTI), The International Association for Health Professions Education (AMEE), Africa Forum for Research and Education in Health (AFREhealth), and the Southern African Association of Health Educationalist (SAAHE). These professional organizations implement VCoP to support their members and domains through regular interactions. Regular interactions are done as board meetings, general assemblies, induction meetings for new members, educational Webinars, delivery of short courses, journal club meetings arranged by special interest groups, research meetings, online and hybrid conferences, symposiums, and congresses. These platforms allow for interprofessional engagement and, the sharing of information between practitioners from different geographic locations and disciplines. Due to structures and level of engagement, VCoP provides a suitable platform for virtual mentoring as novice members are promoted to identify mentors, link up with more experienced staff, and engage in a mentorship relationship. This way, a mentor may have a group of mentees who meet regularly with the support of virtual platforms. Moreover, with advances in technology, health professionals are now able to search for mentors via online platforms such as research profiles on ORCiD, ResearchGate, Web of Science, Scopus, and even by reading publications from journals or e-books.

Apart from VCoP offered by professional organizations, people at the workplace form communities that meet regularly to pursue special interests. Special interests may include a celebration of personal and professional achievements, for communication purposes, discussing company benefits and workplace-related issues, motivating each other and internal learning (Budrytė & Vainauskienė, 2023). Additionally, colleagues may have regular online meetings outside their routine work hours or during their day - off to discuss opportunities for further studies, funding, wellness, and health-related issues. They may use virtual communication channels such as Google Meet, WhatsApp, Google Chat, Microsoft Team Slack channel, and Zoom presentations. Joining a VCoP with colleagues at work may help to situate learning in the workplace, and improve interactions among colleagues and management, which also have a positive impact on productivity. Due to interaction among colleagues, VCoP at the workplace helps identify mentors and people with similar interests to continue further engagement outside the workplace related to VCoP.

Recently, the COVID-19 pandemic has promoted the use of virtual platforms to replace face-to-face interaction, and this has led to some engagements to form VCoP (Shaw et al., 2022). Some of the conferences and congresses used to take place via face-to-face mode only before the COVID-19 pandemic started to adopt a hybrid mode and some continued to be online only. Due to involuntary professional and social isolation brought about by the COVID-19 pandemic, VCoP platforms were used by professionals for relieving stress, as a humorous tool, and to provide comfort and support to each other (Bissessar, 2022). Moreover, VCoP were integral components to fulfilling Maslow's needs during the pandemic (Fayez et al., 2023).

Engagement in VCoP allows online or virtual mentoring to health professionals. Due to health professionals who work in remote, under-served and far-to-reach areas where suitable mentors are not available locally for in-person mentoring endeavours, joining VCoP can afford them an opportunity for virtual mentoring. This can be done through attending online continuing professional activities such as case presentations and discussions. In some cases, professionals participate in research projects led by well-established researchers as part of mentoring. Interaction and engagement in VCoP provide virtual mentoring platforms through Microsoft Teams, YouTube, Zoom, Skype, Trello, Slack, Twitter, Facebook, BlueJeans, WeChat, WhatsApp, and QQ. LINE and KAIKO talk (McReynolds et al., 2020). Some of those provide for asynchrony and synchronous engagement and meetings, while others are messaging applications. To fulfil the principles of situated learning, communities of practice, and legitimate peripheral participation, these platforms allow for mentees to learn in a socio-cultural environment, which is created virtually, engage with other members for a common purpose or shared domain and even transit from being peripheral to central members. Moreover, to fulfil the concepts of ZPD and scaffolding which are the guiding philosophy of mentoring, web-based applications in VCoP for virtual mentoring can allow mentors to facilitate narrowing the gap between what the mentee can do on their own without assistance, and what they can do with the assistance of their mentor. Consequently, these web-based applications used in VCoP can facilitate mentors to provide extra assistance needed to learn or master new knowledge and skills.

For effective use of VCoP as a mentoring tool in health professions and education, the following tips should be followed;

- join a virtual community of practice
- become a central member of the virtual community of practice, never remain at peripheral
- recognize the value of mentoring offered via virtual communities of practice
- identity potential mentors within the virtual community
- approach and introduce self to potential mentors

- be approachable to potential mentees and be available to accommodate the
- use available opportunities to introduce your profile
- attend meetings regularly and participate in online engagements
- be open to participate in activities conducted via a virtual community
- respond to calls for opportunities such as fellowships, research partnerships and courses on offer
- be open to participating in exchange programme proposed via virtual communities of practice
- provide constructive feedback to others and be receptive to feedback.
- familiarize yourself with technology and applications utilized in the virtual communities of practice group

These tips may be helpful for health professionals seeking to use VCoP as mentoring in their education and practices for professional development. They can be applied to both mentors and mentees. The following section presents solutions and recommendations based on the goal of the chapter.

SOLUTIONS AND RECOMMENDATIONS

The virtual communities of practices have the potential to be used successfully as mentoring tools in health professions education and practices, provided mentors and mentees are well guided on how to use the platforms. Therefore, more effort should be put into developing strategies on how that can be done as well as models or frameworks to be followed. Preferably, these strategies, models or frameworks should be designed considering challenges experienced from different geographic locations due to contextual and sociocultural and economic issues that may affect smooth establishment and implementation of mentoring via virtual communities of practices. Moreover, higher education institutions offering health professions programme should be flexible to allow for professionals' time to engage in mentoring activities through virtual communities of practices. Equally, healthcare facilities management should exercise flexibility to allow practitioners and or health professionals time to engage in virtual mentoring activities, especially those scheduled within their working hours. On the same note, higher education institutions and health care facilities should be innovative and appoint a focal person who will be responsible for identifying virtual communities of practice available for health professionals, hence mentoring activities that can be done virtually to reduce travelling costs and time away from work.

FUTURE RESEARCH DIRECTIONS

As future research direction, there is a need for empirical data on experiences and perceptions of mentoring through virtual communities of practices and also review studies such as scoping review, integrative literature review and concept analysis of key concepts to enhance common understanding. This is because, through conduction of literature for this chapter, the author has identified there are still major gaps in those areas, especially that there is limited focus on the field of health professions education and practice. The researcher further recommends participatory action research which may allow for the full involvement of research participants as this increases the opportunity to obtain rich data. These recommendations could support development of mentoring in health professions education and practice, which may promote evidence-based practices. These may also help in the development of frameworks and other guiding documents on how VCoP may be used for mentoring in healthcare settings.

CONCLUSION

This chapter conceptualized virtual communities of practices and mentoring. The review of the literature revealed that the theoretical and philosophical underpinnings of VCoP are situated learning, communities of practice, Vygotsky's sociocultural theory of human learning, legitimate peripheral participation, zone of proximal development and scaffolding. In addition, the chapter included a discussion on how virtual communities of practice may be utilized as mentoring tools in health professions education and practices. The use of VCoP as a mentoring tool favours health professionals who work in remote, under-served and far-to-reach areas where suitable mentors are not available locally for in-person mentoring endeavours. Tips are given in this chapter on how health professionals can make virtual mentoring a success.

REFERENCES

Abedini, A., Abedin, B., & Zowghi, D. (2021). Adult learning in online communities of practice: A systematic review. *British Journal of Educational Technology*, 52(4), 1663–1694. 10.1111/bjet.13120

Alali, H., & Salim, J. (2013). Virtual Communities of Practice Success Model to Support Knowledge Sharing behaviour in Healthcare Sector. *Procedia Technology*, *11*, 176–183. 10.1016/j.protcy.2013.12.178

Anafarta, A., & Apaydin, C. (2016). The Effect of Faculty Mentoring on Career Success and Career Satisfaction. *International Education Studies*, 9(6), 22. 10.5539/ies.v9n6p22

Barnett, S., Jones, S. C., Bennett, S., Iverson, D., & Bonney, A. (2012). General practice training and virtual communities of practice - A review of the literature. *BMC Family Practice*, 13(1), 1–13. 10.1186/1471-2296-13-8722905827

Bentley, C., Browman, G. P., & Poole, B. (2010). Conceptual and practical challenges for implementing the communities of practice model on a national scale - a Canadian cancer control initiative. *BMC Health Services Research*, 10(3), 1–8. https://www.biomedcentral.com/1472-6963/10/3. 10.1186/1472-6963-10-320051125

Bermejo-Caja, C. J., Koatz, D., Orrego, C., Perestelo-Pérez, L., González-González, A. I., Ballester, M., Pacheco-Huergo, V., Del Rey-Granado, Y., Muñoz-Balsa, M., Ramírez-Puerta, A. B., Canellas-Criado, Y., Pérez-Rivas, F. J., Toledo-Chávarri, A., Martínez-Marcos, M., Alejo-Díaz-Zorita, C., Barbero-Macías, C. A., Borrell-Punzón, F., Bueno-Rodriguez, B., Colmena-Martin, B., & Villanueva-Sanz, C. (2019). Acceptability and feasibility of a virtual community of practice to primary care professionals regarding patient empowerment: A qualitative pilot study. *BMC Health Services Research*, 19(1), 1–10. 10.1186/s12913-019-4185-z31221215

Bissessar, C. (2022). The role of virtual community of practice in alleviating social and professional isolation during emergency remote teaching. *Equity in Education & Society*, 1(1), 114–125. 10.1177/27526461211068512

Budrytė, M., & Vainauskienė, V. (2023). Virtual Communities of Practice as a Knowledge Sharing Tool: Recommendations for International Business. *Management of Organizations: Systematic Research*, 89(1), 15–30. 10.2478/mosr-2023-0002

Burgess, A., van Diggele, C., & Mellis, C. (2018). Mentorship in the health professions: A review. *The Clinical Teacher*, 15(3), 197–202. 10.1111/tct.1275629318730

Chang, B. (2021). Situated Learning – Foreign Sites as Learning Contexts. *Journal of Comparative & International Higher Education*, 13(2), 5–22. 10.32674/jcihe.v13i2.2615

Clapper, T. C. (2015). Cooperative-Based Learning and the Zone of Proximal Development. *Simulation & Gaming*, 46(2), 148–158. 10.1177/1046878115569044

Clement, S. (2018). Concept Analysis of Virtual Mentoring. *COJ Nursing & Healthcare*, 1(5), 111–116. 10.31031/COJNH.2018.01.000525

da Silva, R. F., Gimenes, I. M. S., & Maldonado, J. C. (2020). The challenge of evaluating virtual communities of practice: A systematic mapping study. *Interdisciplinary Journal of Information, Knowledge, and Management*, 15, 39–64. 10.28945/4505

Dietl, J. E., Derksen, C., Keller, F. M., & Lippke, S. (2023). Interdisciplinary and interprofessional communication intervention: How psychological safety fosters communication and increases patient safety. *Frontiers in Psychology*, 14, 1164288. Advance online publication. 10.3389/fpsyg.2023.116428837397302

Dowling, S., Earl, S., & Stokes, D. (2018). *Mentoring Handbook: Project and Programme management, Community of Practice*. University College London. www.ucl.ac.uk

Fani, T., & Ghaemi, F. (2011). Implications of Vygotsky's zone of proximal development (ZPD) in teacher education: ZPTD and self-scaffolding. *Procedia: Social and Behavioral Sciences*, 29, 1549–1554. 10.1016/j.sbspro.2011.11.396

Fayez, O., Ismail, H., & Aboelnagah, H. (2023). Emerging Virtual Communities of Practice during Crises: A Sustainable Model Validating the Levels of Peer Motivation and Support. *Sustainability (Basel)*, 15(7), 1–19. 10.3390/su15075691

Frenk, J., Chen, L. C., Chandran, L., Groff, E. O. H., King, R., Meleis, A., & Fineberg, H. V. (2022). Challenges and opportunities for educating health professionals after the COVID-19 pandemic. *Lancet*, 400(10362), 1539–1556. 10.1016/S0140-6736(22)02092-X36522209

Gammelgaard, J. (2010). Knowledge retrieval through virtual communities of practice. *Behaviour & Information Technology*, 29(4), 349–362. 10.1080/01449290903548406

Ghamrawi, N. (2022). Teachers' virtual communities of practice: A strong response in times of crisis or just another Fad? *Education and Information Technologies*, 27(5), 5889–5915. 10.1007/s10639-021-10857-w35095322

Gonen, A., Lev-Ari, L., Sharo, D., & Amzalag, M. (2016). Situated learning: The feasibility of an experimental learning of information technology for academic nursing students. *Cogent Education*, 3(1), 1–8. 10.1080/2331186X.2016.1154260

Grima, F., Paillé, P., Mejia, J. H., & Prud'Homme, L. (2014). Exploring the benefits of mentoring activities for the mentor. *Career Development International*, 19(4), 469–490. 10.1108/CDI-05-2012-0056

Groot, F., Jonker, G., Rinia, M., Ten Cate, O., & Hoff, R. G. (2020). Simulation at the Frontier of the Zone of Proximal Development: A Test in Acute Care for Inexperienced Learners. *Academic Medicine*, 95(7), 1098–1105. 10.1097/ACM.0000000000003265 32134783

Grosik, S. A., & Kanno, Y. (2021). Peripheral or Marginal Participation? University-Based Intensive English Programs as an Entryway to U.S. Academia. *Journal of International Students*, 11(4), 914–931. 10.32674/jis.v11i4.1828

Haas, A., Abonneau, D., Borzillo, S., & Guillaume, L. (2021). Afraid of engagement? Towards an understanding of engagement in virtual communities of practice. *Knowledge Management Research and Practice*, 19(2), 169–180. 10.1080/14778238.2020.1745704

Hajah, P., Norainna, S., Pengiran, B., & Basar, H. (2018). Situated learning theory: The key to effective classroom teaching? *International Journal for Educational, Social, Political &Cultural Studies*, 1(1), 49–60.

Hill, S. E. M., Ward, W. L., Seay, A., & Buzenski, J. (2022). The Nature and Evolution of the Mentoring Relationship in Academic Health Centers. *Journal of Clinical Psychology in Medical Settings*, 29(3), 557–569. 10.1007/s10880-022-09893-635761033

Jaeger, F. N., Bechir, M., Harouna, M., Moto, D. D., & Utzinger, J. (2018). Challenges and opportunities for healthcare workers in a rural district of Chad. *BMC Health Services Research*, 18(1), 1–11. 10.1186/s12913-017-2799-629310644

Klinge, C. M. (2015). A Conceptual Framework for Mentoring in a Learning Organization. *Adult Learning*, 26(4), 160–166. 10.1177/1045159515594154

Koutsoukos, M., Kiriatzakou, K., Fragoulis, I., & Valkanos, E. (2020). The Significance of Adult Educators' Mentoring in the Application of Experiential and Participatory Teaching Techniques. *International Education Studies*, 14(1), 46. 10.5539/ies.v14n1p46

Lave, J., & Wenger, E. (1991). *Situated learning: Legitimate peripheral participation*. Cambridge University Press. 10.1017/CBO9780511815355

Li, L. C., Grimshaw, J. M., Nielsen, C., Judd, M., Coyte, P. C., & Graham, I. D. (2009). Evolution of Wenger's concept of community of practice. *Implementation Science : IS*, 4(1), 1–8. 10.1186/1748-5908-4-1119250556

Manzi, A., Hirschhorn, L. R., Sherr, K., Chirwa, C., Baynes, C., & Awoonor-Williams, J. K. (2017). Mentorship and coaching to support strengthening healthcare systems: Lessons learned across the five Population Health Implementation and Training partnership projects in sub-Saharan Africa. *BMC Health Services Research*, 17(S3), 1–12. 10.1186/s12913-017-2656-729297323

Mcalpine, J., Mcalpine, J. J., Larkins, S., & Nagle, C. (2023). Exploring the evidence base for Communities of Practice in health research and translation : A scoping review. *Health Research Policy and Systems*, 21(55), 1–11. 10.1186/s12961-023-01000-x37337214

McLoughlin, C., Patel, K., O'Callaghan, T., & Reev, S. (2018). The use of virtual communities of practice to improve interprofessional collaboration and education: Findings from an integrated review. *Journal of Interprofessional Care*, 32(2), 136–142. 10.1080/13561820.2017.137769229161155

McReynolds, M. R., Termini, C. M., Hinton, A. O.Jr, Taylor, B. L., Vue, Z., Huang, S. C., Roby, R. A. S., Shuler, H., & Carter, C. S. (2020). The art of virtual mentoring in the twenty-first century for STEM majors and beyond. *Nature Biotechnology*, 38(12), 1477–1482. 10.1038/s41587-020-00758-733273732

Moore, M. (2011). Vygotsky's Cognitive Development Theory. In Goldstein, S., & Naglieri, J. (Eds.), *Encyclopedia of Child Behavior and Developmen*. Springer. 10.1007/978-0-387-79061-9_3054

O'Brien, B. C., & Battista, A. (2020). Situated learning theory in health professions education research: A scoping review. *Advances in Health Sciences Education : Theory and Practice*, 25(2), 483–509. 10.1007/s10459-019-09900-w31230163

Patel, M., Singhal, N., & Sockalingam, S. (2023). The Impact of the Transition to Virtual Environments on Medical Students Mentoring At-Risk Youth. *Academic Psychiatry*, 47(3), 292–296. 10.1007/s40596-023-01771-z37016175

Pramila-Savukoski, S., Jarva, E., Kuivila, H. M., Juntunen, J., Koskenranta, M., Kääriäinen, M., & Mikkonen, K. (2024). Generic competence among health sciences students in higher education – A cross-sectional study. *Nurse Education Today, 133*. 10.1016/j.nedt.2023.106036

Pyrko, I., Dörfler, V., & Eden, C. (2019). Communities of practice in landscapes of practice. *Management Learning*, 50(4), 482–499. 10.1177/1350507619860854

Qutab, S., Iqbal, A., Ullah, F. S., Siddique, N., & Khan, M. A. (2022). Role of virtual communities of practice (VCoP) in continuous professional development of librarians: A case of Yahoo mailing group from Pakistan. *Library Management*, 43(5), 317–333. 10.1108/LM-02-2021-0017

Ranmuthugala, G., Plumb, J., Cunningham, F., Georgiou, A., Westbrook, J., & Braithwaite, J. (2011). How and why are communities of practice established in the healthcare sector? *A Systematic Review of the Literature, 11*, 273. https://www .biomedcentral.com/1472-6963/11/273

Samarasekera, D. D., Nyoni, C. N., Amaral, E., & Grant, J. (2022). Challenges and opportunities in interprofessional education and practice. *Lancet*, 400(10362), 1495–1497. 10.1016/S0140-6736(22)02086-436522199

Schwerdtle, P., Morphet, J., & Hall, H. (2017). A scoping review of mentorship of health personnel to improve the quality of health care in low and middle-income countries. *Globalization and Health*, 13(1), 1–8. 10.1186/s12992-017-0301-128974233

Shabani, K., Khatib, M., & Ebadi, S. (2010). Vygotsky's Zone of Proximal Development: Instructional Implications and Teachers' Professional Development Karim. *English Language Teaching*, 3(4), 237–248. www.ccsenet.org/elt. 10.5539/ elt.v3n4p237

Shaw, L., Jazayeri, D., Kiegaldie, D., & Morris, M. E. (2022). Implementation of Virtual Communities of Practice in Healthcare to Improve Capability and Capacity: A 10-Year Scoping Review. *International Journal of Environmental Research and Public Health*, 19(13), 7994. Advance online publication. 10.3390/ijerph1913799435805649

Skarbalienė, A., Skarbalius, E., & Gedrimė, L. (2019). Effective Communication In The Healthcare Settings: Are The Graduates Ready For It? *Management*, 24(Special Issue), 137–147. 10.30924/mjcmi.24.si.9

Struminger, B., Arora, S., Zalud-Cerrato, S., Lowrance, D., & Ellerbrock, T. (2017). Building virtual communities of practice for health. *Lancet*, 390(10095), 632–634. 10.1016/S0140-6736(17)31666-528816126

Terry, D. R., Nguyen, L. H., Peck, B., Lecturer, S., & Smith, A. (2020). Communities of practice : A systematic review and meta- synthesis of what it means and how it really works among nursing students and novices. *Journal of Clinical Nursing*, 29(3-4), 370–380. 10.1111/jocn.1510031714649

Vaisshalli, G. R., Gupta, A., Bhapkar, A. G., Dixit, A., Singh, S. P., & Agarwal, P. (2022). Challenges in Healthcare Sector. *International Journal for Modern Trends in Science and Technology*, 8(01), 43–46. 10.46501/IJMTST0801008

Valenti, S., & Sutton, S. (2020). Strengthening virtual communities of practice (VCoPs): An Evidence-based approach. *Journal of Education for Library and Information Science*, 61(1), 106–125. 10.3138/jelis.61.1.2018-0045

Vermeir, P., Vandijck, D., Degroote, S., Peleman, R., Verhaeghe, R., Mortier, E., Hallaert, G., Van Daele, S., Buylaert, W., & Vogelaers, D. (2015). Communication in healthcare: A narrative review of the literature and practical recommendations. *International Journal of Clinical Practice*, 69(11), 1257–1267. 10.1111/ijcp.1268626147310

Vygotsky, L. (1978). *Mind in Society*. Havard University Press.

Wenger, E. (1998). *Communities of practice: Learning, meaning, and identity*. Cambridge University Press. 10.1017/CBO9780511803932

Woo, D. J. (2015). Central practitioners' developing legitimate peripheral participation in a community of practice for changing schools. *Australasian Journal of Educational Technology*, 31(2), 164–176. 10.14742/ajet.314

Yang, L. (2020). Silver-lining of COVID-19: A Virtual Community of Practice for Faculty Development. *All Ireland Journal of Higher Education*, 12(3), 1–9.

Zakrajsek, A., & Schuster, E. (2018). Situated Learning and Interprofessional Education: An Educational Strategy Using an Apprenticeship Model to Develop Research Skills for Practice. *Health and Interprofessional Practice*, 3(3), 1–11. 10.7710/2159-1253.1147

Ziegler, A., Gryc, K. L., Hopp, M. D. S., & Stoeger, H. (2021). Spaces of possibilities: A theoretical analysis of mentoring from a regulatory perspective. *Annals of the New York Academy of Sciences*, 1483(1), 174–198. 10.1111/nyas.1441932634268

KEY TERMS AND DEFINITIONS

Communities of Practice: They are groups of people who share passion or concerns over something they do and learn how to do it better through regular interactions. This implies that there should be an interest in a common practice to qualify as a community.

Legitimate Peripheral Participation: Is a process through which an individual becomes a member of communities of practice, and eventually transits from being a marginal practitioner to a central practitioner or member.

Mentoring: Is a personal development learning tool which denotes the relationship between two people who are in any way not linked within a line management structure.

Scaffolding: Is a pedagogical practice whereby the facilitator can assist a learner with understanding content or mastering skills by availing additional resources needed to support the learning process.

Situated Learning Theory: Is a social–cultural process in learning in which the learning environment is "situated" in a specific context which usually requires collaboration and social interaction within the "community of practice".

Virtual Mentoring: Is a teaching-learning process and mentorship which is technology-assisted, and takes place through a reciprocal, career-developing relationship between a mentor and mentee, who are diverse in professional status and credentials.

Zone of Proximal Development: This simply pronounces the difference between what the learners can learn on their own without assistance, and what they can learn with the direction of a facilitator or other learners.

Chapter 10
The Media Plays On:
How an Archives Company Leveraged Community During a Time of Shutdown

Christopher J. Mason
https://orcid.org/0009-0002-9982-8109
Iron Mountain Media and Archive Services, USA

Dana L. Smerda-Mason
New Jersey City University, USA

ABSTRACT

The COVID-19 pandemic challenged people across the globe and forced change across every industry. Many people were home due to quarantine requirements and to help pass this time turned to media of many forms for their entertainment and social interactions. At a time where new content could not be professionally created due to safety requirements, the entertainment industry was forced to visit their archives and collaborate with specialists to solve this emerging concern. This chapter focuses on the virtual communities developed by the archivists at Iron Mountain Media and Archive Services to implement strategies to service this need through the digitization of legacy media and other assets that they manage for their customers. Through creativity and innovation, these professionals created 21st century solutions through virtual communities to challenges related to training, transportation, digitization, and developed a plan to provide social and emotional support to the masses through the ability to connect with newly available media streaming demands.

DOI: 10.4018/979-8-3693-1111-0.ch010

IT'S ONLY ROCK AND ROLL IF YOU CAN FIND IT

In a time of certainty, professionals rely on one another in the workplace to achieve business objectives set by their company each year. What may seem to be launched at the beginning of the year as a new set of criteria for an organization's productivity and progress, quickly morphs into the lived personal objectives that drive professional and personal growth for each individual involved in the process. Employees offer their contribution to each goal in the form of subject matter expertise to provide their best in an annual process. These criteria become the center of community among employees, and side-by-side these individuals commit to a common interest.

Sometimes this requires additional training, and individuals engage in professional development to hone their skills in a needed area. Other times, it relies on a particular type of collaboration where each individual adds their signature abilities like spices to a world-class recipe. The challenges of the heat, and pressure of meeting these goals ultimately brings out the best in each individual, and produces the final dish to be served in the form of a successful year ahead, born out of teamwork and collaboration among a community of professionals. Unity is savored throughout the organization as these professionals have become a community of practice (Wenger, 2024).

That process is no different for the professionals working in the Media and Archive Services Division of an archive company known as Iron Mountain. This sector is made up of an eclectic collection of employees that represent seasoned management, driving members of operations, sales and account management professionals, as well as studio engineers with expertise in both audio and video restoration, fine arts experts, photographers, inventors and builders; many of whom have decades of experience in the entertainment industry working for top-name record labels, directors, the estates of artists and creatives, as well as recording studios.

Iron Mountain's mission is to preserve media from the past and to protect it so future audiences can be entertained and have access to their history for generations to come (Iron Mountain Incorporated, 2023). This division takes this decree to a new level of appreciation for the past, due to the nature of the artifacts that they work to preserve. Their customers are people from the entertainment industry that rely on them to know how to handle and safely store one-of-a-kind materials in a niche field. For example, there is a fine arts division that provides white-glove service for storing, moving, and restoring fine art, where there are art handlers, who are special engineers with art history backgrounds that custom build cases for each priceless piece so that it can be transported or stored safely.

Another aspect focuses on the preservation, cataloging, safely storing, and restoration of audio and video assets. These highly skilled engineers work full-time in the studio to preserve audio and video assets that can range in content anywhere from recorded historical speeches, to the original master recordings of a famous popular music group. In terms of video, they have the ability to add sound to silent recordings, enhance the visual quality of an old film, and apply many other creative techniques to films that constitute the pillars of global entertainment history. Many of these assets are currently saved on old original formats such as tape, or whatever the industry standard at the time of the initial recording had been. Over time they are in danger of different forms of deterioration based on how they were stored over the years, and so many artists have the options of transferring old recordings to a modern digital format.

Iron Mountain Media and Archive Services employs a veteran engineer who has invented and patented various processes for restoration and remediation of audio and video from disintegrating tape and other deteriorating formats. His work allows the organization the opportunity to resurrect often old and previously unheard recordings of artists who have since passed on. Digitizing media from old analogue tape formats allows companies and creators of content the ability to utilize the latest in audio and video engineering technology to remaster, preserve, or rerelease their content with enhancements that were not available historically at the time it was recorded. This allows these artists to have the ability to monetize their masterpieces through new projects and licensing agreements with streaming platform vendors, which extends the life of all audio created for generations to come.

To some, this type of work may not seem as flashy and popularized as the celebrity clients from the entertainment industry that this division services; yet it plays a vital role in the preservation of recorded content that has historical, educational, or cultural value. It is this team of professionals that commit to working together behind the scenes to develop a reliable support for a variety of aspects of the media arts world.

Each day they are in their offices and studios playing their individual role that make up the network of archivists that come in all varieties. This is a thriving community of practice servicing a unique field of artists, and together their work preserves our culture and civilization that will echo the memories of artistic contributors long after they are gone. Together they are armed and ready with the latest industry-standard skills and creative problem-solving strategies to meet the needs of whatever challenges modernization and the rolling on of time present in their wake.

The Unpredictable Shift

March of 2020, was an unforgettable time of unprecedented change across the globe. The COVID-19 pandemic was ravaging nations across the world, and a dangerous health crisis threatened the lives of everyone. Government mandates were established as a safety measure, banning travel from different countries, impacting trade and the supply chain, as well as preventing people from conducting themselves in normal in-person settings. In the United States, many companies closed their doors and furloughed employees. Essential workers were permitted to report in to their places of employment, but the head-count was reduced, and social distancing was put in place to prevent the spread of disease. The landscape of the professional workplace had changed overnight, requiring many individuals to reinvent their process of productivity (Kaushik, 2020).

The employees of Iron Mountain Archive and Media Services were not immune to this crisis. As a profession that services the physical assets of customers in different parts of the world through archiving, digitization, and remediation, relying on experts for in-person service and solutions was critically impacted. What initially started as a two-week quarantine period in March continued to be extended incrementally. As the new reality began to emerge, Iron Mountain Media and Archive Services professionals banded together and committed to designing a solution to support a safe working environment that could service their existing customer needs.

The first step was the easiest and involved the sales, account management, and customer service departments within this division. These employees prepared to work remotely from their homes, and were able to conduct business using company cell phones, laptops, and proprietary secure networking. These individuals were able to stay connected with their individual clients and their specified needs by making meetings virtual through either the Zoom or Google Meet platforms.

All divisions of Iron Mountain had just completed their corporate migration to Google Workspace at the end of 2019. Employees were just becoming acclimated to the features and functions of a Google ecosystem for business, implementing applications such as Google Drive, Chat, Meet, Jamboard, Keep, and other aspect of the Google ecosystem that helped make virtual collaboration possible (Khriyenko & Cochez, 2011). This shift seemed to happen at the perfect time; while there was still more to acclimate to, having this type of a system in place allowed employees to collaborate effectively with more accessibility. The community of practice that was once solely structured in a fixed face-to-face environment was now able to communicate effectively amongst the distancing challenges dictated by the pandemic.

These three departments working remotely provided a safer option for the members of the operations team that were considered essential employees during this time. The nature of their work required them to be on site at all times, while still communicating with remote members of the team. They were responsible for the proper handling and care of each of the physical assets on site, in addition to the physical delivery to customers, and other Iron Mountain facilities housing studio work. Employees in other departments that were able to operate remotely significantly reduced the number of individuals that reported in to each location. This help uphold proper social distancing protocols, ultimately alleviating the health and safety concerns for each party of essential workers. The operations teams had staggered scheduling, allowing smaller teams to continuously work in a safer environment.

Studio engineers and technicians were in a hybrid working situation. The on-site studios continued to stay in use, and many of the technicians were able to rotate between being in-person to working remotely from their homes. To make this possible, tasks and projects were recategorized by the equipment needed to complete them. Equipment that was portable was gathered up and sent home with each technician to anticipate their needs in the type of projects they would be handling, so they could be both safe and productive. This leant itself to an innovative idea referred to as the Studio in a Box.

Experienced studio engineers trained others within the department on unfamiliar equipment by sharing homemade videos with solutions through Google Drive, as well as connecting on Google Meet. At a moment's notice when a challenge arose, Google Chat was the preferred method to exchange quick guidance in advising one another of suggestions to bring about the solution. Inexperienced studio technicians who were more recently hired still needed training, and by having the Studio in a Box, they were able to train at home with the virtual guidance of a team of experienced colleagues.

Annual summit meetings were traditionally held in the first quarter of the year to set and communicate goals and objectives to employees. Due to social distancing, this practice shifted to virtual platforms hosted by Iron Mountain Archive and Media Services through both Google Meet and Zoom. Professional training and collaborative time was recreated through the use of virtual breakout rooms, to provide a space for colleagues to discuss their experience and learn from one another, as well as offer support emotionally and intellectually. These meetings were able to be more inclusive by opening up the invitation list to more employees throughout the organization, since the logistical challenges and costly travel were not a factor with this format.

Additionally, employees of Iron Mountain Archive and Media Services are members of various industry originations such as Association of Moving Images and Archivist (AMIA) and Audio Engineer Society (AES), to name a few. To keep current on industry changes and trends in this uncertain time, and also help build relationships, Iron Mountain developed panel discussions with subject matter experts from these organizations, as well as invited customer stakeholders to join in the discussion, and made these opportunities available to all employees. Iron Mountain employees also attended virtual events hosted by other industry organizations.

This was a way to help bring members of the media arts community together to develop solutions to the current industry needs to ensure that Iron Mountain had current information and could pivot to accommodate changes dictated by the pandemic. Since the service that the company provides is technical in nature, attending these sessions in lieu of face-to-face conferences worked towards maintaining the company's credibility with engineers and archivists and acted as a professional development opportunity for all in attendance.

The administrative management of Archive and Media Services understood that working and living under the changes and restrictions brought on by COVID-19 would be particularly draining, and difficult for employees both professionally and personally (Srinivasa, 2020). As a result, the vice president developed weekly meetings that took the form of a fireside chat. It was at these regularly scheduled virtual meetings that news updates were provided to provide a much transparency for planning as possible. Additionally, space was held at these events for discussions and community, to help team members feel supported and cared for by their colleagues. This was echoed throughout the objectives of the employee resource groups, and continued to resonate through corporate messaging and social media.

The manager of marketing was responsible for building and maintaining the company's website and social media presence. In addition to these platforms, the company relied on an internal social media platform exclusively designed for Iron Mountain employees across all divisions. The name of this platform was called *Currents*, and it provided news updates, commenting options, and discussion platform for internal support among team members. Here, executives shared monthly blog information, and this helped foster a sense of community among all members of the organization, while focusing on a collective interest that differed from the essential nature of training and production.

These collective efforts to embrace change across all levels of the division, allowed for unique solutions from this division to be able to plan to keep up with the needs of customers during this irregular time of need. At the same time, the health and wellness of employees could be at the forefront of operational decisions, which was necessary to keep the division producing at this time.

The Demand of Content Through Streaming

What the employees of Iron Mountain Media and Archive Services did not anticipate was the increase in demand for this division's services that was to come shortly after they established their innovative strategy to work safely and effectively through the pandemic. Streaming had become an important part of how the current generation consumed entertainment content across a variety of media platforms. This popularity was easily recognized during the pandemic, as the circumstances of the time made obvious the need for instant access to streamable content.

To get a comprehensive view of the streaming content business model it is important to look at the history of two companies that were early disruptors in that market, YouTube and Netflix. The history of streaming video content dates back February 2005 when three PayPal employees: Chad Hurley, Steve Chen, and Jawed Karim worked on developing a video-dating website (Vonderau, 2016). On this platform a user could upload videos of themselves talking about the type of partners they were interested in meeting. Originally the platform was called *"Tune In, Hook Up,"* and the three partners offered $20 to each woman that uploaded a dating video. The lack of excitement for this idea indicated that a change in strategy was necessary (Sisson, 2020), and so they moved on to videos for other purposes; public to videos of all kinds for public viewing.

The three drew on the motivation of viewers watching original footage created by subscribers who established their own channels, then expanded to individuals posting recordings of live events. For example, celebrities performing the halftime Super Bowl show, or footage of natural disasters captured by local residents. After the model was changed, the site was receiving an average of 30,000 viewers a day. In six months' time, the platform hosted over two million users daily. By the end of the first year the platform became so popular that over 200,000 videos were being uploaded for the growing 25 million viewers tuning in regularly (Sisson, 2020). Society was catching on to a new way of consuming entertainment.

While still a novel idea that had grown in popularity, YouTube was relatively unknown until December 2005, when Saturday Night Live's last episode for the year featured a short video called "Lazy Sunday" through their platform. This video attracted the attention of many viewers who wanted to rewatch the video and turned to Google to search for it. Searches drove viewers to the YouTube site resulting in the viral use of the streaming platform, igniting its popularity. This caught the attention of Google, which purchased the platform, for $1.65 billion in stock (Lamare, 2018).

YouTube was quickly adopted by the younger generation who were interested in sharing videos and feedback in this emerging form of a social media. Viewers could influence others to view and follow specific pages and content on the platform, including their own, which eventually became a revenue source for content creators. As a result, YouTube had an immediate impact on popular culture and how society began to consume entertainment content.

Viewers searched YouTube to watch various content and engage in social connection, instead of tuning in to a traditional television station as an independent activity. From homemade videos to political campaigns, a new trend was strengthening as viewing became autonomous and social (Trang, 2022). New talent among artists was being discovered, such as Justin Bieber after his mother posted a video of him singing, and PSY from South Korea, when his video for Gangnam Style received over three billion views in a span of four years (Denison, 2020). Through adaptability and the support of the public, an industry of streaming content and new entertainment expectations had been built.

While YouTube initially began as a video sharing platform it has now expanded and launched YouTubeTV, which rivals Netflix, Hulu, and Amazon for monthly subscribers. These vendors directly impact the media industry by giving consumers more options to watch content autonomously, transforming the customer experience. Subscribers no longer have to pay inflated monthly fees, and be tethered to a packaged that offers channels that they have no interest in. For smaller monthly fees subscribers can have direct access to stream television shows and movie content created by various networks, production studios, and music promoters. The revenue generated from monthly subscriptions helps the streaming platform pay for licensing fees for copyrighted material owned by media companies and producers of content (Arditi, 2021).

Before YouTube launched its video sharing platform, Reed Hastings and Marc Randolph, launched Netflix in the late 1990's (Voigt, Buliga, & Michl, 2016). Originally, the business model was to be the equivalent of Amazon in the movie rental industry. Netflix eventually launched their streaming platform, but during the early years they only offered mail order shipping for DVD rentals. Retail video stores were prevalent in most neighborhoods at this time, with the most prominent being Blockbuster Video. For a fee a consumer could visit a video store for access to a variety of movies available in store to rent for a few nights, charging for each movie, and typically being responsible for returning it on time to avoid having to pay late charges.

Hastings and Rudolph had the idea of charging a monthly flat fee allowing consumers to select from an array of movies from the Netflix website and have them shipped directly to their home. This changed the buyer's experience as it eliminated late fees, having to leave home, and having only a limited amount of time to watch a movie. Netflix maintained warehouses and distribution centers where the DVDs were stored. The DVDs arrived at their clients' homes by mail typically within one to three days (Sisson. 2020), which created a built-in level of convenience for the consumer, revolutionizing the home rental model.

In 2007, Netflix made a shift to introduce the "watch now" feature, launching the on-demand streaming platform. The popularity continued to increase and in 2013 Netflix helped create a binge-watching culture with releasing entire series on its platform. This service was dramatically different than previous options available to consumers through traditional television (Arditi, 2021). Streaming content sparked a cultural phenomenon of watching shows from an entire series consecutively until there was nothing was left to watch. This resulted in a cultural shift, and the word "binge-watching" entered our society's lexicon when the Collins English dictionary chose it as the word of the year in 2015 (British Broadcasting Company, 2015). This phenomenon has only intensified as more show series continue to become available, and has led to original productions created by streaming providers themselves such as Netflix.

By 2019 the streaming on demand business generated $17 billion dollars globally and the physical rental business had largely fallen by the wayside (Sisson, 2020). Within the following year the pandemic left many without work, external socialization, or healthy activity with which to engage. During this time of isolation, society relied on streaming content to keep themselves entertained (Johnson, 2021). Netflix and other similar streaming platforms continued to benefit financially at this time, and new varieties of services such as Disney+ and Peacock were launched as well. Movie theaters needed to close for safety so new releases would skip the theater and be released directly to a streaming platform offered by theater companies. The demand for the digital delivery of these converted assets significantly increased as a result.

Original content was also not being created. Television and movie production were not immune to the risk of COVID-19, and many movies, concerts, and shows were immediately put on hold until a safer time occurred and people could gather for work again (Johnson, 2021). This was a unique sub-crisis, because for the first time historically a majority of people were home consuming digital content at unprecedented, binge-watching speed to help keep themselves occupied. As they looked to the entertainment field to support their need for distraction for these difficult times, the media industry was quickly running out of original content ready to be released.

This tragic time caused businesses to find creative alternatives to how they had previously serviced their customers and many were looking to the Netflix model for ideas and inspiration. As a result, Iron Mountain Archive and Media Services relied on their ability to safely work, as a means of filling this need. Many of their existing customers had content in the form of old analogue footage that was still on a variety of legacy tape formats such as beta, VHS, HD Cam, 3⁄4 U-Matic tape, D2, magnetic tape, Linear Tape Open, as well as 35-, 16-, and 8-millimeter film. Although they were not the only media company to be able to service these types of industry needs, they were uniquely positions to be one of the only with the equipment, logistical solutions, and digital converting services which provided a much-needed holistic approach in the field.

Unless an old show or movie had been peviously transferred to a digital format, the content remains on outdated tape formats, only playable by devices that have long since become obsolete or have been decommissioned. Iron Mountain Archive and Media Services had invested in purchasing old playback devices for legacy media and various media formats to be able to convert the content to a digital file, which made it easily streamable on a video sharing platform. Along with the technology to convert the tapes, expert employees were able to conduct training, and provide advice on the spot through Google Workspace to aid younger engineers, less experienced in these modes of technology, with real-time professional support in understanding the complexities in handling old tape formats and technological operation.

These professionals forged ahead and provided digital conversion services for the content creators in the movie, television, and recording industries. The easiest way to start was by digitizing media from old tape formats, since much of this content was already stored on-site in a proper climate-controlled environment for longevity. This is common practice, because storing original recorded material on native formats serves as a safeguard in the event of natural disasters and digital files corruption. It is also not uncommon for creators to revisit these original assets when new technology is introduced that could enhance the original entertainment experience.

For example, in 1992 Dolby Laboratories introduced Dolby 5.1 to the market, better known as surround sound. A 5.1 channel system replaced the four-channel system that had been used throughout the 1970's and 1980's known as Dolby Stereo (Kerins, 2011). By the mid 1990's it became standard that all cinematic recordings rely solely on Dolby 5.1, and the industry was changed. As a result, existing content could now be remastered using this version of technology for a richer sound.

Industry engineers are trained subject matter experts who have established relationships with content creators, and were able to collaborate with them to create the necessary effects on an original asset to the creator's specifications. When finished, this allowed companies and creators of content the ability to remaster original works and rerelease them. Looking back on this industry innovation, we can see parallels in the process of updating assets through digitization to provide another means of releasing media for public consumption. With the ability to digitize original media to a modern format, artists were given the opportunity to monetize legacy assets through licensing agreements with streaming platform vendors. For the first time, many older films and media content were able to be released that had previously been unavailable to the public through this instant platform.

Innovation Born Out of Crisis

Updated practices that came as a result of COVID-19 restrictions. Google Workspaces remains in place, and corporate proficiency among colleagues is enhanced by the collaborative nature of the platforms. Additionally, this helps support the ability for more people to work remotely, and still be effective in their professional responsibilities with more proficiency than prior to the pandemic. Effective remote work has positively impacted this division of Iron Mountain in a few ways.

The configuration of space prior to the pandemic had all employees traditionally in their regional office locations operating in their respective workspaces to accomplish office or studio activities. The division was at capacity in terms of operational services, and maintained their traditional service offerings related to audio, video, and fine arts. Thanks to these adjusted work environment options for select engineer tasks, account management, sales, and customer service, physical space on site has fortuitously become available.

Studio engineers assigned to critical operations have been able to repurpose these newly unused office environments, and convert them to much needed studio space to meet the needs of workflow demands. More of a variety of projects can be in process at a time, which helps meet clients' needs with better time and cost efficiency. Additionally, this has allowed the division to innovate and expand their service portfolio of offerings to include photography services, and make an impact in different and emerging facets of the media industry. By having more variety of services across various regional sites, the division is saving time, energy, and preserving the safety of the assets involved, avoiding extraneous logistical commitments.

The concept of Studio in a Box was originally developed as an emergency response, in a time of crisis. It served as a creative way of accomplishing important customer projects, as well as a training method for developing newly promoted studio engineers and is still in place today. This concept has grown beyond its initial intended purpose, to where Iron Mountain Media and Archive Services can provide a mobile studio option for customer projects. As a global organization, Iron Mountain has locations servicing the industry world-wide.

Some locations specialize in different aspects of industry, and it is not uncommon that customers local to these sites request studio services. Studio in a Box now affords them the ability to travel with everything they need to meet the scope of a project to a facility that does not currently have studio capabilities. The Studio in a Box has since been developed into a mobile agile workstation, capable of operating anywhere in the world for any client-driven project. The community of practice that supports the training initiative associated with learning at a distance is now capable of occurring world-wide.

This flexibility in the digital world continues to popularize already existing services such as digital delivery. The need for digital delivery of assets has expanded beyond the traditional streaming of content to movie theaters, now that the pandemic is over and digitization can more easily occur anywhere. It remains as an enhanced and popular solution requested by customers as the new normal sets in post-pandemic.

Although the virtual summit sessions held during the first quarter of the year have returned to an in-person format, the company has found benefit in the educational experiences that occurred through the panel discussions and presentations between internal and external participants. As a result, monthly virtual training sessions are provided in the form of a series called *Learning Tables,* designed to bring employees together with different presenters to work on upskilling, and enhancing professional development sessions. Internal team members are encouraged to share knowledge on their areas of subject matter expertise, and outside trainers and experienced professionals are invited to contribute as well as a complimentary means of producing professional development content. This form of social learning is in alignment with web-based learning that promotes collaboration among professionals for a shared interest, the needs of which can drive the further development of these online collaborative spaces (Hill, Song, & West, 2009).

The social media presence across the division continues to develop and showcase a positive company presence in the industry. In addition to that, the platform known as *Currents,* as an internal community hub has been replaced and updated to a new and more dynamic platform called PEAK as a means of continuing the organizational trend of embracing 21st century learning. This platform has taken this concept a step further by incorporating elements of a learning community, information hub, as well as an internal social media network all in one easily accessible platform developed to support employees.

Realizing the benefits that came from the chaos of the pandemic in the area of collaboration helps bring employees together through innovative means. This has lead to solutions that were developed through professionals having space to engage within a community of practice (Wenger-Traynor, 2024). Understanding the professional benefits from these learning communities has helped within this division of Iron Mountain, and effort is being made to create a more formal infrastructure to support the community of practice with greater efficiency.

Coupled with the *Learning Tables* professional development series, employees are supported with the autonomous accessibility for important training and information (Kruszelnicki, 2019). Many assets, particularly legacy assets that were created prior to the digital era, require special handling, as well as a clear understanding of the various functions of a compatible playback device. This information is more easily shared across the division, and can be accessed autonomously with ease at the time an employee needs it most.

In addition to these learning and development options, Iron Mountain Media and Archive Services is developing a formal mentor program to help with employee retention, upskilling, and support (Hill & Bahniuk, 1998). They plan to rely on their local experts in the organization to develop the specifics, and utilize the experience of senior employees to share their knowledge in support of all members of the community, especially those who are new to the team. The pandemic has made lasting change in how training, growth, and business operates within this organization and new information and support is required. It may be in the form of a posted resource, or it may be through the ability to connect with an expert in the community to get a quick answer. It is undeniable, that these new channels support the success of the work environment for all employees within the community.

CONCLUSION

Virtual communities look different in every industry, but provide unique aid that helps individuals strive to overcome the impossible. Through aspects of project completion, customer service and development, as well as innovative training and productivity solutions, the employees in the Media and Archive Services division of Iron Mountain were able to innovate impactful solutions in a time of crisis. Aspects of social learning were incorporated, as well as communities of practice to develop virtual communities as a means of enrichment, professional development, and survival during the COVID-19 shutdown.

Over time, these strategies that emerged became refined in ways that helped redefine how media was disseminated. Older legacy assets were digitized and updated in ways that they could be shared with the world conveniently and safely through streaming platforms. Consumers relied on this content for entertainment and social and emotional distraction during a challenging time in history. Born out of these efforts, were new strategies, service offerings, and both personal and professional growth that continues to contribute to the strength of the division in the post-pandemic world. Each of these aspects are pillars in reestablishing the new normal, and ushering in a new era of media preservation and consumption.

REFERENCES

Arditi, D. (2021). *Streaming culture*. Emerald Publishing, Ltd. 10.1108/9781839827686

BBC. (2015, November 5). Binge-watch is Collin's Dictionary word of the year. BBC Entertainment and Arts. https://www.bbc.com/news/entertainment-arts-34723515

Bhandari, N. A. (n.d.). Using a professional development model to enhance instructional models. Virginia Tech. Retrieved from https://higherlogicdownload.s3.amazonaws .com/SPED/04bdc7a0-1ec9-4eaa-b61c-677439532d1a/UploadedImages/Journal _2012/CEC%20Art%202%20Bhandari%20Using_a_PD_Model_to_Enhance _Instructional_Practices%5B.pdf

Contentful. (2024). Digital content delivery platforms. https://www.contentful.com/ use-case/digital-delivery-platform/

Denison, C. (2020). 15 years of YouTube: How a failed dating site became the king of online video. *Yahoo Finance*. https://finance.yahoo.com/news/15-years-youtube -failed-dating-151144194

Desimone, L., Garet, M. (2015). Best practices in teachers' professional development in the United States. *Psychology, Society, and Education, 7*(5). DOI:10.25115. PSYE.V7I3.515

Desimone, L. M. (2009). Improving impact studies of teachers' professional development: Towards better conceptualizations and measures. *Educational Researcher*, 38(3), 181–200. 10.3102/0013189X08331140

Dictionary. (2024). Analog record. *Dictionary of archives terminology*. https:// dictionary.archivists.org/entry/analog-record.html

Hill, J. R., Song, L., & West, R. E. (2009, May 15). Social learning theory and web-based learning environments: A review of research and discussion of implications. *American Journal of Distance Education, 23*(2). https://doi-org.draweb.njcu .edu/10.1080/08923640902857713

Hill, S. K., & Bahniuk, M. H. (1998). Promoting career success through mentoring. *Review of Business*, 19(3), 4–7.

Imagen. (2020). Obsolete tape formats. https://imagen.io/resources/obsolete-tape - formats/

IncNow. (2020). Why form an LLC in Delaware. https://www.incnow.com/delaware - llc/#:~:text=You%20can%20form%20an%20LLC,Agents%20and%20Corpora- tions%2C%20Inc

Iron Mountain Incorporated. (2023). https://www.imes.media

Johnson, M.Jr. (2021, April 21). Hollywood survival strategies in the post-COVID 19 era. *Humanities & Social Sciences Communications*, 8(100), 100. 10.1057/ s41599-021-00776-z

Kaushik, M. (2020). Post COVID-19 world: A paradigm shift at workplace. *TEST Engineering and Management, 83.*

Kerins, M. (2011). *Beyond Dolby (Stereo): Cinema in the digital sound age.* Indiana university press.

Khriyenko, O., & Cochez, M. (2011). *Open environment for collaborative cloud ecosystems.* ResearchGate. cs.jyu.fi/ai/papers/OECCE-2011.pdf

Kruszelnicki, W. (2019, November 19). Self-directedness and the question of autonomy: From counterfeit education to transformative adult learning. *Studies in Philosophy and Education*, 39(2), 187–203. 10.1007/s11217-019-09697-6

Lamare, A. (2018). How streaming started: YouTube, Netflix, and Hulu's quick ascent. *The Business of Business.* https://www.businessofbusiness.com/articles/ a- brief-history-of-video-streaming-by-the-numbers/

McComb. (2015, January 3). *Improving teaching through collegial support.* Huffpost. Retrieved from https://www.huffpost.com/entry/improving-teaching-through -collegial-support_b_6089654

Monsoor, I. (2020) Netflix usage and statistics. *The business of apps.* https://www .businessofapps.com/data/netflix- statistics/#:~:text=The%20number%20subscrib- ing%20to%20three,47%25%20of%2065%2B%20users

Newswire, P. R. (2020). Video streaming market size is projected to reach USD 149.34 Billion by 2026. *Cision PR Newswire.* https://www.prnewswire.com/news -releases/video-streaming- market-size-is-projected-to-reach-usd-149-34-billion -by-2026--valuates-reports- 301142025.html

Sisson, P. (2020). The perfect virtual video store isn't Netflix – it's DVD. *Vox.* https://vox.com/culture/2020/4/23/21230324/Netflix-dvid-rental-classic-movies

Srinivasa, M. R. (2020). (2020, October). COVID-19 pandemic and emotional health: Social psychiatry perspective. *Indian Journal of Social Psychiatry*, 36(5), 24. Advance online publication. 10.4103/ijsp.ijsp_293_20

Video streaming market size, Share & Growth Report, 2030. Video Streaming Market Size, Share & Growth Report, 2030. (2020). https://www.grandviewresearch.com/ industry-analysis/video-streaming-market

Voit, K., Buliga, O., & Michl, K. (2016, July). Entertainment on demand: The case of Netflix. *Business model pioneers.* Springer.

Vonderau, P. (2016). The video bubble: Multichannel networks and the transformation of YouTube. *Convergence (London)*, 22(4), 361–375. 10.1177/1354856516641882

Watson, A. (2020). Share of adults who subscribe to a streaming service in the United States as of May 2020, by age group. *Statista.* https://www.statista.com/statistics/742452/media-streaming-services-penetration-rate age/#:~:text=Share%20 of%20adults%20who%20subscribe,U.S.%202019%2C%20by%2 0age%20group&-text=A%20survey%20held%20in%20the,above%20who%20said%20th e%20same

Wenger, E. (2000). Communities of practice and social learning systems. *Organization*, 7(2), 225-246. 10.1177/135050840072002

Wenger, E., White, N., & Smith, J. D. (2009). Digital habitats: Stewarding technology for communities. CPsquare.

Wenger-Trayner, E., & Wenger-Trayner, B. (2015). Introduction to communities of practice. Retrieved from https://wenger-trayner.com/introduction-to-communities -of-practice/

Wenger-Trayner, E., & Wenger-Trayner, B. (2024, January 9). *Can a community of practice exist only online?* Wenger-Trayner: Global theorists and consultants. https://www.wenger-trayner.com/online-communities-of-practice/

Wenger-Trayner, E., & Wenger-Trayner, B. (2024, January 11). *What is social learning?* Wenger-Trayner: Global theorists and consultants. https://www.wenger -trayner.com/what-is-social-learning/#:~:text=Etienne's%20work%20on%20social %20learning,others%20or%20use%20certain%20tools

Wood, L. (2020). United states over the top OTT market 2020-2025: High penetration of smart TV and the presence of major OTT providers. *Business Wire.* https://www .businesswire.com/news/home/20201113005493/en/United-States-Over-the- To p-OTT-Market-2020-2025-High-Penetration-Of-Smart-TV-And-The-Presence-Of-Major-OTT-Providers---ResearchAndMarkets.com

KEY TERMS AND DEFINITIONS

Analog Recording: is a method of capturing sound by directly imprinting it onto a physical medium such as audio, video tape, phonograph records, and text on paper. The process involves using a microphone to convert the original sound into electrical analog signals and are stored on a physical medium. Examples of analog formats include photographic prints, motion picture film, early audio and video tape, phonograph records, and text on paper.

Communities of Practice: Groups of individuals that share an interest and collaboratively learn to develop their skills in this interest through their interaction (Wenger-Trayner, 2015).

Digital Delivery: Recorded content converted to a digital file transferred and is distributed from creators via various platforms such as mobile phones, computed or tablets to meet the consumers' preference.

Digitizing: The process of converting recorded content stored on a physical medium into a digital file.

Dolby 5.1: Also known as surround sound. Was released as new recording technology in 1992, and became industry standard around 1995 for the film industry. This replaced Dolby 4.0 which was known as stereo recording and had been industry standard since the 1970's (Kerins, 2011).

Legacy Assets: Any recorded content on a physical media element that pre-dates digital production.

Media: Mass communication in the form of broadcasting, publishing, and the Internet.

Social Learning Theory: People learn from observing the experiences of others as well as the consequences, and can successfully develop by the influence of the successes and failures of others (Hill, Song, & West, 2009).

Studio in Box: Coined phrased utilized by Iron Mountain Media and Archival Services during the COVID-19 pandemic shutdown. This phrase describes how Iron Mountain was able to productize converting analog recordings into a digital file with the least amount of equipment and software making it portable to completed digital transfers remotely and anywhere in the world.

Conclusion

Learning has been occurring among individuals since the dawning of time. As a means of survival, groups of people living together have benefitted from the sharing methods, and traditions. This is evidenced by the way tribes moved and settled across various regions of the world, passing along important knowledge from elders down to the youngest members of the community.

The type of knowledge shifted from survival to different forms of innovation as communities established and matured over time. Culture and education became more formalized in terms of what information was important to preserve and pass on. These types of curricular focus changed over the years, based on what was important for an individual to know in the era and social class in which they were living. For example, Children born to high society families were educated to master different skills than the children living on a farming estate. Gender also was a factor, and for centuries communities decided that there were specific roles most appropriate for males and females within the group that would benefit the community.

Learning specified skills and traditions positioned one for success in their particular path in life, and the community to which they belonged was there to guide them and benefit from their success as well. As the needs of the community and the world around evolved, so did the skills and type of community support. A wider variety of communities emerged that an individual could belong to, all making their unique contributions to the world. In modern times, we can view many professional examples from labor unions, to professional organizations, as well as informal groups focusing on hobbies or interests such as historical societies, or motorcycle clubs. Communities continue to evolve and meet the needs of their members, while also providing a place to expand knowledge on a particular interest within the supportive environment of a group.

A significant amount of change has occurred between generations that were raised throughout the 20th century, and today. Where children may have used notebooks and pencils in the mid 1900's, much of what they learn is now recorded on cloud-based documents and easily shared online with their educators from home. Communities that once met solely through in-person settings to exchange ideas, can now be joined by individuals world-wide through social media groups. The variety and accessibility to knowledge and communities has been forever changed since the advent of modern technology. Learning communities of yesterday can all be enhanced through technological components that now can make learning autonomous and accessible anywhere at any time with a single click on a mobile device.

The impact virtual communities continue to have on life in the 21st century is one that is hard to ignore. Within the first twenty years of the century society has learned unique ways to integrate the reliance on technology to support community engagement. Access to the Internet on a household basis helped individuals connect with information online, but eventually led to the development of social interaction that utilized this type of technology. The evolution of which provided the ability for people to connect socially, create media, enroll and engage in online programs for school, as well as professional training. The marriage of these social components of online technology opened the world to new means of connection through learning.

The nature of the COVID-19 challenged the ability of induvials to utilize these avenues to continue life through a long period of quarantine. When it was not safe to gather socially, many communities started exchanging through various forms of online platforms. Education moved to a virtual model, where students from Kindergarten all the way through higher education used new platforms to access educational content, and community to help them achieve in times of emergency. Several authors associated with this book showcased creative means of producing school concerts, focusing on naturally collaborative and hands-on subjects related to STEAM, important solutions to meet the needs of all students as well as supporting educators with solutions for learning in a fast-paced professional environment while relying on virtual communities in the field.

Others focused on the business world, where upskilling to stay current in a changing world was imperative not only to keep the supply chain going, but also to make sure that business services could be provided with regularity. In some cases, companies found creative solutions to work with social distancing, by integrating new platforms for collaborating and servicing their customers, which in turn, serviced a vulnerable global population with supplies, as well as entertainment at a time they needed it most. Authors raised important points to help understand the changes and benefits that came out of this time related to the physical and digital natures of the business world.

While the world shut down with precautionary measures, essential workers in the healthcare and research fields were called to action. Our authors focus on means of collaborating as a community for research purposes with virtual technologies, as well as training healthcare workers with just-in-time techniques. This period in history challenged experts in these fields immensely, with the need to discover more, collaborate more, and learn new techniques at a distance to be able to perform them with expert efficiency. The virtual nature of these fields helped save lives and move society through a difficult time in history, to one of hope and better health.

The purpose of this book was to illuminate areas where virtual communities were utilized in aspects of professional practice, as a testament to the vast impact that the combination of community with modern technology can have. Progress in this area has come quickly in the 21st century, and in a short time society was challenged with finding unique solutions for virtual community and collaboration. This has contributed to a new normal emerging for learning and development, where communities can now rely on tried-and-true technological methods to share information and deliver instruction. This is not only localized to areas of education, but healthcare, business, informal community groups, as well as larger global organizations. Information can be shared and connections can be made for personal and professional development with anyone that has access to virtual technologies, and thanks to the innovation in this field, accessibility is more wide-spread than ever.

As people acclimate to a post pandemic world, they are challenged to utilize the benefits at their fingertips to continue to grow in positive ways. There is a societal opportunity to use what we have learned to establish new means of connection that could redefine how people in the world operate across a variety of fields. Looking back on these chapters, a glimpse of cutting-edge progress is provided, based on a call to action at that time in history. It is important to continue to look to the future to ask ourselves what our capabilities are, as well as what new structures need to be established for the future, and challenge this new status quo to continue developing solutions through virtual collaboration.

Compilation of References

Abedini, A., Abedin, B., & Zowghi, D. (2021). Adult learning in online communities of practice: A systematic review. *British Journal of Educational Technology*, 52(4), 1663–1694. 10.1111/bjet.13120

About Soundtrap. (2024). Soundtrap. https://www.soundtrap.com/about

AbuKhousa, E., El-Tahawy, M. S., & Atif, Y. (2023). Envisioning architecture of metaverse intensive learning experience (MiLEx): Career readiness in the 21st century and collective intelligence development scenario. *Future Internet*, 15(2), 53. 10.3390/fi15020053

Adams, C. (2019). TPACK model: The ideal modern classroom. In Power, R. (Ed.), *Technology and the curriculum: Summer 2019*. Power Learning Solutions.

Aguillo Caño, I. F., Uribe Tirado, A., & López López, W. (2017). Visibilidad de los investigadores colombianos según sus indicadores en Google Scholar y ResearchGate. Diferencias y similitudes con la clasificación oficial del sistema nacional de ciencia - COLCIENCIAS. *Revista Interamericana de Bibliotecologia, 40*(3), 221–230. https://doi-org.nassdoceresources.remotexs.in/10.17533/udea.rib.v40n3a03

Alali, H., & Salim, J. (2013). Virtual Communities of Practice Success Model to Support Knowledge Sharing behaviour in Healthcare Sector. *Procedia Technology, 11*, 176–183. 10.1016/j.protcy.2013.12.178

Ali, M. Y., Wolski, M., & Richardson, J. (2017). Strategies for using ResearchGate to improve institutional research outcomes. *Library Review*, 66(8/9), 726–739. 10.1108/LR-07-2017-0060

Allen, I. E., & Seaman, J. (2016). *Online report card: Tracking online education in the United States*. Babson Survey Research Group and Quahog Research Group, LLC. https://files.eric.ed.gov/fulltext/ED572777.pdf

Compilation of References

Amees, M., & Singson, M. (2015). Faculty contributions and activities on Academic Social Networking Sites: a study onResearchGate. In *Proceedings of National Conference on Future Libraries. Issues and Challenges.* Retrieved from https://www.researchgate.net/profile/Mangkhollen-Singson/publication/284726628_Faculty_contributions_and_activities_on_Academic_Social_Networking_Sites_a_study_on_ResearchGate/links/565830cb08aefe619b208da6/Faculty-contributions-and-activities-on-Academic-Social-Networking-Sites-a-study-on-ResearchGate.pdf

Anafarta, A., & Apaydin, C. (2016). The Effect of Faculty Mentoring on Career Success and Career Satisfaction. *International Education Studies*, 9(6), 22. 10.5539/ies.v9n6p22

Anderson, V., Gifford, J., & Wildman, J. (2020). An evaluation of social learning and learner outcomes in a massive open online course (MOOC): A healthcare sector case study. *Human Resource Development International*, 23(3), 208–237. Advance online publication. 10.1080/13678868.2020.1721982

Andrikopoulou, A., Rowley, J., & Walton, G. (2022). Research Data Management (RDM) and the Evolving Identity of Academic Libraries and Librarians: A Literature Review. *New Review of Academic Librarianship*, 28(4), 349–365. 10.1080/13614533.2021.1964549

Angelle, P. S. (2008). Communities of practice promote shared learning for organizational success. *Middle School Journal*, 39(5), 52–58. 10.1080/00940771.2008.11461654

Anon. (n.d.-a). Data Management & Open Science. *Vrije Universiteit Brussel.* Retrieved December 15, 2023 (https://www.vub.be/en/our-research/our-vision-and-mission/optimal-research-environment/data-management-open-science)

Anon. (n.d.-b). What Is Research Data Management. Retrieved December 15, 2023 (https://datamanagement.hms.harvard.edu/about/what-research-data-management)

Antonello, A., & Cook, M. (2023). Environmental historians, policy, and governance. In *The Routledge handbook of environmental history* (p. 399–412). 10.4324/9781003189350-32

Anyim, W. O. (2021). Use of academic social networking sites among lecturers in state universities. *Journal of Media, Culture and Communication, 1*(1), 1-13.

Arditi, D. (2021). *Streaming culture.* Emerald Publishing, Ltd. 10.1108/9781839827686

Arkorful, V., & Abaidoo, N. (2014). The Role of e-Learning, the Advantages and Disadvantages of Its Adoption in Higher Education. *International Journal of Education and Research*, 2, 397–410.

Arslan-Ari, I., Ari, F., Grant, M., & Morris, W. (2018). Action research experiences for scholarly practitioners in an online education doctorate program: Design, reality, and lessons learned. *TechTrends*, 62(5), 441–449. 10.1007/s11528-018-0308-3

Ashiq, M., Usmani, M. H., & Naeem, M. (2022). A systematic literature review on research data management practices and services. *Global Knowledge. Memory and Communication*, 71(8/9), 649–671. 10.1108/GKMC-07-2020-0103

Ashong, C. Y., & Commander, N. E. (2012). Ethnicity, gender, and perceptions of online learning in higher education. *Journal of Online Learning and Teaching*, 8(2), 98–110. https://jolt.merlot.org/vol8no2/ashong_0612.pdf

Asmi, N. A., & Margam, M. (2018). Academic social networking sites for researchers in Central Universities of Delhi: A study of ResearchGate and Academia. Global Knowledge. *Memory and Communication*, 67(1/2), 91–108. 10.1108/GKMC-01-2017-0004

Avery, D. R., & Thomas, K. M. (2004). Blending content and contact: The roles of diversity curriculum and campus heterogeneity in fostering diversity management competency. *Academy of Management Learning & Education*, 3(4), 380–396. 10.5465/amle.2004.15112544

Avidov-Ungar, O., & Zion, R. (2019). The characteristics and perceptions of teachers engaged in leading professional communities. *Teacher Development*, 23(3), 325–344. 10.1080/13664530.2019.1607772

Babette, A. (2018). The development of STEAM educational policy to promote student creativity and social empowerment. *Arts Education Policy Review*, 119(2).

Baker, L. R., Phelan, S., Woods, N. N., Boyd, V. A., Rowland, P., & Ng, S. L. (2021). Re-envisioning paradigms of education: Towards awareness, alignment, and pluralism. *Advances in Health Sciences Education : Theory and Practice*, 26(3), 1045–1058. 10.1007/s10459-021-10036-z33742339

Baldwin, S. J., & Ching, Y.-H. (2021). Accessibility in online courses: A review of national and statewide evaluation instruments. *TechTrends*, 65(5), 731–742. 10.1007/s11528-021-00624-6

Banaji, M. R., & Greenwald, A. G. (2019). *Blindspot: Hidden biases of good people*. Random House Publishing Group.

Bandura, A. (1991). Social CognitiveTheory of Self-regulation. *Organizational Behavior and Human Decision Processes*, 50(2), 248–287. 10.1016/0749-5978(91)90022-L

Barber, P. H., Hayes, T. B., Johnson, T. L., & Marquez-Magana, L. (2020). Systemic racism in higher education. *Science*, 369(6510), 1440–1441. 10.1126/science.abd714032943517

Barker, P., & Campbell, L. M. (2016). Technology Strategies for Open Educational Resource Dissemination. In *Open Education: International Perspectives in Higher Education* (pp. 51-71). Cambridge, UK: Open Book Publishers. 10.11647/OBP.0103.03

Barnett, S., Jones, S. C., Bennett, S., Iverson, D., & Bonney, A. (2012). General practice training and virtual communities of practice - A review of the literature. *BMC Family Practice*, 13(1), 1–13. 10.1186/1471-2296-13-8722905827

Barni, D., Daioni, F., & Benefene, P. (2019, July). Teacher's self-efficacy: The role of personal values and motivations for teaching. Frontiers in psychology. Retrieved from https://www.frontiersin.org/articles/10.3389/fpsyg.2019.01645/full#:~:text=Teachers'%20self%2Defficacy%2C%20namely,being%20in%20the%20working%20environment

Compilation of References

Barron, J. (2007). Lessons from the bandstand: Using jazz as a model for a constructivist approach to music education. *Music Educators Journal*, 94(2), 18–21. 10.1177/002743210709400205

BBC. (2015, November 5). Binge-watch is Collin's Dictionary word of the year. BBC Entertainment and Arts. https://www.bbc.com/news/entertainment-arts-34723515

Bentley, C., Browman, G. P., & Poole, B. (2010). Conceptual and practical challenges for implementing the communities of practice model on a national scale - a Canadian cancer control initiative. *BMC Health Services Research*, 10(3), 1–8. https://www.biomedcentral.com/1472 -6963/10/3. 10.1186/1472-6963-10-320051125

Bermejo-Caja, C. J., Koatz, D., Orrego, C., Perestelo-Pérez, L., González-González, A. I., Ballester, M., Pacheco-Huergo, V., Del Rey-Granado, Y., Muñoz-Balsa, M., Ramírez-Puerta, A. B., Canellas-Criado, Y., Pérez-Rivas, F. J., Toledo-Chávarri, A., Martínez-Marcos, M., Alejo-Díaz-Zorita, C., Barbero-Macías, C. A., Borrell-Punzón, F., Bueno-Rodriguez, B., Colmena-Martin, B., & Villanueva-Sanz, C. (2019). Acceptability and feasibility of a virtual community of practice to primary care professionals regarding patient empowerment: A qualitative pilot study. *BMC Health Services Research*, 19(1), 1–10. 10.1186/s12913-019-4185-z31221215

Bhalla, S., Bahar, N., & Kanapathy, K. (2023). Knowledge collaboration among fashion designers: An A Priori conceptual model. *The Electronic Journal of Knowledge Management, 21*(3). https://academic-publishing.org/index.php/ejkm/article/view/2928/2180

Bhandari, N. A. (n.d.). Using a professional development model to enhance instructional models. Virginia Tech. Retrieved from https://higherlogicdownload.s3.amazonaws.com/SPED/04bdc7a0 -1ec9-4eaa-b61c-677439532d1a/UploadedImages/Journal_2012/CEC%20Art%202%20Bhandari %20Using_a_PD_Model_to_Enhance_Instructional_Practices%5B.pdf

Birkbeck, G., Nagle, T., & Sammon, D. (2022). Challenges in research data management practices: A literature analysis. *Journal of Decision Systems, 31*(sup1), 153-167. 10.1080/12460125.2022.2074653

Bissessar, C. (2022). The role of virtual community of practice in alleviating social and professional isolation during emergency remote teaching. *Equity in Education & Society*, 1(1), 114–125. 10.1177/27526461211068512

Black, G. (2021). Implementing action research in a teacher preparation program: Opportunities and limitations. *Canadian Journal of Action Research, 21*(2), 47-71.

Blair, D. V. (2009). Stepping aside. *Music Educators Journal*, 95(3), 42–45. 10.1177/0027432108330760

Bozeman & Boardman. (2014). *Research Collaboration and Team Science: A State-of-the-Art Review and Agenda*. SpringerLink.

Braunston, T. (2018). 10 ways to enhance professional development with an LMS. *Knowledge anywhere.*https://www.knowledgeanywhere.com/resources/article-detail/10-ways-to-enhance -professional-development-with-lms

Brooks, J., Grugulis, I., & Cook, H. (2020). Rethinking Situated Learning: Participation and Communities of Practice in the UK Fire and Rescue Service. *Work, Employment and Society*, 34(6), 1045–1061. 10.1177/0950017020913225

Broom, D. (2023). Four-day work week trial in Spain leads to healthier workers, less pollution. *World Economic Forum*. https://www.weforum.org/agenda/2023/10/surprising-benefits-four -day-week/

Brown, L. (2004). Diversity: The challenge for higher education. *Race, Ethnicity and Education*, 7(1), 21–34. 10.1080/1361332042000187289

Budrytė, M., & Vainauskienė, V. (2023). Virtual Communities of Practice as a Knowledge Sharing Tool: Recommendations for International Business. *Management of Organizations: Systematic Research*, 89(1), 15–30. 10.2478/mosr-2023-0002

Burgess, A., van Diggele, C., & Mellis, C. (2018). Mentorship in the health professions: A review. *The Clinical Teacher*, 15(3), 197–202. 10.1111/tct.1275629318730

Burns, M., Naughton, M., Preast, J., Wang, Z., Gordon, R., Robb, V., & Smith, M. (2018). Factors of professional learning community implementation and effect on student achievement. *Journal of Educational & Psychological Consultation*, 28(4), 394–412. 10.1080/10474412.2017.1385396

Cairncross, S., & Mannion, M. (2001). Interactive multimedia and learning: Realizing the benefits. *Innovations in Education and Teaching International*, 38(2), 156–164. 10.1080/14703290110035428

Cairns, L. G. (2022). Learning and work: theories and developments. In M. Malloch, L. Cairns, K. Evans, & B. O'Connor (Eds.), *The SAGE handbook of learning and work* (pp. 5-33). Sage Publishing. 10.4135/9781529757217.n2

Cairns, L., & Malloch, M. (2011). Theories of work, place and learning: New directions. In M. Malloch, L. Cairns, K. Evans, & B. N. O'Connor (Eds.), *The SAGE handbook of workplace learning* (First ed., pp. 3 - 16). SAGE Publications Ltd.

Calvert, S. L., Strong, B. L., & Gallagher, L. (2005). Control as an engagement feature for young children's attention to and learning of computer content. *The American Behavioral Scientist*, 48(5), 578–589. 10.1177/0002764204271507

Camarinha-Matos & Afsarmanesh. (2008). Concept of Collaboration. Academic Press.

CAST. (2018). Universal design for learning guidelines version 2.2. https://udlguidelines.cast.org/

Centor, E. (2024). Why training needs assessment is important to an organization. *Trainsmart Inc.* https://www.trainsmartinc.com/why-training-needs-assessment/

Chai, C. S. (2018). Teacher professional development for science technology engineering and math (STEM) education: A review from the perspectives of technical pedagogical content. *The Asia-Pacific Education Researcher*, 28(1). 10.1007/s40299-018-0400-7

Compilation of References

Chang, B. (2021). Situated Learning – Foreign Sites as Learning Contexts. *Journal of Comparative & International Higher Education*, 13(2), 5–22. 10.32674/jcihe.v13i2.2615

Chase, M., Macfadyen, L., Reeder, K., & Roche, J. (2002). Intercultural challenges in networked learning: Hard technologies meet soft skills. *First Monday*, 7(8). Advance online publication. 10.5210/fm.v7i8.975

Chawinga, W. D., & Zinn, S. (2021). Research Data Management in Universities: A Comparative Study from the Perspectives of Librarians and Management. *The International Information & Library Review*, 53(2), 97–111. 10.1080/10572317.2020.1793448

Chen, P.-Y. (2020). Academic Social Networks and Collaboration Patterns. *Library Hi Tech*, 38(2), 293–307. 10.1108/LHT-01-2019-0026

Chien, F. (2023). The role of corporate governance and environmental and social responsibilities on the achievement of sustainable development goals in Malaysian logistic companies. *Ekonomska Istrazivanja*, 36(1), 1610–1630. 10.1080/1331677X.2022.2090407

Christofi, K., Chourides, P., & Papageorgiou, G. (2023). Cultivating Strategic Agility - An Empirical Investigation in Best Practice. *Global Business and Organizational Excellence*, 00, 1–17. 10.1002/joe.22241

Chrome Music Lab. (n.d.). https://musiclab.chromeexperiments.com/About

Clapper, T. C. (2015). Cooperative-Based Learning and the Zone of Proximal Development. *Simulation & Gaming*, 46(2), 148–158. 10.1177/1046878115569044

Clement, S. (2018). Concept Analysis of Virtual Mentoring. *COJ Nursing & Healthcare*, 1(5), 111–116. 10.31031/COJNH.2018.01.000525

Cochran, J. D., Campbell, S. M., Baker, H. M., & Leeds, E. M. (2014). The role of student characteristics in predicting retention in online courses. *Research in Higher Education*, 55(1), 27–48. 10.1007/s11162-013-9305-8

Cohen, G. L., Garcia, J., Purdie-Vaughns, V., Apfel, N., & Brzustoski, P. (2009). Recursive processes in self-affirmation: Intervening to close the minority achievement gap. *Science*, 324(5925), 400–403. 10.1126/science.117076919372432

College of the Holy Cross. (2023). Montserrat. https://www.holycross.edu/holy-cross-approach/montserrat

Colombi, E., & Knosp, S. (2017). Teaching Dance with Online Course ManagementSystems. *Journal of Distance Education*, 17, 73–76.

Colomer, J., Serra, T., Cañabate, D., & Bubnys, R. (2020). Reflective learning in higher education: Active methodologies for transformative practices. *Sustainability (Basel)*, 12(9), 3827. 10.3390/su12093827

Conradty, C., & Bogner, F. X. (2020) STEAM teaching professional development works: Effects on students' creativity and motivation. *Smart Learning Environments,7*(26).

Contentful. (2024). Digital content delivery platforms. https://www.contentful.com/use-case/digital-delivery-platform/

Contu, A., & Willmott, H. (2003). Re-Embedding Situatedness: The Importance of Power Relations in Learning Theory. *Organization Science*, 14(3), 283–296. 10.1287/orsc.14.3.283.15167

Cooke, F. L., & Rogovsky, N. (2023). Human-centred approach to increasing workplace productivity: Evidence from Asia. *International Labour Organization.* https://www.ilo.org/wcmsp5/groups/public/---dgreports/---inst/documents/publication/wcms_906606.pdf

Cooper, K., Stanulis, R., Brondyk, S., Hamilton, E., Macaluso, M., & Meier, J. (2016). The teacher leadership process: Attempting change within embedded systems. *Journal of Educational Change*, 17(1), 85–113. 10.1007/s10833-015-9262-4

Correa, T., & Jeong, S. H. (2011). Race and online content creation. *Information Communication and Society*, 14(5), 638–659. 10.1080/1369118X.2010.514355

Crawford, R. (2017). Rethinking teaching and learning pedagogy for education in the twenty-first century: Blended learning in music education. *Music Education Research*, 19(2), 195–213. 10.1080/14613808.2016.1202223

Cuello, H. (2023). Assessing the validity of four-day week pilots. *Joint Research Centre.*https://joint-research-centre.ec.europa.eu/system/files/2023-04/JRC133008_jrc133008_dclass_wp_assessing_four-day_week_pilots_final.pdf

da Silva, R. F., Gimenes, I. M. S., & Maldonado, J. C. (2020). The challenge of evaluating virtual communities of practice: A systematic mapping study. *Interdisciplinary Journal of Information, Knowledge, and Management*, 15, 39–64. 10.28945/4505

Dalton, W. (2019). What is STEM? Pearson accelerated pathways. Retrieved from https://pearsonaccelerated.com/blog/stem

Danish National Forum for Research Data Management. (n.d.).The FAIR principles. Retrieved from https://www.howtofair.dk/what-is-fair/

Davis, M. D., Witchcraft, S. M., Baird, S. O., & Smits, J. A. (2017). *The science of cognitive behavioral therapy*. Academic press., 10.1016/B978-0-12-803457-6.00003-9

Day week global (2023). https://www.4dayweek.com/

de Carvalho, A. A., Cirera, R. dos R. & Mengalli, N. M. (2023). FoLo - fear of logging off: Medo de ficar sem conexão. *26ª carta de conjuntura.*https://www.uscs.edu.br/boletim/1603

De Regt, H. W. (2020). Understanding, values, and the aims of science. *Philosophy of Science*, 87(5), 921–932. 10.1086/710520

Compilation of References

De Wit, H. (2011). *Trends, issues and challenges in internationalisation of higher education.* Centre for Applied Research on Economics and Management, Hogeschool van Amsterdam. https://www.eurashe.eu/wp-content/uploads/2022/02/wg4-r-internationalization-trends-issues -and-challenges-hans-de-wit.pdf

Denison, C. (2020). 15 years of YouTube: How a failed dating site became the king of online video. *Yahoo Finance.* https://finance.yahoo.com/news/15-years-youtube-failed-dating-151144194

Desimone, L., Garet, M. (2015). Best practices in teachers' professional development in the United States. *Psychology, Society, and Education, 7*(5). DOI:10.25115.PSYE.V7I3.515

Desimone, L. M. (2009). Improving impact studies of teachers' professional development: Towards better conceptualizations and measures. *Educational Researcher*, 38(3), 181–200. 10.3102/0013189X08331140

Dewey, J. (1979). *Experiência e educação.* Companhia editora nacional.

Dictionary. (2024). Analog record. *Dictionary of archives terminology.* https://dictionary.archivists .org/entry/analog-record.html

Dietl, J. E., Derksen, C., Keller, F. M., & Lippke, S. (2023). Interdisciplinary and interprofessional communication intervention: How psychological safety fosters communication and increases patient safety. *Frontiers in Psychology*, 14, 1164288. Advance online publication. 10.3389/fpsyg.2023.116428837397302

Dong, Y., Xu, C., Song, X., Fu, Q., Chai, C. S., & Huang, Y. (2018). Exploring the effects of contextual factors on in-service teachers' engagement in STEM teaching. *The Asia-Pacific Education Researcher*, 28(1), 25–34. 10.1007/s40299-018-0407-0

Dowling, S., Earl, S., & Stokes, D. (2018). *Mentoring Handbook: Project and Programme management, Community of Practice.* University College London. www.ucl.ac.uk

Dutra, D. L., Santos, H. R. M., & Silva, R. S. (2013). Inovação em processos de aprendizagem. https://www.researchgate.net/publication/263426362_Inovacao_em_Processos_de_Aprendizagem

Eberhardt, J. L. (2019). *Biased: Uncovering the hidden prejudice that shapes what we see, think, and do.* Penguin Books.

Echeburúa, E. (2013). Overuse of social networking. In Miller, P. M. (Ed.), *Principles of Addiction* (pp. 911–920). Academic Press. 10.1016/B978-0-12-398336-7.00092-9

Edgar, S. N. (2017). *Music education and social emotional learning: The heart of teaching music.* G. I. A. Publishing.

Education-Colleges.com. (2021). Retrieved from https://www.education-colleges.com/bachelors -degree-ba- bs/#:~:text=All%20states%20in%20the%20U.S.,and%2C%20eventually%2C%20 for%20teaching.

Evering, D., Pratt, I., & Brodeur, J. J. (2022). The current state of research data management (RDM) at McMaster. Academic Press.

Facebook, P. (2012). *Economist*, 402(8771), 80.

Fani, T., & Ghaemi, F. (2011). Implications of Vygotsky's zone of proximal development (ZPD) in teacher education: ZPTD and self-scaffolding. *Procedia: Social and Behavioral Sciences*, 29, 1549–1554. 10.1016/j.sbspro.2011.11.396

Fayez, O., Ismail, H., & Aboelnagah, H. (2023). Emerging Virtual Communities of Practice during Crises: A Sustainable Model Validating the Levels of Peer Motivation and Support. *Sustainability (Basel)*, 15(7), 1–19. 10.3390/su15075691

Field, A. (2018). Solutions to the STEM teacher shortage. *The network: CISCO's technology news site.* Retrieved from https://newsroom.cisco.com/feature-content?type=webcontent&articleId=1916176

Figlio, D., Rush, M., & Yin, L. (2013). Is it live or is it internet? Experimental estimates of the effects of online instruction on student learning. *Journal of Labor Economics*, 31(4), 763–784. 10.1086/669930

Fleming, N. D. (2011). *Teaching and learning styles: VARK strategies.* Neil D. Fleming.

Freire, P. (1989). A importância do ato de ler: Em três artigos que se completam. *Coleção Polêmicas do Nosso Tempo.* Autores associados: Cortez.

Freire, P. (2003). *Pedagogia da esperança: Um encontro com a pedagogia do oprimido.* Paz e terra.

Frenk, J., Chen, L. C., Chandran, L., Groff, E. O. H., King, R., Meleis, A., & Fineberg, H. V. (2022). Challenges and opportunities for educating health professionals after the COVID-19 pandemic. *Lancet*, 400(10362), 1539–1556. 10.1016/S0140-6736(22)02092-X36522209

Gairín, J., Rodríguez-Gómez, D., & Barrera-Corominas, A. (2020). Hints for rethinking communities of practice in public administration: An analysis from real practice. In I. Management Association (Ed.), *Open Government: Concepts, Methodologies, Tools, and Applications* (pp. 342-363). IGI Global. 10.4018/978-1-5225-9860-2.ch018

Gale, T., & Mills, C. (2013). Creating spaces in higher education for marginalised Australians: Principles for socially inclusive pedagogies. *Enhancing Learning in the Social Sciences*, 5(2), 7–19. 10.11120/elss.2013.00008

Gammelgaard, J. (2010). Knowledge retrieval through virtual communities of practice. *Behaviour & Information Technology*, 29(4), 349–362. 10.1080/01449290903548406

Garlock, L. (2020). Contributions of Jazz to Modern Music. *Copyright Alliance.* https://copyrightalliance.org/contributions-of-jazz-to-modern-music/#:~:text=Rock%2C%20R%26B%2C%20Hip%2Dhop,R%26B%20or%20Latin%20styled%20tunes

Garriott, P. O., Ko, S.-J., Grant, S. B., Jessen, M., & Allan, B. A. (2023). When race and class collide: Classism and social-emotional experiences of first-generation college students. *Journal of College Student Retention*, 25(3), 509–532. 10.1177/1521025121995483

Gaskins, R., & Williams, A. (2022) *Set your team on fire: The three elements of a professional learning community*. Academic Press.

Geng, J., Jong, M. S., & Chai, C. S. (2018). Hong Kong teachers' self-efficacy and concerns about STEM education. *The Asia-Pacific Education Researcher*, 28(1), 35–45. 10.1007/s40299-018-0414-1

Ghamrawi, N. (2022). Teachers' virtual communities of practice: A strong response in times of crisis or just another Fad? *Education and Information Technologies*, 27(5), 5889–5915. 10.1007/s10639-021-10857-w35095322

Gherardi, S. (2000). Practice-based theorizing on learning and knowing in organizations. *Organization*, 7(2), 211–223. 10.1177/135050840072001

Ginsberg, M., & Wlodkowski, R. (2009). *Diversity and motivation: Culturally responsive teaching in college* (2nd ed.). Joseey-Bass.

Girl Scout Research Institute. (2019). Decoding the digital girl: Defining and supporting girls' leadership. Retrieved from https://www.girlscouts.org/content/dam/girlscouts-gsusa/forms-and-documents/about-girl-scouts/research/GSUSA_GSRI_Decoding-the-Digital- Girl_Full-Report.pdf

Gohn, D. M. (2009). *Educação musical a distância: propostas para o ensino e aprendizagem de percussão* (Doctoral Dissertation). Universidade de São Paulo, São Paulo.

Gonen, A., Lev-Ari, L., Sharo, D., & Amzalag, M. (2016). Situated learning: The feasibility of an experimental learning of information technology for academic nursing students. *Cogent Education*, 3(1), 1–8. 10.1080/2331186X.2016.1154260

Gorska, A., Korzynski, P., Mazurek, G., & Pucciarelli, F. (2020). The role of social media in scholarly collaboration: An enabler of international research team's activation? *Journal of Global Information Technology Management*, 23(4), 273–291. 10.1080/1097198X.2020.1817684

Greene, P. (2022). There is no teacher shortage. So why is everyone talking about it. *Forbes*.

Gremli, J. (1996). Tuned in to learning styles. *Music Educators Journal*, 83(3), 24–27. 10.2307/3398974

Grierson, A. L., & Woloshyn, V. E. (2012). Walking the talk: Supporting teachers' growth with differentiated professional learning. *Taylor and Francis online*. 10.1080/19415257.2012.763143

Griffith, A. N., Hurd, N. M., & Hussain, S. B. (2019). "I didn't come to school for this": A qualitative examination of experiences with race-related stressors and coping responses among Black students attending a predominantly White institution. *Journal of Adolescent Research*, 34(2), 115–139. 10.1177/0743558417742983

Griffiths, A.-J., Alsip, J., Hart, S. R., Round, R. L., & Brady, J. (2021). Together We Can Do So Much: A Systematic Review and Conceptual Framework of Collaboration in Schools. *Canadian Journal of School Psychology*, 36(1), 59–85. 10.1177/0829573520915368

Grima, F., Paillé, P., Mejia, J. H., & Prud'Homme, L. (2014). Exploring the benefits of mentoring activities for the mentor. *Career Development International*, 19(4), 469–490. 10.1108/CDI-05-2012-0056

Groot, F., Jonker, G., Rinia, M., Ten Cate, O., & Hoff, R. G. (2020). Simulation at the Frontier of the Zone of Proximal Development: A Test in Acute Care for Inexperienced Learners. *Academic Medicine*, 95(7), 1098–1105. 10.1097/ACM.0000000000003265321347833

Grosik, S. A., & Kanno, Y. (2021). Peripheral or Marginal Participation? University-Based Intensive English Programs as an Entryway to U.S. Academia. *Journal of International Students*, 11(4), 914–931. 10.32674/jis.v11i4.1828

Guyotte, K., Sochacka, N., Costantino, T., Walther, J., & Kellam, N. (2014). STEAM as social practice cultivating creativity in transdisciplinary spaces. *Art Education*, 67(6), 12–19. 10.1080/00043125.2014.11519293

Haas, A., Abonneau, D., Borzillo, S., & Guillaume, L. (2021). Afraid of engagement? Towards an understanding of engagement in virtual communities of practice. *Knowledge Management Research and Practice*, 19(2), 169–180. 10.1080/14778238.2020.1745704

Hailu, M., & Wu, J. (2021). The use of academic social networking sites in scholarly communication: Scoping review. *Data and Information Management*, 5(2), 277–298. 10.2478/dim-2020-0050

Hajah, P., Norainna, S., Pengiran, B., & Basar, H. (2018). Situated learning theory: The key to effective classroom teaching? *International Journal for Educational, Social, Political &Cultural Studies*, 1(1), 49–60.

Hamad, F., Al-Fadel, M., & Al-Soub, A. (2021). Awareness of Research Data Management Services at Academic Libraries in Jordan: Roles, Responsibilities and Challenges. *New Review of Academic Librarianship*, 27(1), 76–96. 10.1080/13614533.2019.1691027

Hammond, Z. (2015). *Culturally responsive teaching and the brain: Promoting authentic engagement and rigor among culturally and linguistically diverse students*. Corwin Press.

Haris, M., Ali, N., & Vaidya, P. (2023). Assessment of ResearchGate to Unfurl the Academic Pursuits of Physics Scholars. *Journal of Scientometric Research*, 12(2), 490–500. 10.5530/jscires.12.2.045

Hart, C. (2012). Factors associated with student persistence in an online program of study: A review of the literature. *Journal of Interactive Online Learning*, 11(1), 19–42.

Hase, S., & Blaschke, L. M. (2022). Heutagogy, work and lifelong learning. In M. Malloch, L. Cairns, K. Evans, & B. O'Connor (Eds.), *The SAGE handbook of learning and work* (pp. 80–98). Sage Publishing. 10.4135/9781529757217.n6

Compilation of References

Herr, D. J. C., Akbar, B., Brummet, J., Flores, S., Gordon, A., Gray, B., & Murday, J. (2019, August). Convergence education- an international perspective. J Nanopart Research. *Vol. 21*(229). *Journal of Nanoparticle Research*, 2019(21), 229. 10.1007/s11051-019-4638-7

Heuer, A. (2020). Research data management. *Information Technology, 62*(1), 1-5. 10.1515/itit-2020-0002

Hewitt, D. (2018). Constructing informal experiences in the elementary general music classroom. *Music Educators Journal*, 104(3), 46–53. 10.1177/0027432117745361

Hill, J. R., Song, L., & West, R. E. (2009, May 15). Social learning theory and web-based learning environments: A review of research and discussion of implications. *American Journal of Distance Education, 23*(2). https://doi-org.draweb.njcu.edu/10.1080/08923640902857713

Hill, S. E. M., Ward, W. L., Seay, A., & Buzenski, J. (2022). The Nature and Evolution of the Mentoring Relationship in Academic Health Centers. *Journal of Clinical Psychology in Medical Settings*, 29(3), 557–569. 10.1007/s10880-022-09893-635761033

Hill, S. K., & Bahniuk, M. H. (1998). Promoting career success through mentoring. *Review of Business*, 19(3), 4–7.

Hogan, K. A., & Sathy, V. (2022). *Inclusive teaching: Strategies for promoting equity in the college classroom*. West Virginia University Press.

Holland, E. (2018) Mentoring communities of practice: what's in it for the mentor?. *International Journal of Mentoring and Coaching in Education*. 10.1108/IJMCE-04-2017-0034

Hopkins, J., Bardoel, A., & Djurkovic, N. (2023). Emerging four day work week trends in Australia: Preview report. *Swinburne University of Technology*. https://apo.org.au/node/323150

Hsu, C.-K., Hwang, G.-J., Chang, Y.-T., & Chang, C.-K. (2013). Effects of video caption modes on English listening comprehension and vocabulary acquisition using handheld devices. *Journal of Educational Technology & Society*, 16(1), 403–414.

Huang, E. Y., Lin, S. W., & Huang, T. K. (2012). What type of learning style leads to online participation in the mixed-mode e-learning environment? A study of software usage instruction. *Computers & Education*, 58(1), 338–349. 10.1016/j.compedu.2011.08.003

Hunter-Doniger, T. (2018). Art infusion: Ideal conditions for STEAM. *Art Education*, 2(71), 22–27. 10.1080/00043125.2018.1414534

Hussain, M., & Jones, J. M. (2021). Discrimination, diversity, and sense of belonging: Experiences of students of color. *Journal of Diversity in Higher Education*, 14(1), 63–71. 10.1037/dhe0000117

Idrizi, E., Filiposka, S., & Trajkovik, V. (2018). VARK learning styles and online education: Case study. http://hdl.handle.net/20.500.12188/24558

Imagen. (2020). Obsolete tape formats. https://imagen.io/resources/obsolete-tape- formats/

Inclusive teaching at a predominantly White institution.(2022). Center for Educational Innovation. https://cei.umn.edu/teaching-resources/inclusive-teaching-predominantly-white-institution

IncNow. (2020). Why form an LLC in Delaware. https://www.incnow.com/delaware- llc/#:~:text=You%20can%20form%20an%20LLC,Agents%20and%20Corporations%2C%20Inc

Iron Mountain Incorporated. (2023). https://www.imes.media

Ivey, S., Lafferty-Hess, S., Ossom-Williamson, P., & Barrick, K. (2023, January 1). Managing, sharing, and publishing data. http://hdl.handle.net/2451/69653

Jaeger, F. N., Bechir, M., Harouna, M., Moto, D. D., & Utzinger, J. (2018). Challenges and opportunities for healthcare workers in a rural district of Chad. *BMC Health Services Research*, 18(1), 1–11. 10.1186/s12913-017-2799-629310644

Jaggars, S. S., & Bailey, T. (2010, July). *Effectiveness of fully online courses for college students: Response to a Department of Education meta-analysis.* Community College Research Center. https://ccrc.tc.columbia.edu/media/k2/attachments/effectiveness-online-response-meta-analysis.pdf

Jeng, W., DesAutels, S., He, D., & Li, L. (2017). Information exchange on an academic social networking site: A multidiscipline comparison on researchgate Q&A. *Journal of the Association for Information Science and Technology*, 68(3), 638–652. 10.1002/asi.23692

Jimenez, R., & O'Neill, V. E. (2023). Workplace Learning Trends: Third-Party Resources as Part of an Organizational Learning Content and Knowledge Strategy. In R. Jimenez & V. O'Neill (Eds.), *Handbook of Research on Current Trends in Cybersecurity and Educational Technology* (pp. 390-405). IGI Global. 10.4018/978-1-6684-6092-4.ch021

Jimenez, R., & O'Neill, V. E. (2022). Strategies to Maximize Asynchronous Learning. In Durak, G., & Çankaya, S. (Eds.), *Handbook of Research on Managing and Designing Online Courses in Synchronous and Asynchronous Environments* (pp. 499–521). IGI Global. 10.4018/978-1-7998-8701-0.ch025

Johannesson, P. (2022). Development of professional learning communities through action research: Understanding and professional learning in practice. *Educational Action Research*, 30(3), 411–426. 10.1080/09650792.2020.1854100

Johnson, B. (2009). Differentiated instruction allows students to succeed. *Edutopia.* https://www.edutopia.org/blog/differentiated-instruction-student-success

Johnson, C. (2017). Teaching music online: Changing pedagogical approach when moving to the online environment. *London Review of Education*, 15(3), 439–456. 10.18546/LRE.15.3.08

Johnson, M.Jr. (2021, April 21). Hollywood survival strategies in the post-COVID 19 era. *Humanities & Social Sciences Communications*, 8(100), 100. 10.1057/s41599-021-00776-z

Jones, S., Pergl, R., Hooft, R., Miksa, T., Samors, R., Ungvari, J., Davis, R. I., & Lee, T. (2020). Data Management Planning: How Requirements and Solutions are Beginning to Converge. *Data Intelligence*, 2(1–2), 208–219. 10.1162/dint_a_00043

Joutsenvirta, T., & Myyry, L. (2010). *Blended learning in Finland*. Faculty of Social Sciences at the University of Helsinki.

Kaari, J. (2020). Researchers at Arab Universities Hold Positive Views on Research Data Management and Data Sharing. *Evidence Based Library and Information Practice*, 15(2), 168–170. 10.18438/eblip29746

Kapp, K. (2012). *The gamification of learning and instruction: Game-based methods and strategies for training and education*. Pfeiffer.

Kasemsap, K. (2016). Utilizing communities of practice to facilitate knowledge sharing in the digital age. In Buckley, S., Majewski, G., & Giannakopoulos, A. (Eds.), *Organizational Knowledge Facilitation through Communities of Practice in Emerging Markets* (pp. 198–224). IGI Global. 10.4018/978-1-5225-0013-1.ch011

Katz, J. S., & Martin, B. R. (1997). What Is Research Collaboration? *Research Policy*, 26(1), 1–18. 10.1016/S0048-7333(96)00917-1

Kaur, A., Awang-Hashim, R., & Noman, M. (2017). Defining intercultural education in Malaysian context for social cohesion. *International Journal of Multicultural Education*, 19(2), 44–60. 10.18251/ijme.v19i2.1337

Kaushik, M. (2020). Post COVID-19 world: A paradigm shift at workplace. *TEST Engineering and Management, 83.*

Keane, J. T., Otter, M., & Violette, J. (2022). Impacting Practice: The Role of Digital Credentials in Social Learning Communities. In Huang, Y. (Ed.), *Handbook of Research on Credential Innovations for Inclusive Pathways to Professions* (pp. 194–213). IGI Global. 10.4018/978-1-7998-3820-3.ch010

Ke, F., & Kwak, D. (2013). Constructs of student-centered online learning on learning satisfaction of a diverse online student body: A structural equation modeling approach. *Journal of Educational Computing Research*, 48(1), 97–122. 10.2190/EC.48.1.e

Kenny, A. (2016). *Communities of musical practice*. Taylor & Francis. 10.4324/9781315572963

Kerins, M. (2011). *Beyond Dolby (Stereo): Cinema in the digital sound age*. Indiana university press.

Khriyenko, O., & Cochez, M. (2011). *Open environment for collaborative cloud ecosystems*. ResearchGate. cs.jyu.fi/ai/papers/OECCE-2011.pdf

Kift, S., Nelson, K., & Clarke, J. (2010). Transition pedagogy: A third generation approach to FYE – A case study of policy and practice for the higher education sector. *The International Journal of the First Year in Higher Education*, 1(1), 1–20. 10.5204/intjfyhe.v1i1.13

Kim, K.-J., & Bonk, C. J. (2002). Cross-cultural comparisons of online collaboration. *Journal of Computer-Mediated Communication*, 8(1), JCMC814. Advance online publication. 10.1111/j.1083-6101.2002.tb00163.x

Kim, S., Hong, J., & Suh, E. (2012). A diagnosis framework for identifying the current knowledge sharing activity status in a community of practice. *Expert Systems with Applications*, 39(18), 130893. 10.1016/j.eswa.2012.05.092

Kinde, A. A., Addis, A. C., & Abebe, G. G. (2021). Research data management practice in higher education institutions in Ethiopia. *Public Services Quarterly*, 17(4), 213–230. 10.1080/15228959.2021.1879707

Klinge, C. M. (2015). A Conceptual Framework for Mentoring in a Learning Organization. *Adult Learning*, 26(4), 160–166. 10.1177/1045159515594154

Kothari, C. R. (2004). *Research Methodology: Methods and Techniques*. New Age International.

Koutsoukos, M., Kiriatzakou, K., Fragoulis, I., & Valkanos, E. (2020). The Significance of Adult Educators' Mentoring in the Application of Experiential and Participatory Teaching Techniques. *International Education Studies*, 14(1), 46. 10.5539/ies.v14n1p46

Krishnamurthi, M. (2003). Assessing multicultural initiatives in higher education institutions. *Assessment & Evaluation in Higher Education*, 28(3), 263–277. 10.1080/0260293032000059621

Krogh, G. V. (2012). Knowledge sharing in organizations: The role of communities. *Handbook of organizational learning and knowledge management*, 403-432.

Kruszelnicki, W. (2019, November 19). Self-directedness and the question of autonomy: From counterfeit education to transformative adult learning. *Studies in Philosophy and Education*, 39(2), 187–203. 10.1007/s11217-019-09697-6

Kuhn, T. S. (1998) *A estrutura das revoluções científicas*. Editora perspectiva.

Kuo, T., Tsai, G. Y., Jim Wu, Y.-C., & Alhalabi, W. (2017). From sociability to creditability for academics. *Computers in Human Behavior*, 75, 975–984. 10.1016/j.chb.2016.07.044

Kutner, M., Jin, Y., Greenberg, E., & Paulsen, C. (2006). *The health literacy of America's adults: Results from the 2003 National Assessment of Adult Literacy* (Report No. NCES 2006483). National Center for Education Statistics. https://nces.ed.gov/pubs2006/2006483.pdf

Lamare, A. (2018). How streaming started: YouTube, Netflix, and Hulu's quick ascent. *The Business of Business*. https://www.businessofbusiness.com/articles/a- brief-history-of-video-streaming-by-the-numbers/

Land, M. H. (2013). Full STEAM ahead: The benefits of integrating the arts into STEM. *Procedia Computer Science*, 20, 547–552. Advance online publication. 10.1016/j.procs.2013.09.317

Lave, J., & Wenger, E. (1991). *Situated learning: legitimate peripheral participation (Learning in Doing: Social, Cognitive and Computational Perspectives)*. Cambridge University Press. 10.1017/CBO9780511815355

Learning Lounge, S. T. E. A. M. (2024, January 10). Links and resources. www.steamlearninglounge.com

Lee, J., Oh, S., Dong, H., Wang, F., & Burnett, G. (2019). Motivations for self-archiving on an academic social networking site: A study on researchgate. *Journal of the Association for Information Science and Technology*, 70(6), 563–574. 10.1002/asi.24138

Leonelli, S. (2020). Scientific research and big data. Retrieved from https://plato.stanford.edu/entries/science-big-data/?ref=hackernoon.com

Liao, C. (2016). From interdisciplinary to transdisciplinary: An arts-integrated approach to STEAM education. *Art Education*. 10.1080/00043125.2016.1224873

Li, L. C., Grimshaw, J. M., Nielsen, C., Judd, M., Coyte, P. C., & Graham, I. D. (2009). Evolution of Wenger's concept of community of practice. *Implementation Science : IS*, 4(1), 1–8. 10.1186/1748-5908-4-1119250556

Lincoln, Y., & Stanley, C. A. (2021). The faces of institutionalized discrimination and systemic oppression in higher education: Uncovering the lived experience of bias and procedural inequity. *Qualitative Inquiry*, 27(10), 1233–1245. 10.1177/10778004211026892

Liu, X., & Ding, N. (2016). Research data management in universities of central China. *The Electronic Library*, 34(5), 808–822. 10.1108/EL-04-2015-0063

Li, Z. (2020). Teaching Introduction to Dance Studies Online Under COVID-19 Restrictions. *Dance Education in Practice*, 6(4), 9–15. 10.1080/23734833.2020.1831853

Louaf, S. Thomas, M., Jankowski, F., Leclerc, C., Barnaud, A., Baufume, S., Guichardaz, A., Joly, H., Labeyrie, V., Leclercq, M., Ndiaye, A., Pham, J., Raimond, C., Rey, A., Saudiy, A., Temple, L. (2022, October 27). Communities of Practice in Crop Diversity Management: From Data to Collaborative Governance. In *Towards Responsible Plant Data Linkage: Data Challenges for Agricultural Research and Development*. (pp. 273-288). Springer.

Lui-Abel, A. (2011). Identifying and classifying corporate universities in the United States. In M. Malloch, L. Cairns, & K. Evans (Eds.), *The SAGE handbook of workplace learning* (pp. 407-419). SAGE Publications Ltd. 10.4135/9781446200940.n30

Main, P. (2022). Google Classroom: A teachers guide. *Structural Learning*. https://www.structural-learning.com/post/google-classroom

Majhi, S., Sahu, L., & Behera, K. (2023). Practices for enhancing research visibility, citations and impact: Review of literature. *Aslib Journal of Information Management*, 75(6), 1280–1305. 10.1108/AJIM-11-2023-532

Majumdar, S. (2022). Studies on the use of academic social networking sites by academics and researchers: A review. *Annals of Library and Information Studies*, 69(2), 158–168. 10.56042/alis.v69i2.61141

Manzi, A., Hirschhorn, L. R., Sherr, K., Chirwa, C., Baynes, C., & Awoonor-Williams, J. K. (2017). Mentorship and coaching to support strengthening healthcare systems: Lessons learned across the five Population Health Implementation and Training partnership projects in sub-Saharan Africa. *BMC Health Services Research*, 17(S3), 1–12. 10.1186/s12913-017-2656-729297323

Markov, S. (2017). *Joy Paul Guilford: One of the founders of the psychology of creativity*. Geniusrevive.com

Masinde, J., Chen, J., Wambiri, D., & Mumo, A. (2021). Research librarians' experiences of research data management activities at an academic library in a developing country. *Data and Information Management*, 5(4), 412–424. 10.2478/dim-2021-0002

Masterson, V. (2022) We could be spending an hour a day in the metaverse by 2026. But what will we be doing there? *World Economic Forum*. https://www.weforum.org/agenda/2022/03/hour-a-day-in-metaverse-by-2026-says-gartner

Mavor, S., & Traynor, B. (2003). Exclusion in international online learning communities. In Reisman, S. (Ed.), *Electronic learning communities: Current issues and best practices* (pp. 457–488). Information Age Publishing.

Mcalpine, J., Mcalpine, J. J., Larkins, S., & Nagle, C. (2023). Exploring the evidence base for Communities of Practice in health research and translation : A scoping review. *Health Research Policy and Systems*, 21(55), 1–11. 10.1186/s12961-023-01000-x37337214

McComb. (2015, January 3). *Improving teaching through collegial support*. Huffpost. Retrieved from https://www.huffpost.com/entry/improving-teaching-through-collegial-support_b_6089654

McLoughlin, C., Patel, K., O'Callaghan, T., & Reev, S. (2018). The use of virtual communities of practice to improve interprofessional collaboration and education: Findings from an integrated review. *Journal of Interprofessional Care*, 32(2), 136–142. 10.1080/13561820.2017.137769229161155

McReynolds, M. R., Termini, C. M., Hinton, A. O.Jr, Taylor, B. L., Vue, Z., Huang, S. C., Roby, R. A. S., Shuler, H., & Carter, C. S. (2020). The art of virtual mentoring in the twenty-first century for STEM majors and beyond. *Nature Biotechnology*, 38(12), 1477–1482. 10.1038/s41587-020-00758-733273732

Mendes, L., & Urbina, L. M. S. (2015). Análise sobre a produção acadêmica Brasileira em comunidades de prática. *RAC*, *19*, 305-327. http://dx.doi.org/10.1590/1982-7849rac20151754

Mendez-Carbajo, D. (2020). Active learning with FRED data. *The Journal of Economic Education*, 51(1), 87–94. 10.1080/00220485.2019.1687377

Mengalli, N. M. (2005). *Intersecção para a comunidade de prática*.https://www.flickr.com/photos/nelimariamengalli/354357844

Mengalli, N. M. (2006). Interação, redes e comunidades de prática (CoP): Subsídios para a gestão do conhecimento na educação. Dissertação (Mestrado em educação: currículo) - Programa de pós-graduação educação: Currículo, pontifícia Universidade Católica de São Paulo. São Paulo.

Mengalli, N. M., & Carvalho, A. A. (2023). *Creation of digital solutions in higher education: Strategies with hands-on and disruptive technologies in phygital transformation. Perspectives on enhancing learning experience through digital strategy in higher education*. IGI Global. 10.4018/978-1-6684-8282-7.ch001

Mengalli, N. M., de Carvalho, A. A., & Galvão, S. M. (2023). *Metaverse ecosystem and consumer society 5.0: Consumer experience and influencer marketing in phygital transformation. Influencer marketing applications within the Metaverse.* IGI Global. 10.4018/978-1-6684-8898-0.ch003

Mengalli, N. M., & Valente, J. A. (2010). *The critical and historical view in communities of practice for the development in education. Cases on collaboration in virtual learning environments: Processes and interactions.* IGI Global. 10.4018/978-1-60566-878-9.ch019

Merriam-Webster. (2024, May 21). Social media. In Merriam-Webster.com dictionary. Retrieved from https://www.merriam-webster.com/dictionary/social%20media

Mishra, P., & Koehler, M. J. (2006). Technological pedagogical content knowledge: A framework for teacher knowledge. *Teachers College Record*, 108(6), 1017–1054. 10.1111/j.1467-9620.2006.00684.x

Mittal, D., Mease, R., Kuner, T., Flor, H., Kuner, R., & Andoh, J. (2022). Data management strategy for a collaborative research center. *GigaScience*, 12, giad049. Advance online publication. 10.1093/gigascience/giad04937401720

Moir, E. (2013). Riding the first-year roller coaster. *Educational Horizons*, 92(1), 6–8. 10.1177/0013175X1309200103

Monsoor, I. (2020) Netflix usage and statistics. *The business of apps.* https://www.businessofapps.com/data/netflix-statistics/#:~:text=The%20number%20subscribing%20to%20three,47%25%20of%2065%2B%20users

Moore, J. (2014). Effects of online interaction and instructor presence on students' satisfaction and success with online undergraduate public relations courses. *Journalism and Mass Communication Educator*, 69(3), 271–288. 10.1177/1077695814536398

Moore, M. (2011). Vygotsky's Cognitive Development Theory. In Goldstein, S., & Naglieri, J. (Eds.), *Encyclopedia of Child Behavior and Developmen.* Springer. 10.1007/978-0-387-79061-9_3054

Moore, M., & Kearsley, G. (2012). *Distance Education: A Systems View of Online Learning* (3rd ed.). Wadsworth.

Nández, G., & Borrego, Á. (2013). Use of social networks for academic purposes: A case study. *The Electronic Library*, 31(6), 781–791. 10.1108/EL-03-2012-0031

National Digital Inclusion Alliance. (n.d.). *Definitions.* National Digital Inclusion Alliance. https://www.digitalinclusion.org/definitions/

National Library of Medicine. (n.d.). Research Data Management. Retrieved from https://www.nnlm.gov/guides/data-glossary/research-data-management

Naushad Ali, P. M., Zehra, S., Vaidya, P., & Mohsin, S. M. (2022). Role of Academic Social Networking Sites in Knowledge Sharing and Research Collaboration among Research Scholars. *DESIDOC Journal of Library and Information Technology*, 42(5), 309–317. Advance online publication. 10.14429/djlit.42.5.18239

Netscher, S., & Katsanidou, A. (2020). Understanding and Implementing Research Data Management. In Wagemann, C., Goerres, A., & Siewert, M. B. (Eds.), *Handbuch Methoden der Politikwissenschaft* (pp. 79–96). Springer VS. 10.1007/978-3-658-16936-7_4

Neves, A. (2001, June 1). Etienne Wenger. *Podcast da knowman KMOL con Ana Neves.* https:// kmol.pt/entrevistas/2001/06/01/etienne-wenger/

Newswire, P. R. (2020). Video streaming market size is projected to reach USD 149.34 Billion by 2026. *Cision PR Newswire.* https://www.prnewswire.com/news-releases/video-streaming-market-size-is-projected-to-reach-usd-149-34-billion-by-2026--valuates-reports-301142025.html

North East Digital Learning Association. (2024, January 10). *Events.* https://nedla.org/page-969292

O'Brien, B. C., & Battista, A. (2020). Situated learning theory in health professions education research: A scoping review. *Advances in Health Sciences Education : Theory and Practice*, 25(2), 483–509. 10.1007/s10459-019-09900-w31230163

O'Connor, B. N., & Lynch, D. (2011). Partnerships between and among education and the public and private sectors. In *The SAGE Handbook of Workplace Learning* (pp. 420–430). SAGE Publications Inc. 10.4135/9781446200940.n31

Office of the U.S. department of education. (n.d.). Wondering if you can get your loans forgiven for your service as a teacher? *Federal student aid.* Retrieved from https://studentaid.gov/manage-loans/forgiveness-cancellation/teacher

Okwumabua, T. M., Walker, K. M., Hu, X., & Watson, A. (2011). An exploration of African American students attitudes toward online learning. *Urban Education*, 46(2), 241–250. 10.1177/0042085910377516

Onyancha, O. B. (2015). Social media and research: An assessment of the coverage of South African universities in ResearchGate, Web of Science and the Webometrics Ranking of World Universities. *South African Journal of Library and Information Science*, 81(1), 8–20. 10.7553/81-1-1540

Ostashewski, N., Reid, D., & Ostashewski, M. (2016). Utilizing Multimedia Database Access: Teaching Strategies Using the iPad in the Dance Classroom. *Journal of Distance Education*, 16, 122–128.

Özdemir, İ. H., Sarsar, F., & Harmon, S. W. (2023). Blended Learning in Higher Education. In R. Jimenez & V. O'Neill (Eds.), *Handbook of Research on Current Trends in Cybersecurity and Educational Technology* (pp. 365-389). IGI Global. 10.4018/978-1-6684-6092-4.ch020

Ozola, S., & Purvins, M. (2013) Teaching/learning theories: How They Are Perceived. *Bulgarian Comparative Education Society,* 133-138.

Parsons, S., Hutchison, A., Hall, L., Parsons, A., Ives, S., & Leggett, A. (2019). US teachers' perceptions of online professional development. *Teaching and Teacher Education*, 82, 33–42. 10.1016/j.tate.2019.03.006

Patel, D. (2016). Research data management: A conceptual framework. *Library Review*, 65(4/5), 226–241. 10.1108/LR-01-2016-0001

Patel, M., Singhal, N., & Sockalingam, S. (2023). The Impact of the Transition to Virtual Environments on Medical Students Mentoring At-Risk Youth. *Academic Psychiatry*, 47(3), 292–296. 10.1007/s40596-023-01771-z37016175

Perrier, L., Blondal, E., Ayala, A. P., Dearborn, D., Kenny, T., Lightfoot, D., Reka, R., Thuna, M., Trimble, L., & MacDonald, H. (2017). Research data management in academic institutions: A scoping review. *PLoS One*, 12(5), e0178261. 10.1371/journal.pone.017826128542450

Perron, G. M., & Duffy, J. F. J. (2012). Environmental and business communities of practice: graduate students comparing community-relevant language: Assessing community of practice identity through language. *Business Strategy and the Environment*, 21(3), 170–182. 10.1002/bse.725

Peterson-Ahmad, M. B., & Luther, V. L. (2022, July 18). *Fostering inclusivity in the college classroom: Looking through a universal design for learning lens.* Faculty Focus. https://www.facultyfocus.com/articles/equality-inclusion-and-diversity/fostering-inclusivity-in-the-college-classroom-looking-through-a-universal-design-for-learning-lens/

Phillips, A. (2019). The Quest for Diversity in Higher Education. *Pepperdine Policy Review, 11*(4), 1-28. https://digitalcommons.pepperdine.edu/ppr/vol11/iss1/4

Picciano, A. G. (2002). 'Beyond student perceptions: Issues of interaction, presence, and performance in an online course'. *Journal of Asynchronous Learning Networks*, 6(1), 21–40.

Plant, R. (2004). Online communities. *Technology in Society*, 26(1), 51–65. 10.1016/j.techsoc.2003.10.005

Powell, K. C., & Kalina, C. J. (2009). Cognitive and social constructivism: Developing tools for an effective classroom. *Education*, 130(2), 241–250.

Power, J., & Kannara, V. (2016). Best-Practice Model for Technology Enhanced Learning in the Creative Arts. *Research in Learning Technology*, 24(1), 30231–30316. 10.3402/rlt.v24.30231

Pramila-Savukoski, S., Jarva, E., Kuivila, H. M., Juntunen, J., Koskenranta, M., Kääriäinen, M., & Mikkonen, K. (2024). Generic competence among health sciences students in higher education – A cross-sectional study. *Nurse Education Today, 133.* 10.1016/j.nedt.2023.106036

Pun, R., & Kubo, H. (2022). What Collaboration Means to Us: Advancing Equity, Diversity, and Inclusion Initiatives in the Library Profession. *Collaborative Librarianship, 13*(1), 2. Retrieved from https://digitalcommons.du.edu/collaborativelibrarianship/vol13/iss1/2/

Purves, R. (2012). Technology and the educator. In McPherson, G. E., & Welch, G. F. (Eds.), *The Oxford Handbook of Music Education* (Vol. 2, pp. 457–475). Oxford University Press. 10.1093/oxfordhb/9780199928019.013.0030

Pyrko, I., Dörfler, V., & Eden, C. (2017). Thinking together: What makes communities of practice work? *Human Relations*, 70(4), 389–409. 10.1177/0018726716661104028232754

Pyrko, I., Dörfler, V., & Eden, C. (2019). Communities of practice in landscapes of practice. *Management Learning*, 50(4), 482–499. 10.1177/1350507619860854

Queen, D. (2023). Could wound care benefit from the artificial intelligence storm taking place worldwide. *International Wound Journal*, 20(5), 1337–1338. 10.1111/iwj.1417137039743

Qutab, S., Iqbal, A., Ullah, F. S., Siddique, N., & Khan, M. A. (2022). Role of virtual communities of practice (VCoP) in continuous professional development of librarians: A case of Yahoo mailing group from Pakistan. *Library Management*, 43(5), 317–333. 10.1108/LM-02-2021-0017

Raffaghelli, J. E., & Manca, S. (2023). Exploring the social activity of open research data on ResearchGate: Implications for the data literacy of researchers. *Online Information Review*, 47(1), 197–217. 10.1108/OIR-05-2021-0255

Rankin, S. R. (2005). Campus climates for sexual minorities. *New Directions for Student Services*, 2005(111), 17–23. 10.1002/ss.170

Ranmuthugala, G., Plumb, J., Cunningham, F., Georgiou, A., Westbrook, J., & Braithwaite, J. (2011). How and why are communities of practice established in the healthcare sector? *A Systematic Review of the Literature, 11*, 273. https://www.biomedcentral.com/1472-6963/11/273

Reichenbach, G. (2015). From STEM to STEAM education. *Power*, 159(6), 6–6.

Reimer, B. (2003). *A Philosophy of Music Education: Advancing the vision* (3rd ed.). Prentice Hall.

Reiter-Palmon, R., & Hunter, S. (2023). Handbook of organizational creativity: Individual and group level influences. Science Direct. https://doi.org/10.1016/C2020-0-04164-0

ResearchGate. (2021). Progress Report 2021. Retrieved from https://www.researchgate.net/progress-report-2021/publisher-solutions

ResearchGate. (2023). About ResearchGate. Retrieved from https://www.researchgate.net/about

Ribiere, V. (2023). *Knowledge management in the metaverse: The future of knowledge management. Knowledge management and organizational learning* (Vol. 12). Springer. 10.1007/978-3-031-38696-1_15

Richardson, C. R. (2023). *Diversity and inclusive teaching*. University of Delaware Center for Teaching and Assessment of Learing. https://bpb-us-w2.wpmucdn.com/sites.udel.edu/dist/c/6655/files/2014/03/Culturally-Responsive-Teaching-1jy7hnk.pdf

Richardson, C. R., & le Blanc, S. (2023). *Diversity and equity in learning*. University of Delaware Center for Teaching and Assessment of Learning. https://bpb-us-w2.wpmucdn.com/sites.udel.edu/dist/c/6655/files/2014/03/Diversity-and-Equity-in-Learning_Jan2016-zm93qx.pdf

Richardson, C. R., & Yang, F. (2015). *Course syllabi: Suggestions for statements to include on your syllabus*. University of Delaware Center for Teaching and Assessment of Learning. https://bpb-us-w2.wpmucdn.com/sites.udel.edu/dist/c/6655/files/2014/03/Course-Syllabi_statements_January2016-2gs8wet.pdf

Compilation of References

Riggins, C., & Knowles, D. (2020). Caught in the trap of PLC lite: Essential steps needed for implementation of a true professional learning community. *Education*, 141(1), 46–54.

Rimol, M. (2022). *Gartner predicts 25% of people will spend at least one hour per day in the metaverse by 2026.* Press Release, Gartner.

Robelen, E. (2011, December 7). STEAM Experts make case for adding the arts to STEM. *Education Week*, 1(6).

Roberts, Van Wyk, & Dhanpat. (2016). *Exploring practices for effective collaboration.* Academic Press.

Robinson, K. (2009). *The element. How finding your passion changes everything.* New York, NY: The Penguin Group.

Robinson, K. (2010, November 4-5). *Keynote address* [Conference presentation]. NJEA 2010 Convention, Atlantic City, NJ, United States.

Rodrigues, Brandão, & Zárate. (2018). Recommending Scientific Collaboration from Research-Gate. Academic Press.

Ross, S. (2014). Diversity and intergroup contact in higher education: Exploring possibilities for democratization. *Teaching in Higher Education*, 19(8), 870–881. 10.1080/13562517.2014.934354

Rovai, A. P., & Gallien, L. B. (2005). Learning and sense of community: A comparative analysis of African American and Caucasian online graduate students. *The Journal of Negro Education*, 74(1), 53–62. https://www.jstor.org/stable/40027230

Rovai, A. P., & Wighting, M. J. (2005). Feelings of alienation and community among higher education students in a virtual classroom. *The Internet and Higher Education*, 8(2), 97–110. 10.1016/j.iheduc.2005.03.001

Rovai, A. P., Wighting, M. J., & Liu, J. (2005). School climate: Sense of classroom and school communities in online and on-campus higher education courses. *Quarterly Review of Distance Education*, 6(4), 361–374.

Rowe, L., Knight, L., Irvine, P., & Greenwood, J. (2023). Communities of practice for contemporary leadership development and knowledge exchange through work-based learning. *Journal of Education and Work*, 36(6), 494–510. 10.1080/13639080.2023.2255149

Rucsanda, M. D., Belibou, A., & Cazan, A. M. (2021). Students' attitudes toward online music education during the COVID 19 lockdown. *Frontiers in Psychology*, 12, 753785. 10.3389/fpsyg.2021.75378534975646

Ruokonen, I., & Ruismäki, H. (2016). E-Learning in Music: A Case Study of Learning Group Composing in a Blended Learning Environment. *Procedia: Social and Behavioral Sciences*, 217, 109–115. 10.1016/j.sbspro.2016.02.039

Ruvalcaba, A. (2020). *I can be myself, [almost] always: A Latinx microclimate in a predominantly White institution of higher education* (Publication No. 27994297) [Master's thesis, Michigan State University]. ProQuest Dissertations Publishing. 10.24059/olj.v23i1.1390

Saldana, J. B. (2014). Comparison of community, practice, domain, and leadership expressions among professional communities of practice [PhD dissertation]. University of Phoenix, ProQuest LLC, Ann Arbor, Michigan.

Samarasekera, D. D., Nyoni, C. N., Amaral, E., & Grant, J. (2022). Challenges and opportunities in interprofessional education and practice. *Lancet*, 400(10362), 1495–1497. 10.1016/S0140-6736(22)02086-436522199

Sanjeeva. (2018). *Research data management: A new role for academic/research librarians.* Academic Press.

Schaffauser, D. (2019). Getting trained to TEACH ROBOTICS: This professional development opportunity helps you with the basics and even includes freely available curriculum. *T H E Journal (Technological Horizons in Education), 20*(6).

Scheurich, J. J., & Young, M. D. (1997). Coloring epistemologies: Are our research epistemologies racially biased? *Educational Researcher*, 26(4), 4–16. 10.2307/1176879

Schwerdtle, P., Morphet, J., & Hall, H. (2017). A scoping review of mentorship of health personnel to improve the quality of health care in low and middle-income countries. *Globalization and Health*, 13(1), 1–8. 10.1186/s12992-017-0301-128974233

Seddon, T. (2022). Liquid learning: re-conceiving the lived-in-world. In *The SAGE handbook of learning and work* (pp. 158–172). SAGE Publications Ltd. 10.4135/9781529757217.n11

Shabani, K., Khatib, M., & Ebadi, S. (2010). Vygotsky's Zone of Proximal Development: Instructional Implications and Teachers' Professional Development Karim. *English Language Teaching*, 3(4), 237–248. www.ccsenet.org/elt. 10.5539/elt.v3n4p237

Shaw, L., Jazayeri, D., Kiegaldie, D., & Morris, M. E. (2022). Implementation of Virtual Communities of Practice in Healthcare to Improve Capability and Capacity: A 10-Year Scoping Review. *International Journal of Environmental Research and Public Health*, 19(13), 7994. Advance online publication. 10.3390/ijerph1913799435805649

Sieck, C. J., Sheon, A., Ancker, J. S., Castek, K., Callahan, B., & Siefer, A. (2021). Digital inclusion as a social determinant of health. *Digital Medicine*, 4(1), 52. Advance online publication. 10.1038/s41746-021-00413-833731887

Silva, E. (2009). Measuring skills for 21st century learning. *Phi Delta Kappan, 90*(9), 630-634. 10.1177/003172170909000905

Silverman, R. E. (2012, October 26). So much training, so little to show for it. *The Wall Street Journal*.https://www.wsj.com/articles/SB10001424052970204425904578072950518558328

Singh, A. (2021). Basic Steps of Doing Research. SSRN *Electronic Journal*. 10.2139/ssrn.3925363

Singh, V. K., Srichandan, S. S., & Lathabai, H. H. (2022). ResearchGate and Google Scholar: How Much Do They Differ in Publications, Citations and Different Metrics and Why? *Scientometrics*, 127(3), 1515–1542. 10.1007/s11192-022-04264-2

Sisson, P. (2020). The perfect virtual video store isn't Netflix – it's DVD. *Vox*. https://vox.com/culture/2020/4/23/21230324/Netflix-dvid-rental-classic-movies

Sjöholm, J. (2014). The art studio as archive: Tracing the geography of artistic potentiality, progress and production. *Cultural Geographies*, 21(3), 505–514. 10.1177/1474474012473060

Skarbalienė, A., Skarbalius, E., & Gedrimė, L. (2019). Effective Communication In The Healthcare Settings: Are The Graduates Ready For It? *Management*, 24(Special Issue), 137–147. 10.30924/mjcmi.24.si.9

Smerda-Mason, D. (2022). Professional development concerns and solutions in STEAM education [Doctoral dissertation, New Jersey City University].

Smith, D. R., & Ayers, D. F. (2006). Culturally responsive pedagogy and online learning: Implications for the globalized community college. *Community College Journal of Research and Practice*, 30(5–6), 401–415. 10.1080/10668920500442125

Smith, M. (1934). Solfège: An essential in musicianship. *Music Supervisors' Journal*, 20(5), 16–61.

Soekiman, S. (2023) The effect of knowledge sharing an individual innovation capability on employee performance with work motivation as an intervening variable. *Oeconomia copernicana*, *14*(2). http://repository.unitomo.ac.id/3465/1/10.pdf

Srinivasa, M. R. (2020). (2020, October). COVID-19 pandemic and emotional health: Social psychiatry perspective. *Indian Journal of Social Psychiatry*, 36(5), 24. Advance online publication. 10.4103/ijsp.ijsp_293_20

Stereotype threat. (n.d.). University of Colorado Boulder Center for Teaching & Learning. https://www.colorado.edu/center/teaching-learning/inclusivity/stereotype-threat

Struminger, B., Arora, S., Zalud-Cerrato, S., Lowrance, D., & Ellerbrock, T. (2017). Building virtual communities of practice for health. *Lancet*, 390(10095), 632–634. 10.1016/S0140-6736(17)31666-528816126

Sue, D. W. (2010). *Microaggressions in everyday life: Race, gender and sexual orientation.* Wiley & Sons.

Summey, T., & Gutierrez, A. (2012). Laptops to go: A student assessment of a library laptop lending service. *Journal of Access Services*, 9(1), 28–43. 10.1080/15367967.2012.629929

Sutton, A. (2023). Cultivating global health: Exploring mindfulness through an organisational psychology lens. *Mindfulness*. Advance online publication. 10.1007/s12671-023-02228-y

Svendsen, B. (2020). Inquiries into teacher professional development: What matters? *Education*, 140(3), 111–141.

Swain, S. (2013). *Diversity education goals in higher education: A policy discourse analysis* (Publication No. 1957) [Doctoral dissertation, University of Maine]. University of Maine: Electronic Theses and Dissertations. https://digitalcommons.library.umaine.edu/etd/1957

Talbot, D. (2003). Multiculturalism. In Komives, S. R., & Woodard, D. B.Jr., (Eds.), *Student services: A handbook for the profession* (pp. 423–446). Jossey-Bass.

Tang, R., & Hu, Z. (2019). Providing Research Data Management (RDM) Services in Libraries: Preparedness, Roles, Challenges, and Training for RDM Practice. *Data and Information Management*, 3(2), 84–101. 10.2478/dim-2019-0009

Tartari, E. (2015). *The Use of Social Media for Academic Purposes in Student' Learning Process.* Academic Journal of Interdisciplinary Studies. 10.5901/ajis.2015.v4n2p393

Tassi, P. (2020, April 23). Fortnite's Travis Scott Concert Was A Stunning Spectacle And A Glimpse At The Metaverse. https://www.forbes.com/sites/paultassi/2020/04/23/fortnites-travis-scott-concert-was-a-stunning-spectacle-and-a-glimpse-at-the-metaverse/

Taylor, S. J., Bogdan, R., & DeVault, M. L. (2016). *Introduction to qualitative research methods: A guidebook and resource.* Wiley.

Terry, D. R., Nguyen, L. H., Peck, B., Lecturer, S., & Smith, A. (2020). Communities of practice : A systematic review and meta- synthesis of what it means and how it really works among nursing students and novices. *Journal of Clinical Nursing*, 29(3-4), 370–380. 10.1111/jocn.1510031714649

The American academy of environmental engineers and scientists. (2022). AAEES website. Retrieved from https://www.aaees.org/studentchapters/

The retirees school volunteer association. (2022). RSVA website. Retrieved from https://rsva.org/

Thelwall, M., & Kousha, K. (2017). ResearchGate articles: Age, discipline, audience size, and impact. *Journal of the Association for Information Science and Technology*, 68(2), 468–479. 10.1002/asi.23675

Toffler, A. (1980). *The third wave.* Morrow.

Ueckert, C. W., & Gess-Newsome, J. (2008). Active learning strategies. *Science Teacher* (Normal, Ill.), 75(9), 47–52. https://search.proquest.com/docview/214624210?accountid=12793

University of Reading. (n.d.). Open and FAIR data. Retrieved from https://www.reading.ac.uk/research-services/research-data-management/preserving-and-sharing-data/open-and-fair-data

University of San Diego. (2023). Living Learning Communities. https://www.sandiego.edu/learning-communities/

University of Toronto Libraries. (2024). Academic Social Networks. Retrieved from https://guides.library.utoronto.ca/researchimpact/networks#:~:text=Academic%20Social%20Networks%20(ASNs)%20are,are%20typically%20free%20to%20use

Compilation of References

Vaisshalli, G. R., Gupta, A., Bhapkar, A. G., Dixit, A., Singh, S. P., & Agarwal, P. (2022). Challenges in Healthcare Sector. *International Journal for Modern Trends in Science and Technology*, 8(01), 43–46. 10.46501/IJMTST0801008

Valenti, S., & Sutton, S. (2020). Strengthening virtual communities of practice (VCoPs): An Evidence-based approach. *Journal of Education for Library and Information Science*, 61(1), 106–125. 10.3138/jelis.61.1.2018-0045

Valizadeh-Haghi, S., Nasibi-Sis, H., Shekofteh, M., & Rahmatizadeh, S. (2022). ResearchGate Metrics' Behavior and Its Correlation with RG Score and Scopus Indicators: A Combination of Bibliometric and Altmetric Analysis of Scholars in Medical Sciences. *Information Technology and Libraries*, 41(1), 1–12. 10.6017/ital.v41i1.14033

VanWyk, A. (2020). Leading curriculum changes in schools: The role of school principals as perceived by teachers. *Perspectives in Education*, 38(2), 155–167.

Vermeir, P., Vandijck, D., Degroote, S., Peleman, R., Verhaeghe, R., Mortier, E., Hallaert, G., Van Daele, S., Buylaert, W., & Vogelaers, D. (2015). Communication in healthcare: A narrative review of the literature and practical recommendations. *International Journal of Clinical Practice*, 69(11), 1257–1267. 10.1111/ijcp.1268626147310

Video streaming market size, Share & Growth Report, 2030. Video Streaming Market Size, Share & Growth Report, 2030. (2020). https://www.grandviewresearch.com/industry-analysis/video-streaming-market

Voit, K., Buliga, O., & Michl, K. (2016, July). Entertainment on demand: The case of Netflix. *Business model pioneers*. Springer.

Vonderau, P. (2016). The video bubble: Multichannel networks and the transformation of YouTube. *Convergence (London)*, 22(4), 361–375. 10.1177/1354856516641882

Vygotsky, L. (1978). *Mind in Society*. Havard University Press.

Vygotsky, L. S. (1978). *Mind in society: The development of higher psychological processes*. Harvard University Press.

Walker, J., & Fontinha, R. (2022). The pandemic has made a four-day working week more attractive to workers and businesses study finds. *Henley Business School*.https://www.henley.ac.uk/news/2022/the-pandemic-has-made-a-four-day-working-week-more-attractive-to-workers-and-businesses-study-finds

Walton, G. M., & Cohen, G. L. (2011). A brief social-belonging intervention improves academic and health outcomes of minority students. *Science*, 331(6023), 1447–1451. 10.1126/science.119836421415354

Wang, H., Fu, T., Du, Y., Gao, W., Huang, K., Liu, Z., Chandak, P., Liu, S., Van Katwyk, P., Deac, A., Anandkumar, A., Bergen, K., Gomes, C. P., Ho, S., Kohli, P., Lasenby, J., Leskovec, J., Liu, T.-Y., Manrai, A., & Zitnik, M. (2023). Scientific discovery in the age of artificial intelligence. *Nature*, 620(7972), 47–60. 10.1038/s41586-023-06221-237532811

Ward, J. H., Bejarano, W., & Haggis, W. (2015). "Open during renovation": Open science and libraries. Substance Abuse Library and Information Studies, 2, 82-89.DOI: https://doi.org/10 .7282/T3TM7DGN

Watson, A. (2020). Share of adults who subscribe to a streaming service in the United States as of May 2020, by age group. *Statista*. https://www.statista.com/statistics/742452/media-streaming -services-penetration-rate age/#:~:text=Share%20of%20adults%20who%20subscribe,U.S.%20 2019%2C%20by%20age%20group&text=A%20survey%20held%20in%20the,above%20who%20 said%20th e%20same

Wenger, E. (2000). Communities of practice and social learning systems. *Organization*, 7(2), 225-246. 10.1177/135050840072002

Wenger, E. (2011). Communities of Practice: A Brief Introduction. http://hdl.handle.net/1794/11736

Wenger, E., White, N., & Smith, J. D. (2009). Digital habitats: Stewarding technology for communities. CPsquare.

Wenger, E. (1999). *Communities of practice: Learning, meaning, and identity.* Cambridge University Press.

Wenger, E. (2009). Communities of Practice and Social Learning Systems: the Career of a Concept. In Blackmore, C. (Ed.), *Social Learning Systems and Communities of Practice.* Springer., 10.1007/978-1-84996-133-2_11

Wenger-Trayner, E., & Wenger-Trayner, B. (2015). Introduction to communities of practice. Retrieved from https://wenger-trayner.com/introduction-to-communities-of-practice/

Wenger-Trayner, E., & Wenger-Trayner, B. (2015). *Introduction to communities of practice: A brief overview of concept and its uses.* https://www.wenger-trayner.com/introduction-to-communities -of-practice/#:~:text=Communities%20of%20practice%20are%20groups,better%20as%20they %20interact%20regularly

Wenger-Trayner, E., & Wenger-Trayner, B. (2024, January 11). *What is social learning?* Wenger-Trayner: Global theorists and consultants. https://www.wenger-trayner.com/what-is -social-learning/#:~:text=Etienne's%20work%20on%20social%20learning,others%20or%20use %20certain%20tools

Wenger-Trayner, E., & Wenger-Trayner, B. (2024, January 9). *Can a community of practice exist only online?* Wenger-Trayner: Global theorists and consultants. https://www.wenger-trayner.com/ online-communities-of-practice/

Wenger-Trayner, E., Fenton-O'Creevy, M., Hutchinson, S., Kubiak, C., & Wenger-Trayner, B. (Eds.). (2014). *Learning in Landscapes of Practice: Boundaries, Identity, and Knowledgeability in Practice-Based Learning* (1st ed.). Routledge., 10.4324/9781315777122

Wenger-Trayner, E., & Wenger-Trayner, B. (2015). Learning in a landscape of practice: a framework. In Wenger-Trayner, E., Fenton-O'Creevy, M., Hutchinson, S., Kubiak, C., & Wenger-Trayner, B. (Eds.), *Learning in landscapes of practice* (pp. 51–78). Routledge.

Compilation of References

Wentzel, K. R. (2010). Students' relationships with teachers. In Eccles, J. S., & Meece, J. L. (Eds.), *Handbook of research on schools, schooling and human development* (pp. 75–91). Routledge.

Whyte, A., & Tedds, J. (2011). Making the case for research data management. DCC Briefing Papers. Digital Curation Centre. Retrieved from https://www.dcc.ac.uk/resources/briefing-papers

Williams, A. E., & Woodacre, M. A. (2016). The possibilities and perils of academic social networking sites. *Online Information Review*, 40(2), 282–294. 10.1108/OIR-10-2015-0327

Williams, D. A. (2013). *Strategic diversity leadership: Activating change and transformation in higher education.* Routledge., 10.4324/9781003447122

Wittman, J. T., & Aukema, B. H. (2020). A Guide and Toolbox to Replicability and Open Science in Entomology. *Journal of Insect Science*, 20(3), 6. 10.1093/jisesa/ieaa03632441307

Wood, L. (2020). United states over the top OTT market 2020-2025: High penetration of smart TV and the presence of major OTT providers. *Business Wire.* https://www.businesswire.com/news/home/20201113005493/en/United-States-Over-the- Top-OTT-Market-2020-2025-High-Penetration-Of-Smart-TV-And-The-Presence-Of- Major-OTT-Providers---ResearchAndMarkets.com

Woo, D. J. (2015). Central practitioners' developing legitimate peripheral participation in a community of practice for changing schools. *Australasian Journal of Educational Technology*, 31(2), 164–176. 10.14742/ajet.314

Woodyard, L., & Larson, E. (2017). *2017 distance education report.* California Community Colleges Chancellor's Office. https://www.cccco.edu/-/media/CCCCO-Website/docs/report/2017-DE-Report-Final-ADA.pdf

Wright, J., Williams, R., & Wilkinson, J. R. (1998). Development and importance of health needs assessment. *National Library of Medicine, 316*(7140). 10.1136/bmj.316.7140.1310

Wu, S., Stvilia, B., & Lee, D. J. (2016). Exploring researchers' participation in online research identity management systems. *Proceedings of the Association for Information Science and Technology*, 53(1), 1–6. 10.1002/pra2.2016.14505301105

Wu, S., Stvilia, B., & Lee, D. J. (2017). Readers, Personal Record Managers, and Community Members: An Exploratory Study of Researchers' Participation in Online Research Information Management Systems. *Journal of Library Metadata*, 17(2), 57–90. 10.1080/19386389.2017.1348783

Xu, Z. (2022). Research Data Management Training in Academic Libraries: A Scoping Review. *Journal of Librarianship and Scholarly Communication*, 10(1). Advance online publication. 10.31274/jlsc.13700

Yang, L. (2020). Silver-lining of COVID-19: A Virtual Community of Practice for Faculty Development. *All Ireland Journal of Higher Education*, 12(3), 1–9.

Yan, W., & Zhang, Y. (2018). Research universities on the ResearchGate social networking site: An examination of institutional differences, research activity level, and social networks formed. *Journal of Informetrics*, 12(1), 385–400. 10.1016/j.joi.2017.08.002

Yilmaz, K. (2011). The cognitive perspective on learning: Its theoretical underpinnings and implications for classroom practices. *The Clearing House: A Journal of Educational Strategies, Issues and Ideas*, 84(5), 204–212. 10.1080/00098655.2011.568989

Yu, M.-C., Wu, Y.-C. J., Alhalabi, W., Kao, H.-Y., & Wu, W.-H. (2016). ResearchGate: An effective altmetric indicator for active researchers? *Computers in Human Behavior*, 55, 1001–1006. 10.1016/j.chb.2015.11.007

Zahid, R., Altaf, A., Ahmad, T., Iqbal, F., Vera, Y. A. M., Flores, M. A. L., & Ashraf, I. (2023). Secure data management life cycle for government big-data ecosystem: Design and development perspective. *Systems*, 11(8), 380. 10.3390/systems11080380

Zakrajsek, A., & Schuster, E. (2018). Situated Learning and Interprofessional Education: An Educational Strategy Using an Apprenticeship Model to Develop Research Skills for Practice. *Health and Interprofessional Practice*, 3(3), 1–11. 10.7710/2159-1253.1147

Ziegler, A., Gryc, K. L., Hopp, M. D. S., & Stoeger, H. (2021). Spaces of possibilities: A theoretical analysis of mentoring from a regulatory perspective. *Annals of the New York Academy of Sciences*, 1483(1), 174–198. 10.1111/nyas.1441932634268

Zimmerman, E. (2018, July 27). The 4 c's of learning in a connected classroom. Edtech focus on K-12. Retrieved from https://edtechmagazine.com/k12/article/2018/07/4-cs-learning-connected-classroom

Zollman, A. (2012). Learning for STEM Literacy: STEM Literacy for Learning. *School Science and Mathematics*, 112(1), 12–19. 10.1111/j.1949-8594.2012.00101.x

Related References

To continue our tradition of advancing information science and technology research, we have compiled a list of recommended IGI Global readings. These references will provide additional information and guidance to further enrich your knowledge and assist you with your own research and future publications.

Abir, J. I., & Shamim, T. F. (2020). What Compels Journalists to Take a Step Back?: Contextualizing the Media Laws and Policies of Bangladesh. In Jamil, S. (Ed.), *Handbook of Research on Combating Threats to Media Freedom and Journalist Safety* (pp. 38–53). IGI Global. https://doi.org/10.4018/978-1-7998-1298-2.ch003

Adesina, K., Ganiu, O., & R., O. S. (2018). Television as Vehicle for Community Development: A Study of Lotunlotun Programme on (B.C.O.S.) Television, Nigeria. In A. Salawu, & T. Owolabi (Eds.), *Exploring Journalism Practice and Perception in Developing Countries* (pp. 60-84). Hershey, PA: IGI Global. https://doi.org/10.4018/978-1-5225-3376-4.ch004

Aggarwal, K., Singh, S. K., Chopra, M., & Kumar, S. (2022). Role of Social Media in the COVID-19 Pandemic: A Literature Review. In Gupta, B., Peraković, D., Abd El-Latif, A., & Gupta, D. (Eds.), *Data Mining Approaches for Big Data and Sentiment Analysis in Social Media* (pp. 91–115). IGI Global. https://doi.org/10.4018/978-1-7998-8413-2.ch004

Ahmad, R. H., & Pathan, A. K. (2017). A Study on M2M (Machine to Machine) System and Communication: Its Security, Threats, and Intrusion Detection System. In Ferrag, M., & Ahmim, A. (Eds.), *Security Solutions and Applied Cryptography in Smart Grid Communications* (pp. 179–214). Hershey, PA: IGI Global. 10.4018/978-1-5225-1829-7.ch010

Akanni, T. M. (2018). In Search of Women-Supportive Media for Sustainable Development in Nigeria. In Salawu, A., & Owolabi, T. (Eds.), *Exploring Journalism Practice and Perception in Developing Countries* (pp. 126–149). Hershey, PA: IGI Global. 10.4018/978-1-5225-3376-4.ch007

Akçay, D. (2017). The Role of Social Media in Shaping Marketing Strategies in the Airline Industry. In Benson, V., Tuninga, R., & Saridakis, G. (Eds.), *Analyzing the Strategic Role of Social Networking in Firm Growth and Productivity* (pp. 214–233). Hershey, PA: IGI Global. 10.4018/978-1-5225-0559-4.ch012

Akmese, Z. (2020). Media Literacy and Framing of Media Content. In Taskiran, N. (Ed.), *Handbook of Research on Multidisciplinary Approaches to Literacy in the Digital Age* (pp. 73–87). IGI Global. 10.4018/978-1-7998-1534-1.ch005

Al-Jenaibi, B. (2021). Paradigms of Public Relations in an Age of Digitalization: Social Media Analytics in the UAE. In Yildiz, O. (Ed.), *Recent Developments in Individual and Organizational Adoption of ICTs* (pp. 262–277). IGI Global. https://doi.org/10.4018/978-1-7998-3045-0.ch016

Al-Rabayah, W. A. (2017). Social Media as Social Customer Relationship Management Tool: Case of Jordan Medical Directory. In Al-Rabayah, W., Khasawneh, R., Abu-shamaa, R., & Alsmadi, I. (Eds.), *Strategic Uses of Social Media for Improved Customer Retention* (pp. 108–123). Hershey, PA: IGI Global. 10.4018/978-1-5225-1686-6.ch006

Algül, A., & Akpınar, M. E. (2022). Hate Speech on Social Media: "Dunyaerkeklergunu" Hashtag on Twitter. In Öngün, E., Pembecioğlu, N., & Gündüz, U. (Eds.), *Handbook of Research on Digital Citizenship and Management During Crises* (pp. 293–305). IGI Global. https://doi.org/10.4018/978-1-7998-8421-7.ch016

Almjeld, J. (2017). Getting "Girly" Online: The Case for Gendering Online Spaces. In Monske, E., & Blair, K. (Eds.), *Handbook of Research on Writing and Composing in the Age of MOOCs* (pp. 87–105). Hershey, PA: IGI Global. 10.4018/978-1-5225-1718-4.ch006

Alsalmi, J. M., & Shehata, A. M. (2022). Official Uses of Social Media. In Al-Suqri, M., Al-Shaqsi, O., & Alsalmi, J. (Eds.), *Mass Communications and the Influence of Information During Times of Crises* (pp. 123–140). IGI Global. https://doi.org/10.4018/978-1-7998-7503-1.ch006

Altaş, A. (2017). Space as a Character in Narrative Advertising: A Qualitative Research on Country Promotion Works. In Yılmaz, R. (Ed.), *Narrative Advertising Models and Conceptualization in the Digital Age* (pp. 303–319). Hershey, PA: IGI Global. 10.4018/978-1-5225-2373-4.ch017

Altıparmak, B. (2017). The Structural Transformation of Space in Turkish Television Commercials as a Narrative Component. In Yılmaz, R. (Ed.), *Narrative Advertising Models and Conceptualization in the Digital Age* (pp. 153–166). Hershey, PA: IGI Global. 10.4018/978-1-5225-2373-4.ch009

Arda, Ö., & Akmeşe, Z. (2021). Media Ethics: Evaluation of Television News in the Context of the Media and Ethics Relationship. In Taskiran, M., & Pinarbaşi, F. (Eds.), *Multidisciplinary Approaches to Ethics in the Digital Era* (pp. 96–110). IGI Global. https://doi.org/10.4018/978-1-7998-4117-3.ch007

Arık, E. (2019). Popular Culture and Media Intellectuals: Relationship Between Popular Culture and Capitalism – The Characteristics of the Media Intellectuals. In Ozgen, O. (Ed.), *Handbook of Research on Consumption, Media, and Popular Culture in the Global Age* (pp. 1–10). IGI Global. https://doi.org/10.4018/978-1-5225-8491-9.ch001

Aslan, F. (2021). Could There Be an Alternative Method of Media Literacy in Promoting Health in Children and Adolescents? Media Literacy and Health Promotion. In G. Sarı (Eds.), *Handbook of Research on Representing Health and Medicine in Modern Media* (pp. 191-199). IGI Global. https://doi.org/10.4018/978-1-7998-6825-5.ch013

Assay, B. E. (2018). Regulatory Compliance, Ethical Behaviour, and Sustainable Growth in Nigeria's Telecommunications Industry. In Oncioiu, I. (Ed.), *Ethics and Decision-Making for Sustainable Business Practices* (pp. 90–108). Hershey, PA: IGI Global. 10.4018/978-1-5225-3773-1.ch006

Assensoh-Kodua, A. (2022). This Thing of Social Media!: Indeed a Platform for Running or Developing Business in the Financial Sector. In Ertz, M. (Ed.), *Handbook of Research on the Platform Economy and the Evolution of E-Commerce* (pp. 389–414). IGI Global. https://doi.org/10.4018/978-1-7998-7545-1.ch017

Atar, Ö. G. (2019). Digital Media Literacy: In-Depth Interview With the Parents of the Students Who Use Digital Media. In G. Sarı (Eds.), *Handbook of Research on Children's Consumption of Digital Media* (pp. 139-155). IGI Global. https://doi.org/10.4018/978-1-5225-5733-3.ch011

Attié, E. A., Bouvet, A., & Guibert, J. (2022). The Stakes of Social Media: Analyzing User Sentiments. In Gupta, B., Peraković, D., Abd El-Latif, A., & Gupta, D. (Eds.), *Data Mining Approaches for Big Data and Sentiment Analysis in Social Media* (pp. 196–222). IGI Global. https://doi.org/10.4018/978-1-7998-8413-2.ch009

Averweg, U. R., & Leaning, M. (2018). The Qualities and Potential of Social Media. In M. Khosrow-Pour, D.B.A. (Ed.), *Encyclopedia of Information Science and Technology, Fourth Edition* (pp. 7106-7115). Hershey, PA: IGI Global. 10.4018/978-1-5225-2255-3.ch617

Baarda, R. (2017). Digital Democracy in Authoritarian Russia: Opportunity for Participation, or Site of Kremlin Control? In Luppicini, R., & Baarda, R. (Eds.), *Digital Media Integration for Participatory Democracy* (pp. 87–100). Hershey, PA: IGI Global. 10.4018/978-1-5225-2463-2.ch005

Barbosa, C., & Pedro, L. (2019). Time Orientation and Media Use: The Rise of the Device and the Changing Nature of Our Time Perception. In Oliveira, L. (Ed.), *Managing Screen Time in an Online Society* (pp. 78–98). IGI Global. https://doi.org/10.4018/978-1-5225-8163-5.ch004

Başal, B. (2017). Actor Effect: A Study on Historical Figures Who Have Shaped the Advertising Narration. In Yılmaz, R. (Ed.), *Narrative Advertising Models and Conceptualization in the Digital Age* (pp. 34–60). Hershey, PA: IGI Global. 10.4018/978-1-5225-2373-4.ch003

Behjati, M., & Cosmas, J. (2017). Self-Organizing Network Solutions: A Principal Step Towards Real 4G and Beyond. In Singh, D. (Ed.), *Routing Protocols and Architectural Solutions for Optimal Wireless Networks and Security* (pp. 241–253). Hershey, PA: IGI Global. 10.4018/978-1-5225-2342-0.ch011

Bekafigo, M., & Pingley, A. C. (2017). Do Campaigns "Go Negative" on Twitter? In Ibrahim, Y. (Ed.), *Politics, Protest, and Empowerment in Digital Spaces* (pp. 178–191). Hershey, PA: IGI Global. 10.4018/978-1-5225-1862-4.ch011

Bekman, M. (2022). Interaction of Internet Addiction with FoMO: The Role of Digital Media. In Öngün, E., Pembecioğlu, N., & Gündüz, U. (Eds.), *Handbook of Research on Digital Citizenship and Management During Crises* (pp. 116–133). IGI Global. https://doi.org/10.4018/978-1-7998-8421-7.ch007

Bishop, J. (2017). Developing and Validating the "This Is Why We Can't Have Nice Things Scale": Optimising Political Online Communities for Internet Trolling. In Ibrahim, Y. (Ed.), *Politics, Protest, and Empowerment in Digital Spaces* (pp. 153–177). Hershey, PA: IGI Global. 10.4018/978-1-5225-1862-4.ch010

Bitrus-Ojiambo, U. A., & King'ori, M. E. (2020). Media and Child Rights in Africa: Narrative Analysis of Child Rights in Kenyan Media. In Oyero, O. (Ed.), *Media and Its Role in Protecting the Rights of Children in Africa* (pp. 125–148). IGI Global. https://doi.org/10.4018/978-1-7998-0329-4.ch007

Black, S. (2019). Diversity and Inclusion: How to Avoid Bias and Social Media Blunders. In Joe, J., & Knight, E. (Eds.), *Social Media for Communication and Instruction in Academic Libraries* (pp. 100–118). IGI Global. https://doi.org/10.4018/978-1-5225-8097-3.ch007

Bolat, N. (2017). The Functions of the Narrator in Digital Advertising. In Yılmaz, R. (Ed.), *Narrative Advertising Models and Conceptualization in the Digital Age* (pp. 184–201). Hershey, PA: IGI Global. 10.4018/978-1-5225-2373-4.ch011

Brown, M. A.Sr. (2017). SNIP: High Touch Approach to Communication. In *Solutions for High-Touch Communications in a High-Tech World* (pp. 71–88). Hershey, PA: IGI Global. 10.4018/978-1-5225-1897-6.ch004

Brown, M. A.Sr. (2017). Comparing FTF and Online Communication Knowledge. In *Solutions for High-Touch Communications in a High-Tech World* (pp. 103–113). Hershey, PA: IGI Global. 10.4018/978-1-5225-1897-6.ch006

Brown, M. A.Sr. (2017). Where Do We Go from Here? In *Solutions for High-Touch Communications in a High-Tech World* (pp. 137–159). Hershey, PA: IGI Global. 10.4018/978-1-5225-1897-6.ch008

Brown, M. A.Sr. (2017). Bridging the Communication Gap. In *Solutions for High-Touch Communications in a High-Tech World* (pp. 1–22). Hershey, PA: IGI Global. 10.4018/978-1-5225-1897-6.ch001

Brown, M. A.Sr. (2017). Key Strategies for Communication. In *Solutions for High-Touch Communications in a High-Tech World* (pp. 179–202). Hershey, PA: IGI Global. 10.4018/978-1-5225-1897-6.ch010

Bryant, K. N. (2017). WordUp!: Student Responses to Social Media in the Technical Writing Classroom. In Bryant, K. (Ed.), *Engaging 21st Century Writers with Social Media* (pp. 231–245). Hershey, PA: IGI Global. 10.4018/978-1-5225-0562-4.ch014

Buck, E. H. (2017). Slacktivism, Supervision, and #Selfies: Illuminating Social Media Composition through Reception Theory. In Bryant, K. (Ed.), *Engaging 21st Century Writers with Social Media* (pp. 163–178). Hershey, PA: IGI Global. 10.4018/978-1-5225-0562-4.ch010

Bull, R., & Pianosi, M. (2017). Social Media, Participation, and Citizenship: New Strategic Directions. In Benson, V., Tuninga, R., & Saridakis, G. (Eds.), *Analyzing the Strategic Role of Social Networking in Firm Growth and Productivity* (pp. 76–94). Hershey, PA: IGI Global. 10.4018/978-1-5225-0559-4.ch005

Caldarola, G., D'Eredità, A., Falcone, A., Lo Blundo, M., & Mancini, M. (2020). Communicating Archaeology in a Social World: Social Media, Blogs, Websites, and Best Practices. In Proietti, E. (Ed.), *Developing Effective Communication Skills in Archaeology* (pp. 259–284). IGI Global. https://doi.org/10.4018/978-1-7998-1059-9.ch013

Carbajal, D., & Ramirez, Q. A. (2022). Applying Theoretical Perspectives to Social Media Influencers: A Content Analysis on Social Media Influencers the LaBrant Family. In Al-Suqri, M., Al-Shaqsi, O., & Alsalmi, J. (Eds.), *Mass Communications and the Influence of Information During Times of Crises* (pp. 69–98). IGI Global. https://doi.org/10.4018/978-1-7998-7503-1.ch004

Castellano, S., & Khelladi, I. (2017). Play It Like Beckham!: The Influence of Social Networks on E-Reputation – The Case of Sportspeople and Their Online Fan Base. In Mesquita, A. (Ed.), *Research Paradigms and Contemporary Perspectives on Human-Technology Interaction* (pp. 43–61). Hershey, PA: IGI Global. 10.4018/978-1-5225-1868-6.ch003

Chepken, C. K. (2020). Mobile-Based Social Media, What Is Cutting?: Mobile-Based Social Media: Extensive Study Findings. In Kır, S. (Ed.), *New Media and Visual Communication in Social Networks* (pp. 113–135). IGI Global. https://doi.org/10.4018/978-1-7998-1041-4.ch007

Chugh, R., & Joshi, M. (2017). Challenges of Knowledge Management amidst Rapidly Evolving Tools of Social Media. In Chugh, R. (Ed.), *Harnessing Social Media as a Knowledge Management Tool* (pp. 299–314). Hershey, PA: IGI Global. 10.4018/978-1-5225-0495-5.ch014

Cole, A. W., & Salek, T. A. (2017). Adopting a Parasocial Connection to Overcome Professional Kakoethos in Online Health Information. In Folk, M., & Apostel, S. (Eds.), *Establishing and Evaluating Digital Ethos and Online Credibility* (pp. 104–120). Hershey, PA: IGI Global. 10.4018/978-1-5225-1072-7.ch006

Cossiavelou, V. (2017). ACTA as Media Gatekeeping Factor: The EU Role as Global Negotiator. *International Journal of Interdisciplinary Telecommunications and Networking*, 9(1), 26–37. 10.4018/IJITN.2017010103

Costanza, F. (2017). Social Media Marketing and Value Co-Creation: A System Dynamics Approach. In Rozenes, S., & Cohen, Y. (Eds.), *Handbook of Research on Strategic Alliances and Value Co-Creation in the Service Industry* (pp. 205–230). Hershey, PA: IGI Global. 10.4018/978-1-5225-2084-9.ch011

Cyrek, B. (2019). The User With a Thousand Faces: Campbell's "Monomyth" and Media Usage Practices. In Kreft, J., Kuczamer-Kłopotowska, S., & Kalinowska-Żeleźnik, A. (Eds.), *Myth in Modern Media Management and Marketing* (pp. 50–68). IGI Global. https://doi.org/10.4018/978-1-5225-9100-9.ch003

Deniz, Ş. (2020). Is Somebody Spying on Us?: Social Media Users' Privacy Awareness. In Kır, S. (Ed.), *New Media and Visual Communication in Social Networks* (pp. 156–172). IGI Global. https://doi.org/10.4018/978-1-7998-1041-4.ch009

Di Virgilio, F., & Antonelli, G. (2018). Consumer Behavior, Trust, and Electronic Word-of-Mouth Communication: Developing an Online Purchase Intention Model. In Di Virgilio, F. (Ed.), *Social Media for Knowledge Management Applications in Modern Organizations* (pp. 58–80). Hershey, PA: IGI Global. 10.4018/978-1-5225-2897-5.ch003

Dolanbay, H. (2022). The Transformation of Literacy and Media Literacy. In Lane, C. (Ed.), *Handbook of Research on Acquiring 21st Century Literacy Skills Through Game-Based Learning* (pp. 363–380). IGI Global. https://doi.org/10.4018/978-1-7998-7271-9.ch019

Dunn, R. A., & Herrmann, A. F. (2020). Comic Con Communion: Gender, Cosplay, and Media Fandom. In Dunn, R. (Ed.), *Multidisciplinary Perspectives on Media Fandom* (pp. 37–52). IGI Global. https://doi.org/10.4018/978-1-7998-3323-9.ch003

DuQuette, J. L. (2017). Lessons from Cypris Chat: Revisiting Virtual Communities as Communities. In Panconesi, G., & Guida, M. (Eds.), *Handbook of Research on Collaborative Teaching Practice in Virtual Learning Environments* (pp. 299–316). Hershey, PA: IGI Global. 10.4018/978-1-5225-2426-7.ch016

Ekhlassi, A., Niknejhad Moghadam, M., & Adibi, A. (2018). The Concept of Social Media: The Functional Building Blocks. In *Building Brand Identity in the Age of Social Media: Emerging Research and Opportunities* (pp. 29–60). Hershey, PA: IGI Global. 10.4018/978-1-5225-5143-0.ch002

Ekhlassi, A., Niknejhad Moghadam, M., & Adibi, A. (2018). Social Media Branding Strategy: Social Media Marketing Approach. In *Building Brand Identity in the Age of Social Media: Emerging Research and Opportunities* (pp. 94–117). Hershey, PA: IGI Global. 10.4018/978-1-5225-5143-0.ch004

Ekhlassi, A., Niknejhad Moghadam, M., & Adibi, A. (2018). The Impact of Social Media on Brand Loyalty: Achieving "E-Trust" Through Engagement. In *Building Brand Identity in the Age of Social Media: Emerging Research and Opportunities* (pp. 155–168). Hershey, PA: IGI Global. 10.4018/978-1-5225-5143-0.ch007

El-Henawy, W. M. (2019). Media Literacy in EFL Teacher Education: A Necessity for 21st Century English Language Instruction. In Yildiz, M., Fazal, M., Ahn, M., Feirsen, R., & Ozdemir, S. (Eds.), *Handbook of Research on Media Literacy Research and Applications Across Disciplines* (pp. 65–89). IGI Global. https://doi.org/10.4018/978-1-5225-9261-7.ch005

Elegbe, O. (2017). An Assessment of Media Contribution to Behaviour Change and HIV Prevention in Nigeria. In Nelson, O., Ojebuyi, B., & Salawu, A. (Eds.), *Impacts of the Media on African Socio-Economic Development* (pp. 261–280). Hershey, PA: IGI Global. 10.4018/978-1-5225-1859-4.ch017

Endong, F. P. (2018). Hashtag Activism and the Transnationalization of Nigerian-Born Movements Against Terrorism: A Critical Appraisal of the #BringBackOurGirls Campaign. In Endong, F. (Ed.), *Exploring the Role of Social Media in Transnational Advocacy* (pp. 36–54). Hershey, PA: IGI Global. 10.4018/978-1-5225-2854-8.ch003

Erkek, S. (2021). Health Communication and Social Media: A Study About Using Social Media in Medicine Companies. In G. Sarı (Eds.), *Handbook of Research on Representing Health and Medicine in Modern Media* (pp. 70-83). IGI Global. https://doi.org/10.4018/978-1-7998-6825-5.ch005

Erragcha, N. (2017). Using Social Media Tools in Marketing: Opportunities and Challenges. In Brown, M.Sr., (Ed.), *Social Media Performance Evaluation and Success Measurements* (pp. 106–129). Hershey, PA: IGI Global. 10.4018/978-1-5225-1963-8.ch006

Ersoy, M. (2019). Social Media and Children. In G. Sarı (Ed.), *Handbook of Research on Children's Consumption of Digital Media* (pp. 11-23). IGI Global. https://doi.org/10.4018/978-1-5225-5733-3.ch002

Ezeh, N. C. (2018). Media Campaign on Exclusive Breastfeeding: Awareness, Perception, and Acceptability Among Mothers in Anambra State, Nigeria. In Salawu, A., & Owolabi, T. (Eds.), *Exploring Journalism Practice and Perception in Developing Countries* (pp. 172–193). Hershey, PA: IGI Global. 10.4018/978-1-5225-3376-4.ch009

Fawole, O. A., & Osho, O. A. (2017). Influence of Social Media on Dating Relationships of Emerging Adults in Nigerian Universities: Social Media and Dating in Nigeria. In Wright, M. (Ed.), *Identity, Sexuality, and Relationships among Emerging Adults in the Digital Age* (pp. 168–177). Hershey, PA: IGI Global. 10.4018/978-1-5225-1856-3.ch011

Fayoyin, A. (2017). Electoral Polling and Reporting in Africa: Professional and Policy Implications for Media Practice and Political Communication in a Digital Age. In Mhiripiri, N., & Chari, T. (Eds.), *Media Law, Ethics, and Policy in the Digital Age* (pp. 164–181). Hershey, PA: IGI Global. 10.4018/978-1-5225-2095-5.ch009

Fayoyin, A. (2018). Rethinking Media Engagement Strategies for Social Change in Africa: Context, Approaches, and Implications for Development Communication. In Salawu, A., & Owolabi, T. (Eds.), *Exploring Journalism Practice and Perception in Developing Countries* (pp. 257–280). Hershey, PA: IGI Global. 10.4018/978-1-5225-3376-4.ch013

Fechine, Y., & Rêgo, S. C. (2018). Transmedia Television Journalism in Brazil: Jornal da Record News as Reference. In Gambarato, R., & Alzamora, G. (Eds.), *Exploring Transmedia Journalism in the Digital Age* (pp. 253–265). Hershey, PA: IGI Global. 10.4018/978-1-5225-3781-6.ch015

Fener, E. (2021). Social Media and Health Communication. In G. Sarı (Ed.), *Handbook of Research on Representing Health and Medicine in Modern Media* (pp. 16-32). IGI Global. https://doi.org/10.4018/978-1-7998-6825-5.ch002

Fernandes dos Santos, N. (2020). The Use of Twitter During the 2013 Protests in Brazil: Mainstream Media at Stake. In Solo, A. (Ed.), *Handbook of Research on Politics in the Computer Age* (pp. 181–202). IGI Global. https://doi.org/10.4018/978-1-7998-0377-5.ch011

Fiore, C. (2017). The Blogging Method: Improving Traditional Student Writing Practices. In Bryant, K. (Ed.), *Engaging 21st Century Writers with Social Media* (pp. 179–198). Hershey, PA: IGI Global. 10.4018/978-1-5225-0562-4.ch011

Friesem, E., & Friesem, Y. (2019). Media Literacy Education in the Era of Post-Truth: Paradigm Crisis. In Yildiz, M., Fazal, M., Ahn, M., Feirsen, R., & Ozdemir, S. (Eds.), *Handbook of Research on Media Literacy Research and Applications Across Disciplines* (pp. 119–134). IGI Global. https://doi.org/10.4018/978-1-5225-9261-7.ch008

Fung, Y., Lee, L., Chui, K. T., Cheung, G. H., Tang, C., & Wong, S. (2022). Sentiment Analysis and Summarization of Facebook Posts on News Media. In Gupta, B., Peraković, D., Abd El-Latif, A., & Gupta, D. (Eds.), *Data Mining Approaches for Big Data and Sentiment Analysis in Social Media* (pp. 142–154). IGI Global. https://doi.org/10.4018/978-1-7998-8413-2.ch006

Gambarato, R. R., Alzamora, G. C., & Tárcia, L. P. (2018). 2016 Rio Summer Olympics and the Transmedia Journalism of Planned Events. In Gambarato, R., & Alzamora, G. (Eds.), *Exploring Transmedia Journalism in the Digital Age* (pp. 126–146). Hershey, PA: IGI Global. 10.4018/978-1-5225-3781-6.ch008

Ganguin, S., Gemkow, J., & Haubold, R. (2017). Information Overload as a Challenge and Changing Point for Educational Media Literacies. In Marques, R., & Batista, J. (Eds.), *Information and Communication Overload in the Digital Age* (pp. 302–328). Hershey, PA: IGI Global. 10.4018/978-1-5225-2061-0.ch013

Gardner, G. C. (2017). The Lived Experience of Smartphone Use in a Unit of the United States Army. In Topor, F. (Ed.), *Handbook of Research on Individualism and Identity in the Globalized Digital Age* (pp. 88–117). Hershey, PA: IGI Global. 10.4018/978-1-5225-0522-8.ch005

Garg, P., & Pahuja, S. (2020). Social Media: Concept, Role, Categories, Trends, Social Media and AI, Impact on Youth, Careers, Recommendations. In Alavi, S., & Ahuja, V. (Eds.), *Managing Social Media Practices in the Digital Economy* (pp. 172–192). IGI Global. https://doi.org/10.4018/978-1-7998-2185-4.ch008

Golightly, D., & Houghton, R. J. (2018). Social Media as a Tool to Understand Behaviour on the Railways. In Kohli, S., Kumar, A., Easton, J., & Roberts, C. (Eds.), *Innovative Applications of Big Data in the Railway Industry* (pp. 224–239). Hershey, PA: IGI Global. 10.4018/978-1-5225-3176-0.ch010

Gouveia, P. (2020). The New Media vs. Old Media Trap: How Contemporary Arts Became Playful Transmedia Environments. In Soares, C., & Simão, E. (Eds.), *Multidisciplinary Perspectives on New Media Art* (pp. 25–46). IGI Global. https://doi.org/10.4018/978-1-7998-3669-8.ch002

Gundogan, M. B. (2017). In Search for a "Good Fit" Between Augmented Reality and Mobile Learning Ecosystem. In Kurubacak, G., & Altinpulluk, H. (Eds.), *Mobile Technologies and Augmented Reality in Open Education* (pp. 135–153). Hershey, PA: IGI Global. 10.4018/978-1-5225-2110-5.ch007

Gupta, H. (2018). Impact of Digital Communication on Consumer Behaviour Processes in Luxury Branding Segment: A Study of Apparel Industry. In Dasgupta, S., Biswal, S., & Ramesh, M. (Eds.), *Holistic Approaches to Brand Culture and Communication Across Industries* (pp. 132–157). Hershey, PA: IGI Global. 10.4018/978-1-5225-3150-0.ch008

Guzman-Garcia, P. A., Orozco-Quintana, E., Sepulveda-Gonzalez, D., Cooley-Magallanes, A., Salas-Velazquez, D., Lopez-Garcia, C., Ramírez-Treviño, A., Espinoza-Moran, A. L., Lopez, M., & Segura-Azuara, N. D. (2022). Ending Health Promotion Lethargy: A Social Media Awareness Campaign to Face Hypothyroidism. In Lopez, M. (Ed.), *Advancing Health Education With Telemedicine* (pp. 165–182). IGI Global. https://doi.org/10.4018/978-1-7998-8783-6.ch009

Hafeez, E., & Zahid, L. (2021). Sexism and Gender Discrimination in Pakistan's Mainstream News Media. In Jamil, S., Çoban, B., Ataman, B., & Appiah-Adjei, G. (Eds.), *Handbook of Research on Discrimination, Gender Disparity, and Safety Risks in Journalism* (pp. 60–89). IGI Global. https://doi.org/10.4018/978-1-7998-6686-2.ch005

Hai-Jew, S. (2017). Creating "(Social) Network Art" with NodeXL. In Hai-Jew, S. (Ed.), *Social Media Data Extraction and Content Analysis* (pp. 342–393). Hershey, PA: IGI Global. 10.4018/978-1-5225-0648-5.ch011

Hai-Jew, S. (2017). Employing the Sentiment Analysis Tool in NVivo 11 Plus on Social Media Data: Eight Initial Case Types. In Rao, N. (Ed.), *Social Media Listening and Monitoring for Business Applications* (pp. 175–244). Hershey, PA: IGI Global. 10.4018/978-1-5225-0846-5.ch010

Hai-Jew, S. (2017). Conducting Sentiment Analysis and Post-Sentiment Data Exploration through Automated Means. In Hai-Jew, S. (Ed.), *Social Media Data Extraction and Content Analysis* (pp. 202–240). Hershey, PA: IGI Global. 10.4018/978-1-5225-0648-5.ch008

Hai-Jew, S. (2017). Applied Analytical "Distant Reading" using NVivo 11 Plus. In Hai-Jew, S. (Ed.), *Social Media Data Extraction and Content Analysis* (pp. 159–201). Hershey, PA: IGI Global. 10.4018/978-1-5225-0648-5.ch007

Hai-Jew, S. (2017). Flickering Emotions: Feeling-Based Associations from Related Tags Networks on Flickr. In Hai-Jew, S. (Ed.), *Social Media Data Extraction and Content Analysis* (pp. 296–341). Hershey, PA: IGI Global. 10.4018/978-1-5225-0648-5.ch010

Hai-Jew, S. (2017). Manually Profiling Egos and Entities across Social Media Platforms: Evaluating Shared Messaging and Contents, User Networks, and Metadata. In Benson, V., Tuninga, R., & Saridakis, G. (Eds.), *Analyzing the Strategic Role of Social Networking in Firm Growth and Productivity* (pp. 352–405). Hershey, PA: IGI Global. 10.4018/978-1-5225-0559-4.ch019

Hai-Jew, S. (2017). Exploring "User," "Video," and (Pseudo) Multi-Mode Networks on YouTube with NodeXL. In Hai-Jew, S. (Ed.), *Social Media Data Extraction and Content Analysis* (pp. 242–295). Hershey, PA: IGI Global. 10.4018/978-1-5225-0648-5.ch009

Hai-Jew, S. (2018). Exploring "Mass Surveillance" Through Computational Linguistic Analysis of Five Text Corpora: Academic, Mainstream Journalism, Microblogging Hashtag Conversation, Wikipedia Articles, and Leaked Government Data. In *Techniques for Coding Imagery and Multimedia: Emerging Research and Opportunities* (pp. 212–286). Hershey, PA: IGI Global. 10.4018/978-1-5225-2679-7.ch004

Hai-Jew, S. (2018). Exploring Identity-Based Humor in a #Selfies #Humor Image Set From Instagram. In *Techniques for Coding Imagery and Multimedia: Emerging Research and Opportunities* (pp. 1–90). Hershey, PA: IGI Global. 10.4018/978-1-5225-2679-7.ch001

Hai-Jew, S. (2018). See Ya!: Exploring American Renunciation of Citizenship Through Targeted and Sparse Social Media Data Sets and a Custom Spatial-Based Linguistic Analysis Dictionary. In *Techniques for Coding Imagery and Multimedia: Emerging Research and Opportunities* (pp. 287–393). Hershey, PA: IGI Global. 10.4018/978-1-5225-2679-7.ch005

Hasan, H., & Linger, H. (2017). Connected Living for Positive Ageing. In Gordon, S. (Ed.), *Online Communities as Agents of Change and Social Movements* (pp. 203–223). Hershey, PA: IGI Global. 10.4018/978-1-5225-2495-3.ch008

Hersey, L. N. (2017). CHOICES: Measuring Return on Investment in a Nonprofit Organization. In Brown, M.Sr., (Ed.), *Social Media Performance Evaluation and Success Measurements* (pp. 157–179). Hershey, PA: IGI Global. 10.4018/978-1-5225-1963-8.ch008

Heuva, W. E. (2017). Deferring Citizens' "Right to Know" in an Information Age: The Information Deficit in Namibia. In Mhiripiri, N., & Chari, T. (Eds.), *Media Law, Ethics, and Policy in the Digital Age* (pp. 245–267). Hershey, PA: IGI Global. 10.4018/978-1-5225-2095-5.ch014

Hopwood, M., & McLean, H. (2017). Social Media in Crisis Communication: The Lance Armstrong Saga. In Benson, V., Tuninga, R., & Saridakis, G. (Eds.), *Analyzing the Strategic Role of Social Networking in Firm Growth and Productivity* (pp. 45–58). Hershey, PA: IGI Global. 10.4018/978-1-5225-0559-4.ch003

Horst, S., & Murschetz, P. C. (2019). Strategic Media Entrepreneurship: Theory Development and Problematization. *Journal of Media Management and Entrepreneurship*, 1(1), 1–26. https://doi.org/10.4018/JMME.2019010101

Hotur, S. K. (2018). Indian Approaches to E-Diplomacy: An Overview. In Bute, S. (Ed.), *Media Diplomacy and Its Evolving Role in the Current Geopolitical Climate* (pp. 27–35). Hershey, PA: IGI Global. 10.4018/978-1-5225-3859-2.ch002

Inder, S. (2021). Social Media, Crowdsourcing, and Marketing. In Singh, A. (Ed.), *Big Data Analytics for Improved Accuracy, Efficiency, and Decision Making in Digital Marketing* (pp. 64–73). IGI Global. https://doi.org/10.4018/978-1-7998-7231-3.ch005

Işık, T. (2021). Media and Health Communication Campaigns. In G. Sarı (Ed.), *Handbook of Research on Representing Health and Medicine in Modern Media* (pp. 1-15). IGI Global. https://doi.org/10.4018/978-1-7998-6825-5.ch001

Iwasaki, Y. (2017). Youth Engagement in the Era of New Media. In Adria, M., & Mao, Y. (Eds.), *Handbook of Research on Citizen Engagement and Public Participation in the Era of New Media* (pp. 90–105). Hershey, PA: IGI Global. 10.4018/978-1-5225-1081-9.ch006

Jamieson, H. V. (2017). We have a Situation!: Cyberformance and Civic Engagement in Post-Democracy. In Shin, R. (Ed.), *Convergence of Contemporary Art, Visual Culture, and Global Civic Engagement* (pp. 297–317). Hershey, PA: IGI Global. 10.4018/978-1-5225-1665-1.ch017

Jimoh, J., & Kayode, J. (2018). Imperative of Peace and Conflict-Sensitive Journalism in Development. In Salawu, A., & Owolabi, T. (Eds.), *Exploring Journalism Practice and Perception in Developing Countries* (pp. 150–171). Hershey, PA: IGI Global. 10.4018/978-1-5225-3376-4.ch008

Joseph, J. J., & Florea, D. (2020). Clinical Topics in Social Media: The Role of Self-Disclosing on Social Media for Friendship and Identity in Specialized Populations. In Desjarlais, M. (Ed.), *The Psychology and Dynamics Behind Social Media Interactions* (pp. 28–56). IGI Global. https://doi.org/10.4018/978-1-5225-9412-3.ch002

Kaale, K. B., & Mgeta, M. B. (2020). Photojournalism Ethics: Portraying Children's Photos in Tanzanian Media. In Oyero, O. (Ed.), *Media and Its Role in Protecting the Rights of Children in Africa* (pp. 149–168). IGI Global. https://doi.org/10.4018/978-1-7998-0329-4.ch008

Kanellopoulos, D. N. (2018). Group Synchronization for Multimedia Systems. In M. Khosrow-Pour, D.B.A. (Ed.), *Encyclopedia of Information Science and Technology, Fourth Edition* (pp. 6435-6446). Hershey, PA: IGI Global. 10.4018/978-1-5225-2255-3.ch559

Kapepo, M. I., & Mayisela, T. (2017). Integrating Digital Literacies Into an Undergraduate Course: Inclusiveness Through Use of ICTs. In Ayo, C., & Mbarika, V. (Eds.), *Sustainable ICT Adoption and Integration for Socio-Economic Development* (pp. 152–173). Hershey, PA: IGI Global. 10.4018/978-1-5225-2565-3.ch007

Karahoca, A., & Yengin, İ. (2018). Understanding the Potentials of Social Media in Collaborative Learning. In M. Khosrow-Pour, D.B.A. (Ed.), *Encyclopedia of Information Science and Technology, Fourth Edition* (pp. 7168-7180). Hershey, PA: IGI Global. 10.4018/978-1-5225-2255-3.ch623

Kasemsap, K. (2017). Professional and Business Applications of Social Media Platforms. In Benson, V., Tuninga, R., & Saridakis, G. (Eds.), *Analyzing the Strategic Role of Social Networking in Firm Growth and Productivity* (pp. 427–450). Hershey, PA: IGI Global. 10.4018/978-1-5225-0559-4.ch021

Kasemsap, K. (2017). Mastering Social Media in the Modern Business World. In Rao, N. (Ed.), *Social Media Listening and Monitoring for Business Applications* (pp. 18–44). Hershey, PA: IGI Global. 10.4018/978-1-5225-0846-5.ch002

Kaufmann, H. R., & Manarioti, A. (2017). Consumer Engagement in Social Media Platforms. In *Encouraging Participative Consumerism Through Evolutionary Digital Marketing: Emerging Research and Opportunities* (pp. 95–123). Hershey, PA: IGI Global. 10.4018/978-1-68318-012-8.ch004

Kavak, B., Özdemir, N., & Erol-Boyacı, G. (2020). A Literature Review of Social Media for Marketing: Social Media Use in B2C and B2B Contexts. In Alavi, S., & Ahuja, V. (Eds.), *Managing Social Media Practices in the Digital Economy* (pp. 67–96). IGI Global. https://doi.org/10.4018/978-1-7998-2185-4.ch004

Kavoura, A., & Kefallonitis, E. (2018). The Effect of Social Media Networking in the Travel Industry. In M. Khosrow-Pour, D.B.A. (Ed.), *Encyclopedia of Information Science and Technology, Fourth Edition* (pp. 4052-4063). Hershey, PA: IGI Global. 10.4018/978-1-5225-2255-3.ch351

Kawamura, Y. (2018). Practice and Modeling of Advertising Communication Strategy: Sender-Driven and Receiver-Driven. In Ogata, T., & Asakawa, S. (Eds.), *Content Generation Through Narrative Communication and Simulation* (pp. 358–379). Hershey, PA: IGI Global. 10.4018/978-1-5225-4775-4.ch013

Kaya, A., & Mantar, O. B. (2021). Social Media and Health Communication: Vaccine Refusal/Hesitancy. In G. Sarı (Ed.), *Handbook of Research on Representing Health and Medicine in Modern Media* (pp. 33-53). IGI Global. https://doi.org/10.4018/978-1-7998-6825-5.ch003

Kaya, A. Y., & Ata, F. (2022). New Media and Digital Paranoia: Extreme Skepticism in Digital Communication. In Aker, H., & Aiken, M. (Eds.), *Handbook of Research on Cyberchondria, Health Literacy, and the Role of Media in Society's Perception of Medical Information* (pp. 330–343). IGI Global. https://doi.org/10.4018/978-1-7998-8630-3.ch018

Kell, C., & Czerniewicz, L. (2017). Visibility of Scholarly Research and Changing Research Communication Practices: A Case Study from Namibia. In Esposito, A. (Ed.), *Research 2.0 and the Impact of Digital Technologies on Scholarly Inquiry* (pp. 97–116). Hershey, PA: IGI Global. 10.4018/978-1-5225-0830-4.ch006

Kharade, S. S. (2022). An Adverse Effect of Social, Gaming, and Entertainment Media on Overall Development of Adolescents. In Malik, S., Bansal, R., & Tyagi, A. (Eds.), *Impact and Role of Digital Technologies in Adolescent Lives* (pp. 26–34). IGI Global. https://doi.org/10.4018/978-1-7998-8318-0.ch003

Kılınç, U. (2017). Create It! Extend It!: Evolution of Comics Through Narrative Advertising. In Yılmaz, R. (Ed.), *Narrative Advertising Models and Conceptualization in the Digital Age* (pp. 117–132). Hershey, PA: IGI Global. 10.4018/978-1-5225-2373-4.ch007

Kocakoç, I. D., & Özkan, P. (2022). Clubhouse Experience: Sentiment Analysis of an Alternative Platform From the Eyes of Classic Social Media Users. In Gupta, B., Peraković, D., Abd El-Latif, A., & Gupta, D. (Eds.), *Data Mining Approaches for Big Data and Sentiment Analysis in Social Media* (pp. 244–264). IGI Global. https://doi.org/10.4018/978-1-7998-8413-2.ch011

Kreft, J. (2019). A Myth and Media Management: The Facade Rhetoric and Business Objectives. In Kreft, J., Kuczamer-Kłopotowska, S., & Kalinowska-Żeleźnik, A. (Eds.), *Myth in Modern Media Management and Marketing* (pp. 118–141). IGI Global. https://doi.org/10.4018/978-1-5225-9100-9.ch006

Krishnamurthy, R. (2019). Social Media as a Marketing Tool. In Mishra, P., & Dham, S. (Eds.), *Application of Gaming in New Media Marketing* (pp. 181–201). IGI Global. https://doi.org/10.4018/978-1-5225-6064-7.ch011

Kumar, D., & Gupta, P. (2021). Communicating in Media Dark Areas. In R. Jackson & A. Reboulet (Eds.), *Effective Strategies for Communicating Insights in Business* (pp. 141-156). IGI Global. https://doi.org/10.4018/978-1-7998-3964-4.ch009

Kumar, P., & Sinha, A. (2018). Business-Oriented Analytics With Social Network of Things. In Bansal, H., Shrivastava, G., Nguyen, G., & Stanciu, L. (Eds.), *Social Network Analytics for Contemporary Business Organizations* (pp. 166–187). Hershey, PA: IGI Global. 10.4018/978-1-5225-5097-6.ch009

Kunock, A. I. (2017). Boko Haram Insurgency in Cameroon: Role of Mass Media in Conflict Management. In Mhiripiri, N., & Chari, T. (Eds.), *Media Law, Ethics, and Policy in the Digital Age* (pp. 226–244). Hershey, PA: IGI Global. 10.4018/978-1-5225-2095-5.ch013

Labadie, J. A. (2018). Digitally Mediated Art Inspired by Technology Integration: A Personal Journey. In Ursyn, A. (Ed.), *Visual Approaches to Cognitive Education With Technology Integration* (pp. 121–162). Hershey, PA: IGI Global. 10.4018/978-1-5225-5332-8.ch008

Lantz, E. (2020). Immersion Domes: Next-Generation Arts and Entertainment Venues. In Morie, J., & McCallum, K. (Eds.), *Handbook of Research on the Global Impacts and Roles of Immersive Media* (pp. 314–346). IGI Global. https://doi.org/10.4018/978-1-7998-2433-6.ch016

Lasisi, M. I., Adebiyi, R. A., & Ajetunmobi, U. O. (2020). Predicting Migration to Developed Countries: The Place of Media Attention. In Okorie, N., Ojebuyi, B., & Macharia, J. (Eds.), *Handbook of Research on the Global Impact of Media on Migration Issues* (pp. 293–311). IGI Global. https://doi.org/10.4018/978-1-7998-0210-5.ch017

Lefkowith, S. (2017). Credibility and Crisis in Pseudonymous Communities. In Folk, M., & Apostel, S. (Eds.), *Establishing and Evaluating Digital Ethos and Online Credibility* (pp. 190–236). Hershey, PA: IGI Global. 10.4018/978-1-5225-1072-7.ch010

Lekic-Subasic, Z. (2021). Women and Media: What Public Service Media Can Do to Ensure Gender Equality. In Jamil, S., Çoban, B., Ataman, B., & Appiah-Adjei, G. (Eds.), *Handbook of Research on Discrimination, Gender Disparity, and Safety Risks in Journalism* (pp. 8–23). IGI Global. https://doi.org/10.4018/978-1-7998-6686-2.ch002

Luppicini, R. (2017). Technoethics and Digital Democracy for Future Citizens. In Luppicini, R., & Baarda, R. (Eds.), *Digital Media Integration for Participatory Democracy* (pp. 1–21). Hershey, PA: IGI Global. 10.4018/978-1-5225-2463-2.ch001

Maher, D. (2018). Supporting Pre-Service Teachers' Understanding and Use of Mobile Devices. In Keengwe, J. (Ed.), *Handbook of Research on Mobile Technology, Constructivism, and Meaningful Learning* (pp. 160–177). Hershey, PA: IGI Global. 10.4018/978-1-5225-3949-0.ch009

Makhwanya, A. (2018). Barriers to Social Media Advocacy: Lessons Learnt From the Project "Tell Them We Are From Here". In Endong, F. (Ed.), *Exploring the Role of Social Media in Transnational Advocacy* (pp. 55–72). Hershey, PA: IGI Global. 10.4018/978-1-5225-2854-8.ch004

Malicki-Sanchez, K. (2020). Out of Our Minds: Ontology and Embodied Media in a Post-Human Paradigm. In Morie, J., & McCallum, K. (Eds.), *Handbook of Research on the Global Impacts and Roles of Immersive Media* (pp. 10–36). IGI Global. https://doi.org/10.4018/978-1-7998-2433-6.ch002

Manli, G., & Rezaei, S. (2017). Value and Risk: Dual Pillars of Apps Usefulness. In Rezaei, S. (Ed.), *Apps Management and E-Commerce Transactions in Real-Time* (pp. 274–292). Hershey, PA: IGI Global. 10.4018/978-1-5225-2449-6.ch013

Manrique, C. G., & Manrique, G. G. (2017). Social Media's Role in Alleviating Political Corruption and Scandals: The Philippines during and after the Marcos Regime. In Demirhan, K., & Çakır-Demirhan, D. (Eds.), *Political Scandal, Corruption, and Legitimacy in the Age of Social Media* (pp. 205–222). Hershey, PA: IGI Global. 10.4018/978-1-5225-2019-1.ch009

Marjerison, R. K., Lin, Y., & Kennedyd, S. I. (2019). An Examination of Motivation and Media Type: Sharing Content on Chinese Social Media. *International Journal of Social Media and Online Communities*, 11(1), 15–34. https://doi.org/10.4018/IJSMOC.2019010102

Marovitz, M. (2017). Social Networking Engagement and Crisis Communication Considerations. In Brown, M.Sr., (Ed.), *Social Media Performance Evaluation and Success Measurements* (pp. 130–155). Hershey, PA: IGI Global. 10.4018/978-1-5225-1963-8.ch007

Martin, P. M., & Onampally, J. J. (2019). Patterns of Deceptive Communication of Social and Religious Issues in Social Media: Representation of Social Issues in Social Media. In Chiluwa, I., & Samoilenko, S. (Eds.), *Handbook of Research on Deception, Fake News, and Misinformation Online* (pp. 490–502). IGI Global. https://doi.org/10.4018/978-1-5225-8535-0.ch026

Masterson, J. R. (2020). Chinese Citizenry Social Media Pressures and Public Official Responses: The Double-Edged Sword of Social Media in China. In S. Edwards III & D. Santos (Eds.), *Digital Transformation and Its Role in Progressing the Relationship Between States and Their Citizens* (pp. 139-181). IGI Global. https://doi.org/10.4018/978-1-7998-3152-5.ch007

Maulana, I. (2018). Spontaneous Taking and Posting Selfie: Reclaiming the Lost Trust. In Hai-Jew, S. (Ed.), *Selfies as a Mode of Social Media and Work Space Research* (pp. 28–50). Hershey, PA: IGI Global. 10.4018/978-1-5225-3373-3.ch002

Mayo, S. (2018). A Collective Consciousness Model in a Post-Media Society. In Khosrow-Pour, M. (Ed.), *Enhancing Art, Culture, and Design With Technological Integration* (pp. 25–49). Hershey, PA: IGI Global. 10.4018/978-1-5225-5023-5.ch002

Mazur, E., Signorella, M. L., & Hough, M. (2018). The Internet Behavior of Older Adults. In M. Khosrow-Pour, D.B.A. (Ed.), *Encyclopedia of Information Science and Technology, Fourth Edition* (pp. 7026-7035). Hershey, PA: IGI Global. 10.4018/978-1-5225-2255-3.ch609

McCallum, K. M. (2020). Immersive Experience: Convergence, Storyworlds, and the Power for Social Impact. In Morie, J., & McCallum, K. (Eds.), *Handbook of Research on the Global Impacts and Roles of Immersive Media* (pp. 453–484). IGI Global. https://doi.org/10.4018/978-1-7998-2433-6.ch022

McGuire, M. (2017). Reblogging as Writing: The Role of Tumblr in the Writing Classroom. In Bryant, K. (Ed.), *Engaging 21st Century Writers with Social Media* (pp. 116–131). Hershey, PA: IGI Global. 10.4018/978-1-5225-0562-4.ch007

McKee, J. (2018). Architecture as a Tool to Solve Business Planning Problems. In M. Khosrow-Pour, D.B.A. (Ed.), *Encyclopedia of Information Science and Technology, Fourth Edition* (pp. 573-586). Hershey, PA: IGI Global. 10.4018/978-1-5225-2255-3.ch050

McMahon, D. (2017). With a Little Help from My Friends: The Irish Radio Industry's Strategic Appropriation of Facebook for Commercial Growth. In Benson, V., Tuninga, R., & Saridakis, G. (Eds.), *Analyzing the Strategic Role of Social Networking in Firm Growth and Productivity* (pp. 157–171). Hershey, PA: IGI Global. 10.4018/978-1-5225-0559-4.ch009

McPherson, M. J., & Lemon, N. (2017). The Hook, Woo, and Spin: Academics Creating Relations on Social Media. In Esposito, A. (Ed.), *Research 2.0 and the Impact of Digital Technologies on Scholarly Inquiry* (pp. 167–187). Hershey, PA: IGI Global. 10.4018/978-1-5225-0830-4.ch009

Melro, A., & Oliveira, L. (2018). Screen Culture. In M. Khosrow-Pour, D.B.A. (Ed.), *Encyclopedia of Information Science and Technology, Fourth Edition* (pp. 4255-4266). Hershey, PA: IGI Global. 10.4018/978-1-5225-2255-3.ch369

Meral, K. Z. (2021). Social Media Ethics and Children in the Digital Era: Social Media Risks and Precautions. In Taskiran, M., & Pinarbaşi, F. (Eds.), *Multidisciplinary Approaches to Ethics in the Digital Era* (pp. 166–182). IGI Global. https://doi.org/10.4018/978-1-7998-4117-3.ch011

Meral, Y., & Özbay, D. E. (2020). Electronic Trading, Electronic Advertising, and Social Media Literacy: Using Local Turkish Influencers in Social Media for International Trade Products Marketing. In Taskiran, N. (Ed.), *Handbook of Research on Multidisciplinary Approaches to Literacy in the Digital Age* (pp. 224–261). IGI Global. https://doi.org/10.4018/978-1-7998-1534-1.ch012

Mhiripiri, N. A., & Chikakano, J. (2017). Criminal Defamation, the Criminalisation of Expression, Media and Information Dissemination in the Digital Age: A Legal and Ethical Perspective. In Mhiripiri, N., & Chari, T. (Eds.), *Media Law, Ethics, and Policy in the Digital Age* (pp. 1–24). Hershey, PA: IGI Global. 10.4018/978-1-5225-2095-5.ch001

Miliopoulou, G., & Cossiavelou, V. (2019). Brand Management and Media Gatekeeping: Exploring the Professionals' Practices and Perspectives in the Social Media. In Meghanathan, N. (Ed.), *Strategic Innovations and Interdisciplinary Perspectives in Telecommunications and Networking* (pp. 56–82). IGI Global. https://doi.org/10.4018/978-1-5225-8188-8.ch004

Miranda, S. L., & Antunes, A. C. (2021). Golden Years in Social Media World: Examining Behavior and Motivations. In Wamuyu, P. (Ed.), *Analyzing Global Social Media Consumption* (pp. 261–276). IGI Global. https://doi.org/10.4018/978-1-7998-4718-2.ch014

Miron, E., Palmor, A., Ravid, G., Sharon, A., Tikotsky, A., & Zirkel, Y. (2017). Principles and Good Practices for Using Wikis within Organizations. In Chugh, R. (Ed.), *Harnessing Social Media as a Knowledge Management Tool* (pp. 143–176). Hershey, PA: IGI Global. 10.4018/978-1-5225-0495-5.ch008

Moeller, C. L. (2018). Sharing Your Personal Medical Experience Online: Is It an Irresponsible Act or Patient Empowerment? In Sekalala, S., & Niezgoda, B. (Eds.), *Global Perspectives on Health Communication in the Age of Social Media* (pp. 185–209). Hershey, PA: IGI Global. 10.4018/978-1-5225-3716-8.ch007

Mosanako, S. (2017). Broadcasting Policy in Botswana: The Case of Botswana Television. In Nelson, O., Ojebuyi, B., & Salawu, A. (Eds.), *Impacts of the Media on African Socio-Economic Development* (pp. 217–230). Hershey, PA: IGI Global. 10.4018/978-1-5225-1859-4.ch014

Mukherjee Das, M. (2020). Harnessing the "Crowd" and the Rise of "Prosumers" in Filmmaking in India. In Biswal, S., Kusuma, K., & Mohanty, S. (Eds.), *Handbook of Research on Social and Cultural Dynamics in Indian Cinema* (pp. 350–359). IGI Global. https://doi.org/10.4018/978-1-7998-3511-0.ch029

Musemburi, D., & Nhendo, C. (2019). Media Information Literacy: The Answer to 21st Century Inclusive Information and Knowledge-Based Society Challenges. In Chisita, C., & Rusero, A. (Eds.), *Exploring the Relationship Between Media, Libraries, and Archives* (pp. 102–135). IGI Global. https://doi.org/10.4018/978-1-5225-5840-8.ch007

Noor, R. (2017). Citizen Journalism: News Gathering by Amateurs. In Adria, M., & Mao, Y. (Eds.), *Handbook of Research on Citizen Engagement and Public Participation in the Era of New Media* (pp. 194–229). Hershey, PA: IGI Global. 10.4018/978-1-5225-1081-9.ch012

Obermayer, N., Csepregi, A., & Kővári, E. (2017). Knowledge Sharing Relation to Competence, Emotional Intelligence, and Social Media Regarding Generations. In Bencsik, A. (Ed.), *Knowledge Management Initiatives and Strategies in Small and Medium Enterprises* (pp. 269–290). Hershey, PA: IGI Global. 10.4018/978-1-5225-1642-2.ch013

Obermayer, N., Gaál, Z., Szabó, L., & Csepregi, A. (2017). Leveraging Knowledge Sharing over Social Media Tools. In Chugh, R. (Ed.), *Harnessing Social Media as a Knowledge Management Tool* (pp. 1–24). Hershey, PA: IGI Global. 10.4018/978-1-5225-0495-5.ch001

Odebiyi, S. D., & Elegbe, O. (2020). Human Rights Abuses Against Internally Displaced Persons (IDPs) in Nigeria: Investigating Media Reportage. In Okorie, N., Ojebuyi, B., & Macharia, J. (Eds.), *Handbook of Research on the Global Impact of Media on Migration Issues* (pp. 180–200). IGI Global. https://doi.org/10.4018/978-1-7998-0210-5.ch011

Okoroafor, O. E. (2018). New Media Technology and Development Journalism in Nigeria. In Salawu, A., & Owolabi, T. (Eds.), *Exploring Journalism Practice and Perception in Developing Countries* (pp. 105–125). Hershey, PA: IGI Global. 10.4018/978-1-5225-3376-4.ch006

Okpara, S. N. (2020). Child Protection and Development in Nigeria: Towards a More Functional Media Intervention. In Oyero, O. (Ed.), *Media and Its Role in Protecting the Rights of Children in Africa* (pp. 57–79). IGI Global. https://doi.org/10.4018/978-1-7998-0329-4.ch004

Olaleye, S. A., Sanusi, I. T., & Ukpabi, D. C. (2018). Assessment of Mobile Money Enablers in Nigeria. In Mtenzi, F., Oreku, G., Lupiana, D., & Yonazi, J. (Eds.), *Mobile Technologies and Socio-Economic Development in Emerging Nations* (pp. 129–155). Hershey, PA: IGI Global. 10.4018/978-1-5225-4029-8.ch007

Pacchiega, C. (2017). An Informal Methodology for Teaching Through Virtual Worlds: Using Internet Tools and Virtual Worlds in a Coordinated Pattern to Teach Various Subjects. In Panconesi, G., & Guida, M. (Eds.), *Handbook of Research on Collaborative Teaching Practice in Virtual Learning Environments* (pp. 163–180). Hershey, PA: IGI Global. 10.4018/978-1-5225-2426-7.ch009

Pant, L. D. (2021). Gender Mainstreaming in the Media: The Issue of Professional and Workplace Safety of Women Journalists in Nepal. In Jamil, S., Çoban, B., Ataman, B., & Appiah-Adjei, G. (Eds.), *Handbook of Research on Discrimination, Gender Disparity, and Safety Risks in Journalism* (pp. 194–210). IGI Global. https://doi.org/10.4018/978-1-7998-6686-2.ch011

Pase, A. F., Goss, B. M., & Tietzmann, R. (2018). A Matter of Time: Transmedia Journalism Challenges. In Gambarato, R., & Alzamora, G. (Eds.), *Exploring Transmedia Journalism in the Digital Age* (pp. 49–66). Hershey, PA: IGI Global. 10.4018/978-1-5225-3781-6.ch004

Patkin, T. T. (2017). Social Media and Knowledge Management in a Crisis Context: Barriers and Opportunities. In Chugh, R. (Ed.), *Harnessing Social Media as a Knowledge Management Tool* (pp. 125–142). Hershey, PA: IGI Global. 10.4018/978-1-5225-0495-5.ch007

Pavlíček, A. (2017). Social Media and Creativity: How to Engage Users and Tourists. In Kiráľová, A. (Ed.), *Driving Tourism through Creative Destinations and Activities* (pp. 181–202). Hershey, PA: IGI Global. 10.4018/978-1-5225-2016-0.ch009

Pérez-Gómez, M. Á. (2020). Augmented Reality and Franchising: The Evolution of Media Mix Through Invizimals. In Hernández-Santaolalla, V., & Barrientos-Bueno, M. (Eds.), *Handbook of Research on Transmedia Storytelling, Audience Engagement, and Business Strategies* (pp. 90–102). IGI Global. https://doi.org/10.4018/978-1-7998-3119-8.ch007

Phiri, S., & Mokorosi, L. (2020). Of Elephants and Men: Understanding Gender-Based Hate Speech in Zambia's Social Media Platforms. In Kurebwa, J. (Ed.), *Understanding Gender in the African Context* (pp. 105–125). IGI Global. https://doi.org/10.4018/978-1-7998-2815-0.ch006

Pillai, A. P. (2019). Nuances of Media Planning in New Media Age. In Mishra, P., & Dham, S. (Eds.), *Application of Gaming in New Media Marketing* (pp. 151–170). IGI Global. https://doi.org/10.4018/978-1-5225-6064-7.ch009

Pillay, K., & Maharaj, M. (2017). The Business of Advocacy: A Case Study of Greenpeace. In Benson, V., Tuninga, R., & Saridakis, G. (Eds.), *Analyzing the Strategic Role of Social Networking in Firm Growth and Productivity* (pp. 59–75). Hershey, PA: IGI Global. 10.4018/978-1-5225-0559-4.ch004

Piven, I. P., & Breazeale, M. (2017). Desperately Seeking Customer Engagement: The Five-Sources Model of Brand Value on Social Media. In Benson, V., Tuninga, R., & Saridakis, G. (Eds.), *Analyzing the Strategic Role of Social Networking in Firm Growth and Productivity* (pp. 283–313). Hershey, PA: IGI Global. 10.4018/978-1-5225-0559-4.ch016

Pokharel, R. (2017). New Media and Technology: How Do They Change the Notions of the Rhetorical Situations? In Gurung, B., & Limbu, M. (Eds.), *Integration of Cloud Technologies in Digitally Networked Classrooms and Learning Communities* (pp. 120–148). Hershey, PA: IGI Global. 10.4018/978-1-5225-1650-7.ch008

Porlezza, C., Benecchi, E., & Colapinto, C. (2018). The Transmedia Revitalization of Investigative Journalism: Opportunities and Challenges of the Serial Podcast. In Gambarato, R., & Alzamora, G. (Eds.), *Exploring Transmedia Journalism in the Digital Age* (pp. 183–201). Hershey, PA: IGI Global. 10.4018/978-1-5225-3781-6.ch011

Ramluckan, T., Ally, S. E., & van Niekerk, B. (2017). Twitter Use in Student Protests: The Case of South Africa's #FeesMustFall Campaign. In Korstanje, M. (Ed.), *Threat Mitigation and Detection of Cyber Warfare and Terrorism Activities* (pp. 220–253). Hershey, PA: IGI Global. 10.4018/978-1-5225-1938-6.ch010

Rao, N. R. (2017). Social Media: An Enabler for Governance. In Rao, N. (Ed.), *Social Media Listening and Monitoring for Business Applications* (pp. 151–164). Hershey, PA: IGI Global. 10.4018/978-1-5225-0846-5.ch008

Redi, F. (2017). Enhancing Coopetition Among Small Tourism Destinations by Creativity. In Kiráľová, A. (Ed.), *Driving Tourism through Creative Destinations and Activities* (pp. 223–244). Hershey, PA: IGI Global. 10.4018/978-1-5225-2016-0.ch011

Resuloğlu, F., & Yılmaz, R. (2017). A Model for Interactive Advertising Narration. In Yılmaz, R. (Ed.), *Narrative Advertising Models and Conceptualization in the Digital Age* (pp. 1–20). Hershey, PA: IGI Global. 10.4018/978-1-5225-2373-4.ch001

Richards, M. B. (2022). Media and Parental Communication: Effects on Millennials' Value Formation. In Malik, S., Bansal, R., & Tyagi, A. (Eds.), *Impact and Role of Digital Technologies in Adolescent Lives* (pp. 64–82). IGI Global. https://doi.org/10.4018/978-1-7998-8318-0.ch006

Robinson, W. R. (2021). The Intellectual Soul Food Lunch Buffet: The Classroom to Student Media Entrepreneurship. In Byrd, L. (Ed.), *Cultivating Entrepreneurial Changemakers Through Digital Media Education* (pp. 108–121). IGI Global. https://doi.org/10.4018/978-1-7998-5808-9.ch007

Ross, D. B., Eleno-Orama, M., & Salah, E. V. (2018). The Aging and Technological Society: Learning Our Way Through the Decades. In Bryan, V., Musgrove, A., & Powers, J. (Eds.), *Handbook of Research on Human Development in the Digital Age* (pp. 205–234). Hershey, PA: IGI Global. 10.4018/978-1-5225-2838-8.ch010

Rusko, R., & Merenheimo, P. (2017). Co-Creating the Christmas Story: Digitalizing as a Shared Resource for a Shared Brand. In Oncioiu, I. (Ed.), *Driving Innovation and Business Success in the Digital Economy* (pp. 137–157). Hershey, PA: IGI Global. 10.4018/978-1-5225-1779-5.ch010

Sabao, C., & Chikara, T. O. (2018). Social Media as Alternative Public Sphere for Citizen Participation and Protest in National Politics in Zimbabwe: The Case of #thisflag. In Endong, F. (Ed.), *Exploring the Role of Social Media in Transnational Advocacy* (pp. 17–35). Hershey, PA: IGI Global. 10.4018/978-1-5225-2854-8.ch002

Saçak, B. (2019). Media Literacy in a Digital Age: Multimodal Social Semiotics and Reading Media. In Yildiz, M., Fazal, M., Ahn, M., Feirsen, R., & Ozdemir, S. (Eds.), *Handbook of Research on Media Literacy Research and Applications Across Disciplines* (pp. 13–26). IGI Global. https://doi.org/10.4018/978-1-5225-9261-7.ch002

Samarthya-Howard, A., & Rogers, D. (2018). Scaling Mobile Technologies to Maximize Reach and Impact: Partnering With Mobile Network Operators and Governments. In Takavarasha, S.Jr, & Adams, C. (Eds.), *Affordability Issues Surrounding the Use of ICT for Development and Poverty Reduction* (pp. 193–211). Hershey, PA: IGI Global. 10.4018/978-1-5225-3179-1.ch009

Sandoval-Almazan, R. (2017). Political Messaging in Digital Spaces: The Case of Twitter in Mexico's Presidential Campaign. In Ibrahim, Y. (Ed.), *Politics, Protest, and Empowerment in Digital Spaces* (pp. 72–90). Hershey, PA: IGI Global. 10.4018/978-1-5225-1862-4.ch005

Schultz, C. D., & Dellnitz, A. (2018). Attribution Modeling in Online Advertising. In Yang, K. (Ed.), *Multi-Platform Advertising Strategies in the Global Marketplace* (pp. 226–249). Hershey, PA: IGI Global. 10.4018/978-1-5225-3114-2.ch009

Schultz, C. D., & Holsing, C. (2018). Differences Across Device Usage in Search Engine Advertising. In Yang, K. (Ed.), *Multi-Platform Advertising Strategies in the Global Marketplace* (pp. 250–279). Hershey, PA: IGI Global. 10.4018/978-1-5225-3114-2.ch010

Seçkin, G. (2020). The Integration of the Media With the Power in Turkey (2002-2019): Native, National Media Conception. In Karlidag, S., & Bulut, S. (Eds.), *Handbook of Research on the Political Economy of Communications and Media* (pp. 206–226). IGI Global. https://doi.org/10.4018/978-1-7998-3270-6.ch011

Senadheera, V., Warren, M., Leitch, S., & Pye, G. (2017). Facebook Content Analysis: A Study into Australian Banks' Social Media Community Engagement. In Hai-Jew, S. (Ed.), *Social Media Data Extraction and Content Analysis* (pp. 412–432). Hershey, PA: IGI Global. 10.4018/978-1-5225-0648-5.ch013

Sharma, A. R. (2018). Promoting Global Competencies in India: Media and Information Literacy as Stepping Stone. In Yildiz, M., Funk, S., & De Abreu, B. (Eds.), *Promoting Global Competencies Through Media Literacy* (pp. 160–174). Hershey, PA: IGI Global. 10.4018/978-1-5225-3082-4.ch010

Sharma, D., & Bhattacharya, S. (2022). Complexity of Digital Media Crowning the Mental Health of Adolescents. In Malik, S., Bansal, R., & Tyagi, A. (Eds.), *Impact and Role of Digital Technologies in Adolescent Lives* (pp. 100–117). IGI Global. https://doi.org/10.4018/978-1-7998-8318-0.ch008

Sillah, A. (2017). Nonprofit Organizations and Social Media Use: An Analysis of Nonprofit Organizations' Effective Use of Social Media Tools. In Brown, M.Sr., (Ed.), *Social Media Performance Evaluation and Success Measurements* (pp. 180–195). Hershey, PA: IGI Global. 10.4018/978-1-5225-1963-8.ch009

Silva, H., & Simão, E. (2019). Thinking Art in the Technological World: An Approach to Digital Media Art Creation. In Simão, E., & Soares, C. (Eds.), *Trends, Experiences, and Perspectives in Immersive Multimedia and Augmented Reality* (pp. 102–121). IGI Global. https://doi.org/10.4018/978-1-5225-5696-1.ch005

Škorić, M. (2017). Adaptation of Winlink 2000 Emergency Amateur Radio Email Network to a VHF Packet Radio Infrastructure. In El Oualkadi, A., & Zbitou, J. (Eds.), *Handbook of Research on Advanced Trends in Microwave and Communication Engineering* (pp. 498–528). Hershey, PA: IGI Global. 10.4018/978-1-5225-0773-4.ch016

Soares, C., & Simão, E. (2020). Software-Based Media Art: From the Artistic Exhibition to the Conservation Models. In Soares, C., & Simão, E. (Eds.), *Multidisciplinary Perspectives on New Media Art* (pp. 47–63). IGI Global. https://doi.org/10.4018/978-1-7998-3669-8.ch003

Sonnenberg, C. (2020). Mobile Media Usability: Evaluation of Methods for Adaptation and User Engagement. *Journal of Media Management and Entrepreneurship*, 2(1), 86–107. https://doi.org/10.4018/JMME.2020010106

Sood, T. (2017). Services Marketing: A Sector of the Current Millennium. In Sood, T. (Ed.), *Strategic Marketing Management and Tactics in the Service Industry* (pp. 15–42). Hershey, PA: IGI Global. 10.4018/978-1-5225-2475-5.ch002

Sudarsanam, S. K. (2017). Social Media Metrics. In Rao, N. (Ed.), *Social Media Listening and Monitoring for Business Applications* (pp. 131–149). Hershey, PA: IGI Global. 10.4018/978-1-5225-0846-5.ch007

Swiatek, L. (2017). Accessing the Finest Minds: Insights into Creativity from Esteemed Media Professionals. In Silton, N. (Ed.), *Exploring the Benefits of Creativity in Education, Media, and the Arts* (pp. 240–263). Hershey, PA: IGI Global. 10.4018/978-1-5225-0504-4.ch012

Teurlings, J. (2017). What Critical Media Studies Should Not Take from Actor-Network Theory. In Spöhrer, M., & Ochsner, B. (Eds.), *Applying the Actor-Network Theory in Media Studies* (pp. 66–78). Hershey, PA: IGI Global. 10.4018/978-1-5225-0616-4.ch005

Tilwankar, V., Rai, S., & Bajpai, S. P. (2019). Role of Social Media in Environment Awareness: Social Media and Environment. In Narula, S., Rai, S., & Sharma, A. (Eds.), *Environmental Awareness and the Role of Social Media* (pp. 117–139). IGI Global. https://doi.org/10.4018/978-1-5225-5291-8.ch006

Tokbaeva, D. (2019). Media Entrepreneurs and Market Dynamics: Case of Russian Media Markets. *Journal of Media Management and Entrepreneurship*, 1(1), 40–56. https://doi.org/10.4018/JMME.2019010103

Tomé, V. (2018). Assessing Media Literacy in Teacher Education. In Yildiz, M., Funk, S., & De Abreu, B. (Eds.), *Promoting Global Competencies Through Media Literacy* (pp. 1–19). Hershey, PA: IGI Global. 10.4018/978-1-5225-3082-4.ch001

Topçu, Ç. (2022). Social Media and the Knowledge Gap: Research on the Appearance of COVID-19 in Turkey and the Knowledge Level of Users. In Aker, H., & Aiken, M. (Eds.), *Handbook of Research on Cyberchondria, Health Literacy, and the Role of Media in Society's Perception of Medical Information* (pp. 344–361). IGI Global. https://doi.org/10.4018/978-1-7998-8630-3.ch019

Toscano, J. P. (2017). Social Media and Public Participation: Opportunities, Barriers, and a New Framework. In Adria, M., & Mao, Y. (Eds.), *Handbook of Research on Citizen Engagement and Public Participation in the Era of New Media* (pp. 73–89). Hershey, PA: IGI Global. 10.4018/978-1-5225-1081-9.ch005

Trauth, E. (2017). Creating Meaning for Millennials: Bakhtin, Rosenblatt, and the Use of Social Media in the Composition Classroom. In Bryant, K. (Ed.), *Engaging 21st Century Writers with Social Media* (pp. 151–162). Hershey, PA: IGI Global. 10.4018/978-1-5225-0562-4.ch009

Trucks, E. (2019). Making Social Media More Social: A Literature Review of Academic Libraries' Engagement and Connections Through Social Media Platforms. In Joe, J., & Knight, E. (Eds.), *Social Media for Communication and Instruction in Academic Libraries* (pp. 1–16). IGI Global. https://doi.org/10.4018/978-1-5225-8097-3.ch001

Udenze, S. (2021). Social Media and Nigeria's Politics. In Aririguzoh, S. (Ed.), *Global Perspectives on the Impact of Mass Media on Electoral Processes* (pp. 83–96). IGI Global. https://doi.org/10.4018/978-1-7998-4820-2.ch005

Uprety, S. (2018). Print Media's Role in Securitization: National Security and Diplomacy Discourses in Nepal. In Bute, S. (Ed.), *Media Diplomacy and Its Evolving Role in the Current Geopolitical Climate* (pp. 56–82). Hershey, PA: IGI Global. 10.4018/978-1-5225-3859-2.ch004

Uprety, S., & Chand, O. B. (2021). Trump's Declaration of the Global Gag Rule: Understanding Socio-Political Discourses Through Media. In Hancı-Azizoglu, E., & Alawdat, M. (Eds.), *Rhetoric and Sociolinguistics in Times of Global Crisis* (pp. 277–294). IGI Global. https://doi.org/10.4018/978-1-7998-6732-6.ch015

van der Vyver, A. G. (2018). A Model for Economic Development With Telecentres and the Social Media: Overcoming Affordability Constraints. In Takavarasha, S.Jr, & Adams, C. (Eds.), *Affordability Issues Surrounding the Use of ICT for Development and Poverty Reduction* (pp. 112–140). Hershey, PA: IGI Global. 10.4018/978-1-5225-3179-1.ch006

van Niekerk, B. (2018). Social Media Activism From an Information Warfare and Security Perspective. In Endong, F. (Ed.), *Exploring the Role of Social Media in Transnational Advocacy* (pp. 1–16). Hershey, PA: IGI Global. 10.4018/978-1-5225-2854-8.ch001

Varnali, K., & Gorgulu, V. (2017). Determinants of Brand Recall in Social Networking Sites. In Al-Rabayah, W., Khasawneh, R., Abu-shamaa, R., & Alsmadi, I. (Eds.), *Strategic Uses of Social Media for Improved Customer Retention* (pp. 124–153). Hershey, PA: IGI Global. 10.4018/978-1-5225-1686-6.ch007

Varty, C. T., O'Neill, T. A., & Hambley, L. A. (2017). Leading Anywhere Workers: A Scientific and Practical Framework. In Blount, Y., & Gloet, M. (Eds.), *Anywhere Working and the New Era of Telecommuting* (pp. 47–88). Hershey, PA: IGI Global. 10.4018/978-1-5225-2328-4.ch003

Velikovsky, J. T. (2018). The Holon/Parton Structure of the Meme, or The Unit of Culture. In M. Khosrow-Pour, D.B.A. (Ed.), *Encyclopedia of Information Science and Technology, Fourth Edition* (pp. 4666-4678). Hershey, PA: IGI Global. https://doi.org/10.4018/978-1-5225-2255-3.ch405

Venkatesh, R., & Jayasingh, S. (2017). Transformation of Business through Social Media. In Rao, N. (Ed.), *Social Media Listening and Monitoring for Business Applications* (pp. 1–17). Hershey, PA: IGI Global. 10.4018/978-1-5225-0846-5.ch001

Vijayakumar, D. S., M., S., Thangaraju, J., & V., S. (2021). Social Media Content Analysis: Machine Learning. In V. Sathiyamoorthi, & A. Elci (Eds.), *Challenges and Applications of Data Analytics in Social Perspectives* (pp. 156-174). IGI Global. https://doi.org/10.4018/978-1-7998-2566-1.ch009

Virkar, S. (2017). Trolls Just Want to Have Fun: Electronic Aggression within the Context of E-Participation and Other Online Political Behaviour in the United Kingdom. In Korstanje, M. (Ed.), *Threat Mitigation and Detection of Cyber Warfare and Terrorism Activities* (pp. 111–162). Hershey, PA: IGI Global. 10.4018/978-1-5225-1938-6.ch006

Wakabi, W. (2017). When Citizens in Authoritarian States Use Facebook for Social Ties but Not Political Participation. In Ibrahim, Y. (Ed.), *Politics, Protest, and Empowerment in Digital Spaces* (pp. 192–214). Hershey, PA: IGI Global. 10.4018/978-1-5225-1862-4.ch012

Wamuyu, P. K. (2021). Social Media Consumption Among Kenyans: Trends and Practices. In Wamuyu, P. (Ed.), *Analyzing Global Social Media Consumption* (pp. 88–120). IGI Global. https://doi.org/10.4018/978-1-7998-4718-2.ch006

Wright, K. (2018). "Show Me What You Are Saying": Visual Literacy in the Composition Classroom. In August, A. (Ed.), *Visual Imagery, Metadata, and Multimodal Literacies Across the Curriculum* (pp. 24–49). Hershey, PA: IGI Global. 10.4018/978-1-5225-2808-1.ch002

Wright, M. F. (2020). Cyberbullying: Negative Interaction Through Social Media. In Desjarlais, M. (Ed.), *The Psychology and Dynamics Behind Social Media Interactions* (pp. 107–135). IGI Global. https://doi.org/10.4018/978-1-5225-9412-3.ch005

Yang, K. C. (2018). Understanding How Mexican and U.S. Consumers Decide to Use Mobile Social Media: A Cross-National Qualitative Study. In Yang, K. (Ed.), *Multi-Platform Advertising Strategies in the Global Marketplace* (pp. 168–198). Hershey, PA: IGI Global. 10.4018/978-1-5225-3114-2.ch007

Yarchi, M., Wolfsfeld, G., Samuel-Azran, T., & Segev, E. (2017). Invest, Engage, and Win: Online Campaigns and Their Outcomes in an Israeli Election. In Brown, M.Sr., (Ed.), *Social Media Performance Evaluation and Success Measurements* (pp. 225–248). Hershey, PA: IGI Global. 10.4018/978-1-5225-1963-8.ch011

Yeboah-Banin, A. A., & Amoakohene, M. I. (2018). The Dark Side of Multi-Platform Advertising in an Emerging Economy Context. In Yang, K. (Ed.), *Multi-Platform Advertising Strategies in the Global Marketplace* (pp. 30–53). Hershey, PA: IGI Global. 10.4018/978-1-5225-3114-2.ch002

Yılmaz, R., Çakır, A., & Resuloğlu, F. (2017). Historical Transformation of the Advertising Narration in Turkey: From Stereotype to Digital Media. In Yılmaz, R. (Ed.), *Narrative Advertising Models and Conceptualization in the Digital Age* (pp. 133–152). Hershey, PA: IGI Global. 10.4018/978-1-5225-2373-4.ch008

Yusuf, S., Hassan, M. S., & Ibrahim, A. M. (2018). Cyberbullying Among Malaysian Children Based on Research Evidence. In M. Khosrow-Pour, D.B.A. (Ed.), *Encyclopedia of Information Science and Technology, Fourth Edition* (pp. 1704-1722). Hershey, PA: IGI Global. 10.4018/978-1-5225-2255-3.ch149

Zbinden, B. (2019). Restricted Communication: Social Relationships and the Media Use of Prisoners. In Oliveira, L., & Graça, D. (Eds.), *Infocommunication Skills as a Rehabilitation and Social Reintegration Tool for Inmates* (pp. 238–267). IGI Global. 10.4018/978-1-5225-5975-7.ch011

Zhou, M., Matsika, C., Zhou, T. G., & Chawarura, W. I. (2022). Harnessing Social Media to Improve Educational Performance of Adolescent Freshmen in Universities. In Malik, S., Bansal, R., & Tyagi, A. (Eds.), *Impact and Role of Digital Technologies in Adolescent Lives* (pp. 51–63). IGI Global. https://doi.org/10.4018/978-1-7998-8318-0.ch005

About the Contributors

* * *

Nowsheeba Ashraf Asmi is a Librarian in the Higher Education Department UT of Jammu and Kashmir, India. She is currently posted as a Librarian at Government College for Women Srinagar. Her research interests include Social Media, Academic Social Networking Sites, Digitization of Cultural Heritage, and Digital Library management. She has authored several publications in reputed Journals and Books. She has presented a good number of papers at National and International Conferences.

Aimen Nazir Bhat has a Masters in Library and Information Science from the University of Kashmir. Her research interests include open access to research, systematic reviews, etc. She has recently completed her dissertation entitled "Treatment and Management of Childhood Obesity: A systematic review."

Remberto Jimenez is an educator at New Jersey City University's Department of Educational Technology. He is also the Director of Learning and Development for an advertising/media firm in New York City. Dr. Jimenez graduated with his Ed.D. in the Educational Technology Leadership program at New Jersey City University. He has earned a Bachelor of Arts in Mathematics from New Jersey City University, a Master of Art, and a Post Master's Certificate in Educational Communications and Technology from New York University. Dr. Jimenez's research interests include Educational Technology, Active Learning, Distance Learning, instructional design, workplace learning, and Student Retention and Persistence.

Nadim Akhtar Khan is an Assistant Professor in the Department of Library and Information Science at the University of Kashmir, India. He has PhD in Library and Information Science, MLIS (Gold Medallist), and PGDCA. His research interests include Open Educational Resources, Metadata Harvesting and interoperability, Institutional Repositories, Digital Libraries and Cultural Heritage. He has attended and presented papers at many national and international seminars.

About the Contributors

Christopher J. Mason has been an employee with Iron Mountain for over 34 years, and has been in the records management industry for over 38 years. He currently serves in the Media & Archive Services division of the company, and holds an MBA in Information Technology Managment, as well as his MS in Management and Leadership from Western Governor's University. He has had the unique experience of serving as management at Iron Mountain in the areas of Operations, Program Management, Project Management, and Account Management across various divisions within the organization. In 1999, Mr. Mason was named the Employee of the Year while serving as an operations manager and was a finalist for this distinction three subsequent times in the following years. He had the pleasure of establishing the first branch of the organization in Ireland and later in 2003 they were named Business Unit of the Year for Europe. As an account manager he was a member of the 30/30 Club for his success in attaining performance indicators over consecutive years, which lead to being a nationally ranked Account Manager in 2011. Mr. Mason is an active member of the organization's LGBTQ employee resource group, serving previously as secretary and most recently as special events planner. He also has had the pleasure of representing the organization through other acts of service while contributing to Moving Mountains, an Iron Mountain program dedicated to volunteerism.

Neli Maria Mengalli is a senior professional who has been working for over twenty years in the educational area, interfacing with the areas of knowledge management, monitoring and measuring social media, society 5.0, phygital transformation, and disruptive technologies. She has worked both in the private sector and in public management. Her postgraduate [master's and doctorate] was carried out at the Pontifical Catholic University of São Paulo with an emphasis on new technologies. A highlight of the works produced is in communities of practice, in the management of online contexts, in disruptive technologies and in transform(active) methodologies. She participated in research groups with the theme of technology at the Pontifical Catholic University of São Paulo and in workshops that associated the language, education, and technology at FASB - Faculdade São Bernardo do Campo. In the professional trajectory are basic education, higher education, course evaluation, advisory in public policies, and mentoring for startups. She was an interlocutor in the implementation of public policies in the educational area.

Vistolina Nuuyoma is a senior lecturer and researcher in the School of Nursing and Public Health, within the Faculty of Health Sciences and Veterinary Medicine, at the University of Namibia, Namibia. She earned her PhD in Nursing Education from the University of Johannesburg in the Republic of South Africa (RSA). Her PhD work focused on strategies to facilitate community engagement in the Faculty of Health Sciences. Vistolina holds a master's degree in health science education from Stellenbosch University in the RSA, and a master's degree in public health from the University of Western Cape in the RSA. Her research interests are teaching and learning in clinical contexts and community settings, community engagement, and scholarship of engagement.

Veronica E. O'Neill is an educator at New Jersey City University's School of Business. Dr. O'Neill graduated with her Ed.D. in the Educational Technology Leadership program at New Jersey City University. She has earned a Bachelor of Arts in Biology/Sociology from the College of the Holy Cross, an MBA in Accounting from Fairleigh Dickinson University, and a Master of Science in Organizational Leadership from Regis University. Dr. O'Neill's research interests include Educational Technology, Active Learning, Distance Learning, and Student Retention and Persistence. Prior to becoming an educator, she had a 26 year career in a major Wall Street firm.

Michael Rivera is the current Vocal Music Teacher at the Wallington School District in New Jersey, teaching Vocal Music to all students from Kindergarten through Grade Six. He is also the director of the Elementary Choir and the Junior/Senior High School Choir. Michael is also an active church musician, having served in a variety of roles, including as Director of Music. Michael graduated with a Master of Arts in Teaching with a Concentration in Music Education from Montclair State University and is currently working towards a Master of Arts in Music from the University of Mary in Bismarck, North Dakota.

Zhivi Williams is a seasoned professional in education, instructional design, diversity, equity, and inclusion. She holds advanced degrees in Theological Studies and Instructional Systems Technology and a Bachelor's in Elementary Education. At Rowan-Cabarrus Community College, she has served as an Instructional Designer/Trainer and Learning and Development Manager, where she develops long-term employee enrichment plans and collaborates with various departments and agencies to enhance educational services. Her work includes organizing interdisciplinary events, inclusivity programs, and well-being initiatives. Zhivi is also active in several committees, including the EDUCAUSE DEI Advisory Committee and the college's Advisory Council for Belonging. Her diversity, inclusion, and education certifications highlight her commitment to professional growth and inclusivity.

Index

Symbols

21st Century Learning 149, 156, 157, 217

A

Academic Social Networking Sites 159, 161, 163, 171, 173, 175, 176, 178
Artificial Intelligence 43, 64, 66, 67, 70, 71, 74, 75, 76, 79, 81, 82, 83, 86, 87, 88, 91, 92, 172, 178, 189
Aural 18, 20, 21, 27

B

Bias 120, 123, 125, 132, 136
BIPOC 117, 118, 119, 121, 123, 124, 125, 126, 131, 132, 133
Business 32, 36, 39, 41, 47, 64, 65, 66, 67, 68, 69, 70, 71, 72, 73, 75, 76, 78, 80, 81, 82, 83, 85, 86, 87, 88, 89, 92, 93, 95, 97, 108, 185, 199, 207, 209, 212, 213, 214, 217, 219, 220, 221

C

Case Studies 29, 30, 123, 190
Case Study 26, 45, 55, 115, 136, 176
Collaboration 31, 49, 53, 56, 57, 58, 61, 65, 66, 69, 79, 89, 91, 93, 98, 100, 106, 110, 119, 136, 142, 143, 148, 149, 150, 151, 152, 163, 164, 166, 169, 170, 174, 175, 176, 177, 179, 180, 183, 186, 187, 191, 202, 205, 207, 209, 217
Communities of Practice 1, 7, 10, 26, 27, 29, 30, 33, 34, 35, 36, 37, 38, 39, 43, 44, 45, 46, 47, 48, 65, 66, 67, 68, 69, 71, 72, 73, 74, 75, 76, 77, 79, 80, 81, 82, 83, 84, 85, 86, 87, 90, 91, 92, 93, 156, 157, 182, 183, 184, 185, 187, 188, 189, 194, 196, 197, 198, 199, 200, 201, 202, 203, 204, 218, 221, 222

Community 1, 2, 3, 6, 7, 9, 10, 11, 12, 13, 16, 17, 20, 21, 23, 24, 25, 29, 30, 31, 32, 33, 34, 35, 36, 37, 38, 39, 40, 42, 43, 44, 45, 46, 47, 48, 49, 53, 54, 56, 57, 58, 60, 61, 62, 63, 64, 66, 67, 68, 69, 70, 72, 73, 74, 75, 76, 77, 78, 79, 80, 81, 82, 83, 85, 86, 87, 88, 92, 96, 98, 100, 102, 103, 108, 117, 119, 125, 126, 130, 131, 136, 137, 138, 139, 141, 145, 147, 148, 149, 150, 151, 152, 153, 157, 159, 160, 162, 164, 167, 169, 179, 180, 185, 186, 187, 188, 190, 191, 196, 197, 199, 200, 202, 204, 205, 206, 207, 208, 209, 211, 216, 217, 218, 221
Community of Practice 3, 6, 7, 10, 29, 30, 31, 32, 35, 36, 39, 40, 42, 43, 44, 46, 47, 48, 56, 64, 66, 67, 68, 69, 70, 72, 73, 74, 75, 76, 77, 78, 79, 80, 81, 82, 83, 85, 87, 88, 92, 148, 152, 153, 157, 187, 190, 196, 199, 200, 202, 204, 205, 207, 208, 209, 216, 217, 221
Constructivism 13, 15, 27, 101, 158, 183
Convergence Education 142, 143, 145, 151, 155, 157
COVID-19 1, 6, 7, 24, 25, 65, 94, 95, 96, 97, 100, 113, 114, 183, 196, 200, 204, 206, 209, 211, 214, 215, 218, 220, 222

D

Dance Education 104, 114
Diversity 90, 117, 118, 119, 120, 122, 123, 124, 125, 126, 127, 129, 130, 133, 134, 135, 137, 138, 139, 149, 177
Domain 10, 35, 36, 42, 43, 44, 47, 48, 65, 66, 67, 72, 76, 81, 87, 151, 159, 171, 186, 196

E

Entertainment Industry 206, 207, 208
Equity 118, 119, 120, 121, 122, 130, 133, 135, 137, 177, 199

I

Inclusion 15, 23, 44, 59, 86, 117, 118, 119, 120, 122, 125, 127, 129, 133, 137, 138, 143, 177

Innovation 12, 40, 66, 72, 73, 74, 75, 79, 83, 84, 91, 100, 108, 131, 136, 140, 142, 164, 171, 206, 215

Iron Mountain 206, 207, 208, 209, 210, 211, 214, 215, 216, 217, 218, 220, 222

K

Kinesthetic 4, 18, 19, 23, 24, 27

Knowledge 2, 7, 8, 9, 11, 12, 13, 14, 15, 16, 17, 23, 24, 25, 27, 28, 29, 30, 31, 32, 33, 34, 35, 36, 37, 42, 43, 44, 46, 48, 50, 53, 56, 59, 62, 64, 66, 67, 68, 69, 71, 72, 73, 74, 75, 76, 78, 79, 80, 81, 82, 83, 84, 85, 86, 87, 88, 89, 91, 93, 98, 99, 100, 101, 102, 104, 105, 106, 107, 108, 109, 110, 120, 124, 130, 131, 140, 141, 142, 143, 146, 147, 148, 149, 150, 151, 157, 160, 166, 167, 168, 169, 172, 173, 176, 183, 184, 185, 186, 187, 188, 189, 190, 191, 192, 193, 196, 199, 200, 201, 217

L

Landscapes of Learning 29, 30

Landscapes of Practice 36, 47, 48, 202

Learning Styles 1, 7, 17, 18, 19, 23, 24, 25, 26, 27, 49, 104, 107, 108, 117, 123, 127, 130

M

Media Industry 213, 214, 216

Mentoring 3, 46, 101, 141, 148, 152, 182, 183, 184, 185, 190, 192, 193, 194, 195, 196, 197, 198, 199, 200, 201, 202, 204, 205, 219

Mentorship 34, 183, 192, 193, 194, 195, 199, 202, 203, 205

Metaverse 66, 68, 71, 73, 79, 81, 82, 83, 87, 88, 89, 90, 91, 96, 115

Multiculturalism 119, 120, 122, 133, 138

Music 1, 3, 4, 5, 6, 7, 8, 9, 10, 11, 12, 13, 14, 15, 16, 17, 18, 19, 20, 21, 22, 23, 24, 25, 26, 27, 94, 95, 96, 97, 98, 99, 102, 103, 104, 108, 109, 110, 111, 112, 113, 114, 115, 208, 213

Music Education 3, 13, 25, 26, 98, 99, 103, 104, 109, 111, 114, 115

N

Netflix 212, 213, 214, 220, 221

O

Online Education 26, 62, 98, 104, 106, 117, 118, 134

Online Learning Communities 103, 107, 136, 145, 147

Organizational Learning 29, 30, 46, 91

P

Phygital Transformation 64, 65, 66, 71, 73, 76, 77, 78, 82, 83, 84, 85, 87, 88, 91, 93

Practice 1, 3, 4, 6, 7, 10, 11, 12, 14, 15, 16, 20, 26, 27, 29, 30, 31, 32, 33, 34, 35, 36, 37, 38, 39, 40, 42, 43, 44, 45, 46, 47, 48, 49, 51, 52, 53, 54, 55, 56, 58, 59, 60, 61, 62, 64, 65, 66, 67, 68, 69, 70, 71, 72, 73, 74, 75, 76, 77, 78, 79, 80, 81, 82, 83, 84, 85, 86, 87, 88, 89, 90, 91, 92, 93, 97, 103, 104, 105, 106, 107, 113, 114, 115, 122, 136, 138, 141, 146, 148, 149, 150, 152, 153, 155, 156, 157, 175, 178, 180, 182, 183, 184, 185, 186, 187, 188, 189, 190, 193, 194, 195, 196, 197, 198, 199, 200, 201, 202, 203, 204, 205, 207, 208, 209, 210, 215, 216, 217, 218, 221, 222

Professional Development 2, 6, 8, 40, 49, 50, 51, 52, 53, 54, 56, 57, 59, 60, 61, 62, 63, 140, 141, 143, 145, 146, 147, 148, 149, 150, 152, 153, 154, 156, 192, 194, 197, 203, 207, 211, 217, 218, 219

Professional Learning Communities 38,

48, 49, 53, 62, 147, 150, 152

R

Reading 4, 18, 21, 24, 28, 51, 56, 57, 58, 59, 73, 83, 92, 120, 121, 124, 129, 131, 142, 168, 178, 179, 180, 195

Research Data Management 159, 160, 161, 163, 167, 170, 173, 174, 175, 176, 177, 178, 179, 180

ResearchGate 90, 92, 159, 161, 164, 166, 167, 168, 169, 170, 173, 175, 176, 177, 178, 179, 195, 220

ResearchGate Metrics 178

Research Impact 164, 171, 172

S

Situated Learning 36, 38, 44, 45, 46, 48, 79, 90, 182, 183, 185, 187, 188, 196, 198, 200, 201, 202, 204, 205

Social Media 96, 97, 102, 109, 110, 111, 112, 141, 152, 160, 161, 162, 163, 166, 169, 174, 176, 177, 178, 180, 181, 211, 212, 217

Social Networking Sites 159, 161, 162, 163, 171, 173, 175, 176, 178, 180, 181

STEAM 140, 141, 143, 145, 149, 150, 151, 152, 153, 154, 155, 156, 158

STEM 141, 142, 143, 144, 154, 155, 156, 157, 158, 202

T

Tech 154, 174, 219

Theater 99, 214

TPack Model 8, 26, 28

Training 11, 32, 39, 40, 41, 43, 50, 52, 53, 57, 58, 59, 62, 63, 67, 74, 90, 92, 99, 100, 106, 122, 142, 145, 146, 147, 148, 149, 150, 152, 153, 161, 163, 166, 171, 178, 179, 183, 191, 192, 199, 202, 206, 207, 210, 211, 215, 216, 217, 218

V

Virtual Communities 6, 7, 56, 61, 65, 67, 70, 79, 81, 82, 85, 86, 87, 88, 140, 148, 151, 182, 183, 184, 185, 189, 194, 196, 197, 198, 199, 200, 201, 202, 203, 204, 206, 218

Virtual Communities of Practice 65, 81, 82, 182, 183, 184, 185, 189, 194, 196, 197, 198, 199, 200, 201, 202, 203, 204

Virtual Mentoring 183, 193, 194, 195, 196, 197, 198, 200, 202, 205

Visual 18, 19, 20, 24, 28, 94, 96, 97, 98, 99, 102, 103, 105, 106, 108, 109, 110, 111, 112, 119, 131, 208

Visual and Performing Arts 94, 96, 97, 98, 99, 103, 105, 106, 108, 109, 110, 111, 112

Visual Arts 105, 106, 112

W

Work 2, 5, 6, 7, 11, 15, 16, 21, 22, 25, 31, 33, 34, 37, 39, 40, 42, 45, 46, 47, 48, 49, 51, 54, 57, 59, 60, 65, 66, 68, 69, 70, 71, 72, 73, 74, 75, 76, 78, 80, 81, 82, 83, 86, 87, 89, 90, 91, 93, 100, 108, 111, 112, 118, 119, 120, 122, 124, 126, 127, 128, 129, 131, 143, 144, 147, 152, 161, 163, 164, 166, 168, 169, 170, 171, 186, 189, 190, 191, 192, 194, 195, 196, 197, 198, 207, 208, 209, 210, 211, 214, 215, 216, 217, 218

Workplace 29, 30, 31, 32, 34, 39, 42, 44, 45, 46, 47, 48, 68, 77, 88, 89, 193, 195, 207, 209, 220

Workplace Learning 29, 32, 45, 46, 47, 48

Y

YouTube 3, 8, 18, 20, 23, 103, 110, 111, 112, 190, 196, 212, 213, 219, 220, 221

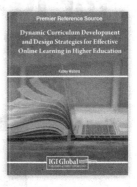
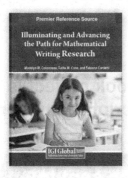

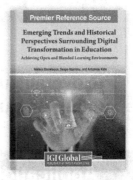

  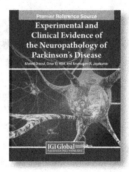 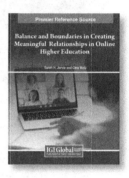

Printed in the United States
by Baker & Taylor Publisher Services